Ancient History Vol. 2

An Enthralling Guide to the Indus Valley Civilization, China, and Japan

Free limited time bonus

Stop for a moment. We have a free bonus set up for you. The problem is this: we forget 90% of everything that we read after 7 days. Crazy fact, right? Here's the solution: we've created a printable, 1-page pdf summary for this book that you're reading now. All you have to do to get your free pdf summary is to go to the following website:

https://livetolearn.lpages.co/enthrallinghistory/

Once you do, it will be intuitive. Enjoy, and thank you!

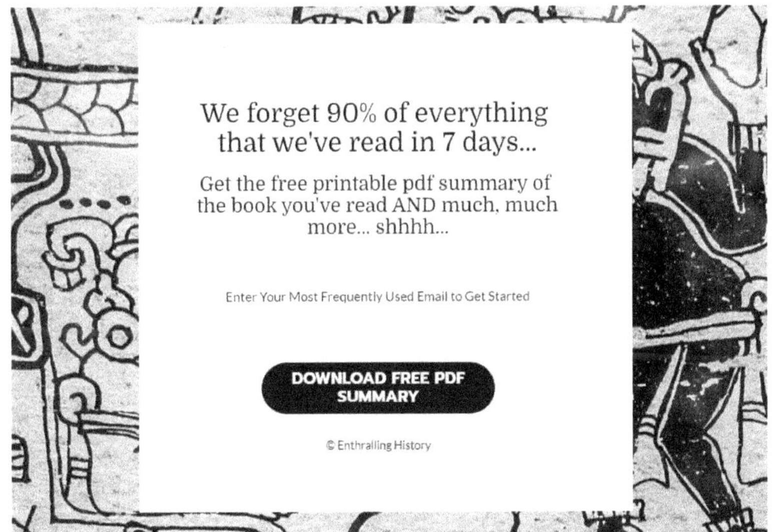

Table of Contents

Part 1: Indus Valley Civilization

An Enthralling Overview of the Harappan Civilization, Starting from the Early Harappan through Mohenjo-daro to the Aryan Invasion and Achaemenid Conquest

Introduction

The Indus Valley civilization, whose people are sometimes called Harappans, was formed in modern-day Pakistan and northwest India around 3300 BCE. This makes it one of the oldest civilizations in the world! Amazingly, the Indus Valley civilization lasted until about 1300 BCE, totaling an impressive two thousand years. During this time, the Harappans started building up their civilization from small towns into massive and organized cities that could hold tens of thousands of people comfortably.[1] This long reign and the civilization's mysterious decline and end makes it an interesting subject for historians to continue studying today.

The Indus Valley was home to several major cities, with some of these ruins being studied today. These sites include Mohenjo-daro, Lothal, Harappa, and more. Each of these sites has something that sets them apart. Both Mohenjo-daro and Harappa have a highly technical grid structure, similar to a modern-day city. It is clear these cities were meticulously planned. Lothal is famous for its docks, which were used for trading.[2] Few of these cities are still standing today, as they had been abandoned for longer than they were used. Still, archaeologists are finding new artifacts at the sites.

---

[1] Hawkes, Jacquetta. *The First Great Civilizations: Life in Mesopotamia, the Indus Valley, and Egypt.* The History of Human Society. New York City, NY: Random House, Inc, 1980.

[2] Hawkes, Jacquetta. *The First Great Civilizations: Life in Mesopotamia, the Indus Valley, and Egypt.*

No one knows who was in charge of making the cities so uniform. Was it a group of architects? A council of elders? The government? There were also beautifully built structures laid out in the town in a specific way within each city. Most of the larger and likely more important buildings were usually created at high elevations in the center of town. Houses were usually made to be about the same size and shape. Farms tended to lay on the lower levels of towns or just outside of them.[3] All of this hints as to how the average Harappan might have lived. The similarity in cities and houses suggests the Indus Valley civilization had a high standard for the equality of its people.

On top of the Harappans' impressive city layout, they also had a water drainage and sewage system that was ahead of its time. Many houses had a bath with a drain that led out of the house into a main drainage system near the street. These drains took sewage away from the city. City centers, sometimes called citadels, had large public baths that anyone could use.[4] These city features show how important hygiene and cleanliness were in the Indus Valley. Many other civilizations would not have a plumbing system this complex or effective for thousands of years after the Harappan civilization came to an end.

Even with all of these highly organized cities and structures, no one knows what kind of government the Indus Valley civilization had or if they even had a government at all! In fact, a lot of the specific rules, regulations, and rituals from the Indus Valley are a complete mystery to scholars. While the Harappans had a written language, no one alive today knows how to read it.[5] This script is called the Indus or Harappan Script.

Of course, there are many theories as to what kind of government the Indus Valley might have had. One theory suggests the Indus Valley didn't have a government at all! This is unlikely, but it is an interesting theory nonetheless. Other theories say the Harappans might have been ruled by

---

[3] Hawkes, Jacquetta. *The First Great Civilizations: Life in Mesopotamia, the Indus Valley, and Egypt.*

[4] Garg, Divya. "Case Study - City Planning and Organization of Indus Valley Civilization." Ischools.org, 2015, https://ischools.org/resources/Documents/Discipline%20of%20organizing/Case%20Studies/Indus Valley-Garg2015.pdf.

[5] Hawkes, Jacquetta. *The First Great Civilizations: Life in Mesopotamia, the Indus Valley, and Egypt.*

their rich or merchant classes, by priest-kings or another religious oligarchy, or had a city-state style of government.[6] No matter what kind of government, if any, the Harappans had, they were able to make great city plans and forge wonderful trade relationships with nearby civilizations.

Other contemporary civilizations, including Mesopotamia and ancient China, did not seem to write about the Harappans much. These two cultures traded with the Harappans often and had written languages historians can read today.[7] However, trade relationships can only provide so many hints as to what the Indus Valley was like.

Historians do know that trade was extremely important in the Indus Valley. Outside of agricultural work, trade was one of the most popular career choices a person could pick. Traders worked alongside farmers and merchants to sell their goods in the Indus Valley and to neighboring civilizations. The Harappans traded with Mesopotamia, modern-day northern India, and China the most. They traded overland and by sea.[8] The Harappans' boats were very impressive for the time. Without their knowledge of watercraft, their trade relationships would have been short-lived and short-distanced.

What sorts of items did the Harappans trade? Inside the Indus Valley, they would have most likely traded foodstuffs and other common household items. Outside the Indus Valley, travelers traded finely made beads, pottery, cloth, and mined metals and jewels. However, even with all of the trading the Harappans did, they didn't use any currency.[9] Their entire economy was trade-based. Even taxes, assuming they had any, would have been paid in grain or other items rather than in gold or silver coins.

The Harappans may have borrowed some ideas from the other cultures they mingled with during trade. They took many ideas from the Mesopotamians, but this is not surprising, as the Indus Valley people's

---

[6] "Indus Valley Civilization." Cultural India, n.d., https://www.culturalindia.net/indian-history/ancient-india/indus-valley.html.

[7] Hawkes, Jacquetta. *The First Great Civilizations: Life in Mesopotamia, the Indus Valley, and Egypt.*

[8] Hawkes, Jacquetta. *The First Great Civilizations: Life in Mesopotamia, the Indus Valley, and Egypt.*

[9] Hawkes, Jacquetta. *The First Great Civilizations: Life in Mesopotamia, the Indus Valley, and Egypt.*

ancestors may have come from Mesopotamia or a similar culture. Because of this possible shared heritage and trade, the two cultures had a lot in common. While no one knows exactly what religion the Harappans practiced, statues found in various ruins in the Indus Valley suggest they may have worshiped a fertility/mother goddess and a god of creatures, similar to what the Mesopotamians worshiped. Some of their architecture is also similar and could have been made similar due to religious reasons.[10] Could some of this have even been a precursor to modern-day Hinduism? Some of the similarities between these two religions are striking, to say the least.

These are just a few examples of all of the wonderful facts, myths, and mysteries that will be discussed throughout the course of this book. Learn all about the history of the Indus Valley, from its humble beginnings in the 3000s BCE to its mysterious end in the 1000s BCE. That's two thousand years to cover, so let's get started!

---

[10] "Indus Valley Civilization."

SECTION ONE:
THE RISE AND FALL OF THE INDUS VALLEY CULTURE

Chapter 1: The Three Main Harappan Cities

The Indus Valley civilization spread throughout modern-day India and Pakistan, easily containing over one thousand cities and towns. Of course, some of these cities have more cultural significance than others. Some of the largest cities were Mohenjo-daro and Harappa, which were both located in modern-day Pakistan. At different times, each of these cities would be the capital of the Indus Valley civilization. Dholavira was another major urban center, but it was located in modern-day India. Dholavira is also the second-largest Indus Valley city that historians know about.[11] More is known about Mohenjo-daro and Harappa than Dholavira. However, historians and archaeologists are still studying the Indus Valley area and learning more about it all the time.

Mohenjo-daro

Mohenjo-daro, also called Mohenjodaro and Moenjodaro, is one of the most famous Indus Valley cities. This city was built along the Indus River in modern-day southern Pakistan. Because of various environmental changes over the last few millennia, the site is now about three kilometers away from the river.[12] In total, the city had an area of

---

[11] Hays, Jeff. "Great Cities of the Indus Valley Civilization." Facts and Details, September 2020, https://factsanddetails.com/india/History/sub7_1a/entry-7116.html

[12] Britannica, T. Editors of Encyclopedia. "Mohenjo-daro." Encyclopedia Britannica, May 16, 2021. https://www.britannica.com/place/Mohenjo-daro.

about 750 acres. At its peak, it could have held up to forty thousand people comfortably.[13] This would make it one of the largest and most populous cities in the world at the time.

Mohenjo-daro's name roughly translates to "Mound of the Dead." The archaeologists who found the city named it this.[14] This name could have come from the fact the city's founders built an artificial base for one area of the town. However, historians do not know for certain what the city's original name was. Some guess that it might have been Kukkutarma.[15] This mound was made of mud bricks and used mud as a type of mortar.

Later, buildings were erected on top of the mound. Many of these buildings were large structures, which could have included both homes and government-like buildings. These buildings were also made of mud bricks.[16] Impressively, the bricks had a uniform shape and weight. This showed the Indus Valley had a complex civil engineering forte.[17] There may have been some wood or hay used in the construction as well, but these would have decayed, so they would not be observable by archaeologists today.

Another amazing feature of Mohenjo-daro was its rectangular grid system and paved roads. These roads were also made out of mud bricks. The city had an impressive sewer system, complete with drainage systems.[18] The sewer system will be discussed in further detail later in the book.

Oddly enough, architects have not been able to find any elaborate palaces, religious buildings, or government buildings in Mohenjo-daro. One of the largest buildings in the city was a public bathhouse. There were smaller administrative buildings in the city and even apartment buildings! Other than these, most of the buildings would have been average houses and marketplaces.[19] Regardless, Mohenjo-daro was one of

---

[13] Tawsam. "Mohenjo-Daro." Atlas Obscura, March 4, 2016, https://www.atlasobscura.com/places/mohenjodaro.

[14] Britannica, T. Editors of Encyclopedia. "Mohenjo-daro."

[15] Tawsam. "Mohenjo-Daro."

[16] Britannica, T. Editors of Encyclopedia. "Mohenjo-daro."

[17] Tawsam. "Mohenjo-Daro."

[18] Britannica, T. Editors of Encyclopedia. "Mohenjo-daro."

[19] Tawsam. "Mohenjo-Daro."

the most advanced cities in the ancient world.

Historians aren't sure when the city's inhabitants began to move away from Mohenjo-daro. There is some evidence that floods from the Indus River may have done damage to the city.[20] However, other historians think the Saraswati River dried up, causing a drought.[21] It is also possible that both of these events happened at different times. Either way, the city collapsed near the end of the Indus Valley civilization around 1900 BCE.

For centuries after the civilization's end, the city was lost to time. The city wasn't found until 1922 when it was discovered by European explorers.[22] However, it is difficult to study ancient architecture because of erosion. In 1966, archaeologists stopped actively digging through the site. Since then, only surface excavations, surveys, and conservation work has been allowed.[23] Even with the decades of archaeological work put in, archaeologists have only uncovered about a third of the entire city.[24] In 1980, UNESCO made the city's ruins into a World Heritage Site.[25] It is impossible to say what new archaeology expeditions will uncover, but historians are sure to keep learning more about the city as time goes on.

Excavated ruins of Mohenjo-daro

Nikesh Chawla. CC BY-SA 4.0, <https://creativecommons.org/licenses/by-sa/4.0>, via Wikimedia Commons, https://commons.wikimedia.org/wiki/File:Excavated_ruins_of_Mohenjo-daro.jpg

---

[20] Britannica, T. Editors of Encyclopedia. "Mohenjo-daro."

[21] Tawsam. "Mohenjo-Daro."

[22] Britannica, T. Editors of Encyclopedia. "Mohenjo-daro."

[23] Tawsam. "Mohenjo-Daro."

[24] Hays, Jeff. "Great Cities of the Indus Valley Civilization."

[25] Britannica, T. Editors of Encyclopedia. "Mohenjo-daro."

Harappa

Harappa was one of the first Indus Valley civilization sites to be discovered by archaeologists in 1921. Because of this, the Indus Valley civilization is sometimes called the Harappan civilization. Harappa is likely the oldest urban center in the Indus Valley; historians think it was first settled around 3300 BCE. Harappa was also built along a river, the Ravi River. This put Harappa right in a flood plain, which made the land fertile and great for farming. It was also in an ideal location to promote trade with other contemporary civilizations.[26] This enabled the people in Harappa to interact with other cultures. This is also why artifacts from other civilizations have been found in Harappa.

Harappa was one of the capitals of the Indus Valley civilization. It is unclear whether it was the capital at the same time as Mohenjo-daro. The city was about half the size of Mohenjo-daro near its beginning, only covering about four hundred acres. Still, about twenty thousand people could live there comfortably. Harappa hit its peak around 2200 BCE, holding close to eighty thousand inhabitants.[27] However, these numbers should be taken with a grain of salt, as they vary among different sources.

Through excavating Harappa's ruins, archaeologists were able to divide the city's development into five stages: Ravi phase (3300–2800 BCE), Kot Diji (2800–2600 BCE), Harappan (2600–1900 BCE), Late Harappan Transitional (1900–1800 BCE), and Late Harappan (1800–1300 BCE). Archaeologists determined the beginning and end dates of these stages based on what types of crafts and technologies were found. By looking at various artifacts, archaeologists guess that Harappa grew from a village to an urban center sometime during the Harappan phase. The archaeologists determined this based on writings and other artifacts from the time period.[28] However, while historians have found writings from the Indus Valley civilization, they cannot yet read them.

During the Ravi phase, people started to move into Harappa. These people likely came from areas relatively close to Harappa rather than traveling far distances. The first people who lived here held a variety of careers and had many different skills. Archaeologists have uncovered all

---

[26] Hays, Jeff. "Great Cities of the Indus Valley Civilization."

[27] Hays, Jeff. "Great Cities of the Indus Valley Civilization."

[28] Hays, Jeff. "Great Cities of the Indus Valley Civilization."

kinds of artwork in the area, from beads to larger sculptures.[29] These items were made out of all kinds of materials but mostly various kinds of stones.

There was likely some trade going on in the area at this time. We can guess this based on one simple question: if the Harappans were making artwork, who were they making them for? These traders likely did not travel too far; they most likely came from Mesopotamia, which was also developing during the same time period. Archaeologists know this because beads made in the Indus Valley have been found at ancient Mesopotamian sites.[30] It is not likely these beads could have gotten there without trade.

The Harappans started to perfect their brick-making during the Kot Diji phase. While there had been some buildings before this time, it was during this phase that the mud bricks became standardized, meaning they had the same shape and size. These bricks lined most of the buildings and streets in Harappa. It was also during this period that Harappans began to build brick walls around the city.

Some of the earliest organized cemeteries are from the Kot Diji period.[31] The buildings and even cemetery plots had different shapes, sizes, and styles. Archaeologists can use this information to determine the different social classes from the time period. This might suggest the Indus Valley people had some sort of economic system by the Kot Diji period.

The Indus Valley civilization continued to expand during the Harappan phase. The people continued to spread out, controlling more land as they did so. During this time, artisans improved their crafts. They started to make glassy ceramics, bone tools, and terracotta items. Even with all of the regulated products in the area, the Indus Valley people did not seem to have one centralized government. Instead, it is more likely that small portions of land were ruled by rich members of society, like merchants and landowners.[32] In this way, the early Indus Valley civilization would have looked a lot like European city-states that appeared millennia later.

---

[29] Hirst, K. Kris. "Harappa: Capital City of the Ancient Indus Civilization."

[30] Hirst, K. Kris. "Harappa: Capital City of the Ancient Indus Civilization."

[31] Hirst, K. Kris. "Harappa: Capital City of the Ancient Indus Civilization."

[32] Hirst, K. Kris. "Harappa: Capital City of the Ancient Indus Civilization."

During the Late Harappan Transitional and Late Harappan periods, people started to move away from the cities and into more rural areas. This started to break up the cities, with the large urban centers getting smaller and other small cities (like suburbs) cropping up around them. This made the cities weaker and more prone to invasion and civil turmoil. All of this, along with climate change, disease, and the loss of trade partners, led to the decline of the Harappan civilization.[33] All in all, the Indus Valley civilization would come to an end sometime around 1300 BCE.

As mentioned, Harappa was discovered by European archaeologists in 1921. However, common people discovered the site decades earlier but likely did not understand its historical significance. Some railroad companies took mud bricks from these sites to use in other projects. This took a heavy toll on the ruins, making it difficult for archaeologists to study. Unlike Mohenjo-daro, Harappa has been open to excavation ever since the 1920s.[34] This has come with both positive and negative side effects. Historians have been able to learn a great deal about life in ancient Harappa. However, archaeologists inadvertently exposed old bricks to the air and weather while digging, causing the site's structures to erode at faster levels than if the archaeologists had not excavated the site.

Unlike some of the other places that will be mentioned in this book, Harappa has been almost continually inhabited. While the Indus Valley civilization may have declined around 1300 BCE, people later moved back into the area. Today, people occupy some of the same streets their ancestors might have thousands of years ago.[35] This is another reason excavations and other studies have been allowed. After all, archaeologists can hardly do more damage to the site than the people who have lived near the site for generations.

---

[33] Hirst, K. Kris. "Harappa: Capital City of the Ancient Indus Civilization."

[34] Hays, Jeff. "Great Cities of the Indus Valley Civilization."

[35] Hirst, K. Kris. "Harappa: Capital City of the Ancient Indus Civilization."

An image of the ruins of Harappa.

Asad Aman, CC BY-SA 4.0, <https://creativecommons.org/licenses/by-sa/4.0>, via Wikimedia Commons, https://commons.wikimedia.org/wiki/File:Harappa_2%28asad_aman%29.jpg

Dholavira

Dholavira lies in modern-day northwestern India, about twenty-five miles south of Pakistan. At the time of its occupation (between 2900 and 1500 BCE), this area was a marshy wetland. This was due to Dholavira's closeness to the Arabian Sea. This land would have been very fertile and a great centralized location for trade. Because of these traits, Dholavira grew to become the second-largest Indus Valley city in modern-day India.[36] Because Dholavira was separated from Mohenjo-daro and Harappa by a great distance, the city grew independently. However, being in the same civilization, all three cities' people would have shared many of the same cultural practices.

There were three main sections of Dholavira. The first area was the layered city. The lower a person lived in the town, the less wealthy they were likely to be. The towns themselves may have also been divided up into smaller sections. Next was the quadrangular middle town. Most of this town was made of residential housing and some small businesses. Lastly was the citadel. The richest members of society would have lived there. Religious and government ceremonies would have also taken place

---

[36] Hays, Jeff. "Great Cities of the Indus Valley Civilization."

there.[37] Historians and archaeologists know which class of people lived where based on the artifacts found in the layers. More expensive artwork and items would have been found near the homes of the rich.

Oddly enough, Dholavira wasn't made out of standardized mud bricks like Harappa and Mohenjo-daro. Instead, most of the buildings were made out of stone. While less regulated and organized, buildings made from stone were more likely to stand the test of time. This is due to stone weathering at a slower rate than mud bricks.[38] This lack of weathering made the city easier for archaeologists to study.

The advanced sewage and water system is one of the most impressive features of Dholavira. This system could divert water from other sources to holding areas. This water could come from many sources, including the Mansar and Manhar streams. The water could then be saved until the residents needed it. This helped the city continue to prosper, even during droughts.[39] The city would have also collected rainwater and water found in wells.

However, as the climate began to change dramatically, it became more difficult to sustain life in Dholavira. The land became too dry for even the city's water systems to fix. People in the city began to migrate away, mostly moving eastward.[40] It is likely they would have eventually settled in other parts of modern-day India.

In 2021, Dholavira became a UNESCO World Heritage Site. Like the other historical cities, Dholavira was extensively studied by archaeologists. During their excavations, archaeologists found organized streets, business buildings, an acropolis, and even shards of stone tablets with ancient writing on them.[41] These findings show that Dholavira was a highly organized city with an intelligent and masterful population.

Major excavations of the city have stopped in recent years. Now, the Indian government and archaeologists work to protect the ruins from

---

[37] Nag, Oishimaya Sen, "Dholavira: Ancient Wonder of Gujarat." World Atlas, January 25, 2021, https://www.worldatlas.com/articles/dholavira-ancient-wonder-of-gujarat.html

[38] Nag, Oishimaya Sen, "Dholavira: Ancient Wonder of Gujarat."

[39] Hays, Jeff. "Great Cities of the Indus Valley Civilization."

[40] Nag, Oishimaya Sen, "Dholavira: Ancient Wonder of Gujarat."

[41] Hays, Jeff. "Great Cities of the Indus Valley Civilization."

outside interference.[42] Archaeologists may still discover more about the city in the meantime; however, the discoveries are likely to be made slower than if an active excavation was still going on.

The ruins of Dholavira.
Rahul Zota, CC BY-SA 4.0, <https://creativecommons.org/licenses/by-sa/4.0>, via Wikimedia Commons, https://commons.wikimedia.org/wiki/File:Dholavira-1.jpg

The Importance of Water

The people of the Indus Valley civilization lived around the Indus River and its tributaries. Some of the most important tributaries include the Rann of Kutch, the Ghaggar-Hakra River, and the Chenab River. This gave the people access to fresh water and helped to create fertile farmlands. Traveling via the river systems also made it easier for other civilizations to trade with the Indus Valley people; most of these traders came from Mesopotamia.[43] Without access to these rivers, the Indus Valley people likely would not have thrived as much as they did.

Looking at the trade the rivers brought to the Indus Valley, it is clear to see how important the rivers were for supporting relationships between the Indus Valley people and their neighbors. As mentioned, the Indus Valley people mostly traded with other civilizations in modern-day India and the Middle East. However, archaeologists have also found evidence

---

[42] Nag, Oishimaya Sen, "Dholavira: Ancient Wonder of Gujarat."

[43] Elshaikh, Eman M. "Indus River Valley Civilizations." Khan Academy, 2017, https://www.khanacademy.org/humanities/world-history/world-history-beginnings/ancient-india/a/the-indus-river-valley-civilizations.

that people from as far away as China may have visited the area since various items from China have appeared in the Indus Valley ruins.[44] The other explanation for the appearance of these items is that people from China traded with other civilizations, and then those civilizations traded with the Indus Valley people.

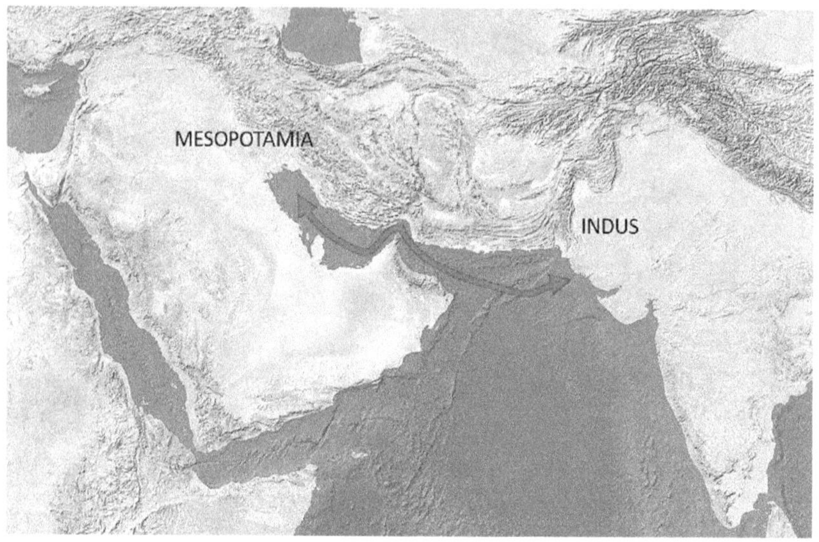

Mesopotamia-Indus.

GFDL, CC BY-SA 3.0 <https://creativecommons.org/licenses/by-sa/3.0>, via Wikimedia Commons, https://commons.wikimedia.org/wiki/File:Mesopotamia-Indus.jpg

Outside of the river systems, the seas around modern-day India were important for trade and travel. The most important larger bodies of water were the Arabian Sea, the Persian Gulf, and the Red Sea. Again, we know the Indus Valley people were able to travel the seas due to their artifacts being found in faraway lands. It is likely they traveled on rafts that had primitive sails and masts on them.[45] However, since these boats would have been made of wood, they all would be decomposed today, leaving no evidence behind.

Intricate Grid Patterns

It seems that every aspect of an Indus Valley city was intricately planned. The Indus Valley people were likely the first, or one of the first, civilizations to have an organized city layout. As mentioned in the sections

---

[44] Elshaikh, Eman M. "Indus River Valley Civilizations."

[45] Elshaikh, Eman M. "Indus River Valley Civilizations."

above, the cities were often broken up into various levels, with different classes living at different elevations. However, that wasn't the only way the cities were organized—they also used a complicated grid system.

Each section of the city was divided into blocks, which were almost exactly like blocks in modern cities. Within each of these blocks, the streets ran in mostly straight lines, parallel and perpendicular to each other; they also connected at corners with right angles. Houses would have been built next to the roads to follow the grid system.[46] All that is left to ask now is, "Why did the Indus Valley people use a grid system?" Was it just to better organize the city or for some other reason?

The answer is a little bit of both. Land was one of the most valuable resources in the Indus Valley. By dividing the area up into parts, more people were likely to have easy access to everything from businesses in the city to the ability to find a water source.[47] The closeness of homes and businesses also made it easier for people to live and work together and improved the local economy since people could trade with each other easily.

Most of the houses in each level of the town would have had the same general size and style. This was done to promote equality among the people. The houses on the higher levels would often be larger than the homes on the level below them, as people who lived on lower levels were often poorer than those who lived above them. No matter where a person lived, their house was likely built on a leveled platform. This helped to make the elevation of each level more or less flat, with some slopes between the levels.[48] The leveling was likely done by laying mud bricks or stone and digging up land from higher elevations and placing it on lower elevations. Remember, these bricks would have had a standard size and weight while shoveling or using rocks would have been less standardized.

[46] Cracker, KAS. "Indus Valley Civilization - Town Planning." Midukkan Tony, March 28, 2021, https://www.midukkantony.com/post/indus-valley-civilization-town-planning.

[47] Garg, Divya. "Case Study - City Planning and Organization of Indus Valley Civilization."

[48] Garg, Divya. "Case Study - City Planning and Organization of Indus Valley Civilization."

Mohenjo-daro (Mound of the Dead)

While historians do not know who organized the cities, they believe there was some kind of centralized government or another group that set the standards for how everything needed to be built. This group would have been organized early on in the civilization's history, as grid pattern cities began to pop up in the Indus Valley as early as 3000 BCE.[49] These early grid systems literally paved the way for Harappa and Mohenjo-daro to be built in such an organized fashion a few hundred years later. Without this organization, it is unlikely the cities would have been able to flourish as much as they did.

Drainage and Sewage Systems

Along with having an organized grid system, the Indus Valley civilization also had an impressive sewer and drainage system. The "pipelines" that ran through the city would have more or less followed the same lines as the grid system used to plan each town. With these two systems working hand in hand, ancient civil engineers were able to plan cities in such a way that the residential areas would not be plagued by smelly sewers.[50] Each home would have also had its own drainage system to take water or urine out of the home. Once the liquid left the home, it

---

[49] Garg, Divya. "Case Study - City Planning and Organization of Indus Valley Civilization."

[50] Garg, Divya. "Case Study - City Planning and Organization of Indus Valley Civilization."

would connect to the city's public drainage system. This drainage system would have been covered by mud bricks and accessed via ancient manhole covers.[51] The ancient Indus Valley drainage system would have been more advanced than many sewer systems found in Europe over a thousand years later.

A drain at Lothal.

Raveesh Vyas. CC BY-SA 2.0, <https://creativecommons.org/licenses/by-sa/2.0>, via Wikimedia Commons, https://commons.wikimedia.org/wiki/File:A_drain_at_Lothal.jpg

An array of man-made canals worked alongside the sewer systems. These canals were used for a variety of reasons, from irrigation to transporting materials via water.[52] Without these canal systems, the area would have been more greatly affected by droughts. While crops could have survived without the canals, the Indus Valley farmers would not have been as successful without them.

---

[51] Cracker, KAS. "Indus Valley Civilization - Town Planning."

[52] Garg, Divya. "Case Study - City Planning and Organization of Indus Valley Civilization."

Chapter 2: Early Indus Period (3300–2500 BCE)

The early years of the Indus Valley civilization, called both the early Indus period and the Ravi period, set the stage for how the Harappan culture would develop over its two-thousand-year history. What shaped this civilization during the early Indus period had almost everything to do with the civilization's geographical location. As mentioned earlier, both the seas and the rivers in and around the Indus Valley were integral to the civilization's success and impacted every part of daily life.

Settlements

The earliest settlers of the Indus Valley likely traveled westward, originating from the mountainous region between or around modern-day Pakistan, Afghanistan, and Iran. Settlers may have even come as far as ancient Mesopotamia, which was mostly located in the modern-day Middle East. The first settlers were likely farmers and other common people.[53] Wealthier groups of people followed in their footsteps later. Once more groups entered the cities, a social hierarchy began to form.

The first villages began to show up in the Indus River Valley around 3300 BCE. They formed around the Ravi River and spread out from there. During this period, Harappa was built, and the Indus Valley

---

[53] Possehl, G. L. "The Early Harappan Phase." *Bulletin of the Deacon College Research Institute,* 60/61, 2003.

civilization started to standardize building methods.[54]

Daily Life

The average person living in the early Indus period would have been a farmer. As time went on, other kinds of careers cropped up. Merchants and craftsmen were some of the most important. Pottery is one of the only remaining practical goods archaeologists have been able to uncover, as other practical goods like clothes (likely made of cotton) and other textiles have since deteriorated. Some artistic items archaeologists have recovered include terracotta beads, seashell and stone jewelry, and decorated pottery and tablets.[55] The most common crafts and materials were likely accessible by the common people. The rarer the items, the more likely that they would have been something the rich would have owned. The other explanation for rare items is that they were not durable enough to stand the test of time.

Indus Valley jar from the Harappan phase, Pakistan, c. 2500–1900 BCE.
Daderot, CC0, via Wikimedia Commons, November 20, 2011,
https://commons.wikimedia.org/wiki/File:Jar,_Indus_Valley_Tradition,_Harappan_Phase,_Quetta_, Southern_Baluchistan,_Pakistan,_c._2500-1900_BC_-_Royal_Ontario_Museum_-_DSC09717.JPG

---

[54] Kenoyer, Jonathan M. "Uncovering the Keys to the Lost Indus Cities." Scientific American, January 1, 2005, https://www.scientificamerican.com/article/uncovering-the-keys-to-the-lost-ind/#:~:text=The%20earliest%20village%20settlement%20at,wealth%20in%20mud%2Dbrick%20tombs.

[55] Kenoyer, Jonathan M. "Uncovering the Keys to the Lost Indus Cities."

Politics

Historians do not know what the political system in the Indus Valley was like. However, since there was standardization in everything from city grid patterns to the sewers, it is likely it had some kind of government. Theories range from the Harappans having many rulers instead of one central one or landowners ruling over the common people. The decentralized government theory is based on the lack of evidence of a king or single ruler. It is plausible the landowners ruled over the common people since houses came in different sizes and some artifacts are rarer than others. This shows a wealth gap, which could have been influenced by politics.[56] Of course, historians will not know for sure what the Indus Valley political system was like until they learn to read the Indus script.

While some weapons have been found in the Indus Valley sites, historians debate whether the Harappan people fought in any wars. This is almost unheard-of for an ancient civilization. Historians do not know if the Harappans didn't go to war because they were purposely a peaceful civilization or because they had no natural enemies due to their position, as they were locked in by mountain ranges.[57]

It is more likely they were peaceful or at least did not get into any large conflicts. After all, they were able to trade via waterways, so if they wanted to attack another civilization, the mountains would not have been enough to stop them. This also applies to any civilization that wanted to fight within the Indus Valley.

Land and Agriculture

Since the first people of the Indus Valley were farmers, it's no surprise agriculture (both subsistence and commercial farming) was central to civilization. Some of the staple foods were barley, wheat, beans, and sesame.[58] During different seasons, they would have grown different foods. Since modern-day Pakistan and India have mild climates, the Indus Valley people would not have been limited to a single growing season. This would have kept a year-round food supply available for the people.

---

[56] Elshaikh, Eman. "Indus River Valley Civilizations." Khan Academy, 2017, https://www.khanacademy.org/humanities/world-history/world-history-beginnings/ancient-india/a/the-indus-river-valley-civilizations

[57] Elshaikh, Eman. "Indus River Valley Civilizations."

[58] Kenoyer, Jonathan M. "Uncovering the Keys to the Lost Indus Cities."

As mentioned earlier, the Indus people were geniuses when it came to water systems and irrigation. Their irrigation system would have been vital to settling a community, feeding the people, and bolstering the economy. Even though the soil in the area was fertile, the land was susceptible to floods and droughts. By having an irrigation system, the Harappans would have been better able to deal with these natural deterrents.[59]

If the Harappans were not able to farm when conditions were not ideal, they would not have been able to stay in the Indus Valley; they might have needed to stay nomadic. This would have changed the history of the Indus Valley and its people forever. Luckily, the people's engineering helped them to stay in the valley and thrive.

Since most of the people in the Indus Valley were farmers, it should be no surprise that the Harappan economy more or less revolved around agriculture. This included plants and animals. By examining various animal remains and artwork, historians know the Indus people domesticated cows, goats, and sheep. These animals would be used for meat, milk, leather, and wool. The Indus people would also hunt and fish to get additional meat.[60] All of these things combined should have given the Indus Valley people everything they needed to survive.

There is little to no evidence the Indus Valley people had their own coins or a concept of money. Instead, they would have traded goods or services. Many of these goods would have been food or somehow related to animals. Trading wool to make clothing is one example of this. Outside of agriculture, they may have traded pottery, jewelry, and fine metals.[61] Trading could have been done within the Indus Valley cities and with other civilizations near modern-day Pakistan and India.

Culture

Some of the oldest clay and terracotta objects, as well as stoneware and tablets, have been dated back to between 3300 and 3200 BCE. What is incredible about this is not that the people were able to make these items but that they were inscribed with letter-like images. The Harappans used

---

[59] Deepak, Prabeer. "Agriculture and Economy of Indus Valley Civilization." Guru, 2020, https://www.ownguru.com/blog/indus-valley-civilization-agriculture/#:~:text=Agriculture%20in%20the%20Indus%20valley,rice%20were%20grown%20in%20summer.

[60] Deepak, Prabeer. "Agriculture and Economy of Indus Valley Civilization."

[61] Deepak, Prabeer. "Agriculture and Economy of Indus Valley Civilization."

a system of writing that was a mix between modern lettering and ancient hieroglyphics, similar to the cuneiform writing used by the Sumerians around the same time period. Historians think the Indus system of writing was independently invented rather than based on cuneiform. However, historians do not know how to translate the Indus script, so it cannot be read today.[62] Cuneiform, on the other hand, can be translated.

Indus Valley seals from Mohenjo-daro.

Historians still do not know if the Harappan people were religious or to what extent they were religious. Unlike many other ancient civilizations, there is no evidence the Harappans built temples or monuments to respect their gods. Most of their artwork shows animals, so there is no depiction of anything godlike. However, historians have found one piece of artwork that shows a Sumerian monster, which may suggest they worshiped some of the same gods as the Sumerians, likely the mother fertility goddess.[63] Then again, finding artwork with Sumerian mythology on it could simply have been the result of the two civilizations trading with each other and not because they shared the same religion. Since historians cannot read the Harappans' writing, they do not know if they wrote about religious rites and gods.

---

[62] Elshaikh, Eman. "Indus River Valley Civilizations."

[63] Elshaikh, Eman. "Indus River Valley Civilizations."

Early Indus Period Burial Practices

Death is as much a part of life as anything else in this world, and the cemeteries in the Indus Valley go a long way in shedding light on what daily life was like and what the people might have believed in. The tombs themselves were small earthen pits that would have dipped a few feet underground. Once the body was placed inside, it would have been covered with stones or mud bricks. The older the graves, the more space they usually had around them. Cemetery plots would have several graves in each one.[64] These plots may have been filled with family members or were simply people who died around the same time.

Dead bodies were not mummified or buried with many valuable objects, but they wore clothes and sometimes jewelry. The bodies were usually wrapped in a cloth. Sometimes, the bodies were buried with pottery or mirrors.[65] The lack of mummification and being buried with many objects is another strange aspect of the Indus Valley people, as they don't quite match up with the rest of the ancient world. While historians don't know why they were buried like this, it may suggest a lack of thought about an afterlife.

Another interesting feature of the human remains in early Indus Valley cemeteries is that the bones do not show signs of cuts or other serious wounds. Weapons were rarely, if ever, buried with bodies.[66] This is further evidence the Harappan people were peaceful and stayed away from war or any other type of serious violence.

Mehrgarh

Mehrgarh is another famous Indus Valley city; it is perhaps one of the oldest. The site was first occupied as early as 7000 BCE. The people who lived here farmed, raised herd animals, and even knew how to use metals in their craftsmanship. Even though the city was founded around 7000 BCE, the Indus Valley civilization didn't form until about 3300 BCE.[67] This means the people who lived here were the ancestors of the people

---

[64] "Harappan Burials." Worldhistory.biz, January 8, 2015, https://www.worldhistory.biz/ancient-history/67121-harappan-burials.html.

[65] "Harappan Burials."

[66] "Early Civilization in the Indus Valley." *Ancient Civilizations Online Textbook.* UsHistory.org, 2022, https://www.ushistory.org/civ/8a.asp.

[67] Hirst, K. Kris. "Mehrgarh, Pakistan and Life in the Indus Valley Before Harappa." ThoughtCo., May 30, 2019, https://www.thoughtco.com/mehrgarh-pakistan-life-indus-valley-171796.

---

who built the Indus Valley civilization. However, these founders are not considered to be a part of the Indus Valley civilization because of a variety of factors, which mostly have to do with the lack of structure in this early time period.

The earliest phase of Mehrgarh is called the Aceramic Neolithic period, which stretches from 7000 to 5500 BCE. This time period is marked by the site's building styles and agriculture. Most of the homes were made out of mud bricks. These would look similar to other homes found in Mesopotamia. There would have been very few large buildings in the city; at this point, Mehrgarh would have been more of a sleepy farming village than anything else. However, there was still more hunting and gathering than farming at this point.

Around this time, the people of Mehrgarh learned to herd cattle, goats, and sheep and farm barley and other cereal crops.[68] For the most part, all of these things were on par with what most ancient civilizations were like in this time period. Nothing was especially fantastic, and nothing was too far behind other civilizations developmentally.

Next up, from 5500 to 4800 BCE, is the Neolithic Period II. During this time, the people living in Mehrgarh had a firm grip on farming, although they were still mostly focused on cereal crops. They kept harvested grains in stone or mud-brick granaries. Homes were still made of mud bricks, but they began to be more uniform in shape. Most of these homes were rectangular. Larger buildings, most likely used by craftsmen, were first built during this time period. With this came the first large-scale bead-making operations and pottery.[69] Again, this was about on par with what most other ancient civilizations were doing at this time.

The most interesting thing here is the shape of the buildings and the development of larger buildings for communal purposes. This shows the people in Mehrgarh were starting to think in the long term when it came to their local economy and city planning. This could have very well paved the way for the intricate grid systems that showed up in the Indus Valley cities thousands of years later.

The Chalcolithic Period III ran between 4800 and 3500 BCE. This was a few hundred years before the Indus Valley civilization officially

---

[68] Hirst, K. Kris. "Mehrgarh, Pakistan and Life in the Indus Valley Before Harappa."

[69] Hirst, K. Kris. "Mehrgarh, Pakistan and Life in the Indus Valley Before Harappa."

began. This generalized time period is often lumped with the Chalcolithic Period VI, which went from 3500 to 3250 BCE, right around the time when the Indus Valley civilization actually began, which means this is where things get interesting. By this time, building styles and placements were starting to become more organized and regulated. Cities were broken up into compact settlements and suburb-like areas. Bricks, usually made of mud, started to come into play. Some buildings were also made with a stone and mud mixture during this time. Craftspeople also started to make more artistic pottery and other crafts.[70] All in all, clay and mud were the main players of these two time periods. Again, the Indus Valley civilization was on par with other ancient civilizations.

During the late period at Mehrgarh, from 3249 until its abandonment around 2600 BCE, the people living in the city improved their craftsmanship, especially in regard to making pottery, leather, and beads. The settlers also started working more with metal, mostly copper. For this reason, the people in the Indus Valley are considered a Bronze Age civilization.[71] Historians suspect the residents of Mehrgarh moved away from the city to the larger city of Naushahro, which was only five miles away. Naushahro had more impressive fortifications and larger buildings.[72] However, there is not one sure cause that historians can point to that tells the story of why the people in Mehrgarh totally abandoned the city. Only further studies of the city will be able to solve this mystery.

The archaeological site of Mehrgarh.

---

[70] Hirst, K. Kris. "Mehrgarh, Pakistan and Life in the Indus Valley Before Harappa."

[71] Hirst, K. Kris. "Mehrgarh, Pakistan and Life in the Indus Valley Before Harappa."

[72] Wood, Michael. *In Search of the First Civilization.* BBC Books, 2005.

Conclusion

The early Indus civilization laid the foundation for everything that came next. By the end of this time period, building styles and grid patterns were starting to solidify. Pottery and other crafts became more decorated and stylistically advanced. From here on, some crafts would become commercialized and made in bulk; beads were one of the most commonly mass-produced goods.[73] Shortly after this time period, settlers would build and move to increasingly larger cities. And from here on out, everything focused on becoming bigger, better, and more organized in the Indus Valley. That is, until the civilization's eventual decline.

---

[73] Hirst, K. Kris. "Mehrgarh, Pakistan and Life in the Indus Valley Before Harappa."

Chapter 3: Mature/Middle Indus Period (2500–1900 BCE)

The next stage in the Indus Valley civilization timeline is known as the Mature Indus Period, Middle Indus Period, and the Integration Era. During this period, cities grew larger but became more organized. Grid patterns, writing, and the regulation of building supplies all came into play. Some evidence shows that social and economic classes started to form, which also impacted how cities were organized. This era could arguably have been the beginning of city-states in the Indus Valley.[74] All in all, this was one of the most productive eras for the Indus Valley civilization. In fact, it was the last era of the Indus Valley civilization before it started to decline.

Agriculture

People began farming in the Indus Valley around 4000 BCE. At first, they focused on farming cereal crops, beans, and spices. As the years went on and the seasons changed, they expanded their agricultural efforts to grow more grains and even cotton.[75] Farming is the beginning of any great civilization, which is clear by the fact the Indus Valley civilization

---

[74] Meadow, Richard H. and Kenoyer, Jonathan, M. "Early Developments of Art and Symbol and Technology in the Indus Valley Tradition." Harappa, 2022, https://www.harappa.com/indus3/e2.html.

[75] Borland, William, Borz-Baba, Luca, and Farid, Sulmon, "Indus Valley Timeline." Sutori, 2017, https://www.sutori.com/en/story/indus-valley-timeline--wT3cJeHpx6TxYUQbC5ZTNXpD.

officially began only a few hundred years after people in the area began growing crops. By growing crops year-round, the area's inhabitants became less migratory, focusing less on living by only hunting and gathering.

In the earlier years of the Indus Valley civilization, farmers would have depended entirely on the fertile soil. Due to all of the rivers and tributaries, the Indus Valley had extremely fertile land. However, over time, the land began to dry out, becoming less and less fertile. To combat this, architects during the Integration Era began to build irrigation systems. These delivered water from rivers and tributaries farther inland than the water could reach naturally. These irrigation channels were usually made of stones, and some still survive today.[76] Without these irrigation channels, farmers would have had to move to sustain their lifestyle and occupation. This may have caused people to move out of the Indus Valley, ending the civilization much faster.

Indus River, Pakistan.

Qaiserqmq. CC BY-SA 3.0, <https://creativecommons.org/licenses/by-sa/3.0>, via Wikimedia Commons, August 17, 2014, https://commons.wikimedia.org/wiki/File:Indus_River_%28Sakardu%29_Pakistan.JPG

With agricultural work being one of the oldest jobs in the ancient Indus Valley, it was also one of the most common. Alongside growing plants, many farmers also tended to domesticated animals. Chickens, cows, goats, and donkeys were some of the most common farm animals. Much of the food and many of the animals would have been consumed

---

[76] Deepak, Prabeer. "Agriculture and Economy of Indus Valley Civilization."

within the Indus Valley, but some of it was traded to outside nations.[77] It is fair to say that farming in the Indus Valley would have survived and thrived without trade, but trade between the Indus Valley and other civilizations would not have lasted long without a surplus of agricultural goods.

Settlements and Urbanization

The Indus Valley became considerably more urbanized during the Integration Era than it had been in previous periods. By the mid-2000s BCE, there were over one thousand cities and smaller settlements within the Indus Valley. Most of these cities were around various large rivers and tributaries, primarily the Indus and Ghaggar-Hakra Rivers.[78] Remember, it was also during this time period that Mohenjo-daro and Harappa sprang up. Both of these cities are prime examples of the Indus people's skill in architecture and city planning. Since those topics have already been discussed in detail earlier, this chapter will focus on other aspects of the Integration Era's architecture, city planning, and specialized buildings.

Most of the populated land in the Indus Valley was leveled in some way. This made building easier and safer, but the leveling process wasn't likely to have been easy. Workers would have had to make hills in various areas. As mentioned in Chapter One, the poorer people tended to live lower in the city, while richer community members lived on the higher levels.

The side (east or west) of a city a building was on would also feature different styles. Homes in the east were usually smaller than homes in the west. The western parts of cities often contained more public buildings and an acropolis.[79] As a side note, the differences in housing were one of the only signs that point to any kind of class distinction.

The more advanced a city's population was, the more variety there was in buildings. Some of the bigger cities had protective walls and other fortifications. These features were used to keep out invaders and prevent floods.[80] Looking at the lack of flooding and conquest, it's fair to say these walls did their job well. The size and population density of each city also

---

[77] Deepak, Prabeer. "Agriculture and Economy of Indus Valley Civilization."

[78] "Indus Valley Civilization."

[79] "Harappan Architecture." Fum. Wiki, n.d.

[80] "Harappan Architecture."

helped to determine how large the houses would be. Many residential buildings were the same size, with slightly larger homes closer to the higher [elevation] levels of the cities.[81] This not only goes to show the Indus Valley civilization had a relatively equal society but also that there was a set standard for how architects were expected to create new structures.

Outside of homes, cities in the Integration Era often had marketplaces, sanitation systems, granaries, community crafts places, and storage areas. Cities along the river or sea would also have dockyards.[82] Most of these buildings were made out of mud bricks. By this time, the shape and weight of bricks had become standardized, which helped to keep the buildings looking uniform. In turn, this helped the cities to become more organized and urbanized.

The Lothal dockyard boundary.

Jashjashjash, CC BY-SA 4.0 <https://creativecommons.org/licenses/by-sa/4.0>, via Wikimedia Commons, November 8, 2012, https://commons.wikimedia.org/wiki/File:The_Lothal_Dockyard_Boundary.jpg

Architecture

Looking at the types of buildings that were in each major city can also paint a picture of what life was like during the Integration Era. Public

---

[81] "Indus Valley Civilization."

[82] "Indus Valley Civilization."

bathhouses were some of the largest buildings in any Indus Valley city. Even though these were made to hold water, they were still made of mud bricks.[83] Bathhouses in the Indus Valley served the same purpose as a bathhouse did in ancient Greece.

The Great Bath, Mohenjo-daro

Granaries were of the utmost importance. Farmers and cities as a whole would keep their stored grains in granaries. These buildings, which were somewhat similar to the purpose of a silo today, kept the grains safe from the elements and animals. They also ensured the food would not spoil as quickly.

Outside of farms, most granaries would be located in the citadel. The rich members of society had the easiest access to grains. Granaries could also be found at ports and docks. The grains there would be specifically used for trade.[84] Ruins of some granaries can still be found in the Indus Valley today.

Speaking of the dockyards, these structures were also impressive. Dockyards would be built away from the currents. Silt was less likely to build up on the dock and cause problems with seafaring. The dockyards

---

[83] "Harappan Architecture."

[84] "Harappan Architecture."

were also equipped with a wooden gate that could be locked and unlocked easily. This helped to keep the watercraft in the dockyard from being affected by high and low tides.[85] This was fairly advanced technology for this time period for civilizations around the world.

While this book has already discussed the irrigation and drainage systems, the Indus Valley people didn't stop there when it came to water-based architecture. They also had man-made canals and man-made lakes. The canals were used primarily for travel and trade, but the man-made lakes were used to store water. Fresh water from other locations would be deposited in these lakes; rainwater was also naturally collected there.[86] Outside of this, the Indus Valley people had wells and other smaller water-storage buildings, as most civilizations at this time had.

An ancient well in Lothal.

Bernard Gagnon, CC BY-SA 3.0 <https://creativecommons.org/licenses/by-sa/3.0>, via Wikimedia Commons, November 27, 2013, https://commons.wikimedia.org/wiki/File:Lothal_-_ancient_well.jpg

Dams were built directly on the water and were another important water-based architectural feat. These dams controlled how much water could enter or leave an area. These were used to prevent flooding, divert parts of rivers, and store water.[87] The dams could have been used with the water storage systems and general draining systems as well. The dams were often made with mud bricks or stone.

---

[85] "Harappan Architecture."

[86] "Harappan Architecture."

[87] "Harappan Architecture."

Lastly, the Harappans had aqueducts. Like aqueducts anywhere else, these channels started at high elevations and gradually descended to lower areas, usually ending in a basin or another water storage area. Some aqueducts diverted into different directions to supply water to different areas in the cities.[88] With all of these different water systems, it appears that most people, if not everyone in the Indus Valley, would have had easy access to fresh water.

Trade

Outside of farming and crafting, trade is thought to be one of the primary occupations of people living in the Indus Valley during the Integration Era. Since the Indus Valley cities did not have a currency, trade and using the barter system was how they ran their economy.[89] Because of this, trade was used both within a community and with the world at large.

When trading with other nations, traders often needed to travel long distances. For the most part, traders traveled over water rather than overland.[90] Traveling by water was considerably easier than traveling overland because of the Indus Valley's geographical location. Most of the large Indus Valley cities were centralized along a river, a river's tributary, or a sea. At the same time, the Indus Valley was somewhat separated from the rest of the world by land, as there were large mountains between the valley and the modern-day Middle East.

Using water for trade and travel directly impacted the Indus Valley's transportation vehicles and water-based technology. The Harappan city of Lothal has one of the oldest-known docks. The Indus Valley also has several man-made canals. They would have needed impressive boats or rafts to carry supplies.[91] However, these boats or rafts would have been made of wood and would have since decayed. Because of this, historians do not know what these watercraft would have looked like.

---

[88] "Harappan Architecture."

[89] "Indus Valley Civilization."

[90] "Indus Valley Civilization."

[91] "Indus Valley Civilization."

Image from the Boat Museum in Kolkata.

Santanupyne, CC BY-SA 4.0 <https://creativecommons.org/licenses/by-sa/4.0>, via Wikimedia Commons, February 19, 2021, https://commons.wikimedia.org/wiki/File:Boat_Museum_in_kolkata_10.jpg

One of the oldest and longest-used ports in the Indus Valley was at Lothal. This dock was built sometime during the 2000s BCE. Another Integration Era port was at Rangpur. Most of the other ancient docks found in the Indus Valley were expected to have been built hundreds of years later, possibly during the final stage of the Indus Valley's occupation.[92] The ruins of the dock at Lothal can still be seen today.

No matter how the Harappans transported their goods, it is impressive how far they traveled and traded. Most trade outside of the Indus Valley took place in Mesopotamia. They also would have traded with countries in western and central Asia, although that was on a smaller scale.[93] Historians know this because Indus Valley artifacts have been found in these places in high enough amounts. Items from these faraway places have also been found in Indus Valley ruins.

Food and animal products were some of the most common trade items. Some of the most valuable agriculture-related goods included cereal crops and cattle.[94] They did not only sell raw goods but processed materials made from animals. Cotton cloth, dried spices, and other foods

---

[92] Rao, S.R. "Shipping and Maritime Trade of the Indus People." *Expedition Magazine* 7.3 (1965): n. pag. *Expedition Magazine*. Penn Museum, 1965 Web. 29 Jun 2022 <https://www.penn.museum/sites/expedition/?p=995>.

[93] "Indus Valley Civilization."

[94] Deepak, Prabeer. "Agriculture and Economy of Indus Valley Civilization."

were some of the most popular processed agricultural goods.[95] These items would have likely been some of the most traded in the Indus Valley and with outside nations.

Pottery and jewelry were the next most popular trade items. Most of the pottery was made of mud or clay. Dishware (pots, plates, cups, bowls, etc.) could have been traded anywhere but most likely did best when they were traded locally.[96] These items could be decorated or plain. The more beautifully and skillfully made the pottery was, the more expensive it would be. Remember, the Indus Valley civilization did not use currency, so there is no way to place a cash value on what certain pottery pieces would be worth in today's currency.

Jewelry was made out of just about anything the Harappans could get their hands on. Beads were made from things as common as terracotta to as rare as lapis lazuli. Gems, metals, and even pearls were used to make beautiful products.[97] Some of the pieces are so beautiful and well made that they look like something that can be found in shops today.

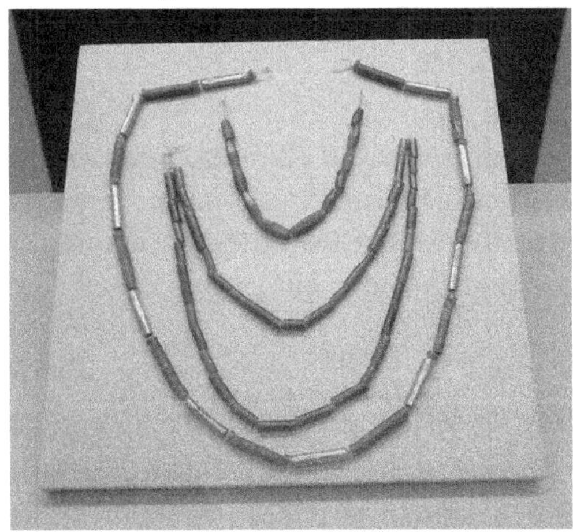

Gold, lapis-lazuli, and carnelian beads found in what was once Ur (Mesopotamia). This piece came from the Indus Valley.

Zunkir. CC BY-SA 4.0, <https://creativecommons.org/licenses/by-sa/4.0>, via Wikimedia Commons September 30, 2019, https://commons.wikimedia.org/wiki/File:Gold,_lapis-lazuli_and_carnelian_beads_-_Ur_OB.jpg

---

[95] "What Did the Indus Valley People Trade?" Tutorials Point, July 30, 2019, https://www.tutorialspoint.com/what-did-the-indus-valley-people-trade#

[96] "What Did the Indus Valley People Trade?"

[97] "What Did the Indus Valley People Trade?"

Of course, the Harappans also traded to gain items. Most of the items they traded for would have been items they could not produce or find in the Indus Valley. The Harappans traded with Mesopotamia, lower areas in modern-day India, and China the most. The Mesopotamians traded gems and minerals. India provided copper and lead. China traded the most diverse items, probably because it was the farthest away, sending the Harappans different kinds of wood and jade.[98] Historians know these civilizations traded these items with each other because items from the Indus Valley have been found in ruins in Mesopotamia, China, and modern-day lower India. Items from these civilizations have also been found in Indus Valley ruins.

By the Integration Era, the Indus Valley civilization had learned how to make standardized weights and scales. Bulk and non-artistic items were weighed to determine their trade value. The items used to "pay" for other items would also be weighed.[99] It is unknown how the worth of artistic items was measured. Their value was more likely to be subjective rather than objective.

Improvements in Science

The Indus Valley people were also fairly advanced in mathematics, which they usually used for architecture, measurements, metallurgy, and travel. They had a set measurement system, similar to how we measure in meters or feet today. By using these measurements along with mathematical calculations, the Harappans could measure land and distance at sea.[100] Being able to do both of these things improved building practices and trade within the civilization and with other nations.

Pottery and Other Crafts

The general level of craftsmanship, as well as the amount of artistic material being made in the Indus Valley, exploded during the Integration Era. Since the Harappans had figured out how to make bronze by this time and their metallurgy, in general, was improving, their craftspeople had begun making more metal-based art, mostly sculptures and small items.[101] These were likely used as decorations, gifts, or toys.

---

[98] "What Did the Indus Valley People Trade?"

[99] "What Did the Indus Valley People Trade?"

[100] "Indus Valley Civilization."

[101] "Indus Valley Civilization."

Bead-making was all but mastered and commercialized by the Integration Era. Large warehouses, similar to factories, were used. Artisans would go there to make beads out of all sorts of materials but mostly used terracotta and stones. To make the beads more beautiful and valuable, the craftspeople glazed them.[102] Once finished, the beads would be used to make other pieces of artwork, like jewelry. Beads were also traded within communities and with other nations. However, they were not used as currency.

Indus Valley carnelian beads excavated in Susa.

ALFGRN. Flickr, CC BY-SA 2.0, https://creativecommons.org/licenses/by-sa/2.0/, April 1, 2019, https://www.flickr.com/photos/156915032@N07/46600944755/

Shells and stones were also common crafting materials. Shells were usually kept in their original form and added to art pieces. Stones, on the other hand, were carved and manipulated in a variety of different ways to make sculptures and other kinds of artwork.[103] Shells were most likely used in jewelry. Women probably wore jewelry more often than men did.

---

[102] "Indus Valley Civilization."

[103] "Indus Valley Civilization."

Pottery and other items made of clay and terracotta had been made in the Indus Valley for centuries, but their production and overall quality began to improve during the Integration Era. Ceramics were covered in all sorts of designs. Some of the most commonly used pottery designs were pictures of animals.[104] Remember, by this time, the Indus Valley people had also come up with their own form of writing. Because of this, much of the artwork of this time (pottery and otherwise) also had writing on it.

Symbols

Describing ancient Indus Valley symbols is complicated because historians cannot read them yet. What historians do know is that the symbols were used as some type of written communication. All in all, there are over four hundred unique "letters" in the Indus Valley written language. However, "letters" may not be the right word to use, as these symbols more likely represent full words or concepts rather than a single sound or syllable. Historians guess this because there are rarely more than a handful of symbols found on any given artifact. The longest string of symbols found on an artifact is only about twenty characters long.[105]

Thus, the Indus Valley written language is closer (as a concept) to modern-day Chinese, Japanese, and other languages that use symbols instead of letters to make words. However, this is most likely a coincidence. There is not enough evidence to say that either culture learned its writing system from the other.

Technology

Many historical records about the Indus Valley civilization put a lot of emphasis on the Harappans' standardized mud brick. To most, this seems like something that would not matter much, but it was, in fact, an architectural wonder in the ancient world. Each brick was made based on the same size and weight ratio. The brick would be four parts long, two parts wide, and one part thick.[106] This gives it a 4:2:1 ratio. By using a ratio, bricks could be made to fit any kind of building. It would also be easy to replace broken bricks since all the other bricks in the same structure would have been the same size.

---

[104] "Indus Valley Civilization."

[105] "Indus Valley Civilization."

[106] "Indus Valley Civilization."

A cut brick from the Harappan Phase, Pakistan, c. 2500–1900 BE.

Daderot, CC0, via Wikimedia Commons,
https://commons.wikimedia.org/wiki/File:Cut_brick,_Indus_Valley_Tradition,_Harappan_Phase,_Chanhu_Daro,_Pakistan,_c._2500-1900_BC_-_Royal_Ontario_Museum_-_DSC09716.JPG

Over time, the Indus Valley people became more and more skilled in metallurgy. By the Integration Era, they had learned how to make bronze, which is why they are now considered to be a Bronze Age civilization. Outside of bronze, they made a variety of objects out of copper, lead, and tin. While they did not use gold often, they knew how to test if gold was real or not.[107] Knowing about the authenticity of gold would have made trade with other nations much more reliable.

Copper sculpture of a coach driver from the Late Harappan period, 2000 BCE.

Miya, M., CC BY-SA 3.0 <https://creativecommons.org/licenses/by-sa/3.0>, via Wikimedia Commons, June 14, 2009, https://commons.wikimedia.org/wiki/File:Coach_driver_Indus_01.jpg

---

[107] "Indus Valley Civilization."

Religion

Historians do not know which religion, if any, the people of the Indus Valley practiced. As discussed, much of Harappan artwork depicts animals rather than anything that looks like a classic god or goddess. However, there is some evidence they may have worshiped a mother/fertility goddess, who was either similar or the same as the one worshiped in Mesopotamia around the same time period.[108] This goddess went by several different names, with the most popular being Nintud. During the time of the Indus Valley's occupation, the mother goddess was one of the most valued deities in Mesopotamian religions. Nintud created mankind, facilitated pregnancy, and could be prayed to in order to ease childbirth.[109] Again, historians do not know for certain if the Harappans worshiped this goddess, but it is likely.

Some seals depict what might be a holy image. One seal shows a figure that looks similar to Lord Pashupati, who is a god of creatures.[110] Today, Pashupati is worshiped in the Hindu religion. Here, he is seen as an aspect of Lord Shiva. This is different from being the lord of Animals, which was how the ancient world might have seen him.[111] With the Hindu religion beginning in India, it is not impossible that the Indus Lord Pashupati could have some relation to the modern-day Lord Shiva.

A seal of Pashupati found in the Indus Valley.
https://commons.wikimedia.org/wiki/File:Shiva_Pashupati.jpg

---

[108] "Indus Valley Civilization."

[109] Brisch, Nicole. "Mother Goddess (Ninmag, Nintud/r, Belet-ili)." Ancient Mesopotamian Gods and Goddesses, Oracc and the UK Higher Education Academy, 2013, https://oracc.museum.upenn.edu/amgg/listofdeities/mothergoddess/.

[110] "Indus Valley Civilization."

[111] Mishra, Sampadananda. "Pashupati is not the Lord of Animals." Bhagavadgita.org, March 27, 2018, https://bhagavadgita.org.in/Blogs/5ab5f10f5369ed0e343a7ca0.

Chapter 4: Late Indus Period (1900–1300 BCE)

The late Indus period saw both a high point in trade with other nations and a gradual decline of the Indus Valley civilization as a whole. The Indus Valley civilization's decline likely started sometime around 1700 BCE and continued until the civilization all but disappeared around 1300 BCE. Historians have different theories on how and why this happened, so let's take a deep dive into the late Indus period.

Trade Relationships with Other Civilizations

We know the Indus Valley people mostly traded with Mesopotamia, lower modern-day India, and China. With all of the trading that went on between these civilizations, they would have needed to have some kind of solid relationship with each other. Remember, there is little to no evidence pointing to the Indus Valley people getting involved in any major wars or other battles. This implies their relationships with their trade partners would have been peaceful.

Mesopotamia: Sumer, Akkad, and More

The Harappans traded with the Mesopotamians for centuries, if not millennia. There were a variety of different ethnic groups and cultures in Mesopotamia. Within Mesopotamia, the Harappans mostly traded with the Sumerians, Akkadians, and the people of Magan. The people of Magan lived the closest to the Indus Valley, so they would have traded with the Harappans most often.[112] The trade with the Magan people allowed goods from the Indus Valley to travel all throughout Mesopotamia.

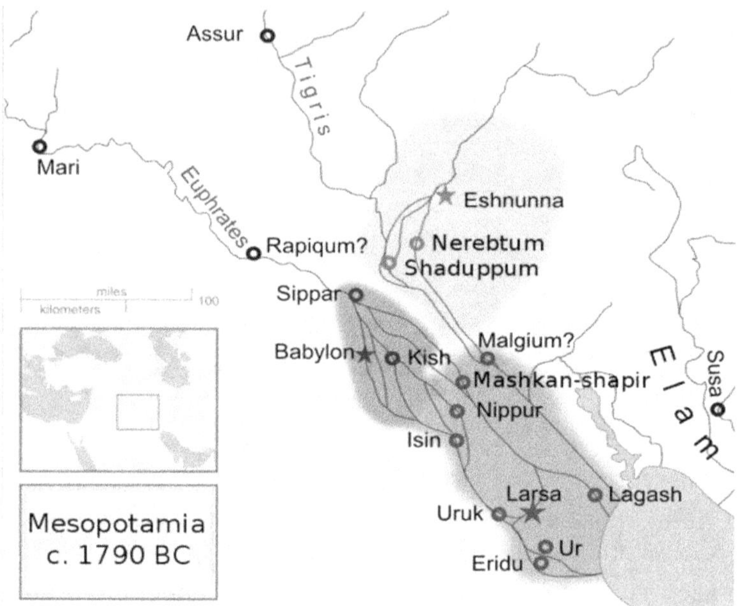

Mesopotamia in c. 1790 BCE.

Zoweee. CC BY-SA 3.0, https://creativecommons.org/licenses/by-sa/3.0/, July 12, 2010, https://en.wikipedia.org/wiki/File:Mesopotamia-1790BC.svg

The oldest-known Indus Valley items found in Mesopotamia were in graves in Ur. These items date back to sometime between 2600 and 2400 BCE. Most of these items were different types of jewelry. Artifacts found elsewhere in Mesopotamia date around or after 2400 BCE.[113] As the years went by, the Indus Valley people continued to travel farther and trade more goods.

One of the areas in Mesopotamia farthest away from the Indus Valley with evidence of a trade relationship is Akkad. The Harappans would have needed to sail up the Euphrates River to get there. Historians guess the Harappans went to Akkad, both because of Indus Valley goods being found there and because the famous Sargon of Akkad once wrote about

---

[112] B., Kanika. "Early Indus Civilization and Its Trade Relations." HistoryDiscussion.net, n.d., https://www.historydiscussion.net/history-of-india/indus-valley-civilisation/early-indus-civilization-and-its-trade-relations-india-history/7058.

[113] B., Kanika. "Early Indus Civilization and Its Trade Relations."

the Meluhha people sailing to trade. The Sumerians also referred to the Meluhha people. Historians now agree the Meluhha, Harappans, and Indus Valley people were all the same.

Historical records from Mesopotamia talk about the different kinds of goods traded with the Meluhha, which match up with archaeological records of what the Harappans and Mesopotamians traded.[114] With historical and archaeological records matching up, we can be pretty certain the ancient written records are true. Luckily, historians can read Mesopotamian writing, which helps to give insight into the Mesopotamians' relationship with the Harappans, even if historians cannot yet read Harappan texts.

As time went on, the Harappans and Mesopotamians' relationship strengthened. Sometime between 2400 BCE and 1700 BCE, merchants from the Indus Valley might have started to take up semi-permanent residences in Mesopotamia to facilitate trade better. The archaeological records that best point to this theory are the seals Indus Valley merchants left behind.[115] Other than this, there is little archaeological evidence of Harappan residency in Mesopotamia. But if Harappans lived in Mesopotamia, they would have mostly used Mesopotamian items, so we cannot discount the possibility this happened.

There are signs of Harappan residency in Mesopotamia as far away as Eshnunna, Akkad. There was more evidence of Harappan merchants here than in other areas. Archaeologists found beads, pottery, and animal sculptures made in the Harappan style. In Eshnunna, there was a drainage and sewer system that was similar to the ones found in Harappa and Mohenjo-daro.[116] This drainage system is one of the best examples of permanent or semi-permanent Harappan occupation in Mesopotamia. The Harappans likely taught local Akkadians how to replicate their drainage systems as well.

The Harappans and Mesopotamians traded everything from timber to metal and gems to live animals. Out of all of these, raw metal and gems were some of the most popular trade items in Mesopotamia. Most of these items were sourced directly from the Indus Valley or imported to the Indus Valley by the Harappans and then taken to be traded within

---

[114] B., Kanika. "Early Indus Civilization and Its Trade Relations."

[115] B., Kanika. "Early Indus Civilization and Its Trade Relations."

[116] B., Kanika. "Early Indus Civilization and Its Trade Relations."

Mesopotamia.[117] Once the Mesopotamians got their hands on Indus Valley goods, they would use the raw materials to make crafts of their own. These might go on to be traded with other nations farther away than the Indus Valley.

First, let's take a look at the inorganic materials the Indus Valley people traded with the Mesopotamians. In this case, the term inorganic will relate to non-living things, such as stones, gems, and other raw materials. Perhaps one of the most commonly traded raw materials was carnelian, a type of red stone. Carnelian stones were mined in the Indus Valley en masse. Once traded, they were often used to make beads and other types of artwork and jewelry. Another popular stone was lapis lazuli, a fairly rare gem. This stone was also mostly used for jewelry and artwork. Copper was also traded often, but it is most likely the Harappans got their copper by trading with other nations, most likely the people from Magan or civilizations that lived in modern-day India.[118] These inorganic materials were traded in both raw and crafted forms. The crafted forms would have been worth more than the raw materials.

Agriculture and lumber-working were two activities that helped to produce organic trade goods. The most popular farm-grown items were sesame and sesame oil. Oddly enough, it is likely this plant originated in Mesopotamia and then traveled to the Indus Valley by trade, only to be traded back to the Mesopotamians centuries later. The Harappans traded various types of wood, including sissoo, mangrove, and teak. Mesopotamia had very few trees, so they relied on trade from the Harappans. Timber was used to make boats, furniture, and decorations.[119] This shows that most agricultural goods were traded within the Indus Valley rather than to outside nations.

Animals and animal products were also traded with Mesopotamia. The Harappans raised and domesticated some of the animals they traded. These mostly included sheep, ibexes, and dogs. However, most of the animals they traded were likely caught. These included lions, elephants, water buffalos, and monkeys. They also traded animal products made by these animals, like wool and ivory.[120] Since the Indus

<hr>

[117] B., Kanika. "Early Indus Civilization and Its Trade Relations."

[118] B., Kanika. "Early Indus Civilization and Its Trade Relations."

[119] B., Kanika. "Early Indus Civilization and Its Trade Relations."

[120] B., Kanika. "Early Indus Civilization and Its Trade Relations."

Valley people traded animals as large as water buffaloes and elephants, they would have needed to have large seafaring vessels.

India

Historians know more about what the Indus Valley people got from trading with other civilizations in India than what these other civilizations got from them. As mentioned, the Harappans traded copper with the Mesopotamians but likely did not mine it themselves. Instead, it is likely they got copper by trading with various tribes in India. Lead was another common mineral they likely got from Indians.[121] A lot of this is up for speculation, as historians cannot read any written records the Harappans left behind about their trade agreements.

Historians do know that the peak of the Indian/Harappan trade relationship lasted between 2000 and 1800 BCE. These dates were determined by the radiocarbon dating of items found in India and the Indus Valley.[122] These dates line up almost perfectly with the beginning of the Late Harappan period.

Even though modern-day India was the closest civilization the Indus Valley people traded with, it seems to be the trade relationship that historians and archaeologists know the least about. This is due to a lack of written historical records (that historians can read) and abundant archaeological evidence.

China

It is impressive that the Chinese and Harappans were able to trade with each other as often as they did due to the large distance between the two civilizations. Unlike Indian traders, Chinese traders kept written records that today's historians can read. Ancient Chinese historians and merchants wrote about conducting trade in the Indus Valley. However, they refer to the area as "Shendu" and "Sindh."[123] With all of this written evidence, historians know more about Indus Valley trade with China than with India.

---

[121] Elshaikh, Eman. "Indus River Valley Civilizations."

[122] Allchin, F. Raymond, Srivastava, A.L., Alam, Muzaffa, Dikshit, K.R, Thapar, Romila, Spear, T.G. Percival, Champakalakshmi, R, Schwartzberg, Joseph E., Subrahmanyam, Sanjay, Wolpert, Stanley A. and Calkins, Philip B. "India." Encyclopedia Britannica, June 29, 2022. https://www.britannica.com/place/India.

[123] IvyPanda. "The History of Indus and Chinese Civilizations Interaction." November 2, 2021. https://ivypanda.com/essays/the-history-of-indus-and-chinese-civilizations-interaction/.

The Chinese merchants likely did most of the legwork when it came to traveling. By the late Indus period, the Chinese had already created intricate trade routes that stretched across western Asia and parts of the modern-day Middle East. Since the Chinese did most of the traveling, it's not a surprise that one of the biggest Indus Valley/Chinese trading towns was Harappa.[124] The Chinese merchants undoubtedly had an impact on Harappan society. While historians do not know for sure, it is possible the Chinese influenced the Indus script, as both scripts use characters instead of letters.

Less is known about the actual items the Chinese and Harappans traded with each other. Historians know the Indus Valley got jade and cedarwood from China.[125] However, not much is known about what China obtained from the Indus Valley. However, historians can assume they gained many of the same items as India and Mesopotamia, including carnelian, food-based oils, various kinds of wood, and artwork made of native Indus Valley materials.

A Lack of War

Some historians suggest the Indus Valley was able to avoid war entirely because it was so isolated from other civilizations. With all of the evidence pointing to the Indus Valley as a trade hub and the fact that merchants could travel hundreds of miles to trade with other civilizations, this theory doesn't hold much weight. Instead, it is more likely that the Indus Valley people were a peaceful group who had no "natural" enemies, not because of their geographical status but because of their friendly relationships with nearby nations.

One of the biggest factors that point to the Indus Valley people being peaceful is their assumed lack of a centralized government. While there were some homes that were larger than others in cities, archaeologists have not been able to pinpoint any one building as a temple or palace.[126] A lack of these buildings points to a lack of class disparity, which most would see as a good thing. Not having any solid proof of a centralized government can also hint toward the theory that the Indus Valley people

---

[124] IvyPanda. "The History of Indus and Chinese Civilizations Interaction."

[125] "What Did the Indus Valley People Trade?"

[126] Taub, Ben. "Was the Indus Valley Civilization Really a Non-Violent, Egalitarian Utopia?" IFL Science, September 19, 2016, https://www.iflscience.com/indus-valley-civilization-really-non-violent-egalitarian-utopia-37974.

might have had city-states. Of course, historians can't be certain of any of this, as they cannot read any Indus writing that might lay out what their government was like.

Many of the smaller cities in the Indus Valley did not have great fortifications or walls around each city. There was little to no proof of any large military-like buildings in the cities as well. Both of these things, or more the lack of these things, showed that the people living in this area were not afraid of their neighbors.[127] Instead of using their building materials on these structures, they were able to focus more on building homes and sanitation systems. It's possible that a lack of threats could be part of the reason the Indus Valley was such an advanced society for its time.

There is also a stunning lack of weapons found in tombs and other areas of Indus Valley cities. Most of the weapons that have been found were more likely to be hunting weapons rather than weapons used in battle.[128] If the Indus Valley civilization did participate in wars, archaeologists would have a much easier time finding weapons. This can point to two possibilities: either the Indus Valley people did not have many weapons, or they destroyed all of their weapons before their civilization disappeared. Which is more likely?

The theory that the Indus Valley did not see any wars is astounding. There is also no evidence of major ashen areas, which means none of the cities in the Indus Valley ever burned down.[129] If the cities had been attacked, burned, and sacked, there would be some evidence of it. Instead, it seems as though the Harappans were great at avoiding conflicts, something that is nearly unheard-of for an ancient civilization.

Transportation

When it came to traveling within each city or for short distances, the Harappans usually walked or used carts.[130] Historians also know the

---

[127] Taub, Ben. "Was the Indus Valley Civilization Really a Non-Violent, Egalitarian Utopia?"

[128] Taub, Ben. "Was the Indus Valley Civilization Really a Non-Violent, Egalitarian Utopia?"

[129] Mhackworth. "No Interest in War: The Harappan Civilization." Real Archaeology. Vassar. September 22, 2017, https://pages.vassar.edu/realarchaeology/2017/09/22/no-interest-in-war-the-harappan-civilization/#:~:text=This%20is%20the%20Harappan%20civilization,ancient%20cities%20to%20do%20so.

[130] "Harappan Culture." Students of History, n.d., https://www.studentsofhistory.com/harappan-

Harappans did not domesticate many rideable animals. They may have ridden donkeys or used them to help transport goods.[131] Overall, the cities were easy to navigate, so most people probably walked to where they needed to go.

The Harappans needed to have reliable seafaring vessels to travel long distances over water. Ancient writings and art show the Indus Valley people had large boats. Well, they were large enough to hold several people at a time and enough cargo to make the trip to Mesopotamia and elsewhere worth taking. Sargon of Akkad was one of the first to mention the Meluhha landing a ship in the dockyard.[132] Knowing this, historians can say with confidence that the Harappans would have mastered making these ships sometime before 2300 BCE.[133] No doubt, they only became better shipbuilders as time went on.

Decline

As with so much else surrounding Harappan culture, their decline and eventual disappearance is something of a mystery. While historians know that something caused the civilization to decline, they don't know what exactly caused it. This is, in large part, due to historians' inability to read Harappan texts. Other cultures around them did not write much about their disappearance. Of course, historians have theories on what could have happened. The theories are discussed briefly below, but they will be discussed in greater detail later in this book.

The first theory is often referred to as the Aryan invasion theory. The theory goes that sometime after 1800 BCE, a tribe called the Aryans started to travel from Central Asia toward modern-day India and Pakistan. Unlike the Harappans, the Aryans were war-like people. The theory says the Aryans came into some of the larger Indus Valley cities, namely Mohenjo-daro, and overwhelmed the people there, as they would have had more weapons and horses. Everyone in the Indus Valley would

---

planned-cities#:~:text=They%20used%20wheeled%20carts%2C%20boats,from%20the%20north%20in%20Afghanistan.

[131] Deepak, Prabeer. "Agriculture and Economy of Indus Valley Civilization."

[132] B., Kanika. "Early Indus Civilization and Its Trade Relations."

[133] Dalley, Stephanie M. "Sargon." *Encyclopedia Britannica*, January 5, 2021. https://www.britannica.com/biography/Sargon.

---

have been killed by the Aryans or forced to assimilate into their culture.[134]

The Aryan invasion theory was most popular between the 1920s to the early 1940s. Its main proponent was an archaeologist named Mortimer Wheeler. While excavating parts of Mohenjo-daro, Wheeler and his team found some unburied skeletons. Wheeler theorized these bodies were unburied because they had died in battle and that no one had been around to give them a proper burial. If these people died in battle, someone had to do the killing, so Wheeler made the Aryans the villains of the Harappan civilization's story.[135]

However, there are many noticeable holes in this theory. That's why it should be noted that this theory was made shortly after Harappa and Mohenjo-daro were first found, so Wheeler (and everyone else) didn't know much about the Indus Valley civilization yet.

The Aryan invasion theory was more or less discredited in the mid-1940s. Once archaeologists learned more about Harappa and Mohenjo-daro, it was seen as less likely that the dead bodies were victims of war. Instead, it was more likely the people were buried quickly, near the end of the civilization.[136] Also, remember that archaeologists over time have barely found any weapons or bodies that were obviously ravaged by war (having cuts in bones or deadly head injuries), which would be found in a culture that was defeated in a major war.

Another theory is the climate change theory. If this theory was true (which historians do not know yet), the climate change that led to the eventual end of the Harappan civilization would have started around 1800 BCE. There are two different theories within this theory: one involving floods and one involving droughts.[137] While these two natural climate changes are opposites of each other, there is a strong possibility that one of these two events took place.

First, let's look at the drought scenario. In this theory, historians believe the Saraswati River started to dry out. Historians know this river

---

[134] "Disappearance of the Indus Valley Civilization." LumenCandela. Lumen Learning, n.d., https://courses.lumenlearning.com/suny-hccc-worldcivilization/chapter/disappearance-of-the-indus-valley-civilization/.

[135] "Disappearance of the Indus Valley Civilization."

[136] "Disappearance of the Indus Valley Civilization."

[137] "Disappearance of the Indus Valley Civilization."

did start to dry out sometime around 1900 BCE.[138] This river would have been located a few hundred miles eastward of the Indus River and would have been more or less the same length. It does not exist today.[139] While this river likely disappeared slowly, its disappearance would have had a tremendous impact on the environment around it—in more ways than one.

With the river drying up, the Indus Valley would have lost a major water source. This would have affected everything from the plant life around the river to the irrigation systems closer to cities. A lack of water would have made it difficult to do everyday tasks, from washing to farming. Without the ability to farm, people living around the Saraswati River would have had to move, import food, or starve.

Moving on to the flood theory, the Indus Valley was used to having a monsoon season. This could sometimes bring flooding if the rain was too heavy. The heavy rains could damage buildings or kill crops.[140] Again, the loss of crops would have been the nail in the coffin. In the end, flooding would have had more or less the same long-term effects as a major drought.

Disappearance

No matter what caused the Indus Valley civilization to come to an end, historians, for the most part, do not think that all of the Harappans died suddenly or that their ethnic group was wiped out. Instead, it is more likely the people living in the Indus Valley slowly moved out of the region to live in surrounding areas. Many Harappans moved to the Ganges Basin. No matter where they went, they assimilated into the native cultures. Still, archaeologists were able to find some artifacts that resembled Harappan practices and arts.[141] These artifacts became some of the main pieces of evidence used to prove the Indus Valley people didn't simply disappear off the face of the earth.

---

[138] "Disappearance of the Indus Valley Civilization."

[139] Mani, B.R. "The 8th Millennium BC in the "Lost" River Valley. Friends of ASI, 2013, https://friendsofasi.wordpress.com/writings/the-8th-millennium-bc-in-the-lost-river-valley/

[140] "Disappearance of the Indus Valley Civilization."

[141] "Disappearance of the Indus Valley Civilization."

SECTION TWO:
DAILY LIFE WITHIN THE
INDUS VALLEY CIVILIZATION

Chapter 5: Agriculture and Farming

Agriculture was extremely important in the Indus Valley throughout its two-thousand-year history. Without a firm grip on agricultural practices, no ancient civilization would have been able to settle in one spot for so long. Agriculture is what turns nomadic camps into stationary settlements. While the Indus Valley's agricultural practices have already been described in previous chapters, this chapter will look at farming and animal rearing on a more magnified scale to explain just how important agriculture was for the Harappans.

Fertile Soil

The Indus Valley lay in between several sources of water, including the Indus River, the Ganga River (also known as the Ganges River), and the Arabian Sea. Both Mohenjo-daro and Harappa were near the shores of the Indus River, with the Lothal dockyard being closer to the Arabian Sea. Water also came from other sources, mostly tributaries of the major rivers. Some of the most important tributaries included the Ravi, Chenab, and Jhelum.[142] All of these different waterways spread throughout and around the Indus Valley, which was why the Indus Valley's soil was so fertile. However, it is not as fertile today as it used to be, mostly due to climate changes over the centuries.

---

[142] Burki, Shahid J. and Ziring, Lawrence. "Pakistan." Britannica, July 1, 202, https://www.britannica.com/place/Pakistan

Monsoon Season

Apart from the rivers and seas, the Indus Valley also had two monsoon seasons, which are sometimes referred to as flood or drought seasons. One monsoon season began in October and continued until February. The winds began in the north and moved westward. Instead of bringing humid weather, it brought dry air. This could sometimes cause droughts and lower the water level in the rivers.

The other monsoon season started in June and ran into early October. These winds started in the south, near the Indian Ocean, and moved eastward. These monsoons brought heavy winds and rains. It could do wonders to support crops, or it could cause flooding if the weather was too severe.[143]

Remember, one of the theories of why the Harappans left the Indus Valley was due to climate change. If this theory is true, then the two monsoon seasons could have been key players in the end of the Indus Valley civilization.

While monsoons could bring destruction, they were also one of the reasons why the soil was so fertile. Monsoons did their best work during the rainy season. During this season, the Indus River usually flooded, providing more water and more minerals to the soil around it.[144] Since the monsoon seasons were predictable, the Harappans grew to rely on the wet monsoon season to boost their crop production and saved up water to prepare for the dry season.

Agriculture as a Way of Life

The fertile soil made it easy for all sorts of crops to grow. Cereal crops, like wheat and barley, were some of the first to be planted. As the farmers became more accustomed to planting more types of food, they started to grow things they could not eat, like cotton.[145] Of course, the exact crops a farmer grew would depend on what they had access to via trade and where exactly in the Indus Valley they lived.

---

[143] "Geography of the Ancient Indus River Valley." Students of History, 2022, https://www.studentsofhistory.com/the-geography-of-ancient-india#:~:text=The%20Indus%20River%20Valley%20is,steady%20supply%20of%20fresh%20water.

[144] Marsh, Matthew G. "Tools of Agriculture in the Indus Civilization." *History of Applied Science & Technology*, 2017, https://press.rebus.community/historyoftech/chapter/tools-of-agriculture-in-the-indus-civilization/

[145] "Geography of the Ancient Indus River Valley."

There isn't an exact timeline that can show when the Harappans started to grow each new variety of plant. Archaeologists know they began with staple cereal crops; soon after that, they learned how to produce different kinds of millets.[146] In a way, this was one of the first instances of selective breeding in agriculture.

As farmers became more experienced, the communities as a whole began to rely less on hunting and gathering and started to focus more on agriculture. Soon, the farmers were planting not only staple crops and grains but also fruits and vegetables. Melons, dates, and grapes were some of the most planted foods. Cotton, which was used to produce cloth, was added later.[147] Before using cotton, the Harappans likely used animal skins for clothing, which was common in many ancient civilizations.

Farming Techniques

The Harappans used their knowledge of the monsoon seasons and plants to plan when they would sow seeds and harvest crops. Most of the time, the farmers planted their seeds in November. This gave the seeds time to mature without being washed away by the floods. The people would then harvest the plants in April.[148] These dates may have changed depending on if the monsoon season did not begin and end when expected.

Archaeologists discovered the Harappans used the furrow method for plowing and planting.[149] Furrowing is the technique of making rows in a field. The rows are laid in a raised pile and lowered trench pattern.[150] This makes it easier to separate plants that need to have deeper and shallower roots and to provide spacing between plants.

---

[146] Marsh, Matthew G. "Tools of Agriculture in the Indus Civilization."

[147] Marsh, Matthew G. "Tools of Agriculture in the Indus Civilization."

[148] Marsh, Matthew G. "Tools of Agriculture in the Indus Civilization."

[149] Amruta, Patil. "Agriculture During Indus Valley Civilization - Ancient India History Notes." University of North Dakota. Prepp, July 6, 2022, https://prepp.in/news/e-492-agriculture-during-indus-valley-civilization-ancient-india-history-notes

[150] Karuga, James. "What is a Furrow (In Agriculture)?" World Atlas, April 25, 2017, https://www.worldatlas.com/articles/what-is-a-furrow-agriculture.html.

An example of a field furrow.
Free for commercial use, Pixabay, https://pixabay.com/service/license/, April 29, 2016,
https://pixabay.com/photos/field-fields-furrow-agriculture-1359496/

Using a furrowing system helped to reduce flooding and soil erosion. Excess rains, which were a common environmental problem during the wet monsoon season, could cause both flooding and erosion. The furrow pattern also protected against erosion caused by wind.[151] So, by using a furrow system, the Harappans' farms would have been more durable during the flood season. The more durable the field was, the more likely the crops would survive.

Animal Husbandry

As time went on, the Harappans learned how to domesticate beasts of burden to help make farming easier. They also used them as a source of meat and other animal products. Cattle and oxen were likely domesticated in Mesopotamia and the present-day Middle East around 6000 BCE. These animals could have been brought over to the Indus Valley by migrating people from the Middle East or through trade. Zebu, also known as humped cattle, were likely domesticated by the Indus Valley people or their predecessors around 4000 BCE.[152] Cattle and oxen

---

[151] Karuga, James. "What is a Furrow (In Agriculture)?"

[152] "Domestication Timeline." American Museum of Natural History, n.d., https://www.amnh.org/exhibitions/horse/domesticating-horses/domestication-timeline

were often used to pull plows in fields. While farming could have been done without the help of domesticated animals, it would have been much more labor-intensive and difficult.

Bactrian two-humped camels and donkeys were also used for labor. Donkeys and camels were used for traveling and hauling equipment.[153] In theory, camels could have been used to pull plows or carts, but cattle would have been a more efficient choice for either of those tasks. Donkeys could pull carts and plows but could not bear as much weight as cattle simply due to their size.

Most other domesticated animals were bred and raised to provide meat, milk, fur, leather, and wool. Goats, sheep, and pigs were all domesticated before the Indus Valley civilization formed.[154] The Asian water buffalo, also known as the river buffalo, was domesticated later, around 3000 BCE. The river buffalo was likely first domesticated by the Indus Valley people.[155] Water buffalo do not look or act like the American buffalo; instead, they act and look more similar to cattle. They would have been used in a similar way as cattle.

Wild water buffalo.
Mammalwatcher, CC0, via Wikimedia Commons
https://commons.wikimedia.org/wiki/File:Wild_water_buffalo_Lunugamvehera_NP.JPG

---

[153] Marsh, Matthew G. "Tools of Agriculture in the Indus Civilization."

[154] "Domestication Timeline."

[155] "Water Buffalo." Johne's Information Center. University of Wisconsin-Madison, 2022, https://johnes.org/other-animals/water-buffalo/

Farming Tools

Farming tools are essential for any civilization that doesn't want to do everything by hand. As mentioned already, the Indus Valley people had plows and likely started to use them shortly after domesticating the zebu cattle.[156] However, the Harappans didn't invent the plow. Many cultures around the world independently invented their own type of plows, but the Harappans learned how to make and use plows from the Sumerians. Their plows were made out of wood, making them light enough for animals to pull.[157] Since the plows were wooden, they have all since decayed. Historians can only guess what they would have looked like based on metal and stone artwork from the time that depict plows and farming.

Similar to the plow, the Harappans also used wheeled carts. These were often pulled by oxen or other beasts of burden. While these were also made out of wood, historians have a better idea of what the carts looked like. Archaeologists have found more metal-based cart artwork and toys than ones modeled after plows. Because of this, archaeologists know the wheels on these carts were made out of solid wood (they were not spoked wheels).[158] The cart is further proof the Harappans knew how to use animals to help with agriculture.

When it was time to harvest the plants, the Harappans would use stone sickles. While the Harappans eventually learned how to use copper and other metals, they continued to use stone in their farming.[159] This is most likely because using stone was much cheaper than using other metals.

After the Harappans learned to grow and harvest grains, they started to use saddle querns and other similar devices. These tools were usually made of stone. People would place whole grains on the stone and crush them into a rough powder to make a flour-like product.[160] Without the use of this tool, the Harappans would not have been able to make bread or other similar foods.

---

[156] Marsh, Matthew G. "Tools of Agriculture in the Indus Civilization."

[157] Amruta, Patil. "Agriculture During Indus Valley Civilization - Ancient India History Notes."

[158] Amruta, Patil. "Agriculture During Indus Valley Civilization - Ancient India History Notes."

[159] Marsh, Matthew G. "Tools of Agriculture in the Indus Civilization."

[160] Amruta, Patil. "Agriculture During Indus Valley Civilization - Ancient India History Notes."

Saddle quern and rubbing stone

Irrigation System Impact on Crop Production

With the Indus Valley going through wet and dry seasons each year, farmers had to plan ways to work around and with the seasonal changes. During the wet season, this meant storing extra water in various reservoirs and other water storage constructions. During the dry season, water that had been saved during the wet season was put to use to avoid a drought.

Before the use of irrigation, natives would have needed to move around the area, settling in areas primarily during the wet seasons. During the drier parts of the year, they practiced a migratory lifestyle. As more irrigation systems were built and farming practices became more advanced, the people in the Indus Valley were able to become less nomadic.[161] However, irrigation systems are not necessary for a civilization to stop being nomadic. Having irrigation systems does help make it easier to stop being nomadic, though.

By using irrigation systems, farmers were able to transport water from rivers to water storage constructions and then to their farms. This helped farmers plant farther away from rivers, allowing them to move closer to cities. With the farms moving inland, it was easier for people in the cities

---

[161] Amruta, Patil. "Agriculture During Indus Valley Civilization - Ancient India History Notes."

to get fresh food. The more advanced irrigation systems became, the more food farmers were able to produce. The more food farmers were able to produce, the larger a city was able to become.[162] All of these factors contributed to the Indus Valley people's slow transition from being nomadic to a more sedentary civilization.

The drainage system at Lothal.

Abhilashdvbk. CC BY-SA 3.0 Unported, <https://creativecommons.org/licenses/by-sa/3.0>, via Wikimedia Commons, August 29, 2012, https://commons.wikimedia.org/wiki/File:The_drainage_system_at_Lothal_2.JPG

Most of the irrigation canals were made of stone or mud bricks. The canals themselves were man-made, but builders took natural water sources into account to make them run more smoothly. Water could enter these irrigation systems since they were usually connected to other water sources. The irrigation canals were open at the top, so rainwater could easily enter them.[163] While this kept a steady water supply in the canals, it did not assure that the water quality was great. The water needed to be purified in one way or another before it could be used for consumption or cleaning.

The irrigation canals didn't bring water to farms all year round. The canals were fullest during the wet season. During the wet season, the canals would not only hold water and bring it to farms but also make sure the water didn't flood into the cities and other areas. During the dry

---

[162] Amruta, Patil. "Agriculture During Indus Valley Civilization - Ancient India History Notes."

[163] "Ancient Irrigation System." Indus River Valley Information, n.d., https://indusrivervalleyinformation.weebly.com/ancient-irrigation-system.html.

---

season, the canals functioned more as a drainage system.[164] This system wasn't fool-proof, but it worked well enough for centuries before climate change made the irrigation systems lose their efficiency.

Granaries

Once crops were harvested, they were stored in large buildings called granaries.[165] The granaries in the Indus Valley had a similar build to those found in Mesopotamia. The granaries were usually made out of stone. The structure as a whole was raised off the ground on a stone or hardened mud platform. This made it more difficult for pests to get inside. There were sometimes walls on the inside of the granaries to separate different types of grains or as a way to have a better estimate of how much grain was stored in the granary.[166] While the Indus Valley people knew how to use standardized weights and measurements by this time, as shown by the mud bricks used to build the granaries, it was unlikely the Harappans could have accurately measured large volumes of items.

Details of walls in a granary area, Harappa.
Muhammad Bin Naveed, CC BY-SA 3.0 <https://creativecommons.org/licenses/by-sa/3.0>, via Wikimedia Commons, September 24, 2014, https://commons.wikimedia.org/wiki/File:Details_of_Walls_in_Granary_Area,_Mound_F_-_Archaeological_site_of_Harappa.jpg

---

[164] "Ancient Irrigation System."

[165] Marsh, Matthew G. "Tools of Agriculture in the Indus Civilization."

[166] Amruta, Patil. "Agriculture During Indus Valley Civilization - Ancient India History Notes."

When a granary had walls inside, the building would be divided into three to six rooms. The granaries were built within the city and lined up with the city's grid system. Some of the largest granaries were located in Harappa and Mohenjo-daro. Other smaller granaries were found in Lothal, Ropar, and other large cities in the Indus Valley.[167] The larger the city, the larger the granary would be. Larger cities likely had more than one granary. Fruits, vegetables, and other perishable goods would not have been stored in granaries. These would be eaten sooner or preserved in another way (such as drying) and kept in pottery.

Economy

Some of the harvested foods, mostly grains, may have been used as a way to pay taxes or wages since the Harappans did not have an official currency.[168] Trade was an important part of the economy, which was, in part, carried by agriculture. Local trade relied more on crops, while long-distance trade relied more on animals and animal products. While traders could have made a living without agricultural goods to trade, they would not have been nearly as economically productive.

All in all, if a person in the Indus Valley wasn't a trader or a craftsman, then they were likely a farmer or worked in agriculture in some way. Without agriculture, the Indus Valley civilization could not have survived for nearly as long as it did. When farming became difficult due to climate change, the Indus Valley society slowly marched toward its end.

---

[167] "The Great Granary of Indus Valley Civilization Has Been Discovered by Which Site." Unacademy. Sorting Hat Technologies Pvt Ltd, 2022.

[168] Marsh, Matthew G. "Tools of Agriculture in the Indus Civilization."

Chapter 6: The Great Bath of Mohenjo-daro

The Great Bath of Mohenjo-daro is thought to have been built sometime around 3300 BCE, right around the official start of the Indus Valley civilization. Archaeologists discovered the Great Bath during the general excavation of the site in the early 1920s. Many other smaller baths have been found all around Mohenjo-daro and other Indus Valley civilization sites. The Harappans were one of the first civilizations to have bathtubs in their homes![169] However, the baths did not use running water.

Regardless, this is solid proof that bathing and cleanliness were very important to the Harappans. Why it was so important, outside of general hygiene, is the bigger question.

---

[169] Britannica, T. Editors of Encyclopedia. "Great Bath." Encyclopedia Britannica, January 26, 2018. https://www.britannica.com/place/Great-Bath-Mohenjo-daro.

Great Bath, Mohenjo-daro.

Structure and Construction

Like most of the other buildings in the Indus Valley, the Great Bath of Mohenjo-daro was mostly made of mud bricks. In total, the Great Bath has an area of 897 square feet. It was built into the ground and was eight feet lower than the other buildings in the town.[170] The Great Bath was large enough to fit several people at once. It is more accurate to say the Great Bath was more like a large swimming pool than a bath.

The Harappans had to do something to waterproof the Great Bath for it to hold as much water as it needed to. To do this, the bricks were mortared together with gypsum rather than mud. Bitumen, a tar-like substance, was used to seal cracks. The bottom of the Great Bath contained a layer of brick, gypsum, and bitumen. One corner of the bath had an outlet that connected to a drain. Since the Great Bath was in the citadel (one of the highest elevations of the town), the water was able to drain downhill. There were also wooden stairs to enter the Great Bath at one point, but these have since degraded.[171] Other than the loss of the

---

[170] Britannica, T. Editors of Encyclopedia. "Great Bath."

[171] Britannica, T. Editors of Encyclopedia. "Great Bath."

wooden stairs, the Great Bath has held up surprisingly well.

The Harappans did not have running water, so the Great Bath had to be filled by hand. There was a well in a room close to the Great Bath. Water from the well would be used to slowly fill the Great Bath.[172] This would have undoubtedly been a time-consuming task. Historians do not know how often the Great Bath was filled or how long the water stayed in the Great Bath before it was drained.

Great Bath, Mohenjo-daro.
Source: Nikesh Chawla. CC BY-SA 4.0 International, <https://creativecommons.org/licenses/by-sa/4.0>, via Wikimedia Commons, September 15, 2016, https://commons.wikimedia.org/wiki/File:Great_bath_-_Mohenjo-daro.jpg

Social Significance

For the most part, the Great Bath would have likely held the same social significance as public baths in ancient Greece and Rome. The Great Bath would have likely been free or inexpensive to use and open to members of the public (likely both men and women).[173] It might have been a little more difficult for the average Harappan to make it to the Great Bath as opposed to the Romans or Greeks going to the bathhouses. After all, there was only one Great Bath. However, similar but smaller baths were located all over the Indus Valley.

On a related note, the Great Bath was in the citadel, which was the area of Mohenjo-daro where wealthier people lived. Assuming that

---

[172] Britannica, T. Editors of Encyclopedia. "Great Bath."

[173] Atmaca, Dogukan. "Roman Baths as Social Congregation Places and Roman Bathing Culture." Mediterranean History & Culture by Dogukan Atmaca. July 3, 2019, https://www.doatmaca.com/post/roman-baths-as-social-congregation-places-and-roman-bathing-culture.

everyone was allowed to use the Great Bath, it would have been much easier for rich members of society to get there compared to farmers, who would need to walk a greater distance.

More than anything else, bathing in the Great Bath would have been important simply because cleanliness was important to the Harappans. Many Harappan homes had baths in them, which is something that wouldn't happen in European countries for millennia![174]

Religious Significance

Some historians believe the Great Bath might have had some religious significance to it. Because of the grandeur of the Great Bath's construction and the various rooms in and around it, some historians believe that priests lived there. In a way, the Great Bath could have been used as a training area for priests. If this theory is true, the priests might have used the water to both literally and figuratively cleanse a person, much like a Christian baptism.[175] However, historians do not know why the Harappans would have needed to be metaphorically cleansed, as historians do not know if the Harappans had a concept of sin.

Remember, historians do not know much about what the Harappans believed in. The Harappans may have believed in a mother and father spirit, similar to what the Mesopotamians believed.[176] However, there is no solid proof the Harappans had priests. Because of this, any guesses about the Great Bath being used by priests or for religious reasons is a matter of speculation.

Conclusion

While a lot is known about the construction of the Great Bath of Mohenjo-daro, very little is known about how it was used. Most likely, it was a place for people to gather, spend time together, and bathe. If there was a religious significance, historians do not yet know what it was. This is yet another mystery of the Indus Valley civilization that is not likely to be solved until historians learn how to read the Harappan script.

---

[174] Britannica, T. Editors of Encyclopedia. "Great Bath."

[175] Kiprop, Joseph. "Interesting Facts about the Great Bath, the World's Oldest Public Pool." World Atlas, January 10, 2019, https://www.worldatlas.com/articles/interesting-facts-about-the-great-bath-mohenjo-daro-the-world-s-oldest-public-pool.html.

[176] "Indus Valley Civilization."

Chapter 7: Social and Political Organization

There is little to no evidence of government buildings, temples, or any other architectural structures that point to the Indus Valley civilization having a government. Does that mean the Harappans lived out their days without any kind of laws or some kind of authority to uphold those laws? The total absence of any kind of governing force is unlikely. However, a lack of a centralized governing force is possible.

Since historians cannot read the Indus script, there is little proof of how exactly the Indus Valley government was structured. However, there are certain aspects of Harappan culture and cities that hint at the Indus Valley having some kind of government.

Evidence of a Government

The simple fact that so much in the Indus Valley was standardized, from their mud bricks to the way the cities were laid out, is the single biggest piece of evidence that the Indus Valley had some kind of government or authority.[177] Someone (or, more likely, a group of several people) would have had to make up the rules and regulations for anything that was consistently standardized. On top of this, someone or a group of people would have had to keep these regulations in line for hundreds of years. How could this be done without some kind of government?

---

[177] Elshaikh, Eman. "Indus River Valley Civilizations."

Let's take a look at some of the things that were consistently standardized over the centuries. The mud bricks are the first thing that comes to mind when it comes to uniformity. Throughout the centuries, many of the bricks were the exact same size and weight. Other bricks were not the exact same size and weight but did have the same size-to-weight ratio.[178] These bricks kept their standardization throughout the existence of the Indus Valley civilization. While it is possible the size of the bricks was not regulated by the government, it would still have needed to be regulated by some organization.

Harappan artifacts.

Large cities in the Indus Valley were more or less organized in the same way as each other. Parts of cities were often leveled and terraced to create man-made changes in elevation. Farmers and other average people likely lived on the lower elevations, while the citadel, other large buildings, and perhaps the richer members of society lived at higher elevations.[179] All of these buildings had to be constructed by someone.

---

[178] Tawsam. "Mohenjo-Daro."

[179] Nag, Oishimaya Sen, "Dholavira: Ancient Wonder of Gujarat."

And since so many buildings were uniform in shape and size and used the same materials, it is unlikely that no one was regulating the architects, even in the early years of the Indus Valley civilization.

Also, let's not forget about the intricate grid patterns that were used throughout most of the larger cities in the Indus Valley. The roads and buildings were placed in such a way that the cities were full of right angles, making traveling and locating buildings easier. The cities in the Indus Valley were similar to organized city blocks in modern countries.[180] Planning city blocks would have taken a team of architectural and city planning experts. Even if there were no government to regulate this, there would have needed to be some kind of city-planning commission to make sure everything was placed where it should be.

Since this pattern kept occurring in cities all over the Indus Valley over the course of hundreds of years, several commissions would have been needed to cater to the needs of each individual city. This piece of evidence points to the theory that the Indus Valley, while likely not having a centralized government, could have operated with several smaller seats of government, like city-states.

The Harappans' trade relationships with other civilizations are another thing that points to the Indus Valley having some kind of government. Trade is a complex activity. While trade can be performed by individual merchants, the merchants aren't the only ones involved in the trade process. It takes a whole organization of people to have successful trade relationships with other civilizations. At the very least, there would have needed to be an organized network of traders and merchants working together.

No matter which civilization is trading, what they are trading, or even what year they are trading, the steps from production to the final sale more or less work the same way every time. First, the resources to make a product need to be grown or collected. This could be done by farmers, miners, and other common people. Once the ingredients are collected, craftspeople then make the new items. Back in ancient times, these items were usually jewelry, clothing, pottery, and other types of artwork. Next, merchants or traders pack up the items and get ready to trade.

Back then, trade was conducted both overland and water. When the trading was done within the Indus Valley, traders likely traveled overland

---

[180] Cracker, KAS. "Indus Valley Civilization - Town Planning."

or sailed up small rivers. When trade was being done with other civilizations, trade was more likely to be done via water, with traders sailing various rivers or across the Arabian Sea.[181]

Depending on what was being traded, there may have been more steps in the trading process. These steps are just the most common.

Since there are little to no written records on how trade networks worked in the Indus Valley, let's take a look at how Mesopotamian trade worked, as these two civilizations were trading around the same time and trading with each other. When trade first started in Mesopotamia, it was done locally on a small scale. As trade became more developed, merchants began traveling farther. By about 1700 BCE, various Mesopotamian trade groups had set up posts in other nations, such as Anatolia.[182] The Indus Valley people would have hit their stride in trade sometime before 1700 BCE (most likely around 1900 BCE), but for the purposes of this example, the trade timeline of these two civilizations line up well enough.[183]

Even in the unlikely scenario of the Harappans traveling to a new land to trade without the sanction or rules of a governing force or other authority, the traders would have had to work with the government of the area they were trading in. Why? Traders often needed to pay taxes to the government they were trading with.[184] So, even if the Harappans didn't need to pay taxes while in the Indus Valley (which is very unlikely), they would have still needed to work with the governments of neighboring civilizations. All of this would go much smoother if the Indus Valley had some kind of government or authority that regulated trade relationships, rules, and taxation.

Historians cannot say for certain whether or not the Harappans paid taxes within the Indus Valley. However, with so many projects in the cities (like buildings), someone needed to be funding them. While the Indus Valley didn't use money as we do today, they still paid for things and worked off debt in other ways, mostly through trade. One Indian

---

[181] "Indus Valley Civilization."

[182] "Mesopotamia Trade: Merchants and Traders."

History on the Next, Salem Media, 2022, https://www.historyonthenet.com/mesopotamian-merchants-and-traders.

[183] B., Kanika. "Early Indus Civilization and Its Trade Relations."

[184] "Mesopotamia Trade: Merchants and Traders."

historian named Bahata Ansumali Mukhopadhyay suggests that some of the Indus Valley characters might represent terms involving taxes.[185] While most of this is up to speculation, a lot of Mukhopadhyay's evidence seems to make sense.

Mukhopadhyay suggests that some of the Indus Valley symbols represent tax symbols and other items. Some symbols might represent various crops, measurements, stones, beads, and more. These symbols were written on tablets and seals.[186] However, while Mukhopadhyay can guess what category the symbols fall into, no one knows exactly what the symbols mean.

There are a few ways that Mukhopadhyay and other historians can guess how these symbols could relate to taxes. One way is by comparing it to cuneiform texts, which historians can already read. The Indus Valley texts can also be compared to different Mesopotamian and Persian texts. While there is no "Harappan Rosetta Stone," the engraved tablets are made in a similar enough way and with a similar enough style of writing that historians can guess they are tax documents.[187] And where there are tax documents, there must be taxes. Where there are taxes, there needs to be someone to collect them. And if there are tax collectors, there has to be a government or some other higher authority figure or group.

Another sign (the last sign that will be covered in this section) that the Indus Valley had a government or authority was the use of seals. In the hundred or so years in which archaeologists have been excavating the Indus Valley, they have found thousands of different seals. Most of these seals have a combination of both artwork and script on them. Some seals have drawings on both sides, while a smaller number have drawings on only one side. While the seals were made out of different materials (gold, terracotta, clay, ivory, stone, etc.), they were usually about two inches tall

---

[185] Mukhopadhyay, Bahata A. "Ancient Tax Tokens, Trade Licenses and Metrological Records?: Making Sense of Indus Inscribed Objects Through Script-Internal, Contextual, Linguistic, and Ethnohistorial Lenses." Delivery PDF, n.d., https://papers.ssrn.com/sol3/papers.cfm?abstract_id=3189473.

[186] Mukhopadhyay, Bahata A. "Ancient Tax Tokens, Trade Licenses and Metrological Records?: Making Sense of Indus Inscribed Objects Through Script-Internal, Contextual, Linguistic, and Ethnohistorical Lenses."

[187] Mukhopadhyay, Bahata A. "Ancient Tax Tokens, Trade Licenses and Metrological Records?: Making Sense of Indus Inscribed Objects Through Script-Internal, Contextual, Linguistic, an Ethnohistorical Lenses."

by two inches wide.[188] This standardization is just more proof that someone was in charge of regulating the seals or that there was a general rule about how seals could be made.

Harappan seals.

Zunkir, CC BY-SA 4.0 <https://creativecommons.org/licenses/by-sa/4.0>, via Wikimedia Commons, https://commons.wikimedia.org/wiki/File:Elephant_harappan_seal_-_BM.jpg

Almost all of the seals have a picture of at least one animal on them. Most of the animals depicted on the seals are ones the Harappans had domesticated or used in trade. Some of the most common animals depicted include water buffalo, rhinos, elephants, and deer. Sometimes, plants were carved on the seals as well. The script was usually written at the top.[189]

Why were these animals used? They were probably used because they were the ones the Harappans had the most contact with. They could have also been used to describe what the seal was meant to be used for, such as trade.

Based on archaeological records, historians know that seals were pressed into soft clay to make an imprint. Historians also know seals were used for trading because Indus Valley symbols appeared in ruins in Mesopotamian and Chinese sites. However, historians are not exactly

---

[188] "Seals of Harappan Civilization." Byju's Exam Prep, 2022, https://byjus.com/free-ias-prep/seals-harappan-civilization/#:~:text=Thousands%20of%20seals%20have%20been,shape%20with%20a%202X2%20dimension.

[189] Menon, Arathi. "An Indus Seal." Smart History, April 22, 2020, https://smarthistory.org/indus-seal/.

sure how the seals were used in trading. Traders may have had unique seals to mark which products were theirs. Some seals have been found with a hole in the top, which could have been used to tie a string through it (these strings were organic and have since deteriorated). Thus, some historians think a seal may have doubled as a sort of identification card.[190]

In the end, it doesn't really matter if the seals were used for trade or as an identification method. Someone still needed to be in charge of overseeing their production. Even if seals were made by an individual (which is unlikely based on how uniform they all are), an authority figure would likely need to check if the seal's design was already registered to another person. Government or not, some kind of bureaucracy was likely at work when it came to these seals.

There is a lot of proof that one person or a group of people kept order in the Indus Valley. The civilization as a whole is too uniform to have all these things be simply coincidences. Nevertheless, when it comes to history, it is important to stay objective. Let's explore the theories for why the Indus Valley might not have had a government.

Evidence for Lack of Government

There is little evidence suggesting the Indus Valley had no government or authority figure(s), but these pieces of evidence should be discussed nonetheless, as it is important to show as many schools of thought as possible. Just because there is less evidence doesn't necessarily mean the civilization had a government.

The largest piece of evidence scholars use to suggest the Indus Valley did not have a government is the fact the Indus Valley did not have any major battles, wars, or even tiffs with nearby civilizations (so far as any archaeological records show).[191] It is almost unheard-of for a civilization or country to exist for more than a few hundred years without some kind of battle, and yet the Indus Valley civilization seems to have been able to last about two thousand years without a battle large enough to leave any evidence.

Governments often have power struggles with other civilizations and even within themselves. If the Harappans went to war with any of their trading partners or nearby nations, there would have been written records

---

[190] Menon, Arathi. "An Indus Seal."

[191] "Indus Valley Civilization."

of it by one of the other civilizations, as long as they had a system of writing. Historians can read ancient Mesopotamian and Chinese writing, which are the two civilizations the Harappans had the most contact with.[192] Odds are, if they were to fight with anyone, they would have fought with them.

Since there are no archaeological or written records about the Harappans fighting with either of these groups, it's safe to say the Harappans avoided war. This is something that would have been very difficult to do with a government that sought expansion, control, or riches, as most governments do.

Authority Theories

Historians know about the governments of Mesopotamia and other civilizations that neighbored the Indus Valley because of their written records. However, with historians' inability to read the Indus script, historians know relatively little about Indus Valley codes, laws, and any other aspect that usually goes into a government. Still, historians have their guesses on what the Indus Valley government might have been like. However, scholars tend to argue, and not all of the theories match up with each other.

One theory states the Indus Valley did not have a government at all. As discussed, there's not much water to keep this theory afloat. The "evidence" for the no-government theory is that most of the dwelling places and graves were about the same size, shape, and level of grandeur. However, the theory ignores the fact that someone would have had to make sure that all of the houses and graves were made to be the same size. There is also the fact that while most houses and graves were the same size, not all of them were the same. Also, some homes had more ornate pottery and decorations than other homes, which shows a difference in wealth between civilians, even if it doesn't necessarily imply a great wealth disparity.[193] There are more holes in this theory than there is anything else. Still, it is important to talk about this theory to show all of the possibilities.

Another theory suggests the Harappans were ruled not by a government but by a ruling class consisting of the wealthy members of

---

[192] "Indus Valley Civilization."

[193] "Indus Valley Civilization."

society. This theory cites the differences in housing in the cities. It is well documented that the citadel had the largest and most well-decorated buildings. The administration buildings and public baths were also often found in the citadels. The people on the lowest elevation were mostly farmers or other agricultural workers.[194] While this kind of town set-up doesn't necessarily point to class segregation, it could hint at it. In civilizations across time and place, rich members of society have been able to afford the best for themselves and make life more enjoyable for themselves, their families, and their friends. With enough money, power, and influence, these rich members of society very well might have been able to function as a government, even if they weren't a "real" government in name.

How could members of society become rich if the Indus Valley civilization didn't use money? Remember, trade was an integral part of Harappan society. While a person in the ancient Indus Valley civilization couldn't go to the market and pay someone five dollars for a pound of beef, they could go to the marketplace and trade someone a pound of grain for a pound of beef. Using this basic understanding of trade, while a rich person in the Indus Valley wouldn't be flush with gold coins, they could own a lot of resources. In a world of trade, grain was gold. Whoever owned all the grain made the rules.

Next, we come to the priest-king theory, also known as the religious oligarchy or the theocracy government theory.[195] As made clear by the names, this theory revolves around the idea that the Indus Valley's government was ruled by religious figures, most likely priests. This theory is a bit tricky to understand and work with because historians are not exactly sure what religion the Harappans followed—assuming they followed a religion at all. Of course, if they did not have a statewide religion, then this theory is null and void.

Proponents of this theory assume that the Harappans had a structured religion and that the religion was a statewide affair. With these things in mind, let's take a closer look at what this theory suggests.

---

[194] "Indus Valley Civilization."

[195] Subrahmanyam, S., Thapar, Romila, Spear, T.G., Percival, Calkins, Philip B., Wolpert, Stanley, A., Srivastava, A.L., Schwartzberg, Joseph E., Champakalashmi, R., Allicin, Frank Raymond, Dikshit, K.R., and Alam, Muzaffar. "India." Encyclopedia Britannica, July 13, 2022, https://www.britannica.com/place/India

The theocracy theory (which is not the official name but what the theory will be referred to as from this point onward) is based, in part, on some aspects of life in Mesopotamia during the same time period. Historians know the Mesopotamians were religious. Part of the Mesopotamians' religious traditions included making large mounds.[196] Many cities in the Indus Valley were placed on man-made mounds.

Could the mounds in the Indus Valley have been related to religious purposes? While possible, it is more likely the mounds were used for architectural purposes. Regardless, many historians tie the mounds to religion and tie the religion to a possible theocracy.

In the theocracy theory, the priest-kings would have been highly revered religious leaders. The term "king" is used to describe their power, not their heredity, like in the modern-day understanding of a monarchy. Each priest-king would be in charge of a region rather than the entirety of the Indus Valley. There would likely be a group of priests that worked together to keep all of the regions effectively functioning as one.[197]

Of course, historians do not know much about Indus Valley religions, so the laws that came from this structure are all theoretical. However, this does tie into the city-state model theory, which is the most popular and most plausible theory for how the Indus Valley people ran their civilization.

The closest example historians have of a city-state near the Indus Valley (both geographically and time-wise) was in Sumeria in Mesopotamia. With these Sumerian city-states, a ruler, similar to a king, would rule a specific city and surrounding area.[198] For example, there may have been different rulers for Mohenjo-daro, Harappa, and other large cities. Other rulers might have watched over less-populous areas while having control of a larger area of land or vice versa.

To keep one continuous civilization, these rulers would have to work together. This is the only way so many things could be kept standardized in different areas in the Indus Valley. The leaders of the city-states could have been elected, been the richest members of society, been priests, or

---

[196] Subrahmanyam, S., et. all. "India."

[197] Subrahmanyam, S., et. all. "India."

[198] "Mesopotamia Sumerian City-States." History's Histories, n.d., https://www.historyshistories.com/mesopotamia-sumerian-city-states.html

been kings in the traditional sense. All in all, no one really knows how the Harappans structured their government. It's just another feature of the Indus Valley that will remain a mystery until historians learn how to read the Indus script.

Freedom of Religion

While historians do not know what exactly the Harappans believed in, historians can speculate the Indus Valley people had freedom of religion. The little evidence archaeologists have found suggests the Harappans were polytheistic, believing in more than one god or goddess. Historians do not know how the Harappans worshiped, but they believed some form of meditation, effigy making, and animal sacrifices were a part of their religion.[199] With so many gods to worship, it is unlikely there was any authority in charge of ensuring that people worshiped certain gods or worshiped the gods at all.

Female figure, possibly a fertility goddess, Harappan Phase, c. 2500–1900 BCE.

Daderot. CC0, via Wikimedia Commons, December 28, 2011,

https://commons.wikimedia.org/wiki/File:Female_figure,_possibly_a_fertility_goddess,_Indus_Valley_Traditio

n,_Harappan_Phase,_c._2500-1900_BC_-_Royal_Ontario_Museum_-_DSC09701.JPG

---

[199] V., Jayaram. "The Religion of the Indus Valley Civilization." Hinduwebsite.com, 2019, https://www.hinduwebsite.com/history/indus.asp

---

Family Life

The earliest settlements in the Indus Valley and in most other early civilizations around the world were started by a few small families working together to create a community. In early settlements (pre-city grids), small houses would be clustered together. The houses would spread out around the first home in a target or circle-like shape. Over time, these communities continued to grow and become more developed. Old homes would often be built over in more "modern" styles. [200] With such close-knit communities, families had to be important. However, historians do not know if families were organized in a nuclear way or otherwise; the earlier in history historians look, the trickier this question is to answer.

Families living in similar areas (low elevation groups to citadel groups) would have owned similar objects. Archaeologists have found pottery and other artifacts of similar quality that show proof of this. [201] Knowing this, it's not crazy to extrapolate that the people living in similar areas would have a similar social level and structure their families in a similar way. People living in similar areas probably had similar jobs. It's possible that older family members taught their trade to younger family members. Farmers would raise farmers, artisans would raise artisans, traders would raise traders, etc.

An anthropology professor from Albion College, Brad Chase, suggests that family relationships in regard to trade may have been an important part of daily life. Trade sometimes took place over large expanses of land. Without the use of cars and other modern vehicles, it could take weeks to get to the final destination. Traders needed a place to stay when they stopped. Staying with family members would be one of the safer solutions. "Family" might not always imply a blood relation, but it would be close to the concept of close family friends. [202] Either way, close, familiar relationships greatly improved the chances of trade being completed successfully and safely. However, this system would not be necessary for trade to work. Also, there is no proof this system was in place; it is just a theory.

---

[200] Chase, Brad. "Family Matters in Harappan Gujarat." Academia, 2018, https://www.academia.edu/37391121

[201] Chase, Brad. "Family Matters in Harappan Gujarat."

[202] Chase, Brad. "Family Matters in Harappan Gujarat."

Chase goes on to suggest that biological families lived together most of the time. These families could involve just parents and children or include grandparents, siblings-in-law, and more. Marriages, or something akin to it, took place between adults.

Who was in charge of running the household? In multigenerational households, older members of the family were likely to pull more weight than the younger generation. Adults likely took care of the elderly, and children were taught to obey their parents. Men or women could have been "in charge" of the household, or they might have held equal power and worked together.[203] Historians do not know how gender roles worked in the Indus Valley, assuming the Harappans used gender roles at all. As it is with the world today, each family was likely a little different. The hierarchy in each household could vary based on the relationships between the people in each house, not to mention countless other factors.

After marriage, one partner would move to either live with their spouse's family or move to live closer to their spouse's family. It is unclear whether the new husband or wife would be more likely to move. A dowry may have been required to marry. The Harappans might have had certain restrictions on marriage, such as not allowing cousins or other relatives to marry.[204] Even if the Harappans did not understand the genetic problems that came from inbreeding, they may have had a taboo against it. Most cultures have some taboos against marrying relatives, but the degree to which it is acceptable (such as whether marrying second cousins is okay) depends on the specific cultural group.

Marriage expectations could have been different depending on where (in time and place) a couple was in the Indus Valley. Generally speaking, singles in smaller towns would have fewer options than people who lived in the cities. This could have created more competition. In both cases, this makes a dowry even more important. Each person needed to prove to the other's family what they could bring to the marriage. In the end, the wealthier family would win out. However, in close-knit families, resources might have been openly shared between both parts of the family.[205] Again, the exact dynamics of the marriage, dowry, and family would be affected by more factors than anyone can count.

---

[203] Chase, Brad. "Family Matters in Harappan Gujarat."

[204] Chase, Brad. "Family Matters in Harappan Gujarat."

[205] Chase, Brad. "Family Matters in Harappan Gujarat."

When looking at ancient Indus Valley relationships, it is always important to try to remember to avoid looking at it from a European viewpoint. Much of the way India's history has been told has been filtered through the lens of colonialism. This drastically changes the story of any colonized people. An example of this would be to assume that women in the Indus Valley were viewed as being "lesser," like in the early days of Europe, where men dominated the household, politics, and so on. While this might have been true in the Indus Valley, historians cannot say for sure. Until more is figured out, it is best not to assume anything. This note is necessary, as most people in the Western world have more of an understanding of European life than Asian and Middle Eastern life and may use their own biases when studying these cultures.

Entertainment

What did the Harappans like to do for fun? While the Harappans would have spent a lot of time working, they would still have plenty of time to take part in more leisurely activities. Like other civilizations at the time, the Indus Valley was full of toys, games, and even musical instruments!

Most of the children's toys that have been found in Indus Valley sites (most of the artifacts came from Mohenjo-daro) were made of clay. Animal figures were some of the most popular toys, with puzzles and games coming in as the next most popular toys. Amazingly, some of these toys had moveable parts. The animal toys were some of the most complicated and were sometimes made with simple mechanics that allowed them to move on their own, like modern-day toy cars that you pull back, then shoot forward on their own.

Along with animal toys, there were usually toy carts and other agricultural-based toys that could be used alongside them.[206] Essentially, one could have a whole farming set of toys. With how important agriculture was in the Indus Valley, it's not surprising that agricultural features made it into the hands of children as toys.

---

[206] Pathania, Shivam. "Toys of Indus Valley Civilization." Amar Chitra Katha Media, June 25, 2021, https://www.amarchitrakatha.com/history_details/toys-of-indus-valley-civilization/#:~:text=Animal%20figurines%2C%20utensil%20sets%2C%20puzzle,other%20visuals%2C%20was%20the%20bull.

Terracotta toys, 3200–1500 BCE

Sailko, CC BY 3.0 <https://creativecommons.org/licenses/by/3.0>, via Wikimedia Commons, October 29, 2019, https://commons.wikimedia.org/wiki/File:India_antica,_periodo_harappa,_oggetti_in_miniatura,_in_terracotta,_3200-1500_ac_ca._02.jpg

Games were a favorite form of entertainment for both children and adults. Historians guess that some games were specially made for children, as they seem easier to play than some of the other games found in various Indus Valley ruins. Mazes and tops were some popular games. They were also usually made of clay. The mazes may have had balls in them at some point, with the aim of the game being to get the ball from one end of the maze to another. However, no balls were found during excavations.[207] Tops and ball mazes are both still popular toys with children today. It's crazy to think that kids have been enjoying the same kind of games for thousands of years!

Games for adults were probably a little more complicated than simple mazes. Archaeologists have found six-sided dice in various Indus Valley ruins. While historians do not know what games the dice were used for, they can guess they were a popular gaming component since they were

---

[207] Pathania, Shivam. "Toys of Indus Valley Civilization."

found all over the Indus Valley.[208] It's quite possible the Harappans played games that were similar to what we play today. The dice could have also been used for gambling.

One historian and musician has put a lot of effort into discovering ancient Harappan instruments and how to play them! Shail Vyas has uncovered how to play a variety of different Indus Valley instruments. One set of instruments is a collection of metal bowls with indentations on them. When flipped upside down, they can be hit like drums to make music. Modern Indian music uses an instrument similar to this, but it is made out of clay.[209] Because of the difference in materials, these instruments would be played in the same way but would sound different.

Stringed instruments were also an important part of the Indus Valley culture. Some stringed instruments had up to ten strings and were similar to a modern-day harp. Shail believes he has learned how to play this instrument. With future time and funding, he hopes to be able to recreate music that was played in the Indus Valley.[210] While this music is unlikely to be exactly like the songs played in the Indus Valley, the general tone and feeling of the music should be similar.

Children had their own version of musical instruments. These were surprisingly common to the musical toys children have today. Some of these toys were rattles and whistles. The rattles were similar to baby rattles or maracas today. The whistles were usually shaped like animals, mostly birds.[211] It's always fascinating to see that, no matter how much humans think they have changed over time, there is much in human culture that has always been and may always be the same.

One of the most captivating pieces of artwork that hint at the Indus Valley civilization's love of music is the miniature statue called the *Dancing Girl*. She was found in the ruins at Mohenjo-daro and is speculated to have been made around 2500 BCE. The statuette has a

---

[208] Pathania, Shivam. "Toys of Indus Valley Civilization."

[209] Tiwari, Soumya V. "Music to the Years: Musical Instruments from the Indus Valley Civilization." Hindustan Times, August 16, 2016, https://www.hindustantimes.com/music/music-to-the-years-musical-instruments-from-the-indus-valley-civilisation/story-WuViIqOST8WMNCSkkayuuN.html

[210] Tiwari, Soumya V. "Music to the Years: Musical Instruments from the Indus Valley Civilization."

[211] Pathania, Shivam. "Toys of Indus Valley Civilization."

relaxed pose, making her look like she is dancing with one hand on her hip. She might be holding a small bowl or drum. Her wardrobe, or lack thereof, is an important sign of the times. She seems to be naked other than wearing a few pieces of jewelry. Her hair is also tied back.[212] This statuette not only shows the importance of music but also how women might have dressed. However, historians do not know if people in the Indus Valley walked around naked often or just for special events.

Dancing Girl found at Mohenjo-daro.
Gary Todd, CC0, via Wikimedia Commons, April 21, 2019,
https://commons.wikimedia.org/wiki/File:Dancing_girl_of_Mohenjo-daro.jpg

---

[212] "Dancing Girl (Mohenjo-Daro) from the Indus Valley Civilization." Joy of Museums Virtual Tours, 2022, https://joyofmuseums.com/museums/asia-museums/india-museums/national-museum-new-delhi/dancing-girl-mohenjo-daro/.

Conclusion

The people in the Indus Valley lived lives that can easily be compared to other cultures from around the same time period, as well as to cultures today. It is interesting to see what items were common in all Indus households and what were mostly found in the citadels. By looking at artifacts, archaeologists can learn more about life in an ancient civilization. But until historians learn how to read the Indus script, studying artifacts is the best way to uncover more about the Harappan culture.

SECTION THREE: HARAPPAN ARTS, CRAFTS, AND IDEOLOGIES

Chapter 8: Arts and Crafts

The people of the Indus Valley were expert craftspeople whose legacy lives on to this day. So far, we have discussed some of the major architectural works and famous statues, like the *Dancing Girl*. Now, it's time to take a closer look at how some of the more common art forms were created, what their purposes were, and what kind of people might have used them.

Jewelry

Jewelry, beads, and fragments of other ornamental clothing have been found in all of the Harappan ruins, showing how popular wearing jewelry was. Historians do not know if jewelry was traditionally worn by men, women, or both genders. Let's take a look at some of the most popular types of jewelry and the various methods and materials that were used to create them.

Bangles were some of the most commonly worn pieces of jewelry. They were made out of all sorts of materials, such as terracotta, clay, copper, and bronze. Terracotta and clay bangles were hardened and covered with lacquer. While much of the paint has since worn away, historians believe the terracotta and clay bangles were often decorated with red and black paints.[213] Depending on how thick the bangles were, they may have had intricate designs. Metal bangles were less likely to have been painted.

---

[213] "Jewellery." Sindhishaan, 2012, https://www.sindhishaan.com/gallery/jewellery.html.

Terracotta and clay bangles were shaped by hand or by small tools. It is easy to see this with whole (undamaged) bangles since they do not form perfect circles. Outside of stylistic choices, this also explains why bangles come in all different shapes and sizes. It's possible they are one of the few things in the Indus Valley that weren't standardized!

Metal bangles, on the other hand, needed to be made with tools since the metal would be too hot to handle by hand. Instead, metal was heated up and banged into a circular shape with a hammer.[214] The metal bangles look more well made than the terracotta bangles. Perhaps this is because they required more specialized work to be made well. They may have also been more expensive, which could add some inherent quality control.

Necklaces were also commonly worn in the Indus Valley. These were usually made out of thin metals or beads on strings. These beads could be made from everything from clay to gold. Some of the beads most indicative of Harappan handiwork are made from carnelian, copper, jasper, steatite, lizardite, and grossular garnet.[215] With these materials, the most common colors for jewelry seem to have been red, orange, brown, and green. Terracotta or clay beads may have also been painted to display other colors.

The materials for these beads could be sourced in the Indus Valley, mined in areas around the Indus Valley (mostly in modern-day northern India), or obtained through trade with other nations.[216] No matter where the materials came from, the beads were shaped to have different sizes and designs.

While the Harappans didn't invent the concept of glazing jewelry, they did develop a new kind of gloss that gave their jewelry an exceptional shimmer and shine. This gloss, also called faience, came in a variety of colors but mostly in shades of red, green, and blue.[217] These may have been the easiest colors to make, or maybe they were just the colors the Harappans thought were most beautiful.

---

[214] "Jewellery."

[215] "Jewellery."

[216] "Jewellery."

[217] "Jewellery."

Oddly enough, jewelry was almost never buried with the dead. This includes both bodies wearing jewelry or jewelry placed in tombs with bodies.[218] The jewelry would not have decayed over time, like the rest of the Harappans' clothing. Instead of being buried with people, the jewelry was likely passed to other family members or sold. This is a striking juxtaposition to the Egyptian civilization, which was in full swing at the same time as the Indus Valley civilization. The Egyptians often buried jewelry and other items with their dead since they thought their dead could use the items in the afterlife.[219] The lack of jewelry in Harappan tombs may hint that either the Harappans didn't have a concept of an afterlife or that they thought they would not be able to take items with them from this world into the next.

Pottery

Harappan pottery is world-famous for its shape, style, and glaze. Creating pottery was a revered skill and an important job for artisans. Like anywhere else in the world, pottery in the Indus Valley was used to store everything from food to flowers. For this section, "pottery" will refer to any bowl or vase-shaped object made of clay.

All Harappan pottery was made of clay, which was locally sourced in the Indus Valley. This clay was of good quality and easily moldable. There were a few different ways in which pottery could be made. What method crafters used depended on their skill level. Some examples of pottery techniques include shaping clay by hand, using molds, and using a pottery wheel. When the clay was in the perfect shape, it was baked in a kiln to harden. Later, it would be glazed in a clear or colored gloss.[220] Pottery may have used the same gloss as jewelry. However, jewelry would not have been made using a throwing (pottery) wheel.

Similar to clay and terracotta jewelry, pottery was often painted red, black, blue, white, and green, with red, white, and black being the most

---

[218] "Jewellery."

[219] Glencairn Museum News. "Sacred Adornment: Jewelry as Belief in Ancient Egypt." Glencairn Museum, November 2, 2020, https://www.glencairnmuseum.org/newsletter/2020/3/6/sacred-adornment-jewelry-as-belief-in-ancient-egypt.

[220] Chhatrapati Shivaji Maharaj Bastu Sangrahalaya. "Harappan Miniature Pottery." Indian Culture, n.d., https://indianculture.gov.in/artefacts-museums/harappan-miniature-pottery#:~:text=Harappan%20pottery%20was%20made%20of,basin%2C%20casket%20and%20so%20on.

---

popular colors.[221] The colors could also be colored with tinted gloss.

Pottery from different regions would sometimes have unique painted designs. The Ghaggar Plains region of the Indus Valley (modern-day Rajasthan) and numerous other sites have been extensively excavated, revealing large caches of pottery. Archaeologists can use the designs on the pottery to guess when it was made. This doesn't so much give archaeologists the exact year a piece of pottery was made but instead which phase (Early, Mature, etc.) it was made in. The more intricate the patterns and drawings, the more recently the pottery was likely made.[222] Interestingly enough, it seems the smaller the pottery was, the more intricate the paintings were. Larger pieces of pottery generally had less detailed designs and used broader brushstrokes.

Outside of using painting styles to determine when the pottery was made, historians can also radiocarbon date the pottery. It can also be studied at a microscopic level. By using microscopic data, scientists can determine where the clay used to make the pottery was sourced.[223] Most of the clay would have been sourced within the Indus Valley, as this would have been easier and less expensive than importing clay.

Some of the pottery archaeologists have found are very small. They could have been used to hold small objects like medicines or spices. However, some historians think they were used as children's toys.[224] Children have toy dishes and food today, so it makes sense that Harappan kids would have their own kitchen sets. It seems like play has not changed much in the last few thousand years.

Animal Miniatures

Agriculture was a major part of life in the Indus Valley, so it is no wonder that so many of their arts and crafts are either in the shape of

---

[221] Bhagat, Sonya. "A Study of the Harappan Pottery Tradition in Saurashtra (With Special Reference to Padri and Tarasara, Shavnagdar District, Gujarat)." *Bulletin of the Deccan College Research Institute* 64/65 (2004): 359–64. https://www.jstor.org/stable/42930666

[222] Dangi, Vivek and Uesugi, Aninori. "A Study on Harappan Painted Pottery from the Ghaggar Plains." The Journal of the Indian Archaeological Society, No. 43, 2013, https://www.academia.edu/9718951/A_Study_on_the_Harappan_Painted_Pottery_from_the_Gha ggar_Plains

[223] Bhagat, Sonya. "A Study of the Harappan Pottery Tradition in Saurashtra (With Special Reference to Padri and Tarasara, Shavnagdar District, Gujarat).

[224] Chhatrapati Shivaji Maharaj Bastu Sangrahalaya. "Harappan Miniature Pottery."

animals or have animals painted or carved on them. Small animal figurines have been found all over the Indus Valley. This can imply they were cheap and easy to produce, making them commonplace in people's homes.

Animal figurines could be made of all types of materials. For the most part, they were made of clay or terracotta. Some figures used sand, ground shells, or organic materials to hold the figure together. The word "miniature" isn't an exaggeration—some were as small as six centimeters high! Some of the bigger sculptures only reached about thirty centimeters high. The later the sculptures were made, the more detailed they tended to be.[225] It's best to imagine them as small tchotchkes someone might display in their home today.

Most of the animals were modeled after farm animals. About 75 percent of the animal figures found in Harappan ruins are cattle or buffalo. Other common animals include dogs, cats, sheep, elephants, deer, and monkeys. Most of the time, the animals are on four legs. Some animal sculptures had matching farm equipment, such as plows, wheels, or cages.[226] This provides great evidence as to what kind of animals the Indus Valley people saw and worked with on a regular basis. It also suggests the Harappans had pet dogs and cats.

However, not all animal sculptures were made to look like real animals. Some looked like mythical creatures that are still commonly known today, like unicorns. Other animal figurines have human-like attributes, such as beards. Some historians suggest these types of figures could have been used for ritual purposes or as amulets.[227] However, it is unclear as to what kind of ritual they would have been used in or how they would have been used in the ritual.

While many animal figurines were probably used for decoration, some were also toys. Some of the most common animal toys were cows and other livestock. Most of the toy sculptures were made of clay, but they were also made of wood, string, or other materials that have since biodegraded.[228] These toys were intimate creations, as they were made by

---

[225] EIA Editors. "Indus Valley Terracotta Animal Figurines." Map Academy, n.d., https://mapacademy.io/article/indus-valley-terracotta-animal-figurines/.

[226] EIA Editors. "Indus Valley Terracotta Animal Figurines."

[227] EIA Editors. "Indus Valley Terracotta Animal Figurines."

[228] "Indus Valley Wheeled Ram Toy," in World History Commons, n.d.,

hand rather than by a throwing wheel. They may have been painted or kept plain.

A toy from Mohenjo-daro.
https://en.wikipedia.org/wiki/File:Mohenjodaro_toy_001.jpg

Sculptures

The Harappans were expert sculptors. However, only a few large sculptures still remain. It is unclear if the Indus Valley people did not create many large sculptures in the first place or if they were destroyed over time. What historians do know is the Harappans used a wide variety of materials to make them.

Stone was one of the most common sculpture materials. Sandstone was especially common. Compared to other stones, sandstone is relatively soft and easy to work with. There are several large sandstone reservoirs and deposits in modern-day Pakistan, so it stands to reason they were always there. This sandstone came in an array of colors, including red, orange, yellow, brown, pink, and grey.[229] The Harappans would have taken advantage of this to create colorful works.

---

https://worldhistorycommons.org/indus-valley-wheeled-ram-toy

[229] Siddiqui, Muhammah H. "Assignment on Sandstone Reservoir in Pakistan." Department of Earth and Environmental Sciences. Bahria University, November 5, 2015, https://www.academia.edu/18491035/Sandstone_Resorvior_in_Pakistan.

One of the most well-preserved examples archaeologists have of Harappan sandstone work is the "Male Torso" sculpture. This piece of art is exactly what it sounds like. It was crafted from a reddish-purple sandstone. The torso shows little wear and tear. However, there are grooves and cracks near the armpits and bottom of the neck. This suggests the sculpture may have had a head and arms at some point.[230] However, if the sculpture ever had a head or limbs, they have never been found.

Harappan Male Torso (Indus Valley).
Gary Todd, CC0, via Wikimedia Commons, November 12, 2015,
https://commons.wikimedia.org/wiki/File:Harappan_Male_torso_(Indus_Valley).jpg

The Harappans were also fond of steatite. They often used this material to make their beads and other decorative goods. One of the most famous Harappan sculptures of all time, the Priest-King, is made of steatite.[231] Other smaller sculptures and figurines would have been made from this material as well.

---

[230] "Sculpture in the Indus Valley." GK Today, December 17, 2013, https://www.gktoday.in/topic/sculpture-in-indus-valley-civilization/#:~:text=Terracotta%20Sculptures,-The%20terracotta%20figurines&text=The%20terracotta%20figurines%20of%20Indus,the%20female%20were%20more%20common.

[231] "Sculpture in the Indus Valley."

Terracotta was also popular. By definition, terracotta is any type of clay that has been fired to harden. Many ancient cultures made terracotta sculptures because the clay was easy to put into molds or shape by hand.[232] The quality of the final product could vary greatly between sculptures; it depended almost entirely on the skill of the craftsperson making it. One of the most famous Harappan terracotta sculptures is the "Mother Goddess," which was found in Mohenjo-daro.

Mother Goddess sculpture.

Quratulain, CC BY-SA 3.0 <https://creativecommons.org/licenses/by-sa/3.0>, via Wikimedia Commons, November 16, 2013, https://commons.wikimedia.org/wiki/File:Picture_of_original_Godess.jpg

Perhaps the most impressive Harappan sculptures were made of bronze. Part of what makes the Harappans' work so important is that the Bronze Age only began around 3000 BCE, right around the same time the Indus Valley civilization was beginning.[233] This means the Harappans would have been some of the first cultures to use bronze in art and other crafts.

---

[232] "Sculpture in the Indus Valley."

[233] Britannica, T. Editors of Encyclopedia. "Bronze Age." Encyclopedia Britannica, May 13, 2022. https://www.britannica.com/event/Bronze-Age.

To make bronze sculptures, the craftsperson would first have to make a mold, which was usually made of clay. The Harappans used this technique to make their sculptures, but they also used something called the lost-wax technique. This technique involved using beeswax to make wire-like pieces of wax strings. These strings could be used to make more detailed and structured shapes than clay alone. Then, clay, dung, or sand was molded onto the wires. When all this was done, it would create a solid mold that would be able to handle the heat of molten bronze.[234] The most popular bronze sculptures are the *Dancing Girl* and the *Bronze Bull.*

Conclusion

There is no doubt the Harappans were masters of their crafts. As the Indus Valley sites continue to be excavated, more art pieces are sure to be uncovered. Any new art pieces that are found are likely to be similar to the ones discussed in this chapter.

---

[234] "Sculpture in the Indus Valley."

Chapter 9: Religious Structure, Iconography, and Burial Practices

The Harappans were something of a mystery when it came to their daily lives and the structure of their government. They were even more mysterious when it came to their religious beliefs. At least, mysterious in the sense that historians still do not know much about what they believed in. While this book has discussed some overarching themes in their religions, this chapter will go more in-depth on some of the various theories behind the Harappan religion.

Religious Theories

It is unknown if the Harappans wrote about their religion since historians cannot read the Indus script. Because of this, historians need to use artifacts the Harappans left behind, namely sculptures and other types of artwork. Historians also look at what the people in nearby areas believed in. This is because civilizations with similar cultures may have had similar or shared religions.

If the Harappans shared a religion with any other culture, it was most likely to have been with the Mesopotamians. As discussed earlier, archaeologists have found a sculpture that looks similar to the Mesopotamian mother goddess.[235] If the Harappans worshiped the mother goddess, then it is possible they may have worshiped some of the

---

[235] "Indus Valley Civilization."

other Mesopotamian gods and goddesses, along with following other aspects of their religion.

The Mesopotamians had a polytheistic religion, meaning they worshiped more than one god or goddess. The first two gods, Apsu and Tiamat, created the world. Once the world was created, other gods and goddesses came to life. However, these younger gods and goddesses often were in conflict with their elders. Their battles and the fallout from them served to create various features of the earth.[236] These stories worked their way into Mesopotamia's general mythology. As with many other ancient cultures, their mythology shaped the way they saw the world around them and interacted with it.

Temples were erected as places to show veneration to the gods and goddesses. If humans worshiped their gods and made sacrifices to them, then the gods would watch over and protect them. Humans could also pray as a form of worship.[237] However, the Harappans did not build any lavish temples or other buildings that might have been places of worship.[238] This works against the theory the Harappans and Mesopotamians had the same religion. Then again, it is possible they worshiped the same gods but in different ways.

The Mesopotamians also believed in the power of divination or predicting the future. Diviners could interpret messages from the gods by looking at the organs of certain animals, the actions of living animals, and the health of people.[239] Divining was a specialized skill that not everyone could do.

The Harappans may have believed in a form of animism. Generally speaking, animism is the belief that all living things (and sometimes nonliving things) have a soul. This worship primarily revolves around animals and plants but can also include things like rivers, mountains, and objects that spirits (human or otherwise) might inhabit.[240] In this religion, there are no higher gods and goddesses; instead, everything has a spirit.

---

[236] Mark, Joshua J. "Mesopotamian Religion." World History Encyclopedia. World History Publishing, February 22, 2011, https://www.worldhistory.org/Mesopotamian_Religion/.

[237] Mark, Joshua J. "Mesopotamian Religion."

[238] Elshaikh, Eman. "Indus River Valley Civilizations."

[239] Mark, Joshua J. "Mesopotamian Religion."

[240] Perkins, McKenzie. "What Is Animism?" Learn Religions, April 5, 2019, https://www.learnreligions.com/what-is-animism-4588366

Because of this, everything can be worshiped. However, this doesn't mean that everything was worshiped. People likely picked and chose which plants, animals, departed human spirits, or nonliving objects they wanted to praise.

Some archaeologists suggest the Harappans were animists because they created so many pieces of artwork and seals that depict plants and animals. Some of their art pieces showed humans and animals together. Some also suggest the Harappans may have worshiped stones if they thought spirits were housed within them.[241] It is not known how these animals, plants, and nonliving objects were worshiped. To understand how it might have been done, we need to look at how animism works in other cultures around the globe.

The suggestion the Harappans were animists seems to hold more weight than the thought they worshiped in the exact same way as the Mesopotamians. Animism doesn't require any temples or religious leaders. This matches up well with the Indus Valley's lack of religious buildings or signs of a centralized religion.

Some animists believed in a supreme god that ruled over all spirits, while other groups did not. In either case, the average animist would have been more concerned with praising and respecting everyday spirits rather than a supreme god. These spirits could affect people on a personal level. The kinder a person was to the spirits, the better their life was likely to be.[242] In turn, if a person disrespected the spirits, they would face bad luck.

Another popular theory is that the Harappans were some of the earliest Hindus or that their religious practices were the inspiration for what would eventually become Hinduism. It is tricky to know for sure. Scholars estimate that Hinduism as an organized religion started sometime between 2300 BCE and 1500 BCE, most likely in the Indus Valley.[243] While this timeline and area match up with the Harappan civilization, it doesn't necessarily mean the Harappan civilization as a

---

[241] Anand. "Socio-Religious Life of the Harappan People." Your Article Library, n.d., https://www.yourarticlelibrary.com/history/socio-religious-life-of-the-harappan-people/47142.

[242] Halverston, Dean. "An Overview Definition of Animism." The Traveling Team. International Students, Inc, 2004, https://www.thetravelingteam.org/articles/animism-overview.

[243] History.com Editors. "Hinduism." History. A&E television Networks, May 19, 2022, https://www.history.com/topics/religion/hinduism

whole was Hindu.

The Rig Veda, the first of the Hindu holy books, was written sometime around 1500 BCE. While this was around the time the Indus Valley civilization was still going on, the book was written in Sanskrit, so we know the Indus Valley people did not write it.[244] It is almost impossible to say whether or not for certain anyone in the Indus Valley civilization ever got to read the Rig Veda, but it is more likely than not that the average Harappan would not have had access to it.

One of the biggest reasons archaeologists believe the Harappans might have had something to do with Hinduism is because of the Pashupati seal. This seal represents a god who was the lord of animals. Historians see this as a proto-Shiva, who is a Hindu god.[245] So, while the Harappans may not have been Hindu, they may have had a religion that somehow tied into Hinduism.

Knowing all of these things about Hinduism and the general timeline of the Indus Valley civilization, it is most likely the Harappans believed in *something*. This could have been animism, proto-gods, or various other spirits. Hinduism would later take some aspects of whatever the Harappans (and other peoples in the area) believed and incorporate them into the religion. So, while it's not fair to say the Harappans were Hindus, it is fair to say they influenced what would become Hinduism.

Lastly, it's possible the Harappans didn't have a religion or believed in some kind of unspecified higher power. If this were the case, the Harappans would not have had any religious ceremonies or even a centralized religion. However, as atheism is more of a lack of a religion than a religion itself, it is hard to prove whether or not the Harappans believed in it.

Iconography

Iconography is a common type of art practice in which certain figures, shapes, and designs represent different concepts, animals, or people. In regards to the Harappans, most of their iconography has been found on seals and pottery. The designs were usually painted on or etched into the

---

[244] History.com Editors. "Hinduism."

[245] Marcus334. "Shiva Pashupati." World History Encyclopedia. World History Publishing, April 26, 2012, https://www.worldhistory.org/image/361/shiva-pashupati/.

work.[246] Various historians and anthropologists have theories on what these figures could mean.

Some of the most common icons in Harappan art were domestic animals. Part of the reason these icons were so popular was that agriculture was so important to Harappan daily life and their economy. Some anthropologists suggest art with domesticated farm animals on them could represent a family totem.[247] This suggests items marked with a specific animal and script showed that a certain family owned the item. This would have been especially common for merchant and trader families.

Animal totems also appeared on buildings, which could suggest these were places where animals were bought, sold, or sacrificed.[248] If animals were sacrificed at these places, that would show they had some kind of religious significance. If the Harappans had any form of ancient religion, it is likely that some kind of sacrifice would have been a common part of their religious practices.

Harappan (Indus Valley) Pottery Figure
Gary Todd. Flickr, Public Domain, https://creativecommons.org/publicdomain/zero/1.0/, November 12, 2015, https://www.flickr.com/photos/101561334@N08/22517672984

---

[246]Sparavigna, Amelia. "Icons and Signs from the Ancient Harappa." Dipartimento di Fisica, Politechnico di Torino, n.d., https://web-archive.southampton.ac.uk/cogprints.org/6179/1/icons-and-signs-harappa.pdf

[247] Sparavigna, Amelia. "Icons and Signs from the Ancient Harappa."

[248] Sparavigna, Amelia. "Icons and Signs from the Ancient Harappa."

Stars were another common icon, as they appeared in all sorts of Harappan artwork. This could suggest the Harappans appreciated the stars, either for their beauty or for astrological reasons.[249] This ties into Vedic astrology well. Vedic astrology has its roots in the Indus Valley and began about 300 BCE.[250] While this was a considerable amount of time after the Indus Valley civilization had ended, it is possible the Vedics held some of the same astrological views as the Harappans. If the Harappans believed in some early form of astrology, it likely would not have been as complex as the later Vedic astrology. Still, it could have influenced Vedic astrology.

The Indus Valley people also used basic shapes to represent ideas. An X represented division, sharing, and roads.[251] It shouldn't come as a surprise that this symbol was often used in the Indus Valley, especially since the Indus Valley had great street and city structures.

A bracket-like symbol represented either the sky, heavens, or rain.[252] Rain was especially important to the Harappans, as they relied on the schedule of the monsoon season to farm effectively. The Harappans held rain and water in high regard. Knowing this, it makes sense they may have used the same symbol to represent rain and the heavens.

Fish were another common symbol. Unlike domesticated farm animals, fish were less likely to represent families and were more likely to represent gods, religion, or the stars. Other line markings or shapes near the fish might have represented a specific star, a number of stars, or planets. These same symbols would later be adopted by the Vedics.[253] This is just another thing that suggests the Harappans had an interest in astrology and that they could have influenced some aspects of Vedic astrology.

Burial Practices

Since the first major discoveries of Indus Valley sites were discovered in the 1920s, only a few hundred Harappan graves have been found. All

---

[249] Sparavigna, Amelia. "Icons and Signs from the Ancient Harappa."

[250] Koch-Westenholz, Ulla. "Mesopotamian Astrology." CNI Publications. Museum Tusculanum Press, 1995.

[251] Sparavigna, Amelia. "Icons and Signs from the Ancient Harappa."

[252] Sparavigna, Amelia. "Icons and Signs from the Ancient Harappa."

[253] Sparavigna, Amelia. "Icons and Signs from the Ancient Harappa."

of these graves are underground, but some were better structured than others. Graves could be rectangular or oval. Better-structured graves were lined with mud bricks. Some archaeologists think Harappans may have sometimes used wooden coffins.[254] However, if the Harappans used coffins, they have since decomposed. It is likely the coffins were a similar shape as they are today, but this is impossible to know for sure.

Cemeteries were usually in mound-like shapes. This is what accounts for Mohenjo-daro being called the "Mound of the Dead." Large mounds were commonly found outside of large cities.[255] The larger the city, the more mounds or larger mounds the area would have.

Harappans were usually buried with items such as pots, jewelry, dishes, trinkets, and food. None of these items would have been very expensive besides the jewelry. As of 2019, archaeologists have not found any Harappan graves with anything especially ornate in it.[256] This suggests two things. Firstly, it suggests the Harappans believed in some kind of afterlife. Being buried with objects is a common sign of this in other cultures, so it stands to reason the Harappans would have buried people with items for the same reason. Secondly, it suggests the Harappans thought they only needed certain items in the afterlife. Their spirits would not need expensive items in the next life. They would only need practical items.

Every once in a while, couples and family members would be buried in the same grave. Because the grave had to fit more than one person, it would be wider than other graves. This was a rare occurrence and would likely only happen if people died at the same time.[257] Archaeologists can determine whether people found in joint graves are related or not with DNA testing. However, it can be difficult to do so with skeletons as old as the ones found in Harappan sites.

---

[254] "Burial Methods of the Indus Valley Civilization." Unacademy. Sorting Hat Technologies Pvt Ltd, n.d., https://unacademy.com/content/bpsc/study-material/history/burial-methods-of-the-indus-valley-civilization/#:~:text=More%20than%20two%20hundred%20bodies,sites%20after%20all%20these%20years.

[255] Prabhakar, V. N. "A Survey of Burial Practices in the Late/Post-Urban Harappan Phase during the Second and First Millennium BCE." Journal of Multidisciplinary Studies in Archaeology 3 (2015): 54–83.

[256] Biswas, Soutik. "Harappa Grave of Ancient Couple Reveals Secrets." BBC, January 9, 2019, https://www.bbc.com/news/world-asia-india-46806084.

[257] Biswas, Soutik. "Harappa Grave of Ancient Couple Reveals Secrets."

Archaeologists can sometimes tell the age of a grave without carbon dating from how organized or not the site is. Over the thousands of years the Indus Valley was occupied, people were buried in similar locations. As time went on, bodies had to be jammed into crowded spaces or buried on top of older graves.[258]

Sometimes, after a person had been dead and buried for long enough, their bones would be transferred from a grave into pottery. This pottery would usually be reburied. In rare cases, bone pots have been found in or under homes. Some of these pots were decorated and had lids, while others were open and left plain. If the pottery was decorated, the designs would often have symbolic meanings. Plants and animals were some of the most common types of designs.[259] The skulls were usually placed at the top of the pot. Usually, there was only one body per pot.[260] Sometimes, all or some of the bones had burn marks on them or had been entirely cremated. Even in these cases, the skull was usually left intact.[261] This was likely done to save space in graveyards. Similar things were done in other cultures around the world.

Pottery found in a cemetery.

---

[258] "Burial Methods of the Indus Valley Civilization."

[259] Prabhakar, V. N. "A Survey of Burial Practices in the Late/Post-Urban Harappan Phase during the Second and First Millennium BCE."

[260] "Burial Methods of the Indus Valley Civilization."

[261] Prabhakar, V. N. "A Survey of Burial Practices in the Late/Post-Urban Harappan Phase during the Second and First Millennium BCE."

Afterlife

How the Harappans viewed the afterlife, if they thought about it at all, likely depended on which religion (if any) they practiced. Below are some of the possibilities of what they may have thought the afterlife looked like, as well as who got to go to the afterlife.

If the Harappans followed the Mesopotamian religion, they would have gone to the underworld when they died. The land of the dead wasn't similar to the Christian concept of heaven or hell. Instead, it was a deary place. A human could not go to the Mesopotamian version of heaven, Dilmun, as it was a place meant only for the gods.[262] Death would have been an accepted but somewhat feared aspect of life. Appeasing the gods in life only made life before death easier but did little to affect life after death.

However, family members could somewhat affect their loved one's afterlife. Making sure a family member had a proper burial helped to put their soul (or a similar concept of a soul) at ease. This made the afterlife easier but also made it less likely the departed person's soul would cause trouble in the land of the living. People could leave offerings (usually food) at their loved one's graves. An appeased spirit would do them no harm once they gave offerings. If the family had trouble after the person died, they could consult a necromancer to see if one of the living members had done something to offend the dead family member.[263] The belief that the spirits of departed loved ones could interfere with the living was another aspect of Mesopotamian mythos that helped to explain why things happened. This was mostly used to explain bad luck and why bad things happened to good people.

If the Harappans had been animists, they likely did not have a concept of an afterlife as a physical place. Instead, they were more likely to believe in something closer to reincarnation or ghosts. Either their spirits would live on in the mortal plane, or their spirits would be recycled to occupy a new vessel.[264] If they were reincarnated, they would go on to live another life. If they became a spirit without a body, they would act more like a ghost or roaming spirit that could interact with the world around them. Either way, there would have been little reason for animist Harappans to

[262] Mark, Joshua J. "Mesopotamian Religion."

[263] Mark, Joshua J. "Mesopotamian Religion."

[264] Halverston, Dean. "An Overview Definition of Animism."

fear death, as it was just a new beginning.

Assuming the Harappans were Hindus or believed in something that was a pre-runner to Hinduism, they would have likely believed in reincarnation as Hindus do today. Souls are not reassigned after death randomly. Souls are judged based on what the person did in life. People who fill their lives with bad deeds will end up worse off than they did in their past life, and people who did many good deeds will end up in a better place than in their past life.[265] The "system" is a bit more complicated than this. What is important is that if the Harappans believed in reincarnation, they would have expected their actions would impact their future lives.

Along with reincarnation, there are also several heavens and hells. If a soul was not reincarnated, it could be sent to one of two heaven-like places. The first was an afterlife filled with their ancestors. Another heaven-like place was filled with the gods. During life, people could give offerings to either their ancestors or the gods. Some gods had their own versions of heaven. People who lived terrible lives would go to hell-like places that were filled with demons. Unlike in Christianity, the condemned person would not be in hell for eternity but only until they paid off their bad karma.[266] We do not know if the Harappans believed in karma, but they may have had a similar concept. Even if they did not believe in karma, they might have had a concept of heaven and hell.

Hindus also believe in ghosts and spirits. People who commit suicide are most likely to become ghosts. Spirits can either be good or bad. They can sometimes possess humans to do good or evil. Both ghosts and spirits tend to stick around important or desolate places.[267] Because the average person will not become a ghost, the Harappans may not have thought about this outcome, instead focusing mainly on reincarnation or heaven and hell.

If the Harappans were atheists, they likely did not believe in any kind of afterlife. Once their lives ended, their soul (if they believed in a soul) would have died too. There would have been no afterlife to prepare for. If they were agnostic, then they may have believed in some kind of life

---

[265] V., Jayaram. "Death and Afterlife in Hinduism." Hinduwebsite.com, n.d, https://www.hinduwebsite.com/hinduism/h_death.asp/

[266] V., Jayaram. "Death and Afterlife in Hinduism."

[267] V., Jayaram. "Death and Afterlife in Hinduism."

after death, but it would more likely be a vague concept instead of a fact. There is an unlimited number of ways they could have prepared for the afterlife.

Conclusion

The Harappans were just as mysterious in life as they were in death, but most of this mystery simply comes from the fact that we cannot read anything they wrote. In the meantime, historians and others need to use the relics the Indus people left behind to guess what they believed in.

SECTION FOUR:
THE LEGACY OF THE INDUS VALLEY CIVILIZATION

Chapter 10: The Collapse of the Indus Civilization (1300 BCE)

Throughout this book, we've learned the Indus Valley people stayed away from war, invasion, and other general threats from other nations. This could have been in part because of their healthy trade relationships with nearby nations or because of the mountain ranges surrounding the Indus Valley, which would have made it difficult to invade. Many other ancient civilizations came to an end because of war or invasion, so it is strange the Indus Valley civilization did not.

Because the Indus Valley civilization did not end with the bang of a war or the sizzle of a disease, its culture died out slowly. This also makes it more difficult to pinpoint what exactly caused the civilization's collapse, as well as what happened to any remaining Harappans afterward. Some popular theories that hold the most weight have to do with a decline in agricultural production. A decline in farming would have made it more difficult for the Harappans to live prosperous lives in the Indus Valley, encouraging them to move elsewhere.

Drought

The Indus Valley civilization relied on the monsoon seasons to know when to plant and harvest their crops. Without being able to rely on this seasonal schedule, Harappan farmers would have struggled to grow enough food.[268] Drought was one of the major problems that could

---

[268] "Geography of the Ancient Indus River Valley."

happen if the monsoon season did not happen according to schedule.

A recent 2018 archaeological study suggests the Indus Valley went through a major drought season that lasted almost nine hundred years! This would have started sometime around 2350 BCE and lasted until about 1450 BCE.[269] This timeline lines up well with the decline and end of the Indus Valley civilization.

Just because the drought season lasted about nine hundred years doesn't mean there were no monsoons or rain for that entire time. Instead, the monsoon rains were not as heavy.[270] This would not have wiped out the civilization right away but would have weakened it over the centuries.

The researchers who discovered this drought period suggested the Harappans would have moved out of the Indus Valley to look for more fertile land. It is possible the Harappans moved to the Ganga-Yamuna Valley, Bengal, Vindhyachal, and Gujarat.[271] Of course, it is likely that many Harappans would have starved to death before the civilization as a whole broke apart and moved to other areas, mostly to modern-day India.

Flooding

Even though the monsoons may have been weaker in the last millennium, the Indus Valley was still prone to flooding. An archaeological expedition in the mid-1960s showed that some Harappan buildings were artificially raised over many years, most likely to bring the buildings above the rising water level.[272] Floodwaters that were high enough to be a threat to buildings would also have likely damaged farms and drowned crops.

The same expedition showed that some floodwater deposits were raised about thirty feet above where the water levels usually were.[273] It is

---

[269] Pandey, Jhimli M. "900 Year Drought Wiped Out Indus Civilization: IIT-Kharagpur." The Times of India, April 16, 2018, https://timesofindia.indiatimes.com/india/900-year-drought-wiped-out-indus-civilisation-iit-kharagpur/articleshow/63776710.cms.

[270] Pandey, Jhimli M. "900 Year Drought Wiped Out Indus Civilization: IIT-Kharagpur."

[271] Pandey, Jhimli M. "900 Year Drought Wiped Out Indus Civilization: IIT-Kharagpur."

[272] Dales, George, F. "Civilization and Floods in the Indus Valley" Expedition Magazine 7.4 (1965): n. pag. Expedition Magazine. Penn Museum, 1965 Web. 23 Aug 2022 <https://www.penn.museum/sites/expedition/?p=1010>

[273] Dales, George, F. "Civilization and Floods in the Indus Valley"

unknown when the water rose to this level, but it most likely rose over time rather than all at once. This means inhabitants would have been able to see that the water levels would become too high to continue living in the Indus Valley safely. Most people would have had time to move without needing to worry about flash flooding. Scientists will likely study the building styles in the future to give us a better guess at when the buildings were raised, which would also give us a good estimate of when the floods happened.

There is no one time that flooding would have been a problem for the Harappans. Just as the monsoon season went in cycles, so did the floods. Historians suggest there could have been up to six major floods in the Indus Valley before the civilization's end.[274] As with the drought situation, the Harappans would have likely moved out of the Indus Valley to avoid the effects of these floods.

Assimilation

Since the Indus Valley civilization came to an end slowly, many Harappans would have left the area to live elsewhere. As mentioned, most of the Harappans likely moved into modern-day India and the surrounding areas. When the Harappans moved, they likely intermarried and had children with the native people from these areas. There are a few different theories as to which cultures the Harappans might have assimilated with.

While the Aryan invasion theory has been more or less discredited, it is possible the Harappans assimilated into the Aryan culture. The Aryans migrated to modern-day India and Pakistan sometime around 1900 BCE to 1500 BCE.[275] This lines up with the decline and fall of the Indus Valley civilization's timeline.

While there is no evidence of a battle with the Aryans in the Indus Valley, there is genetic evidence the Aryans were in the area. One geneticist, Razib Khan, says that research shows Aryan ancestry in genetic data all around India.[276] This shows the Aryans did go into India, where

---

[274] Dales, George, F. "Civilization and Floods in the Indus Valley"

[275] Mark, Joshua J. "Indus Valley Civilization." World History Encyclopedia. World History Publishing, October 7, 2020, https://www.worldhistory.org/Indus_Valley_Civilization/

[276] Basak, Saptarshi. "Deconstructing the 'Aryan Invasion' Debate Surrounding IIT Kharagpur's Calendar." The Quint, December 30, 2021, https://www.thequint.com/news/india/deconstructing-the-aryan-invasion-debate-surrounding-iit-kharagpurs-calendar

they likely would have come into contact with the Harappans.

There is some debate on whether or not the Harappans migrated from modern-day Pakistan into modern-day India. The bulk of this debate is due to a lack of written evidence. One historian, Richard Meadow, argues there is not enough documentation from any group that shows the Harappans moved into southern India. However, Iravatham Mahadevan, an Indian scholar who studied ancient inscriptions, suggests there is enough evidence, both written and otherwise. Apparently, old Tamil poems talk about a migration from Pakistan to India. He also suggests that if a large-scale migration happened, it likely would have been overland instead of by ship.[277] Unless the Harappans left behind bronze items or pottery during their migration, there would be little to no physical evidence left. Any wooden boats or organic material they used on their journey would have long since biodegraded.

There is also debate on whether or not the Harappans and Vedics had anything to do with each other. The movement of people described in the Rig Veda does not match up with the sedentary lifestyle of the Harappan people. On top of this, religion was very important to the Vedics, and historians still do not know which religion the Harappans followed or if they even followed any.[278] This suggests the Harappans had little to no contact with the Vedics.

On the other hand, archaeologists have found Harappan seals that seem to depict Pashupati, a proto-Hindu version of Shiva.[279] While this could be a coincidence, it could also point to the idea that some Harappan religious values were adopted by the Vedics. The most likely way this would have happened is if the Harappans assimilated with the Vedics at some point.

The seals are not the only signs the Indus Valley civilization had some impact on the Vedics. Some other Harappan ideas and practices were

---

[277] "Do We Have Any Evidence of a Migration from the Indus to South India?" Harappa, n.d., https://www.harappa.com/answers/do-we-have-any-evidence-migration-indus-south-india.

[278] Vahia, Mayank. "Is There Any Relation Between Vedic and Indus Civilization as many Indus and Saraswati Sites Have Been Found in the Region Which is Called Saptasindu in Vedas?" Harappa, n.d., https://www.harappa.com/answers/there-any-relation-between-vedic-and-indus-civilization-many-indus-and-saraswati-sites-have.

[279] Vahia, Mayank. "Is There Any Relation Between Vedic and Indus Civilization as many Indus and Saraswati Sites Have Been Found in the Region Which is Called Saptasindu in Vedas?"

adopted by the Vedics, such as using fire altars, taking ritual baths, and adoration for the stars.[280] While this could all be a coincidence, it is most likely the Harappans (or ancestors of the Harappans) and the Vedics came into contact with each other at some point. If they did end up meeting, they most likely intermarried and had children together, mixing their lineages and carrying Harappan DNA.

Conclusion

Like with much of the history of the Indus Valley, no one really knows for sure what caused the civilization to come to an end. Climate change (which is not necessarily the same as global warming) is the most likely villain. Whether it caused flooding or drought, the Harappans would have been faced with a major change that would have negatively affected their agricultural schedule.

Without being able to count on the once-reliable monsoon season, the Harappans would have had to move to a place where the climate was steadier. While moving, they would have run into people from other cultures. Since there are no records of the last of the Harappans dying out, they probably married and had children with the people in these areas. This would allow some aspects of their culture to live on, even if the Harappans in name were all but gone.

---

[280] Pattanaik, Devdutt. "Was Harappan Civilization Vedic or Hindu?" Daily Beta. India Today Group, December 15, 2016, https://www.dailyo.in/variety/harappan-civilisation-hinduism-vedic-age-dharma-aryans-hindu-supremacists-marxists-14564

Conclusion

The Indus Valley civilization lasted about two thousand years without any war or major conflicts. The people who made up this civilization, the Harappans, were primarily farmers. Their knowledge of agriculture, combined with the predictable monsoon seasons, allowed them to settle in a fertile valley.

Harappan farmers mastered how to plant different cereal crops and learned how to domesticate various types of animals. The Harappans were also great fishers. Agriculture became the dominant force in the Indus Valley's economy. Without it, the Indus Valley civilization couldn't survive. In the end, it was most likely climate change that altered the Harappans' ability to farm, which forced them to leave the Indus Valley.

Once the Harappans settled in one place, they were able to build magnificent cities and buildings, some of which are still standing (albeit in ruins) today. Even with all of their talents in building and city planning, the Harappans never built temples. This could suggest they did not have a centralized religion that would have required temples. However, it doesn't mean the Harappans didn't have the ability to build temples, as they built many other large structures, including homes and bathhouses.

Without being able to read the Indus script, historians need to examine what the Harappans left behind. They are famous for their beautiful pottery and figures, which were mostly made from terracotta and similar minerals. The Harappans were also a Bronze Age society, which, by definition, means they eventually learned how to work with bronze. They used bronze to make sculptures, tools, and jewelry.

The Harappans used the items they made and the food they grew inside the Indus Valley and traded with nearby civilizations. Historians have the most evidence of the Harappans trading with the Mesopotamians, but we also know the Harappans traded with the peoples of modern-day northern India and China. When it came to trading, the Harappans sailed to Mesopotamia on large boats, traveled overland to get to India, and had the Chinese merchants come to them. Their trade relationships were more than likely positive because there are no records of conflict with other nations or any physical evidence of a conflict. Plus, the trade relationships lasted for hundreds of years.

When not farming, making items, or trading, the Harappans relaxed in places like the Great Bath. These baths were likely used in a similar way as ancient Roman bathhouses. If the Harappans didn't want to do that, they could also play games or play with toys.

While historians know a lot about the daily life of the Harappans, we still do not know what kind of government or religion they had, if any. These and many other facts about the Indus Valley people will remain a mystery until we have a better understanding of how to read the Indus script. Until then, further excavations of Harappan sites will provide more clues as to how these ancient peoples lived.

Part 2: Ancient China

An Enthralling Overview of Chinese History, Starting from the Settlement at the Yellow River through the Xia, Shang, Zhou, and Qin Dynasties to the Han Dynasty

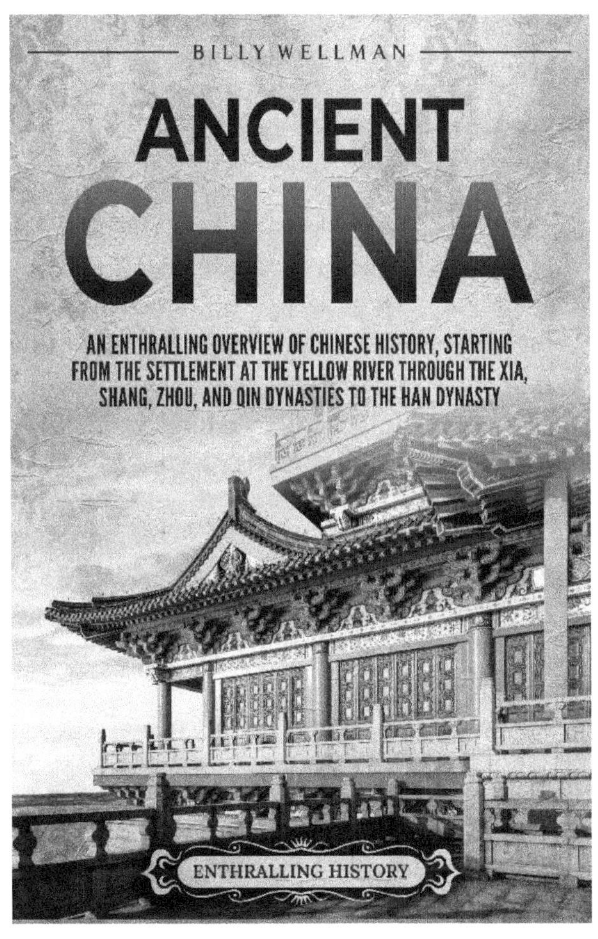

Introduction

We have all witnessed the incredible economic development of China in the last few decades. But this is only a very small fraction of Chinese history. China has the longest continuous cultural development of all modern countries. Yes, the ancient Egyptian civilization is older than the Chinese civilization, but ancient Egypt came under the influence of other religions, which suppressed their older traditions. China, on the other hand, has remained connected to its roots, which span back to the Paleolithic Age (the Old Stone Age) and possibly even further.

It's quite remarkable that Chinese people today can somewhat understand even the oldest inscriptions dating from the period of the Shang dynasty (2nd millennium BCE). This is what we mean by the *continuity* of a culture. Age-old inscriptions found on oracle bones and turtle shells from the Shang dynasty bear Chinese characters similar to those still used today.

Fast forward one millennium, and we're in the period of the famous Confucius (the 6th to 5th centuries BCE), who does not lag behind the great minds of ancient Greece. In fact, Confucius predates a majority of ancient Greek philosophers, apart from the Milesians (Thales, Anaximander, and Anaximenes).

Jumping forward five hundred years, we encounter the great Han dynasty, which is famous for bringing forth the Golden Age of China (today, we might rightfully say the first "Golden Age"). The Han ruled between the 3rd century BCE and the 3rd century CE. They are very much responsible for the modern Han identity of the Chinese. During this period, there was a highly ordered Chinese society with a centralized government, distinct and diverse social classes, and a well-functioning administration.

This book, for the most part, will remain between the prehistoric roots of Chinese culture and the fall of the Han dynasty (covering a period of more than ten thousand years, from the 10th millennium BCE to the 1st millennium CE). It is virtually impossible to write a fairly short yet good book on all of Chinese history, as it is a challenge to do so just for the country's prehistory. But from the Han dynasty onward, so many things happened in China until the ultimate dissolution of the Chinese Empire in the early 20th century under the Qing dynasty. And even after that, there was the ensuing Warlord era, revolutionary chaos, and the victory of the Chinese Communist Party.

History is fractal in nature. When you look a bit more carefully, things start unraveling in all sorts of directions, and you're amazed at their sheer complexity. However, there is a sort of "recency" bias, namely, more recent events tend to be remembered in a more detailed manner. It is for this reason that most people focus on the 20th-century history of China, Mao Zedong, and China's ultimate economic success. But if you look with the right kind of eyes, even far back to prehistoric times, you'll start understanding this fractal nature of (pre)history. And this is exactly what we'll be doing in this book. We'll take distant events, which at first glance seem so minuscule, maybe even nonsignificant, and we'll put them under the microscope to observe how one event grows and divides into numerous other events, establishing unfathomable links between themselves.

By doing this, we'll be able to understand the essence of modern China and how this great culture endured for so many centuries. There were many great cultures throughout history, such as the ancient Greeks, Persians, Romans, and Maya, to name a few. But the Chinese culture is the only one that survived mostly intact. There is something in Chinese culture that allows it to continue existing even though other cultures crumbled under the burden of the sands of time. And to learn what that something is, we have to look back, way back. Maybe we won't be able to find that something. Maybe we'll find out that there are actually many things that make the Chinese culture so special. And maybe, just maybe, we'll learn how to use this knowledge to further improve the world we are living in. In any case, it will be an interesting ride! Sit back, relax, and come with us on a travel through time. Destination: paleolithic China (pre-10,000 BCE).

SECTION ONE:
EARLY YELLOW RIVER SETTLEMENTS AND THE XIA DYNASTY

Chapter 1: Paleolithic China, Early Yellow River, and Yangtze River Settlements

To understand the formation and significance of early Yellow River settlements, we have to juxtapose them with their precursors, the Paleolithic societies in China. It's important to note that we don't exactly know to what extent Paleolithic and Neolithic peoples in China are related, nor do we know to what extent modern Han Chinese are related to people who lived in China thousands of years ago.

Human and human-like fossils from the Paleolithic Age are found throughout the whole of China. The Zhoukoudian cave system, on its own, preserved a wealth of fossils dating from various sub-periods of the Paleolithic Age.[281] This age is by far the longest in the development of humans. The so-called Peking Man who inhabited the Zhoukoudian caves is at least 700,000 years old, possibly even older.[282] The cave system is home to the remains of *Homo erectus*, a species that was perhaps the

---

[281] Chang, Kwang-Chih. "In Search of China's Beginnings: New Light on an Old Civilization: A Golden Age of Archaeology is piecing together a new Chinese prehistory and history that differ in fundamental ways from the traditional story." *American Scientist* 69, no. 2 (1981): 148-160.

[282] A very loose term used to denote human remains found in Zhoukoudian Caves. There are many layers of archaeological findings in these caves, and it is not clear how these layers relate between themselves.

first to start using and constructing simple stone tools. Even though members of *Homo erectus* weren't entirely like modern humans, they walked upright and used tools. In any case, they inhabited Eurasia a long, long time ago. The Peking Man isn't even the oldest fossil remains of human-like primates. The oldest is the Yuanmou Man, which dates back to at least 1.7 million years ago.[283] The Yuanmou Man was also a *Homo erectus*.

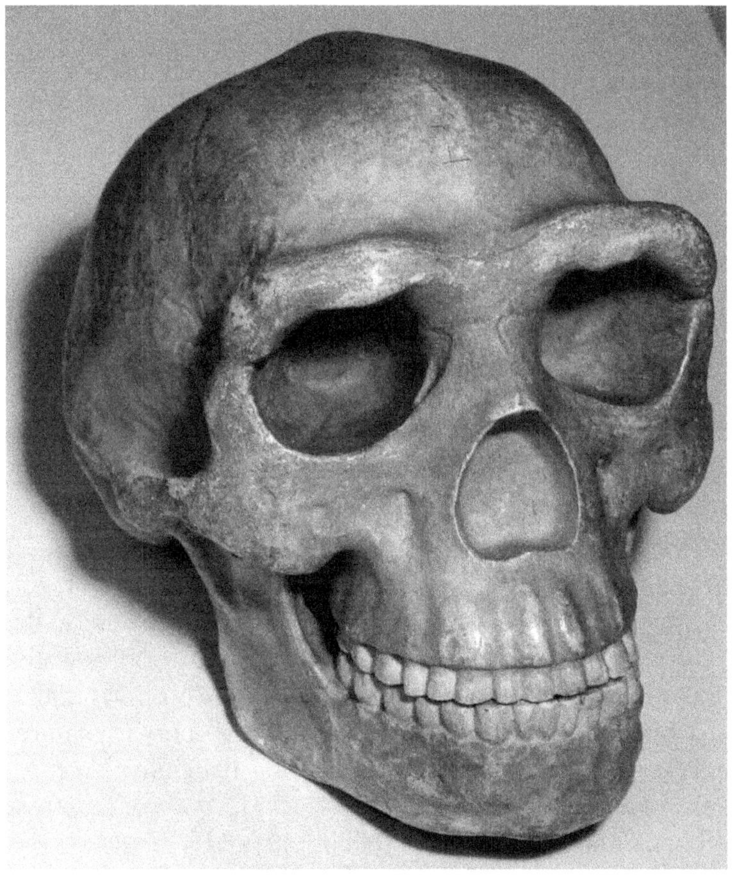

Peking Man skull (reconstruction).
Kevin Walsh; https://creativecommons.org/licenses/by/2.0/.
https://www.flickr.com/photos/86624586@N00/10191736

---

[283] Pu, Li, Chien Fang, Ma Hsing-Hua, Pu Ching-Yu, Hsing Li-Sheng, and Chu Shih-Chiang. "Preliminary study on the age of Yuanmou man by palaeomagnetic technique." *Scientia Sinica* 20, no. 5 (1977): 645-664.

Remains of a human tibia bone, Yuanmou area.

The oldest inhabitants of China, as was typical for the Paleolithic Age in general, were hunter-gatherers who lived in small communities. They constructed and used stone tools for hunting and other purposes. Apart from that, we don't know much about these "proto-people." It's possible they engaged in cannibalism.[284] However, these people formed communities and probably hunted in organized groups.

Fossils dating back to around thirty-five thousand to thirty thousand years ago provide evidence of a gradual change in Chinese Paleolithic cultures. Stone refinement techniques became more sophisticated, and it is from this period that we obtain the first evidence of arts and symbolic activities, which are an important "marker" of human nature.[285] This gradual movement, which occurred late in the Paleolithic Age, is marked by the rise of *Homo sapiens*. Numerous *Homo sapiens* fossils were unearthed in China, some being 200,000 years old.

The Paleolithic Age is one big mystery in the development of humanity. Drastic cultural progress happened in the Neolithic Age (New Stone Age). Therefore, the evidence for the Neolithic Age is much more

---

[284] Boaz, N., and R. Ciochon. "The scavenging of "Peking Man." *Natural History* 110, no. 2 (2001): 46-51.

[285] Gao, Xing. "Paleolithic cultures in China: uniqueness and divergence." *Current Anthropology* 54, no. S8 (2013): S358-S370.

abundant, as people started using more complex ways to express themselves and their mastery of their surroundings. The Paleolithic Age, on the other hand, is relatively scarce with respect to archaeological findings, so we can only make loose conjectures about how Paleolithic people lived. This is why there are many interpretations of the Paleolithic Age, and many authors have used it in different ways to prove their claims.

For instance, Sigmund Freud believed that way back in prehistory, people's most powerful impulses, sex and aggression, were manifested in much more straightforward ways compared to today.[286] Freud went as far as to claim that the Oedipus complex, which, according to him, exists in an implicit and symbolic form in all of us, was manifested in a much more real way. Because Paleolithic communities were formed around one powerful male who "possessed" all females and was the leader of the group, Freud presumed that other males (e.g., the sons of an alpha male) grew jealous and wanted to get rid of the alpha male. So, they killed their own (real or symbolic) father and ate his flesh in a sort of ritual that bound them together in their guilt.[287] Freud goes as far as to claim that this prehistoric Oedipus complex served as a basis for a less violent society. Those who killed the alpha male were held together with strings of communal guilt, and they gradually learned how to divide power amongst themselves more rationally to avoid internal strife. Due to guilt and fascination with the power of a long-gone alpha male, people were compelled to make a sort of totem, which they venerated. This is how Freud explains an important moment in the early formation of religions.

Whether you believe in this story or not, Freud really did try to understand the psychology of prehistoric people. Though he may have overestimated the importance of the Oedipus complex (both for individual and phylogenetic[288] development), he succeeded in painting a believable prehistoric scene. Prehistoric communities (especially early in the Paleolithic Age) were kept together by sheer necessity, physical

---

[286] Freud, Sigmund. Moses and monotheism. *Leonardo Paolo Lovari,* 2016.

[287] This is another conjecture about the Paleolithic Age, namely the "alpha male" theory. While it's very likely that physical prowess was of the utmost importance back then, we still don't know a lot about the social hierarchy of the Paleolithic Age. In other words, it's possible that early prehistoric communities had a strong male leader, but we don't really know the extent of his power and control over his "subordinates."

[288] Development of a species.

dominance of one (or a handful) of members, and fear. Impulses that we have driven to the unconscious were likely expressed in a more direct manner back then. Language, if it even existed in the Paleolithic Age, was also coarse and probably very different from the languages we speak today. They probably varied even across fairly small areas. It's also due to the relative coarseness of early languages that people had to find other, more direct means to express their desires.

The Paleolithic Age is, thus far, the longest period in the development of humanity. And yet we have to remain content with conjectures, hypotheses, and suppositions when it comes to explaining how people lived in this (very long) period. This early period of the development of humanity will probably forever remain veiled in the mystery of time, and it will always be a period that necessitates a peculiar combination of scientific and artistic types of thinking to be explained.

Early Yellow River and Yangtze River Settlements in the Neolithic Age

A lot of things happened (not only in China but also in Europe and the Middle East) that made the Paleolithic people gradually adopt a different lifestyle. Although the people didn't abandon hunting and foraging, they started learning how to control their sources of life. Namely, they started controlling their two main sources of food, plants and animals, leading to the birth of agriculture and domesticated animals. As is the case with most things that happened in prehistory, we don't really know how this shift happened. There are many possible scenarios of how people discovered they could domesticate wild animals or sow seeds of a plant. Once again, these were probably gradual processes and varied greatly across different geographical locations.

In any case, around ten thousand years ago, the Neolithic Age was well under way in China. There are many markers of the Neolithic cultures, with pottery, large permanent settlements, organized cultivation, and the processing of plants being some of the most important markers.

Nanzhuangtou is perhaps the oldest Neolithic Chinese culture. The Nanzhuangtou culture was situated in China's modern-day northern Hebei province. This culture is around ten thousand years old, perhaps even older, and it gave us the first evidence of millet consumption and cultivation.[289] Members of the Nanzhuangtou also domesticated dogs (one

---

[289] Yang, Xiaoyan, Zhikun Ma, Jun Li, Jincheng Yu, Chris Stevens, and Yijie Zhuang. "Comparing subsistence strategies in different landscapes of North China 10,000 years ago." *The Holocene* 25,

of the first animals to be domesticated, globally speaking), and they also made and used pottery.[290] Generally speaking, the Nanzhuangtou culture is so different compared to other evidence of human activity from the Paleolithic Age.

Location of modern-day Hebei province, the location of the Nanzhuangtou culture.
TUBS, CC BY-SA 3.0 <https://creativecommons.org/licenses/by-sa/3.0>, via Wikimedia Commons; https://commons.wikimedia.org/wiki/File:Hebei_in_China_(%2Ball_claims_hatched).svg

With the Peiligang culture (around eight thousand years ago), Chinese agriculture saw an immense developmental step. This culture was situated in modern-day Henan province in the basin of the Yellow River. Members of the Peiligang culture cultivated a wide variety of plants, such as broomcorn and foxtail millet.[291] Agriculture requires careful planning and management of resources. The Peiligang people possibly engaged in

---

no. 12 (2015): 1957-1964.

[290] Jing, Yuan. "The origins and development of animal domestication in China." *Chinese Archaeology* 8, no. 1 (2008): 1-7.

[291] Bestel, Sheahan, Yingjian Bao, Hua Zhong, Xingcan Chen, and Li Liu. "Wild plant use and multi-cropping at the early Neolithic Zhuzhai site in the middle Yellow River region, China." *The Holocene* 28, no. 2 (2018): 195-207.

---

organized tilling of soil and soil improvement, as well as weeding out unnecessary and obnoxious plants that would take nutrients and light from the crops. Irrigation and watering were also basic activities for the Peiligang people. Irrigation and control of the big rivers, such as the Nile or Yellow River, were probably the first large-scale engineering feats of humanity. And while the Egyptians were learning how to control the great power of the Nile, the ancient Chinese were learning how to control their immense rivers, such as the Yellow River and the Yangtze River. The Peiligang people didn't only eat their domestic crops. They also relied heavily on various sorts of nuts and fruits, such as walnuts, hazelnuts, acorns, jujube, plums, and others.

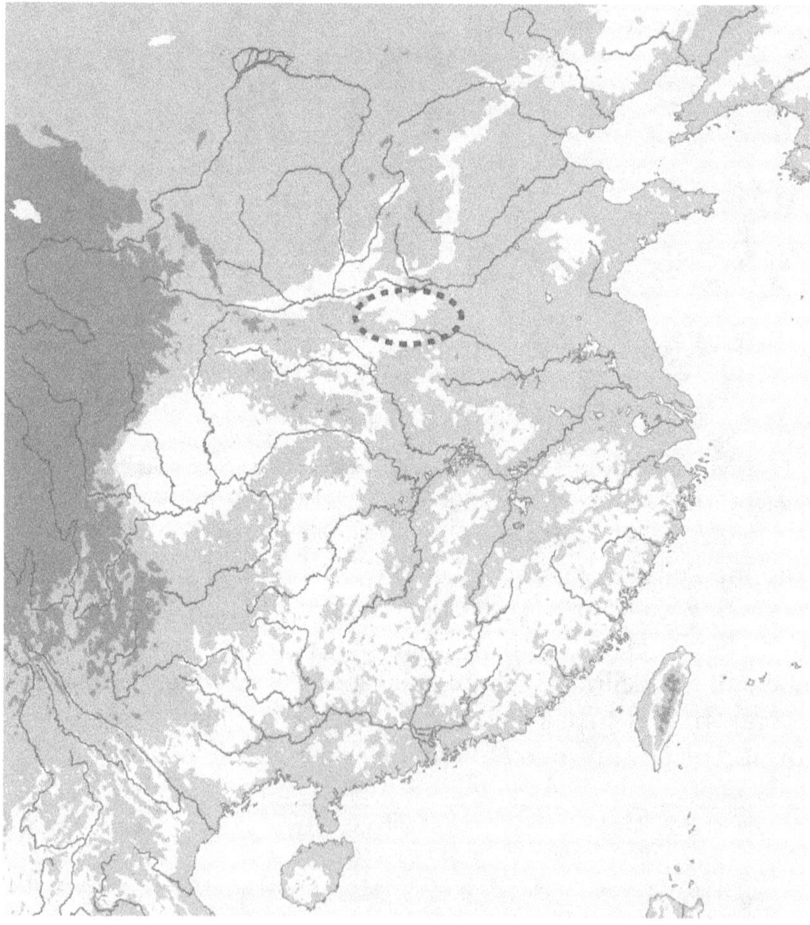

The location of the Peiligang culture in modern-day Henan province in mainland China.
Kanguole, CC BY-SA 4.0 <https://creativecommons.org/licenses/by-sa/4.0>, via Wikimedia Commons; https://commons.wikimedia.org/wiki/File:Peiligang_map.svg

The Peiligang people were skilled potters. To make pottery, one has to learn how to build a fire that can reach very high temperatures and sustain that heat. People becoming more skilled in controlling fire was another crucial engineering feat of the Neolithic Age. Neolithic people, the Peiligang included, were able to build ovens that could produce and sustain temperatures needed for baking pottery. These were possibly underground ovens, which, thanks to the insulation properties of soil, were crucial in creating good pottery.

Peiligang pottery in Shanghai Museum. This piece has characteristic "ears" and dates from a later period of the Peiligang culture, from the 7th or 6th millennia BCE.
User:Captmondo, CC BY-SA 3.0 <http://creativecommons.org/licenses/by-sa/3.0/>, via Wikimedia Commons; https://commons.wikimedia.org/wiki/File:PeiligangCulture-RedPotWithTwoEars-ShanghaiMuseum-May27-08.jpg

The Peiligang people made all sorts of vessels, tripods, double-handed jars, cups, dishes, bowls, and other things.[292] Their pottery is rarely adorned with works of art, though some have geometrical ornaments as decoration. We also have numerous spades, axes, sickles, and grinding stones dating from this period, which are testaments to the Peiligang

---

[292] Guoping, Sun. "Recent research on the Hemudu culture and the Tianluoshan site." *A companion to Chinese archaeology* (2013): 555-573.

culture's technological development and diversity in crafts. Interestingly, the tools of one type seem to have roughly been the same size, which means that sharing craftsmanship knowledge was already standardized to a certain extent in Peiligang culture. It's possible that some people already specialized in making pottery, while others specialized in making stone tools or simply worked as farmers. They also domesticated dogs, pigs, sheep, chickens, and cattle.

Although we don't know much about the social life of the Peiligang people, it is likely they lived in more or less permanent villages and had an elaborate system of religious beliefs. Archaeologists have uncovered numerous sacrificial pits, with domestic animals used as sacrifices. Chickens were often used as sacrificial offerings, especially roosters, which probably means that male chickens had some sort of symbolic value for the Peiligang. Sacrifices were frequent and probably were an important part of everyday life.

The Neolithic Age is sometimes seen as an idyllic period, a period when people lived in harmony with their environment and each other. Remember, they were still in the Stone Age, and though weapons existed in the Stone Age, they weren't as effective as the weapons that would come later. The people weren't as numerous, and there wasn't a pressing need to find new territory, as there was enough land for everyone.

However, it's likely that the Neolithic Age saw a drastic increase in population. People learned how to make and preserve food on their own and weren't as dependent on hazardous searches for food or hunting. Moreover, the Neolithic Age probably saw the first significant accumulation of wealth. And when you have wealth, you also have people who want to obtain it by any means possible. These two factors prove crucial for explaining the period that comes right after the Neolithic Age, the Age of Metal. With more and more people and more and more wealth, the scene was set for a more turbulent and violent age. The accumulation of wealth allowed for a more intricate separation of classes within society, with some people being wealthier and others less so.

The evidence of Neolithic cultures in the basin of the Yangtze River stems back to at least ten thousand years ago.[293] The earliest evidence of

---

[293] Wang, Jiajing, Jiangping Zhu, Dongrong Lei, and Leping Jiang. "New evidence for rice harvesting in the early Neolithic Lower Yangtze River, China." *Plos one* 17, no. 12 (2022): e0278200.

rice cultivation in the Lower Yangtze comes from the Shangshan culture (ten thousand years), in the form of stone tools, such as scrapers and burins (stone flakes with sharp tips). There were also sharp tools that were used to harvest plants. The ingenious methodology of archaeologists makes it possible to test if a stone tool was used for harvesting plants. In the case of the Shangshan, archaeologists have found numerous stone tools with acute edges. Plants leave residue on stone tools (and to prove just how and to what extent, modern archaeologists have to make real-life experiments) and wear-and-tear marks (just what kind of marks is also something we learn through modern experiments).

The Shangshan people were the first sedentary group of people in the region of the Lower Yangtze; in other words, they weren't nomads but formed permanent villages. One such Shangshan village is around thirty thousand square meters in size, with designated spaces for living, storage, burials, and waste disposal. But this was just the start of agriculture. and We'll have to wait another few thousand years to pass before we see "fully fledged" agriculture and civilization in the Yangtze River Basin.

The Liangzhu culture (4,300 to 5,300 years ago) was the most technologically advanced of all the Neolithic cultures in the Lower Yangtze region before the great flood. Yes, even back then, people had problems with climate change. It seems that around 4,300 years ago, people in China experienced great climate perturbations ending in catastrophic floods.[294] They brought an end to the well-developed Liangzhu culture, which had its own capital city that was defended by walls and adorned with palaces. The Liangzhu people were probably well known in their age for their jade industry (we have some beautiful evidence of their craft) and a good water-management system.

---

[294] Zhang, Haiwei, Hai Cheng, Ashish Sinha, Christoph Spötl, Yanjun Cai, Bin Liu, Gayatri Kathayat et al. "Collapse of the Liangzhu and other Neolithic cultures in the lower Yangtze region in response to climate change." *Science Advances* 7, no. 48 (2021): eabi9275.

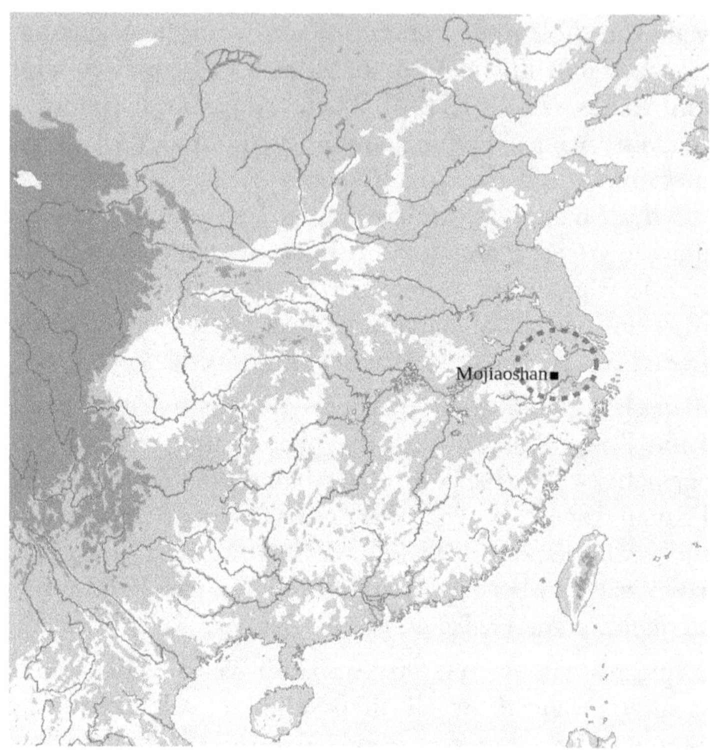

The location of the Liangzhu culture in the Lower Yangtze, modern-day Zhejiang province.
Kanguole, CC BY-SA 4.0 <https://creativecommons.org/licenses/by-sa/4.0>, via Wikimedia Commons; https://commons.wikimedia.org/wiki/File:Liangzhu_map.svg

With Liangzhu, we're already in a world more similar to the one we're living in today. If we skip back "just" ten thousand years before, we would be back in the Paleolithic Age, which is much stranger and more distant to humans today. But in the Liangzhu culture, we encounter the makings of the modern age, such as elaborate social stratification, complex death and burial rituals, and more. In fact, social stratification and burials are closely related; by exploring the cemeteries of the Liangzhu, we are able to make inferences about their social structure.

The Liangzhu people were very careful about their cemeteries. They were always located on higher ground, and if there wasn't such a location nearby, the Liangzhu would build a mound or a hillock for the purpose of burials. Their social stratification was preserved even in death. The elites were placed at the top of the hillock, and less elite members went to the bottom.[295] Most evidence relating to the Liangzhu comes from

---

[295] Ling, Qin. "The Liangzhu culture." *A companion to Chinese archaeology* (2013): 574-596.

cemeteries since these were situated on higher grounds, making them easier to find them. Villages that were placed on lower ground became covered by layers of sediment. Archaeologists found numerous everyday objects in burial sites, such as stone axes, jade objects, and pottery. Ceramic pots, tripods, stemmed dishes, jars, and basins have also been found in abundance. Interestingly, males were buried with stone axes and jade objects, while women were buried with circular and plate ornaments.

One of the ways the Liangzhu expressed wealth was by the number of objects in a burial site. The more things a person could afford to send to the other world, the richer they were. Jade seems to have been a status symbol. The Liangzhu produced jade objects, adorned them, and distributed them. The three main motifs were dragons, humans, and sacred animals and appeared separately on jade objects, perhaps indicating their different meanings in the Liangzhu religion. Similar motifs appeared on Liangzhu pottery. The differences between the jade and pottery representations of, say, dragons can be taken as evidence of craft specialization among the Liangzhu. By analyzing the decoration of jade and pottery objects, archaeologists have concluded that these were decorated by different craftsmen.

A luxurious jade object with intricate ornamental decorations made by Liangzhu craftsmen. Located in the Provincial Museum of Zhejiang.

Let's briefly turn toward more monumental achievements of the Liangzhu. Near modern-day Hangzhou, remains of a Liangzhu urban center were discovered. The most important discovery in this sense is the long city wall, which enclosed an area of about 290 hectares. The wall was probably around four meters high and had a very solid rock base. This wall is not only a testament to the construction capabilities of the Liangzhu but also to the increasing need to defend wealth. As we've already mentioned, during the Neolithic Age, humans really started to accumulate wealth. While the people had an intricate status differentiation within communities, they also had increasing differences between various groups.

It's possible that war, as we know it today, originated around the time of the Neolithic Age. Indeed, the most important achievements of the Neolithic Age, namely a sedentary lifestyle, the accumulation of wealth, and the emergence of status differentiations within and between groups, can be seen as the prerequisites of organized warfare.[296] It's true that aggression, conflicts, massacres, skirmishes, and things like that existed since the dawn of humanity, but the emergence of organized warfare is probably a newer "invention" dating back to the Neolithic Age. The Neolithic humans were also skilled craftsmen and were able to make increasingly effective weapons. Yes, these weapons were made of stone or wood, so they wouldn't be as effective as weapons made of bronze or iron. The world had to wait for the Age of Metal and the further perfection of the art of warfare before things got really bloody.

A model of the Liangzhu capital. The bottom right quarter represents the rectangular walled area, with something like a palace or castle in the middle. The walled area itself is surrounded by buildings that would have had various economic purposes.

猫猫的日记本, CC BY-SA 3.0 <https://creativecommons.org/licenses/by-sa/3.0>, via Wikimedia Commons; https://commons.wikimedia.org/wiki/File:Model_of_Liangzhu_Ancient_City_01_2013-10.JPG

---

[296] Runnels, Curtis N., Claire Payne, Noam V. Rifkind, Chantel White, Nicholas P. Wolff, and Steven A. LeBlanc. "Warfare in Neolithic Thessaly: A case study." Hesperia: *The Journal of the American School of Classical Studies at Athens* 78, no. 2 (2009): 165-194.

Let's briefly discuss another great achievement of the Neolithic Age, the one we're still using in more or less the same form today: the invention of alcoholic beverages. Fairly early in Neolithic China, some eight thousand years ago, people started to experiment with alcohol fermentation.[297] All sorts of beverages were made from plants like broomcorn millet, Job's tears (Adlay millet), beans, ginger, rice, lily, yam, and others. The Chinese people used various fermentation techniques, such as cereal malts, moldy grains, and special herbs. One invention was crucial for the discovery of alcohol fermentation: pottery. Special vessels for alcoholic beverages were made in early Neolithic China. Without such vessels, it would have been impossible to preserve any kind of liquid for extended amounts of time. The earliest Chinese alcoholic beverages (and Neolithic alcoholic beverages in general) probably had fairly low alcohol percentages. The world had to wait a bit longer for the emergence of stronger alcoholic beverages until the distillation process was invented. The Neolithic drinks were probably somewhat similar to beer or wine, though, as we've seen in the case of China, many different variations were possible. Moreover, we don't really know what purpose these early drinks served. Scholars hypothesize that alcoholic beverages in Neolithic China probably had medicinal, social, and spiritual uses.

And this is the broad landscape of Neolithic China. It was a marvelous period in the development of humanity. In the space of "only" a few thousand years, the Neolithic Age brought tectonic changes to humanity and propelled China (and others) into the historical period (as in the written age). But before we deal with the first written evidence from China, let's turn to one big mystery that still exists because of the blurred lines between myth and history—the Xia dynasty.

---

[297] Liu, Li, Jiajing Wang, Maureece J. Levin, Nasa Sinnott-Armstrong, Hao Zhao, Yanan Zhao, Jing Shao, Nan Di, and Tian'en Zhang. "The origins of specialized pottery and diverse alcohol fermentation techniques in Early Neolithic China." *Proceedings of the National Academy of Sciences* 116, no. 26 (2019): 12767-12774.

Chapter 2: The Xia Dynasty: Myth or History?

According to an age-old story, the Xia dynasty was an illustrious dynasty that ruled over a prehistoric Bronze Age Chinese culture. Scholars aren't unanimous when it comes to the existence of this dynasty and whether we can establish a connection between the Xia dynasty and one or several Bronze Age cultures of China, which are numerous.[298] First, let's give a little bit of context.

We have jumped from the Neolithic Age straight to the mythical Xia dynasty. The end of the Neolithic Age in China was marked by the invention of copper tools and weapons, which, in general, can be considered the first metal to be crafted into tools by humans.[299] Copper items, such as spearheads, started to emerge in the 3rd millennium BCE (five thousand years ago) in modern-day western China.[300] Copper isn't

---

[298] Thorp, Robert L. "Erlitou and the search for the Xia." *Early China* 16 (1991): 1-38.

[299] There's a reason copper was the first metal to be extracted and crafted by humans. Unlike most other metals, it can be found in a relatively pure form in nature. In order to use other types of metals, more elaborate extraction methods had to be put into place. Moreover, copper has a lower melting point compared to iron or alloys like steel. Interestingly, bronze, which was a metal invented immediately after copper, has a similar melting point to copper. Thus, the furnaces had to evolve correspondingly.

[300] Bunker, Emma C. "The Beginning of Metallurgy in Ancient China" *Web Archive.* Available at: https://web.archive.org/web/20070206143502/http:/exhibits.denverartmuseum.org/asianart/articles/metalwork/art_li_mat.html

that sturdy, and people soon found a way to make it more durable. They added tin, creating bronze. This was a period of experimenting with mixing different metals and observing the outcome. The Chinese quickly became skilled metal craftsmen, and in Chinese classical literature, we have evidence of how people back then were aware of how mixing metals in different proportions had differing outcomes.

Around four thousand years ago in prehistoric China, numerous Bronze Age cultures emerged, among them the famous Erlitou culture. The Erlitou people lived in the basin of the Yellow River, modern-day Henan province. Needless to say, they mastered agriculture and had large permanent settlements and an urban center. They were also skilled in making various bronze objects, such as wine vessels. The remains of a palace were also found, testifying to the existence of an Erlitou elite. The palace was surrounded by a sturdy wall built by compressing the earth and other materials together. Here's an expert description of this building:

"The compound stood on a broad pounded earth platform ... Walls enclosed this area, but little except their footings survives. Roofed galleries were probably created by the addition of parallel rows of columns both inside and outside the walls. At the center of the south wall was a large opening in the wall measuring 34 m across interpreted as a gate, but this portion of the site is so poorly preserved that little about the appearance of this gate can be deduced ... Another gate (or an attached chamber?) may have occupied a position in the notched northeast segment of the east wall.

An elevated main hall, apparently the single structure within this compound, was raised near the north wall, some 70 m north of the putative south gate and equidistant from both edges of the platform. Its foundation block, 36 m wide and 25 m deep, was built prior to the surrounding platform. Columns on the foundation block were spaced at intervals of 3.8 m, nine running across the north and south faces, and four (double counting the end columns) at the east and west ends."[301]

This is a description of a fairly complex building, which probably was under some form of control by the elites or elders. Unfortunately, we don't know much about the exact use of the building. Experts presume it had a complex set of functions, from civic to religious. In any case, the large enclosed space inside the palace was enough for ten thousand

---

[301] Thorp, Robert L. "Erlitou and the search for the Xia."

people, so it's possible this space had religious and/or other social purposes.[302] Scholars infer this conclusion from early Chinese texts that come from the Zhou dynasty. For instance, in the *Book of Documents*, a collection of some of the oldest surviving texts from ancient China, it is mentioned that the "king ordered the multitude all to come to the courtyard." Thus, it is probable that was the purpose of Erlitou courtyards too.

Erlitou burial rites must have been fairly complex and once again testify to an intricate differentiation of social strata. In the richest tombs, various sorts of objects were found, such as bronze vessels, jade objects, ceramic jars and basins, pouring vessels, and the like. Weapons were also found, as well as a skeleton of a dog in a small coffin.

Inversely, numerous "slave" or "sacrifice" burials were found, presumably of people who were of lower status.

Needless to say, the Erlitou culture is best known for being one of the earliest to produce bronze objects. Numerous bronze cups were unearthed that were made of a thin layer of bronze molded from multiple pieces. The Erlitou people also learned to make bronze axes, knives, and bells, some of which were decorated with complex ornaments. Several bronze plaques with turquoise decorations were also found; they are further testaments to "quantum leaps" in metallurgical knowledge and skill.

Erlitou bronze tripod, the so-called *jue*. Some authors believe this was a wine vessel, and it's possible that it had a very specific ritual purpose. Part of the collection of the Archeological Research Institute of the Chinese Academy of Social Sciences.

---

[302] Ibid.

But where does the legendary Xia fit? First, let's explore the historical documents mentioning the Xia. It's crucial to note that the legendary Xia didn't have a writing system, so any evidence of Xia has to be either archaeological or in subsequent writings. The Xia is mentioned in legends and myths that have found their way into later texts that came mainly from the Zhou period (some three thousand years ago).[303] The earliest historical evidence from ancient China (Shang dynasty) comes to us in the form of oracle bone inscriptions, which bear no mention of the Xia. Thousands of these oracle bones were found. They precede the Zhou dynasty by some five hundred years and are arguably closer to the mythical Xia, so it is curious that none of the unearthed bones mention the Xia. However, the bones do occasionally bear mentions of the Shang dynasty, so it is reasonable to assume that if the great Xia dynasty existed and been important, at least some bones would have contained inscriptions referring to the Xia, owing to its historical closeness to the Shang (and purported cultural continuity between the Xia and Shang). But so far, this hasn't been the case.

It is for this and other reasons that numerous scholars believe the Xia dynasty was a fabrication of the Zhou. But what would be the motive for this? Some scholars emphasize the parallels between the legendary Yu (who is reportedly the most important Xia ruler) and King Wen of Zhou, who were both instructed and guided by deities.[304] This kind of analogy might have served to "justify" the Zhou overthrow of the Shang, showing that it was mandated from the heavens. Needless to say, this is only a hypothesis. It's questionable whether the Zhou simply made up the whole story or whether they simply decided to focus on a specific legend that served their purpose. Some authors evoke the concept of "social memory" and that passages that mention the Xia have a purpose of preserving the memory of ancient times and societal changes, not necessarily the purpose of providing accurate historical accounts about a certain dynasty.[305] In this sense, the Xia can be a sort of "mnemonic" tool, a way to synthesize numerous historical events into one single culture and dynasty.

---

[303] Chen, Minzhen. "Faithful History or Unreliable History: Three Debates on the Historicity of the Xia Dynasty." *Journal of Chinese humanities* 5, no. 1 (2019): 78-104.

[304] Ibid.

[305] Ibid.

Now, we're at the same point as when we started our discussion on the Xia. The Xia dynasty exists somewhere in between myth and reality, legend and history. Some of the stories linked to the Xia are not without a historical basis, as we'll see in the next chapter on Yu the Great, the legendary Xia king. Hardships and achievements attributed to the Xia dynasty were most certainly things the ancient Chinese people experienced. On the other hand, it is still impossible to prove the existence of a culture or dynasty named Xia or the existence of a king named Yu the Great. Attempts have been made to establish a link between the Erlitou culture and the Xia, but the results are ambiguous at best. Any real existence of a king (or emperor) named Yu who propelled China into a period of exponential development is even more dubious. The developmental path ascribed to the Xia and Yu was most certainly trotted by the Chinese. But whether it was the Xia who were responsible for these developments is still questionable.

Chapter 3: Yu the Great

Now that we've cleared up (or further perpetuated) the question of the historicity of the Xia dynasty, let's look at Yu the Great, the legendary emperor of the Xia. As mentioned, the textual evidence for the Xia comes from a much later period, from the Zhou dynasty. These are exceedingly hermetic texts full of ancient cosmology and mythology. Before we move on to describe the achievements ascribed to Yu the Great, let's briefly explore his lineage.

The Xia supposedly come from ten totemic sun-birds who lived in the Mulberry Tree. All ten sun-birds rose from the Mulberry Tree and went westward to the western counterpart of their own Mulberry Tree. Then there was a man called Yellow Lord (Huang Di). Yellow Lord is a complex figure in his own right and is steeped in hermetic Chinese methodology, perhaps even more than his successor, Yu the Great. In some versions of the myth, he is credited as the ancestor of numerous tribes, including the Xia. His surname was either You Nai Shi or Han Yuan Shi, which is a testament to his totemic nature. In classical Chinese, *nai* can mean "three-legged turtle or dragon." *Han Yuan* is "black turtle," which has heavenly qualities. So, the Yellow Lord is an entity somewhere in between a totem and a human being.

The Yellow Lord had a wife named Lei Zu ("Woman of the Western Mound"), and the two had a son called Chang Yi, who inherited the kingdom of the Yellow Lord. Chang Yi is also associated with the west and with water. Chang Yi's home was the Ruo River, which flowed from the western version of the Mulberry Tree. According to one version of the myth, Chang Yi had a son named Han Liu. "Han Liu had a long throat and small ears, a human face with a pig's snout, a scaly body, thighs like wheel rims and pettitoed feet."[306]

Thus, Han Liu was a creature akin to a dragon, similar to Zhuan Xu (also spelled Zhuanxu), who was also Chang Yi's son, according to a slightly different version of the myth.

Moreover, both Han Liu and Zhuan Xu are associated with the Ruo River, which is their purported home. The descendants of Zhuan Xu are referred to as the people with three faces, who are immortal. He also had an adversary, Gong Gong. It seems that Gong Gong is accredited as the source of great floods, which the ancient Chinese (and people elsewhere) experienced, using it as the basis for their myths and legends. Zhuan Xu had a son, Gun, who attempted to solve the flooding problem but was unable to do so. The myth has it that Gun followed the signs of turtles and owls. Unfortunately for Gun, his solutions weren't effective, and he was executed by the king, who was probably his father. However, Gun's death wasn't his end, as he was transformed into *nai* (the aforementioned three-legged turtle or dragon). After that, his son, Yu (who would become Yu the Great), was born.

Similar to how Gun followed patterns laid out by turtles and owls, Yu followed the pattern of yellow dragons. He also built up a high land and led the digging of numerous canals to allow water to flow around settlements and not into them. This must have been an immense project that took years and an incredible human (and animal) workforce to complete. Yu the Great also led the dredging of riverbeds, which allowed for a more abundant water flow and perhaps even the increased navigability of rivers. Besides digging canals and dredging the riverbeds, Yu is credited with important reforms. For instance, he divided the country into nine provinces: Jizhou (冀州), Yanzhou (兖州), Qingzhou (青州), Xuzhou (徐州), Yangzhou (揚州), Jingzhou (荊州), Yuzhou (豫州), Liangzhou (梁州), and Yongzhou (雍州).

In a similar way to Gun, Yu also transformed into *nai*, a mythical being. After seeing him in his new form, Yu's wife, the Lady of Tu

---

[306] Allan, Sarah. "The myth of the Xia Dynasty." *Journal of the Royal Asiatic Society* 116, no. 2 (1984): 242-256.

Mountain, ran away and turned into stone. It was only after this that she gave birth to Yu's son, Qi. The name "Qi" can mean "beginning," and Qi is often credited as being the first hereditary ruler of China and the last to have a miraculous birth. Qi's son, Tai Kang, continued the Xia dynasty, which yielded many great kings. One of the last was a king named Kong Jia, about whom we have a little bit more information compared to other Yu's successors.

It seems that Kong Jia was the king who started the decline of the Xia. Kong Jia was interested in magic and the supernatural. The heavens sent him two dragons, but Kong Jia was unable to attend to them. One of them died. This dragon was unknowingly served as a meal to Kong Jia, who ate it, sealing his fate. In another version of the myth, the Xia ruler "dwelt at the Western River. Heaven had an ominous disaster: the ten suns came out together."[307] Soon, the Xia disappeared, only to be replaced by the Shang. It's not a coincidence that the ten suns were symbols of the Shang, and the ominous event that happened to the Xia ruler announced the arrival of a new dynasty, the first Chinese dynasty for which we have solid historical evidence.

---

[307] Ibid.

SECTION TWO:
THE SHANG DYNASTY
(c. 1600–1050 BCE)

Chapter 4: The Battle of Mingtiao

Although the decline of the Xia was visible from the time of Kong Jia, it was only with his successor, Jie, that the dynasty ceased to exist. A man called Tang finally overthrew the Xia in an act of open rebellion, which ended in the decisive Battle of Mingtiao. The battle was won by Tang, who became the first ruler of the Shang dynasty.[308] The battle is said to have taken place sometime around 1600 BCE. The Xia, as we've seen, became decadent, and even the heavens were sending signs of their upcoming demise. The end came in the form of Tang.

Perhaps there was more to Tang than simply being someone who represented the mandate of heaven. Some authors believe he was the leader of a widespread rebellion against the Xia and who might have, over time, become a sort of elite who governed the less-privileged people. In this sense, Tang could have been an expression of a wider rebellion against, for instance, the Xia dynasty's taxation and extravagance.

Unfortunately, we don't know the real circumstances of the Battle of Mingtiao. If there was something like a rebellion against the hegemony of the Xia, it's likely that numerous cultural groups participated and that Tang was simply one of the leaders.

Tang

There's a very interesting tale about Tang preserved on bamboo slips that were discovered by the authorities as they were being smuggled into

---

[308] Mark, Joshua J. "Ancient China." *Ancient History Encyclopedia* (2012).

Hong Kong. These bamboo slips came from a much later period called the Warring States Period (5th to 3rd century BCE).[309] The story is called (somewhat poetically) "When Red Pigeons Gathered at Tang's House," and it goes like this. Tang was at his house when he saw red pigeons flocking on his roof. Tang took his bow and arrow and shot one pigeon, which he gave to his servant Xiaochen, ordering him to make a soup from the red pigeon. Xiaochen proceeded to make the soup, but before he was able to serve it to his master, Tang's wife, Ren Huang, arrived. Tang's wife wanted a taste of the red pigeon soup, but Xiaochen was hesitant. He was afraid that his master would find out and have him killed. But Ren Huang threatened to kill Xiaochen if he didn't let her taste the soup.

So, poor Xiaochen was forced to allow Ren Huang to taste the soup. After doing so, she was able to see all things in the world; her glance penetrated everywhere. Xiaochen took what was left of the soup, and he, too, experienced the same effects. Tang found out what happened, which prompted Xiaochen to flee to the Xia. Although he managed to run away from Tang, the Shang king enchanted Xiaochen, and the latter became very sleepy and was unable to pursue his plan. At that moment, a flock of ravens came to Xiaochen, wanting to eat him. However, they found out that Xiaochen couldn't be eaten. So, the leader of the ravens, a sort of spiritual medium, stepped in front and sent other ravens to the court of the Xia, where the Xia lord was making his offerings in the hope of gaining better health.

The spiritual medium raven possessed Xiaochen, which, in a way, negated the spell cast by Tang. The possessed Xiaochen reached the Xia, whose lord didn't know the reason for his own illness. But the possessed Xiaochen did know it: a man called Thearch employed black magic to make the Xia lord ill by ordering two white rabbits and two yellow snakes to dwell beneath the Xia lord's bedroom. Two mounds were also made beneath his bedroom. All these made the Xia lord ill. His heart wasn't working as it should have, and the lord's body started showing sores, which precluded him from resting.

The black magic items were removed, and the Xia lord regained his health. But one rabbit got away; to keep this rabbit away from the city,

---

[309] Allan, Sarah. "'When Red Pigeons Gathered on Tang's House": A Warring States Period Tale of Shamanic Possession and Building Construction set at the turn of the Xia and Shang Dynasties." *Journal of the Royal Asiatic Society* 25, no. 3 (2015): 419-438.

people started building parapets.

Needless to say, there are many ways to interpret this story. Sarah Allan, a scholar of ancient China, believes that this story takes the mythical content (Tang's magical powers, etc.) and blends it with the rites of building parapets to provide a sort of justification and historic-mythical basis for the rite.

Despite the Shang dynasty being the first Chinese dynasty for which we have actual written proof (found mainly on oracle bones), it is still steeped in myth. Studying Shang oracle bones and later textual evidence helped scholars to uncover an important founding figure, the minister Yi Yin. Similar to Xiaochen in the aforementioned story, Yi Yin was described as Tang's cook and someone who assisted in sacrifice rites. Some scholars believe that Yi Yin is a typical figure in ancient myths and legends of China. He was of low origins but was nevertheless brought up by the emperor and allowed to reach the highest office. It is also believed that such a motive stressed the importance of delegating or sharing power at the very top. The emperor was surely the top man, but he was unable to do anything unless he had support from the groups who were ruled by him.

In a very indirect way, the Yi Yin motif is a testament to the incredible cultural diversity of ancient China. As you might understand by now, there wasn't a simple succession of cultures; rather, China (and the world) had many cultures coexisting together. They probably engaged in extensive contact with one another, whether through trade or wars. It's likely that during certain periods, one or two cultures emerged as "leaders." To this day, China is an incredibly complex country with many different provinces, traditions, and ethnic groups. Back in the Bronze Age, it's likely that things were pretty much the same; perhaps, things were even more complicated and less centralized, considering the speed of communication and the transmission of knowledge. So, whoever was at the top had to be there with the approval of those he governed.

The Shang were at the top for quite a long time, owing to their cultural development, mastery of crafts, and willingness to learn from other cultures. We must not forget that the Shang cities were situated fairly close to the Erlitou sites, and there were likely extensive exchanges between the Shang and the Erlitou and between other ancient Chinese groups. The ingenious Shang, to whom we owe the very first written documents from ancient China, nevertheless encountered the same fate as the one they bestowed on the Xia. But let's first see their achievements before shifting to the decline of the Shang and the rise of the Zhou.

Chapter 5: Cultural and Military Developments

While most historians prefer to remain silent with respect to the Battle of Mingtiao, we know a lot more about one of the main protagonists of the battle: the Shang. The development of the Shang has been well preserved, and archaeologists have been able to track the early days of the Shang back to 2000 BCE.[310] The so-called "proto-Shang" were discovered in the Henan and Hubei provinces of China. In the early phases of development, the Shang inhabited modern-day Hubei; as time went on, they moved more to the south, crossing the Yellow River at one point and settling in modern-day Henan. It is presumed that the Shang went from a nomadic lifestyle, relying heavily on livestock, to a more agriculture-based, sedentary lifestyle.

---

[310] Hou, Liangliang, Yaowu Hu, Xinping Zhao, Suting Li, Dong Wei, Yanfeng Hou, Baohua Hu et al. "Human subsistence strategy at Liuzhuang site, Henan, China during the proto-Shang culture (~ 2000–1600 BC) by stable isotopic analysis." *Journal of Archaeological Science* 40, no. 5 (2013): 2344-2351.

Shang territory in the modern-day Chinese provinces of Hubei and Henan.
Lamassu Design Gurdjieff, CC BY-SA 3.0 <https://creativecommons.org/licenses/by-sa/3.0>, via Wikimedia Commons; https://commons.wikimedia.org/wiki/File:Shang_dynasty.svg

This leads us to the establishment of a very important Shang city called Zhengzhou. Zhengzhou is the name of a modern Chinese city situated at the old Shang archaeological site.[311] With the Zhengzhou site, we are probably entering the year 1600 BCE, so this ancient city might have been the first capital of the Shang dynasty after the legendary Xia were defeated. At Zhengzhou, a large wall made from rammed earth was discovered, measuring almost seven kilometers in length. But there are other Shang sites, such as Xiaoshuangqiao and Huanbei, which are both fairly large and surrounded by thick earth-rammed walls. The development of elaborate defensive structures shows that conflicts between groups were, more or less, a thing of everyday life in this period. Wealth and luxury had to be protected by any means possible. And while

---

[311] Guangkuo, Yuan. "The discovery and study of the Early Shang culture." *A companion to Chinese archaeology* (2013): 323-342.

the Bronze Age, which was heralded by the Shang in ancient China, brought very important developmental changes to humanity, it's quite likely there were some groups of people who simply wanted to "hijack" the developmental path and jump up a few steps by eradicating more advanced cultures and taking over their achievements.

The larger cities, almost by a rule, were surrounded by smaller settlements, which, in a way, orbited around the illustrious cultural centers. The surrounding settlements probably weren't exclusively "Shang." They probably had a very diverse mixture of people. In this light, the establishment of capital cities seems even more important, as it allows one to establish himself (and sometimes herself) as the "boss" in the area. The collection of tributes and taxes (if they existed back then) and more careful control of the area would also have been possible.

Social Hierarchy

To inspect the social hierarchy, we have to turn toward a place where, for all intents and purposes, the social hierarchy ceases to exist: death. But much like people aren't equal while they are alive, they don't cease being unequal in death. Ancient people were very careful to preserve the social hierarchy, even in the afterlife. The wealthiest members of the Shang were buried in large graves (around ten square meters). Wooden coffins were used to hold the bodies of the upper class, and some had both outer and inner wooden coffins. The coffins themselves were sometimes decorated or painted. Numerous prestigious objects were found in these graves. Archaeologists have discovered jade daggers, bronze tripods and jars, food containers, and bronze tools and weapons. Some graves of the elite also contained proto-porcelain.

As we move toward the bottom of the hierarchy, we uncover more modest graves that are smaller in size and usually contain ceramic objects. Some graves are smaller than one square meter, which means the body can only fit in a contracted, fetal-like position. These graves rarely have any objects.

The Shang were probably the first to start utilizing bronze on a larger scale. The aforementioned Erlitou culture was one of the first to produce bronze, but the use of bronze was restricted to a few types of fairly small objects, such as knives. The Shang, on the other hand, started using bronze for making tools like shovels and axes. Bronze shovels and axes are more effective than stone or wooden tools. Different bronze foundries were discovered in Shang settlements. There were probably many craftsmen specializing in smithing, and different workshops specialized in different types of tools. Moreover, there wasn't one single "recipe" for bronze. The proportion of copper and tin in the bronze alloy varies significantly. Some pieces of Shang bronze also contain lead, which is perhaps a testament to the willingness of the Shang to experiment and improve their metal further.

A bronze Shang ax that was possibly used for combat and ritual purposes.

In a similar way, there were numerous experts who made ceramics. They also aimed to improve their craft, which is why we are able to find the so-called "proto-porcelain" of the Shang.

This doesn't mean that some of the more ancient crafts were extinct by the time of the Shang. For instance, numerous bone workshops were uncovered. Animal and human bones were used for the production of all sorts of everyday objects, such as needles, arrowheads, rings, hooks, and the like. There has been some evidence of human sacrifice by the Shang, so the use of human bones for the production of tools isn't that surprising. Interestingly, in such workshops, ivory was also found. It's likely the Shang had to import ivory from far away, meaning they had extensive communication with nearby cultures and much more distant ones.

Chapter 6: Politics and Religion

Probably the most important source of the Shang cultural practices are the famous oracle bones, which bear the first known writing system of ancient China. More than eight hundred oracle bones bear mentions of the Qiang, who were distinct from the Shang and probably subordinated to the latter.[312] The Qiang war captives had the grueling fate of being human sacrifices for the Shang. Although the exact reason behind the Shang dynasty's human sacrifices will probably remain obscure, there are ways to explain this phenomenon, all of which potentially bring insight into the religious and political system of the Shang.

A likely theory is that human sacrifices served as a way to legitimize the Shang dynasty's political control over the population. In this sense, the Shang (or any other ethnic group) cannot exist without positioning them in relation to other ethnic groups. The Qiang might have served as an antithesis of the Shang, providing a way for the Shang to establish themselves as the victors, the ones who exert power over others. This interpretation gives us a different kind of perspective on the topic of human sacrifice, which is important since modern people tend to ascribe such behavior to the depths of prehistory. People avoid interpreting this behavior, instead calling it pure barbarism, cannibalism, and the like.

The oracle bones probably had a complex purpose. They were likely used by the Shang in their court rituals in the following fashion.

---

[312] Shelach, Gideon. "The Qiang and the question of human sacrifice in the late Shang period." *Asian Perspectives* (1996): 1-26.

Alternative divinations were inscribed on a turtle shell, saying, for instance, "It will rain tomorrow" and "It won't rain tomorrow." Hot charcoal or another source of heat was then inserted into the previously hollowed-out parts on the back of the turtle shell. The hot charcoal inevitably made cracks in the turtle shell. The pattern of cracks with respect to the inscriptions was then interpreted by a diviner.[313] The exact content of the oracle bone inscriptions gives us a glimpse into the everyday worries and struggles of the Shang. "This night there will be no disaster." "The whole day we will not encounter great wind." "The whole day there will be no harm."[314] This content can be interpreted as not just predicting the future but also as a way to *affect* the future and, more importantly, free people from suffering.

In these rituals of the Shang, the early connection between religion and struggles with the environment is evident. And once again, we return to Freud, who believed that it was thanks to the harshness of the early environment of humans that deities came into existence. When a person has nothing to turn to, when they are completely at the mercy of environmental conditions, they might seek spiritual ways to improve their life.[315] The Shang oracle bones bear evidence of this initial struggle between humans and nature.

A pit containing numerous oracle bones excavated at Yinxu, Anyang, China.
Chez Câsver (Xuan Che), CC BY 2.0 <https://creativecommons.org/licenses/by/2.0>, via Wikimedia Commons; https://commons.wikimedia.org/wiki/File:Oracle_bones_pit.JPG

---

[313] Keightley, David N. "Shang divination and metaphysics." *Philosophy East and West* 38, no. 4 (1988): 367-397.

[314] Ibid.

[315] Freud, Sigmund. The future of an illusion. *Broadview Press*, 2012.

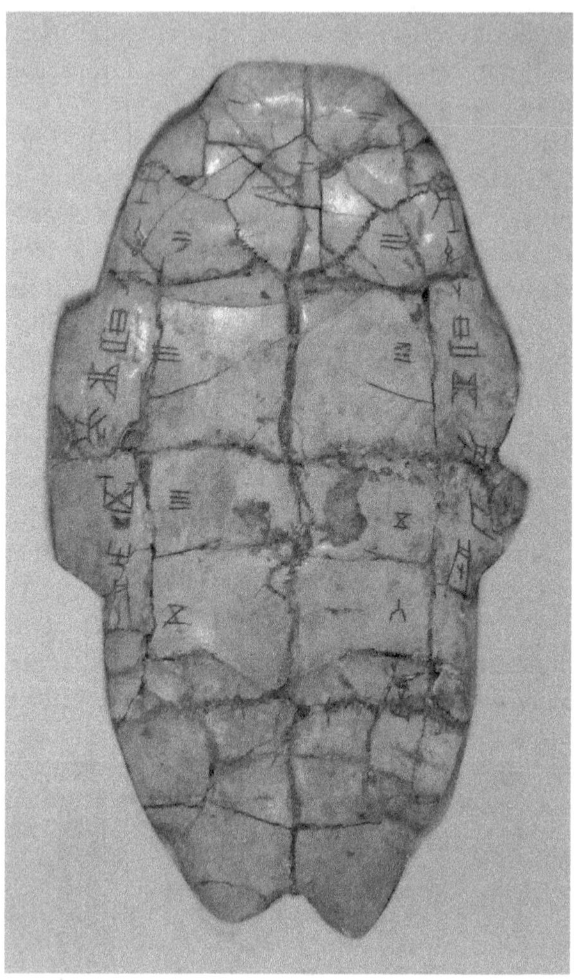

A very typical Shang oracle bone from a tortoise. This bone comes from the period of King Wu Ding. The two alternative predictions are interpreted as follows: "Gu divined: Ban will have misfortune" and "Gu divined: Ban will have no misfortune."

Let's now turn to a more concrete analysis of oracle bones related to the Qiang, which will help us uncover the mysteries of the Shang. You'll also understand just how much work goes into understanding even a single Chinese character preserved on oracle bones.

According to most scholars, the character pronounced as "Qiang" has the following meaning: "Western Rong sheep herdsmen."[316] The Qiang

---

[316] Shelach, Gideon. "The Qiang and the question of human sacrifice in the late Shang period. p. 4

character is made from two separate characters, one denoting "man" and the other "sheep." The Qiang probably lived in northwest China and had a pastoral lifestyle. In that sense, they were on the periphery of Shang influence and were culturally distinct. Whereas the Shang were more agriculturally based, the Qiang were herdsmen. Thanks to their technological developments, notably the extensive use of bronze, the Shang were probably more effective soldiers and were able to keep the surrounding societies subjugated, at least for a certain amount of time. For instance, although chariots are absent from early Shang sites, they appear in the later period (around 1000 BCE) and must have been used in both war and hunting.

The Qiang weren't the only neighboring culture to be mentioned on oracle bones. In fact, dozens of societies are mentioned on oracle bones in a context that implies they enjoyed more or less extensive political freedom and autonomy from central Shang rule. Therefore, the structure of the Shang civilization wasn't entirely unlike the fiefdoms of the medieval age. Their domination over neighbors wasn't simply characterized by war and subjugation but also by negotiations and extensive cultural contact. For instance, the Shang nobles mixed with the nobilities of neighboring groups. Inversely, non-Shang were adopted into the clan or dynasty, and non-Shang were also able to take high political and religious positions.

There was certainly extensive trading going on between the Shang and their neighbors. The turtle shells for oracle bones were extensively procured from the outside. Other important materials, such as salt, tin, and copper, were also obtained from neighbors.

In this sense, the Qiang emerged as very important neighbors, at least for the Shang, since they are the only ones mentioned on oracle bones as being human sacrifices. The Qiang must have done something to precipitate a harsher response from the Shang.

At the site called Yinxu (Anyang), the biggest Shang city, numerous human sacrificial pits were excavated, with people sometimes accompanying the nobles in their afterlife. Although we don't know the ethnicity of the people found in these sacrificial pits, it's likely that the Qiang war prisoners participated in similar rituals or were buried in the sacrificial pits found in Yinxu. What we do know for certain is that the oracle bones that mention the Qiang talk about the Shang and their allies hunting for the Qiang. The Qiang were often decapitated, at least according to the oracle bones, and numerous headless skeletons have been found in Shang sacrificial pits. Most of the people found in sacrificial pits were men, which further fosters the hypothesis that they were war captives.

But why did the Shang perform these rituals? Scholars are not certain, but there are some very likely hypotheses. For example, human sacrifices might have been a way to communicate with ancestors. This interpretation receives support from text discovered on oracle bones. Moreover, as is often the case with sacrifices, the Shang may have done them to please the spiritual beings who had power over human life. When the Shang noticed signs that harmony in the world was being lost, they might have felt compelled to offer something to the supreme spiritual beings to alter what seemed to be their impending annihilation.

But this is only a part of the story. To get the full picture, we have to turn toward the construction of the Shang state. At the top, of course, was a king surrounded by his noble family and members of the elite. The elites from other societies were allowed inside the Shang dynasty and vice versa. Below the elites was probably the military: somewhat wealthy people who had enough money to equip themselves for war and were directly controlled by the elites. Then came the craftsmen and artisans, who were of the utmost importance for cultural development. At the very bottom were (relatively) free farmers; they were probably the most numerous. It seems the Shang didn't have institutionalized slavery. In ancient Greece or Rome, war captives were often sold into slavery. The Shang didn't have institutionalized slavery, at least as far as we know, and thus had to find another "purpose" for their war captives.

Some Shang Kings

The Shang dynasty lasted for around six hundred years, and it is by no means possible to give a good account of all the Shang rulers here. However, we can turn to some of the more interesting stories about some of the Shang rulers, which were preserved in an ancient book called the *Records of the Grand Historian*, written by one of the first Chinese historians, Sima Qian (c. 145–86 BCE). In this book, Sima covers a period of around 2,500 years. Although Sima Qian is considered one of the first Chinese historians, the things he talks about have to be taken critically; this is very similar to other early historians, such as the Greek Herodotus, whose *Histories*, although incredibly interesting and captivating, isn't always completely reliable.

You may recall that the Shang story began with a ruler named Tang. At one point in Sima Qian's book, he writes the following words:

"After T'ang, when Emperor T'ai-wu came to the throne of the Shang dynasty, a mulberry and a paper mulberry sprang up together in the court of his palace and in the space of one night grew so large that a person could not reach around them with his arms. The emperor was frightened, but his minister I Chih said, 'Evil omens cannot prevail over virtue!' Then Emperor T'ai-wu strove for greater virtue in his rule and the two mulberries died. I Chih praised the emperor to the shaman Hsien. It was at this time that the shaman Hsien came to power."[317]

Many generations later came another Shang leader called Wu-ting. Sima Qian refers to him as someone who restored the Shang state and was dubbed the "Great Patriarch." He had a minister, Fu Yiieh, which is a regular theme in early Chinese history, with a king often having a very important minister who helps run the government. Sima sometimes refers to Wu-ting as someone who helped restore the Shang country, which might mean there was a period in which the Shang dynasty was threatened by external or internal enemies.

Unfortunately, the Shang experienced a similar decline as the Xia before them, and this time, the fate of Shang was sealed. According to legend, just five generations after the virtuous Wu-ting, King Wu-Yi went against the will of the spirits, and for this misdeed, the heavens sent thunder to kill him. The last Shang ruler, Di Xin, pejoratively referred to as Emperor Chou or Zhou, which can mean horse crupper (so, it is likely this nickname was a serious insult).[318] Sima Qian has a few words to say about Emperor Zhou, stating that people venerated this emperor while he was alive, but after he died, people had more respect for simple farmers!

Unfortunately, we don't know exactly how and why Emperor Zhou was depraved. Sima Qian tells us that he was "licentious," but other than that, we don't know too much. Many stories have been ascribed to Emperor Zhou, which have him engaged in all sorts of immoral deeds.

---

[317] Qian, Sima. "Records of the Grand Historian of China" Available at: https://archive.org/stream/in.ernet.dli.2015.532974/2015.532974.records-of_djvu.txt

[318] A crupper is a sort of leash that goes around the horse's tail and prevents the saddle from sliding forward. Due to its position, this leash gets contaminated by excrement, hence its negative connotation.

However, it's likely these are false stories aimed more to explain the downfall of Shang than to capture historical reality.

Chapter 7: The Fall of the Shang Dynasty

The Shang experienced the same fate as the one ascribed to the Xia: they were overthrown by a rising neighbor. And just as a grand battle signified the end of the Xia, another grand battle marked the end of the Shang: the Battle of Muye. We know comparatively quite a lot more about the Battle of Muye than about the Battle of Mingtiao. This is, of course, because the Battle of Muye is more recent, taking place by 1046 BCE. The Battle of Mingtiao happened around six hundred years earlier. By 1046 BCE, Chinese cultures had already adopted the use of writing.

The story of the Battle of Muye is as follows. While the Shang society was plunging deeper into decadence and decline, a new source of progress emerged, the Zhou. They lived west of the Shang in modern-day Shaanxi province.[319] In the next chapter, we'll talk more in depth about the Zhou culture and its development prior and after becoming the dominant culture in China. It's likely the Zhou were becoming more frustrated with their vassal-like position in relation to the Shang. The Zhou were skilled craftsmen and had effective weapons and fairly good military organization. It was only natural for them to start considering themselves worthy of leading the Chinese world. For now, suffice it to say that around 1046 BCE, the Zhou and Shang fought a decisive battle. Led by King Wu, the Zhou rushed toward the main Shang cities, numbering

---

[319] LI, Xiaobing (ed.). "China at War: An Encyclopedia." ABC-CLIO, 2012.

forty-five thousand infantrymen. The Zhou also had a well-developed cavalry, around three thousand cavalrymen. The Shang were much more numerous, numbering 170,000 men, most of whom were slaves.[320] The Zhou directly attacked the Shang infantry. After seeing their elites being decimated by the Zhou, the Shang slaves gave up, and a lot of them probably defected to the other side. The Shang emperor fled and soon committed suicide. The Shang state was abolished, as some scholars put it, and a new dynasty arose: the Western Zhou.

The Shang was the first Chinese culture to leave traces of a somewhat organized writing system. The oracle bone inscriptions are testaments to an extremely old writing system—only the writing systems of ancient Egypt and ancient Middle Eastern states (and perhaps the still undeciphered Linear A Minoan writing system) are older. The Shang era gave us an incredibly complex writing system, which served as a basis for the modern Chinese characters.

Hundreds of thousands (perhaps even millions) of years have passed since the emergence of a new, human-like species that dwelled on Earth in search of food and shelter. For thousands and thousands of years, people had relatively similar lifestyles, used relatively simple stone tools, and hunted and gathered the food they could find. Then, after a period of just a few thousand years, evidence of the New Stone Age is present, with more advanced stone-processing methods, domestication of animals, inceptions of a sedentary lifestyle, and agriculture. Add a few thousand years more, and we're in the Bronze Age. People learned how to combine different metals to craft more durable tools. They also became skilled agriculture workers, craftsmen, and soldiers. Then, as a crown to all these achievements, humans invented what's perhaps the greatest invention of all: writing systems.

The exponential nature of human development should be evident by now. But by talking about this, we also have to be aware of the proper historical context. Although the use of writing systems is an incredible intellectual feat for beings that nine thousand years prior only knew how

---

[320] Initially, the Shang didn't have institutionalized slavery. It seemed that as time went on, they relied more and more on slaves, and ultimately, they paid dearly for this. We can encounter similar examples of slavery-related problems throughout history. Sparta had a big problem in periods when the slaves drastically outnumbered the free population. Rome saw numerous slave revolts, some of which were extremely dangerous for the stability of the nation. In other words, slavery, besides being extremely unethical, turned out to be a not-so-wise business plan.

to craft simple stone tools, the ritual significance of early inscriptions is obvious. In China, the earliest inscriptions are inextricably linked to the spiritual universe. Writing something down was an act of creating a better future, an act of influencing unpredictable nature. In this sense, the early Chinese inscriptions are steeped in the mythical, religious, and spiritual. However, the writing didn't only have this purpose. Shang bronze vessels also have writing on them. Coming from the late Shang period, these bronze vessel inscriptions have a somewhat practical nature, although they are still steeped in the ritual world. They tell us about the name of the clan of the person who owned the (probably prestigious) bronze vessel and also the name of the craftsman who made it.[321]

Soon after the end of the Shang, the oracle bones almost completely disappear, and the writing is encountered in numerous other contexts. Perhaps this points to one of the reasons why the Shang disappeared in the first place. They weren't practical enough, and once they reached the top, they stagnated. The Zhou, who were maybe more practical at the time, took their chance and propelled China into a new era of development.

---

[321] Boltz, William G. "Early Chinese Writing." *World Archaeology* 17, no. 3 (1986): 420-436.

SECTION THREE:
THE ZHOU DYNASTY
(c. 1050–221 BCE)

Chapter 8: Western and Eastern Zhou Dynasties

The Zhou (or Chou) most certainly didn't come out of the blue. This culture existed and developed for a long time before it took over the helm of China. The early Zhou (c. 1400 BCE) lived in the Loess Plateau, which is an arid region just south of modern-day Mongolia. In the 2nd millennium BCE, the Loess Plateau was essentially a steppe, with forest vegetation here and there. The altitude of the original Zhou place of living was around one thousand meters above sea level. Over time, the Zhou started moving southward and eastward, reaching fertile regions surrounding the rivers.[322] It is possible the Zhou were compelled to move southeastward by two broad factors: migrations of nomads from the north and increasing climatic aridity. Due to these reasons, the Zhou decided to seek a better environment for themselves, finally settling in the Fufeng region (modern-day western Shaanxi), building the capital Qiyi there. They continued moving eastward, finally reaching and overturning the Shang dynasty around one thousand years before the birth of Christ.

---

[322] Huang, Chun Chang, Shichao Zhao, Jiangli Pang, Qunying Zhou, Shue Chen, Pinghua Li, Longjiang Mao, and Min Ding. "Climatic aridity and the relocations of the Zhou culture in the southern Loess Plateau of China." *Climatic Change* 61 (2003): 361-378.

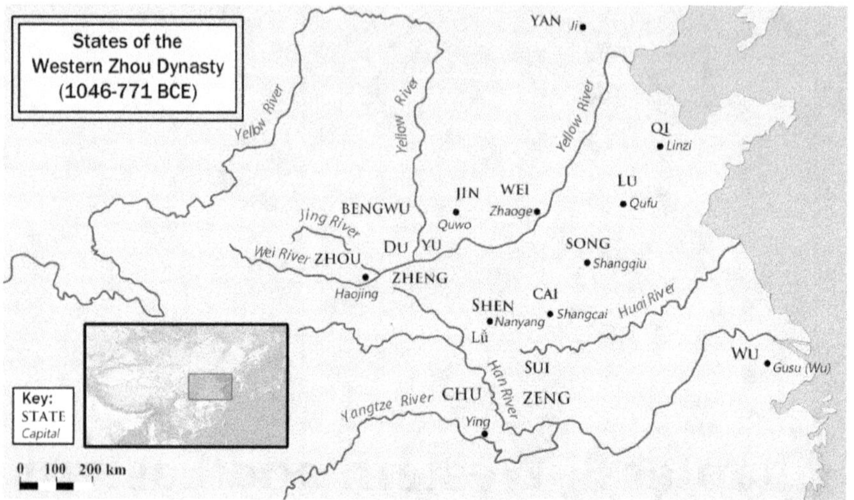

Map of Western Zhou and their neighbors. Note that this is only a rough estimate and took place over a fairly long period.

Philg88, CC BY-SA 3.0 <https://creativecommons.org/licenses/by-sa/3.0>, via Wikimedia Commons; https://commons.wikimedia.org/wiki/File:EN-WesternZhouStates.jpg

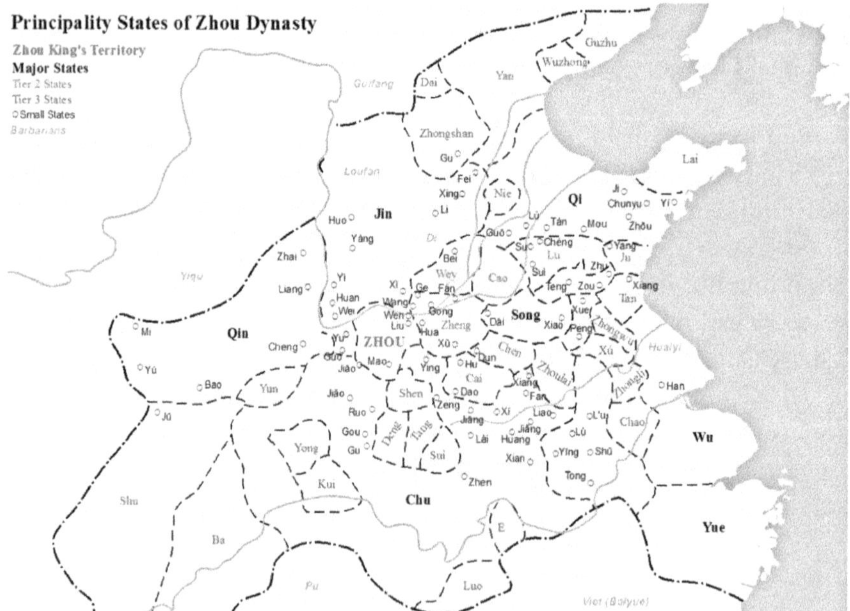

Map of Eastern Zhou and their neighbors.

SY, CC BY-SA 4.0 <https://creativecommons.org/licenses/by-sa/4.0>, via Wikimedia Commons; https://commons.wikimedia.org/wiki/File:States_of_Zhou_Dynasty.png

The Zhou adopted and modified the Shang writing system, and they brought their supreme deity, Tian, or Heaven, with them.[323] The mandate of heaven justified their overthrow of the Shang, much as the mandate of heaven oversaw the overthrow of the Xia by the Shang. From the early days of the Zhou, we find bronze vessels bearing inscriptions relating to this mandate of heaven or "Great Command from Heaven."

Initially, the Zhou settled in the more central regions of China, the aforementioned Shaanxi province. Their most important cities there were Zongzhou (Hao) and Fengjing (Feng or Fengxi), situated on the opposite banks of the Feng River, sometimes collectively referred to as Fenghao. It's likely that the Zhou emanated a sort of royal power from their prestigious cities, exerting authority over neighboring nations in a similar way as the Shang.

Unfortunately for the Western Zhou, which is how we refer to this initial period of the Zhou dynasty, their neighbors saw no reason not to do the same things as the Zhou. They invaded the wealthy cities and took on the role of leaders of the region. Finally, in 771 BCE, a group from the north, the Quan Rong, invaded the Western Zhou cities and killed King You (Gongsheng).[324] This occasion marks the end of the Western Zhou and the beginning of the Eastern Zhou.

As is always the case with the downfalls of great empires, there were many factors at play for the Western Zhou. It's possible that invaders from the west were catching up with them in terms of technology, weapons, and military organization. The Western Zhou likely grew comfortable with their position as a regional force and failed to make the necessary changes to stay on top.

The Eastern Zhou period is marked by the decreasing central authority of the royal family and the rise of powerful neighboring states. But even the Western Zhou established a sort of feudal system with their subordinate neighboring states, such as Ba, Zheng, and Yu.[325] During the Eastern Zhou, the importance and autonomy of neighboring states further

---

[323] Rawson, Jessica. "Ordering the exotic: ritual practices in the late western and early eastern Zhou." *Artibus Asiae* 73, no. 1 (2013): 5-76.

[324] Khayutina, Maria. "Western Zhou cultural and historic setting." *The Oxford Handbook of Early China* (2020): 365.

[325] Childs-Johnson, Elizabeth, ed. *The Oxford Handbook of Early China*. Oxford University Press, USA, 2020.

---

increased over the course of the so-called Spring and Autumn Period (771–481 BCE). With the Warring States Period (481–221 BCE), the aspirations of neighboring regions became even more prominent, and the period ended with the total defeat of the Zhou.

The Zhou Military

The Zhou owe their ascent to their powerful military. The elite members of the Zhou were inextricably tied to the military and must have served as the leaders of individual military units. They were likely also tasked with supplying their units with the necessary provisions. The Zhou probably had standing armies that were ready to act whenever necessary. The skill of archery was held in high esteem, and the elite members were supposed to be skilled archers. Furthermore, archery competitions were organized, and during the rule of King Mu, a sort of elite academy for archers was founded. The royal family regularly handed out beautiful bows and arrows to worthy individuals as a sign of allegiance and military prowess.

Thanks to advancements in the fabrication and processing of bronze, the Zhou were able to make durable chariots that were drawn by four horses (compared to the two-horse chariots of the Shang). Chariots had symbolic and practical purposes. They were used as a sign of wealth and status, not unlike people who use higher-end vehicles today to prove their elite status. However, chariots also had a very practical purpose. Chariot military units were formed, and they were able to wreak havoc among enemy infantry units. In fact, there's evidence that chariots were considered so dangerous that commanders would rather have them destroyed than have them fall into enemy hands. An interesting connection between ancient and modern wars can be made here.[326] Indeed, one of the implicit statements of this book is that modern societies aren't essentially different from societies established from the Neolithic Age onward.

During the period of the Eastern Zhou, the use of iron became more widespread use. For instance, graves from the Warring States Period hid numerous iron items, such as weapons and luxurious objects.[327] From

---

[326] In 1940, the British sank the French fleet docked at Mers-el-Kebir (then French Algeria) to prevent it from falling into German hands.

[327] Wagner, Donald B. "The earliest use of iron in China." *BAR International Series* 792 (1999): 1-9.

roughly the same period, iron foundries (for instance, in Hebei, central eastern China) were also unearthed, which are testaments to an organized, systematic production of iron in the 3rd century BCE. The Wu and Chu states possess the oldest traces of widespread iron use and production, with evidence of smelting processes being traced back as far back as the 5th century BCE. Interestingly, the oldest evidence of iron use comes from the Shang/early Western Zhou, and it has been proven that these iron artifacts have a meteoritic origin, meaning they literally came from space. The artifacts in question are bronze ax heads that were fostered with iron.

However, it is quite likely that the later production of iron in the Wu and Chu states and the propagation of iron across all of China are unrelated to the initial use of meteoritic iron. Around three centuries before the birth of Christ, iron reached the Zhou and quickly replaced bronze as the most-used metal for producing various items. There were possibly other sources of iron production, possibly from the northern steppe cultures. In fact, a grave was found in Shaanxi dating from the 6th century BCE containing gold-iron swords and knives. By this time, the Western Zhou were pushed eastward. The grave also contained evidence that corresponded more to steppe cultures. In other words, this must have been a cultural group under the influence of both the steppe and Chinese cultures.

In the early days of experimentation with iron (8th century BCE), iron wasn't of good quality and must have been inferior to bronze. It was possibly used as decoration for prestigious weapons. It was only in the 6th century BCE that more durable iron was produced in the southern states of Wu and Chu. The smithing techniques of Wu and Chu were related to the production of bronze agricultural tools. It's possible that during these early days, iron products were fairly brittle, though fairly resistant to wear and tear, compared to bronze. But China wouldn't have to wait long for the perfection of iron production.

The Zhou made other important breakthroughs, such as the use of the crossbow. The crossbow was used by Chinese militaries during the Warring States Period, which lasted from the 5th to the late 3rd century BCE.[328] Presumably, a man, Chi'in Shih, from a state called Chu invented the crossbow, probably during the 6th century BCE. The crossbow entered, relatively speaking, widespread use, as it was adopted by other

---

[328] Cartwright, Mark. Crossbows in Ancient Chinese Warfare. *World History Encyclopedia*.

states. For instance, the military of the state of Qi also adopted the crossbow by the time of the Battle of Maling (341 BCE), and it was thanks to crossbows that they won the battle against the Wei state.

Needless to say, it wasn't easy to make a good crossbow back then, and it must have been fairly expensive. This is why only chosen and well-trained soldiers were bestowed with the opportunity of using crossbows. For the most part, the Chinese militaries were fairly standard with the infantry typical of the period.[329]

---

[329] Greeks and Romans used crossbow-like weapons during roughly the same period. Greeks had their *gastraphetes*, and Romans had their large *ballista*. It's not clear whether there is a connection between Chinese and European crossbow-like weapons, as is often the case with ancient connections between Europe and the Far East.

Chapter 9: Cultural Developments

The most important historical evidence from the Zhou period comes in the form of bronze vessels bearing different sorts of inscriptions. In this sense, the discovery of more than one hundred bronze vessels in a single pit by farmers in 1977 near Mount Qi in the Fufeng region was instrumental since it provided archaeologists and linguists with an abundance of material to work with.[330]

More specifically, 103 bronze vessels were found there, and 74 had inscriptions. It seems they all came from a single line of craftsmen-scribes, the Wei family. The Wei family is presumed to have originated within the Shang elite, but they became integrated into the Zhou after the latter defeated the Shang. One particular bronze vessel, a water pan cast by a man named Qiang, is particularly interesting since it bears what some scholars refer to as the first conscious attempt in China to write history. The pan is famous among archaeologists and is usually referred to as the "Shi Qiang pan." It was presumably made around 900 BCE.

---

[330] Shaughnessy, Edward L. *Sources of Western Zhou history: inscribed bronze vessels.* Univ of California Press, 1992.

The famous Shi Qiang pan. Below is the translation of the inscriptions on the vessel. Also, note the drastic progress in the quality of bronze objects from the Erlitou to the Zhou. Located in the Baoji Bronzeware Museum.

Here is a portion of what was inscribed on the pan:

"Accordant with antiquity was King Wen! (He) first brought harmony to government. The Lord on High sent down fine virtue and great security. Extending to the high and low, he joined the ten thousand states.

Capturing and controlling was King Wu! (He) proceeded and campaigned through the four quarters, piercing Yin and governing its people. Eternally unfearful of the Di (Distant Ones), oh, he attacked the Yi minions.

Model and sagely was King Cheng! To the left and right (he) cast and gathered his net and line, therewith opening and integrating the Zhou State.

Deep and wise was King Kang! (He) divided command and pacified the borders.

Vast and substantial was King Zhao! (He) broadly tamed Chu and Jing; it was to connect the southern route.

Reverent and illustrious was King Mu! (He) patterned (himself) on and followed the great counsels."[331]

The scribe Qiang goes on with his odes to the Zhou royal family and ends with a brief mention of himself. He writes about his hopes for a long life adorned with wealth, which would allow him to serve the Zhou in the best way possible.

In general, the bronze vessel inscriptions regularly mention the Zhou royal family and the fact that it was chosen to rule. The Zhou rulers were presented as "stabilizers" or "protectors" of their region. Much like the Shang, they were connected to the neighboring elites through political marriage. It seems the kings were considered the absolute owners of all the lands; although this might have been the case, once the lands were granted to the elites, they probably had almost absolute power over the land and even the right to exchange or sell it.

Agriculture permeated practically all aspects of life during the Zhou period. Not only was it a major source of food and wealth, but it was also the essence of numerous Zhou rituals. In turn, the proper observance of rituals was related to the well-being of the royal family and the whole state. A major ritual involved ceremonial plowing, in which the elites had to participate personally. A large piece of land called "Thousand Acres," as ancient texts have it, was dedicated specifically for these ritual purposes. Moreover, the bronze vessels were a major part of the rituals and a crucial connection between the royal family and the elites. Namely, the heads of neighboring states were required to prove their subordination in periodic rituals in the Zhou court, and in return, the Zhou kings gifted their "vassals" with beautiful bronze vessels.

A bronze sword from the Eastern Zhou dynasty. The blade is still fairly sharp, testifying to the perfection of bronze production in the later period of the Zhou.

---

[331] Shaughnessy, Edward L. Sources of Western Zhou history: inscribed bronze vessels. Univ of California Press, 1992.p. 4

For all intents and purposes, the Zhou emanated an allure of prestige, luxury, and dominance. They were able to accumulate large amounts of wealth and used this wealth to ensure their own status. Powerful women who owed their influence to their wealth and social status and not necessarily to military prowess started to emerge. For instance, Queen Wang Jiang seems to have been very influential in the court, as she directed various political activities and relationships of the royal house. In other words, the women during the Zhou period weren't simply an exchange currency or a guarantee of connections between the Zhou and their neighbors.

Philosophical Developments

Over the course of the Zhou era, especially during the Spring and Autumn Period and the Warring States Period, numerous philosophical schools of thought were developed. Scholars sometimes refer to the period between 550 and 200 BCE as the "Hundred Schools of Thought" or "Hundred Philosophers."[332]

Confucius is by far the best-known philosopher from this period, and he proved to be one of the most important influences on Chinese philosophy in general, akin to the way Plato and Aristotle shaped European philosophy. Confucius was a strong believer in benevolent leadership, cherishing the "sage-king" ideal personified in legendary emperors of prehistoric China.[333] One of Confucius's ideas was personal virtue. An absolute ruler's virtue should transpire through the whole community, meaning that if the ruler was virtuous, the people he led would be willing to abide by the rules and be good subjects.

Confucius wasn't born in the state of Zhou. He came from the state of Lu (modern-day Shandong province), one of the states (nominally) subordinate to Zhou. He was born around 551 BCE. Confucius was a master of a number of skills and arts that were considered essential during the period, such as music, archery, calligraphy, arithmetic, and charioteering. He must have known numerous works of art and science by heart, which was, generally speaking, a must for ancient scholars.

---

[332] Tu, Wei-Ming. "Confucius and Confucianism." Confucianism and the Family: A Study of Indo-Tibetan Scholasticism (1998): 3-36.

[333] It's an incredible coincidence that Plato was writing his famous *Republic*, where he too formulated his ideas about benevolent leaders and sage-kings, roughly during the same period as Confucius.

Confucius was also one of the early teachers in China. There were surely many teachers before him, but Confucius was probably one of the first to consciously choose this way of life, with the goal of improving individuals and society as a whole. One of the ways to do this was to teach sons of noble people and improve them as people, thus providing the basis for just and virtuous leadership.

Confucius's method was in stark contrast with the hermits, who were also known as wise men but chose to abandon society. Confucius wanted to improve his society for the better and was intensely involved in political debates of the day. He was involved in the government's public works and served as a minister of justice. After serving the state of Lu for some time, he left his home state, somewhat disillusioned by the royal lifestyle of the Lu elite. He toured China, and it is thanks to this that he became well known, even during his days. By the time of his death (c. 479 BCE), he amassed around three thousand people who defined themselves as his followers.

One of the most important Confucian scriptures, the *Analects*, captures the discourse and reasoning of Confucius as it must have been received by his followers. In the *Analects*, we encounter Confucius, who is very close to a saint (he was often revered as such by the Chinese population in the centuries to come). In this sense, Confucius is similar to Socrates. Both were seen as being more than sages and men with incredible mastery over themselves. Like Socrates, Confucius didn't exert his intellectual influence upon his followers; his spiritual influence was just as important.

Confucius had a vigorous and inquisitive mind, and he was always thinking about ways to improve himself and learn new things. In the *Analects*, he says, "It is these things that cause me concern: failure to cultivate virtue, failure to go deeply into what I have earned, inability to move up to what I have heard to be right, and inability to reform myself when I have defects."[334]

During roughly the same period, a counterpart to Confucianism emerged called Taoism. While Confucianism dealt with concrete issues of living in a state, improving oneself, and becoming virtuous, Taoism was more concerned with the philosophy of nature. Taoism is an incredibly complex cluster of religious and philosophical viewpoints, and it was

---

[334] Tu, Wei-Ming. "Confucius and Confucianism." p.11

developed for centuries. Instead of diving deep into the diversity of Taoism teachings and its perplexing history, we will only note that it is, in a way, more esoteric than Confucianism since it deals with the underlying principles of the whole universe.

Legalists were another group of ancient Chinese intellectuals who stood in stark contrast to both Confucians and Taoists. Legalists were influenced by the political instability of the Warring States Period and formulated justifications for autocratic systems. For instance, Legalists were behind the autocratic regime of the Ch'in state, which, in turn, served as the basis for the establishment of the empire and fostering the position of the emperor. Legalists gave practical advice concerning the surveillance of the population and punishment of anti-government actions.

Consider the following excerpt from the work of Li Si, who relied heavily on the founders of the Legalist school of thought, Shen-tzu and Han-tzu:

"Wise rulers alone are capable of dealing severely with those who commit minor crimes, [making it clear that] even minor crimes are severely punished and that much more severely would those who commit major crimes be dealt with. Consequently, the people dare not transgress ... As a wise sovereign rules autocratically, authority does not reside in the hands of his ministers. Only then can he obliterate the path of virtue, muzzle the mouths of fast eloquence, curb the deeds of high-spirited men, keep the empire in ignorance, and exercise his faculties of seeing and hearing by himself alone."[335]

In other words, the Legalists were concerned with fostering the central government and the position of the supreme ruler. In their opinion, power should be much more personal and concentrated in the hands of a single man. It is easy to feel dismayed at such words, but we have to put them in their historical context. During the Warring States Period, numerous Chinese states battled for supremacy. This period determined who would lead China in the centuries to come. Under such circumstances, the Legalists provided the philosophical basis for the flourishing of imperial, absolutist tendencies, as they believed a single centralized ruler would be the only one capable of putting an end to the

---

[335] Hsiao, Kung-chuan. "Legalism and autocracy in traditional China." *Chinese Studies in History* 10, no. 1-2 (1976): 125-143.

civil wars.

There was another important intellectual contribution to Chinese culture during this time: Sun Tzu's *The Art of War*, probably one of the most famous books ever written. Sun Tzu lived in the 6th century BCE, just before the Warring States Period. *The Art of War* shows just how much warcraft had progressed, even before the Warring States Period, by which time China must have already witnessed numerous armed conflicts. It took some time, from the early Neolithic Age to the ripe Iron Age, for people to perfect the craft of organized warfare. The primary incentives for war—gaining new lands and wealth, development of solid weapons, and strife for prestige—all converged by the latter half of the 1st millennium BCE in China, and the scene was set for a great war, one that would determine China's future. But before we move on to describe this period (the end of the Zhou and the emergence of the Qin), we'll briefly focus on *The Art of War*, which will give us a nice basis for thinking about the Warring States Period.

The very first words of Sun Tzu in *The Art of War* are, "The art of war is of vital importance to the State."[336] However, this book isn't an ode to war. It's a very rational and practical guide on how to wage war and, most importantly, how to avoid battle when possible. For instance, Sun Tzu tells us that, when possible, it's better to avoid besieging walled cities. The setting up of a siege takes a lot of time, and then an army will need even more time to try and break into the city, by, for instance, making a mound against the city walls. Moreover, he tells us that it's always better to take a country while keeping it intact, and it's better to capture a group of soldiers than to battle them.

Then we have advice on how many miles an army can cover on a daily basis and when and how men should march without most of their equipment so they can move faster. Sun Tzu also valued proper reconnaissance; he believed that no army should be moved anywhere before the terrain was properly investigated. In addition, Sun Tzu talks positively about the use of different types of signals, such as flags, banners, signal fires, and drums, to remain in control of the army.

Sun Tzu's *The Art of War*, in a way, is a collection of loosely related sayings, each of which is a few lines long. In other words, this is not

---

[336] Tzu, Sun. The Art of War. Available at:
https://sites.ualberta.ca/~enoch/Readings/The_Art_Of_War.pdf

necessarily a completely coherent system for leading an army but more like a collection of wise statements that any general should have in his memory. One of our favorite lines from this book is, "When you surround an army, leave an outlet free. Do not press a desperate foe too hard." This is an incredibly concise yet rich statement, pertinent not only to warfare but also to human relationships in general. This is the reason Sun Tzu's work is admired even today, some 2,500 years of military development later. He was not only a supporter of good reconnaissance but also supported the use of spies. It is at this point that Sun Tzu's sane, practical spirit comes to the forefront: "Knowledge of the enemy's dispositions can only be obtained from other men." According to Sun Tzu, the spiritual world has no place in warfare. Too often, omens and prophecies turn out not to be true.

Chapter 10: Fall of the Zhou Dynasty

By the 5th century BCE, the authority of the Zhou was crumbling. Inversely, the influence of the Han, Wei, and Zhao states increased, and the Zhou were forced to officially recognize these three states so they could take a more active part in defending the Zhou in their constant struggles against northern and western invaders, such as the Xiongu and Loufan who were threatening the Zhou and other Chinese states from the north or the Qiang who were coming from the west. When the armies of these (and other) states grew strong enough, and at the moment the Zhou were no longer able to force the neighboring states back into submission, the Warring States Period started. It was a sort of free-for-all battle that lasted for centuries.[337] As the 4th century BCE was setting its foot on the scene of history, four more states emerged: Qi, Qin, Chu, and Yao. There were many other smaller states, but the three mentioned before (Han, Wei, and Zhao), together with Qi, Qin, Chu, and Yao, were the most powerful and tended to absorb the smaller ones. Alliances, truces, skirmishes, and open wars were extremely numerous, hence the name of the period.

The scale of warfare in this period is staggering and probably unmatched by almost anything that was happening in Europe during

---

[337] Cartwright, Mark. Warring States Period. *World History.* Available at: https://www.worldhistory.org/Warring_States_Period/

---

roughly the same period.[338] The sheer size of armies and battles in this period shows us two things: the incredible fertility of the Chinese land and the high civilizational development of China, which was able to feed, arm, and, in some instances, pay many soldiers. It's possible that in some states, for instance, Qi and Qin, the number of infantry soldiers was close to one million.

The Qin were allies of the Zhou, who somehow clung to their old glory for most of the Warring States Period. In the 4th century BCE, the Qin still defended (to a certain extent) the interests of the dying Zhou state. But soon, they, too, would turn against their old masters. Numerous other states had ambitions similar to the Qin. The great Zhou were growing weaker, and power was simply waiting for someone worthy enough to come and grab it.

The Zhou were extremely important for the development of Chinese culture. Zhou cities served as centers of cultural development. The Zhou made important breakthroughs, and their great cities served as a place where different cultural influences met and gradually formed the cradle of Chinese culture. This finally materialized in the form of a precarious balance between the authority of the Eastern Zhou and developing neighboring states, which, after a while, made their own grand entrance into history. The Zhou inherited the bronze culture from the Shang and granted their successors a well-developed iron culture.

---

[338] Herodotus, for instance, gives very high numbers for the Greco-Persian Wars (5th century BCE), while modern historians tend to think critically about the hundreds of thousands of Persians who allegedly invaded Greece. In later years, the number of fighters in the Punic Wars, which saw tens of thousands of soldiers on each side, was perhaps more likely, although Polybius, our main source for the Punic Wars, sometimes exaggerates.

SECTION FOUR:
THE QIN DYNASTY
(221–206 BCE)

Chapter 11: Rise of the Qin Dynasty and Qin Shi Huangdi

Although the Qin lasted for a significantly shorter amount of time in comparison to previous dynasties, they were nevertheless very important for the development of the concept of an "empire" and an "emperor." The Qin started the long tradition of Chinese emperors.

But let's start with the basics. The Qin were situated, roughly speaking, in the area previously controlled by the Zhou (modern-day Shaanxi province). It is extremely challenging to speculate about the ethnicity of the Qin, though it's likely that they were initially perceived as barbarians but slowly adopted the cultural achievements of the Zhou (and other states) and also worked on their own cultural achievements.

As mentioned, they were initially allies of the Zhou, with Duke Xin, the Qin ruler in the 4th century BCE, being awarded his title by the Zhou for protecting their interests. The Qin rulers were also influenced heavily by the Legalist tradition, which provided a sort of ideological backing for later territorial expansions. But by the 3rd century BCE, the Qin had initiated conflicts with the Zhou, and the Qin took over the remainder of the Zhou by 260 BCE.

Zheng rose to the Qin throne in 246 BCE when he was only thirteen years old. He was the son of the Qin king and a concubine that the king had met while in captivity in the state of Zhao. It may seem that Zheng might have been an unlikely successor due to being a son of a concubine, but direct royal lineage wasn't the only important thing in Chinese dynasties, and concubines had an important influence on the lives of many emperors.

Eight years after Zheng ascended the throne, in 234 BCE, Li Si was appointed as the Qin prime minister. The Qin now had two very capable and ambitious gentlemen at the wheel. Spurred by the recent subjugation of the Zhou, the Qin went on to subjugate other important states, such as Han (230 BCE), Wei (225 BCE), Yan (222 BCE), and Qi (221 BCE). Centuries of civil conflicts, coupled with a political and ideological vacuum that was coming to the forefront as the Zhou were growing weaker, made room for a different political system and a different ideology. Legalism, the ideological foundation of the Qin, which favored dictatorial, centralized control of subordinated states and the formation of a cult of personality, was a very logical product of the Warring States Period. After centuries of conflicts, countless broken alliances, and unstable truces, Legalism came as a breath of fresh air and a herald of newfound stability.

Qin was not the only state that looked favorably on Legalist scholars; other states also grasped the importance of this new stream of thought. But the Qin had both symbolical and real power manifested in their subjugation of the Zhou and their military power, which, coupled with strict Legalist ideology, were enough for the formation of the first Chinese empire.

Moreover, it's not a coincidence that young Zheng of Qin would become the first Chinese emperor. Often, we see an unfathomable and insatiable thirst for control in people who ascend to power when young. It's as if those who are revered and feared by their subordinates have no other path in life than to pursue their grandiosity. Sometimes, this results in debauchery, vice, and utter decadence. But Zheng was of a different breed. He was a capable leader with grand aspirations, becoming the first Chinese emperor. Sima Qian, who was far from favorable with Zheng, sometimes referred to him as "possessing the mind of a tiger or wolf."[339] Sima Qian nicely summarized the age of the Qin as the "World of Bronze," alluding to the prevailing power of arms over culture. Sima Qian juxtaposed the "World of Bronze" with the "World of Bamboo," a world

---

[339] Feng Kai & Liu Lu, The stigmatized Qin Shihuang

and the formation of Han culture, Qin Han studies,

2019 (00), pp.297-306.

of culture, knowledge, and morals. While bronze was used for crafting arms, bamboo was an important source of writing material, hence its association with culture.[340]

As we've seen, by the year 221 BCE, all the other warring states had come under the control of the Qin. The leader of the Qin, Zheng, became the first Chinese emperor, gaining the title of Shi Huangdi, which literally means the "first emperor." The way he dealt with neighboring states was starkly different compared to how the Zhou dealt with their vassals. Shi Huangdi ordered the complete disarmament of subjugated states. Arms were collected, most certainly not without occasional quarrels and unrest, and brought to the Qin capital (Xianyang). The arms were then melted and used for making things, such as bells and statues.

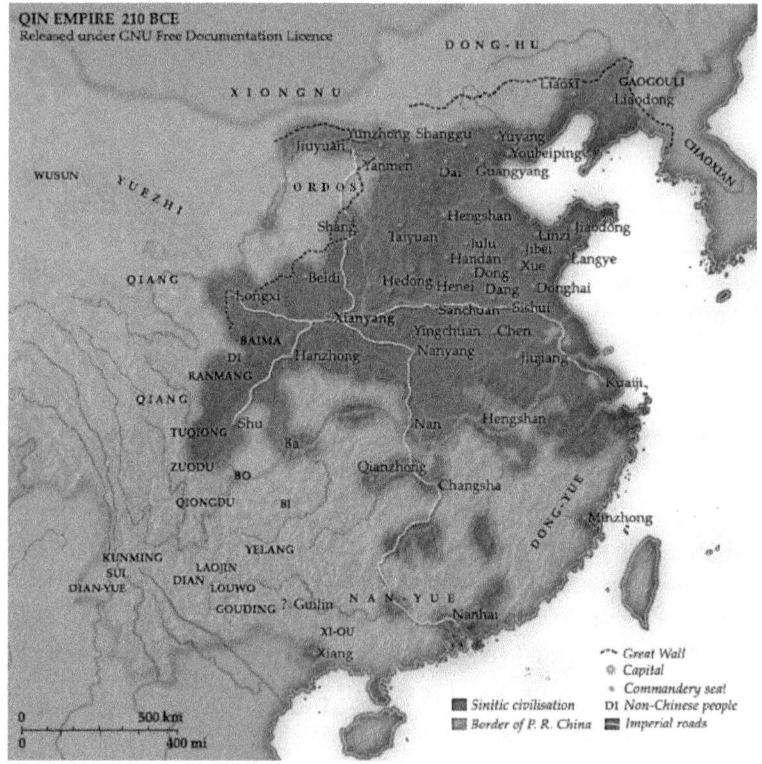

Map of the Qin dynasty at its height.

I, PHGCOM, CC BY-SA 3.0 <http://creativecommons.org/licenses/by-sa/3.0/>, via Wikimedia Commons; https://commons.wikimedia.org/wiki/File:QinEmpireWithOrdos.jpg

---

[340] Berkowitz, Alan. "Worlds of Bronze and Bamboo: Sima Qian's Conquest of History." (2001): 600-606.

Chapter 12: The Expansion of China and the Fall of the Qin Dynasty

Emperor Zheng didn't stop with the "unification" of China or, better put, the formation of the first Chinese empire. He conquered new lands that had been regarded as "barbaric" by the Zhou cultural sphere. Soon after becoming the emperor, he launched an invasion of modern-day southern China. The scene for virtually all events recounted up until this moment was modern-day north-central China. But with Emperor Zheng, the empire expanded its borders toward the south.

There were also northern conquests that were aimed primarily at putting an end to the perennial Chinese problem of northern invasions. These conquests were a prerequisite for the Great Wall of China and were led by a very important individual, General Meng Tian, who was directly appointed as the chief commander by the emperor. It is true that during the Warring States Period, various states started building large defensive walls to stop enemy forces from entering the country. Meng Tian probably took what was already available and built new fortifications, stabilizing the empire, at least against an external enemy.

However, internally, there were many struggles. As is often the case when a strong, charismatic, and authoritative leader dies, it's hard to fill his place, especially when the court is full of treacherous individuals. Qin Shi Huangdi died in 210 BCE due to an illness; he was around fifty years old at the time. Although he managed to avoid multiple assassination attempts, he couldn't run away from fate. Some scholars even believe that he desired to find the elixir of eternal life, which was what killed him since mercury was thought to be an important ingredient. It's possible that Qin Shi was poisoned by mercury, which prematurely ended his life.

When Emperor Zheng died in 210 BCE, he wasn't succeeded by Fusu, his oldest son, but by his second eldest son, Ying Huhai, later known as Qin Er Shi ("Qin the Second"). It's likely that a very powerful man and Emperor Zheng's previous advisor and chancellor had a hand in this. His name was Li Si. He was possibly one of the most important people in the empire's establishment and the administrative and government changes that were necessary for that establishment.[341] It's likely he played a role in the dubious events that came just after the death of the first emperor, namely the deaths of the emperor's oldest son, Fusu, and the military commander Meng Tian. Li Si was also involved in the appointment of Ying Huhai as emperor. The younger successor must have been easier to control compared to the older brother. Huhai must have had his own interest in becoming the emperor independent of Li Si, so we should not reject Huhai as an important factor in the removal of Fusu and Meng Tian, although these events will unfortunately remain clouded by the mists of time.

Unfortunately for Li Si, other people eyed his place as the empire's chancellor, and he was executed when various charges against him, including the capital charge of treason, were raised by the new chancellor, Zhao Gao, in 208 BCE. Zhao Gao, in turn, was able to remove Qin Er Shi. The emperor suffered the same fate as his older brother and Meng Tian, both of whom were forced to commit suicide. Qin Er Shi committed suicide in 207 BCE.

Ziying (or Liying) came to the throne not as an emperor but as a king under the watchful eye of Zhao Gao. This shows us just how much the influence of the Qin was reduced after the death of the first emperor. His exact relationship with previous emperors isn't clear, and he might have been either Fusu's son, the second emperor's brother, or the first emperor's nephew.[342] Ziying had Zhao Gao assassinated a few days after

---

[341] Kulmar, Tarmo. "On the nature of the governing system of the Qin Empire in ancient China." *Folklore: Electronic Journal of Folklore* 59 (2014): 165-178.

[342] Goldin, Paul Rakita, ed. *Routledge Handbook of Early Chinese History.* Routledge, Taylor &

he was appointed as the king. But Ziying didn't rule for a long time (according to some sources, he ruled for only forty-six days).

The neighbors of the Qin, which were recently subjugated by the Qin, took their chance and attacked the weakened empire. The Han leader, Liu Bang, penetrated into Qin territory and defeated the imperial army. Ziying's life was spared, but he was not alive for long, as another important warlord, Xiang Yu of the Chu, had Ziying and his whole family executed in 206 BCE.

Francis Group, 2018. p. 146-159.

Chapter 13: Cultural Developments

Under the leadership of Li Si, basic economic matters were brought into order. For instance, Li Si heralded the standardization of the coinage system, as well as the closely related weight and measuring systems. The Chinese states had their own coins of various kinds before, but it was from 221 BCE and with Li Si that an organized, systematic production of standardized coins, weights, and measures was initiated. Moreover, Li Si (or his government) understood the importance of standardizing the writing system, which allowed for more seamless written communication within the vast empire.

These factors served as the basis for a relatively short period of economic well-being during the first Chinese empire. After centuries of conflicts, people could finally enjoy peace and accumulate wealth. The empire itself, needless to say, benefited from this and launched important projects, such as the aforementioned Great Wall. The Qin didn't build the Great Wall as it stands today. But the concept of the Great Wall and the initial (though very grandiose) constructions, which, at the time, must have been enough to keep invaders away, were started by the Qin and, more specifically, by the first emperor.

During the Warring States Period, the Qin mastered the employment of large masses of people for military purposes. Now they employed large masses of people to build the Great Wall. The building of the Great Wall wasn't really that much safer than war, and it's likely that thousands of people died as a result of being forced to work on it.

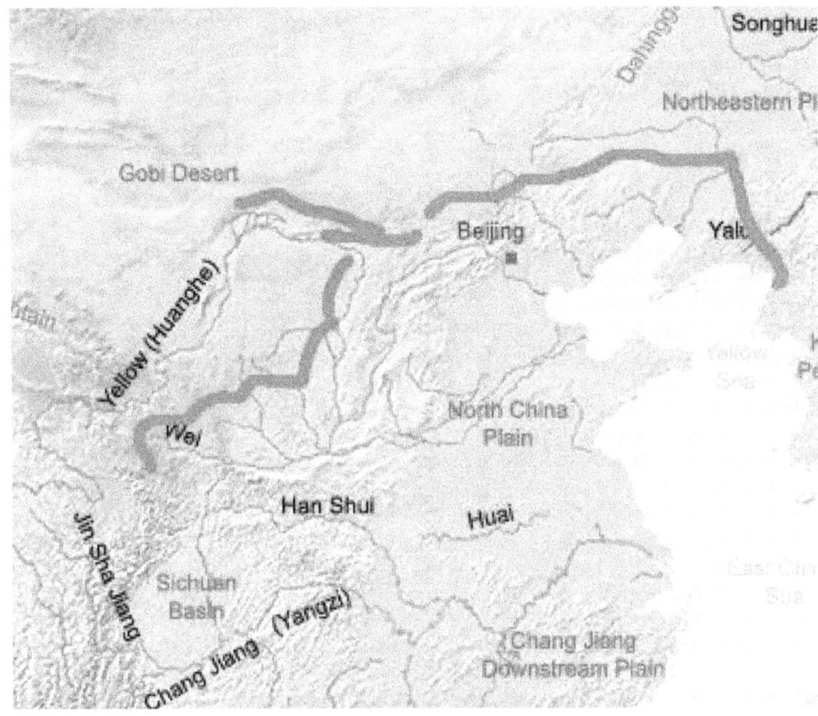

Walls built during the Qin dynasty as the first line of defense against foreign invasions. The earliest foundations of some of these walls are older than the Qin.

Ksyrie at the English Wikipedia, CC BY-SA 3.0 <http://creativecommons.org/licenses/by-sa/3.0/>, via Wikimedia Commons; https://commons.wikimedia.org/wiki/File:GreatWallofQinDynasty.png

We remember the Qin for another grand project—the famous Terracotta Army. It's safe to say that the first emperor wanted to prolong his life and fame as much as he could. Having failed to find the elixir of life, he wanted to make the afterlife as glorious as possible for himself.[343] Several thousand baked clay soldiers were found buried together with the first emperor. The soldiers must have been made with a variety of molds, but it would be an overstatement to say that each and every one of them is unique. Rather, the craftsmen must have devised a system of making a number of different soldiers by varying a set of fixed characteristics.

---

[343] Fiskesjö, Magnus. "Terra-cotta Conquest: The First Emperor's Clay Army's Blockbuster Tour of the World." p. 166

The famous Terracotta Army of the First Emperor located in the mausoleum of the first emperor, modern-day Shaanxi province.

A Terracotta soldier. Note the close attention to detail, especially considering the number of unearthed soldiers.

A bronze chariot also found in the mausoleum of the first emperor.

The tomb itself is complex and illustrious, a perfect eulogy for the mighty emperor. The emperor was buried with a number of real-world companions. Sima Qian talks about the tomb and mentions that it was filled with dangerous traps for intruders. Reportedly, there was a large body of mercury hidden somewhere in the tomb, waiting for intruders. Interestingly, there are no mentions of the terracotta soldiers, not in Sima Qian's or in other texts. It is for this reason that we cannot accept that all the terracotta soldiers were made by Emperor Shi Huangdi. Of course, we wouldn't go as far as to state that they are fake or anything like that, but there should be a degree of objective criticism with respect to this fascinating archaeological find, just as there should be with any archaeological find.

Chapter 14: The End of Feudalism

As Legalism became the basis of the Qin dynasty, the end of Feudalism inevitably happened. No longer were neighboring states seen as somewhat independent vassals; they became integral parts of the first Chinese empire. In other words, the unity of the state was of the utmost importance; there was no space for divisions or dissenting voices.[344] The importance of a supreme ruler grew more and more. The Legalists believed that it was impossible for a humane leader to enforce laws and build a harmonious society. The people needed a strong hand, someone who would enforce laws cruelly and indefatigably. This all seems good on paper, but as we've seen, the Qin Empire dissolved very quickly. Even during its short reign, there were uprisings that were suffocated by ruthless power.

Some Confucian values were demonized and considered as subverting the interest of the monarch and his empire. Charity, philanthropy, rhetoric, and art were frowned upon as giving rise to dissenting voices. These practices had the potential to free people's spirits and result in an open rebellion against the emperor.

In turn, the severity of reprimands and punishments grew, even for what we may consider minor offenses. But the laws were the cruelest toward acts perceived as rebellious or in some way endangered the state's unity or the emperor's authority. For such offenses, capital punishments

---

[344] Kulmar, Tarmo, et al. "On the nature of the governing system of the Qin Empire in ancient China." p.168

were common, and they were often executed in an abominable way. People were torn and cut to pieces, their bones broken, or buried alive, to mention just a few of their ingenious yet cruel methods. Additionally, forced labor was widely used as a punishment; for instance, people could be sent to build the Great Wall. Mutilations were common as well, as numerous people had their noses or ears cut off. They could also be branded like cattle or blinded.

All these measures seemed to have been necessary to establish the emperor's authority. Because of the Warring States Period, the Legalists believed that a strong leader needed a weak populace. The imperial regime introduced so-called "joint" or "collective" responsibility. Namely, the offenses of a single person were extended to his family, who were also punished for the crime. In rural areas, several households and families were involved in this cruel circle of joint responsibility. The aristocracy wasn't free of this kind of joint responsibility, and unlike the peasants, whom the state could hardly surveil in an efficient fashion, the aristocracy was carefully monitored. All signs of disloyalty were swiftly suppressed. A new division of territory was introduced that would serve as the basis for the administration of later empires. The Qin Empire was divided into commanderies, counties, and municipalities/townships. The new administrative regions of the empire allowed for more centralized control over subjugated areas and less influence from traditional regional powers. People were appointed as heads of commanderies or counties due to their merit and reputation with the centralized administration, and their powers weren't hereditary.

We can establish certain parallels between this fairly short episode in China's history and some later periods, especially the Cultural Revolution and Mao Zedong's rule.[345] Cruelty, paranoia, and absolute loyalty to the monarch. There was no space for free debate. And this leads us to one of the most powerful and shameful instruments in the arsenal of dictators: the destruction of intellectuals and their works.

---

[345] Mao's dictatorship is one such period that comes to mind.

Chapter 15: The Burning of Books and the Burying of Scholars

Confucians and Legalists were very much two worlds apart. Although they had similar attitudes toward the importance of the monarch and the necessity of establishing authority, they disagreed on just about everything else. The Confucians were proponents of a much milder style of governance, one that was benevolent to the populace. The monarch's supremacy was an important element in the Confucian intellectual world, but his supremacy was counterweighted by the king's immaculate virtues. The populace was also expected to follow a similar path as the king, which would help improve the state by ensuring the average person was good, thoughtful, and virtuous.

The Legalists sharply disagreed with Confucians when it came to these ideas. The Legalists likely regarded the Confucians as esoteric philosophers who only roused the youth and undermined the authority of the state and the emperor.[346] The clash between the two schools of thought was inevitable, and in 213 BCE, things came to a head when Confucian books were burned and destroyed.[347]

---

[346] Confucius experienced similar difficulties during his lifetime, although he died in old age and probably of natural causes. However, the parallel between Confucius and Socrates can be seen in what happened to the followers of Confucius, as they were persecuted and executed during the Qin period.

[347] Kulmar, Tarmo, et al. "On the nature of the governing system of the Qin Empire in ancient

Officials and bureaucrats were carefully scrutinized. Anyone who openly stated that life was better in the pre-empire days could be executed, as well as those who didn't report a crime they knew about.

This crackdown on Confucians is sometimes referred to as the "Burying of Scholars," and the expression isn't metaphorical—around 460 Confucians were indeed buried alive. Confucians were also sent to build the Great Wall. Interestingly, it seems that only those who continued to talk about politics and religion were punished. Confucians who focused more on science weren't the regime's primary targets.

The political works of Confucianism weren't the only texts to be destroyed. Li Si, the man behind the regime, understood the importance of history for the neighboring states and their identity. It is for this reason that numerous ancient records of other states were destroyed to prevent the rise of separatist tendencies and ensure a more circumscribed form of patriotism.

Li Si was also behind what we would refer to today as the emperor's cult of personality. The state made sure that the populace received news about the emperor's impeccable and divine nature. Numerous inscriptions from the period were found. Here is one example:

"The emperor was a wise and prudent ruler, who worked from early morning till late night for the good of his people; all men and women were law-abiding, and everyone fulfilled their duties; there was peace and order in the empire."

Some reports ascribe superhuman reading powers to the emperor (Qin Shi Huangdi), who is said to have been able to read thirty kilograms (sixty-six pounds) of manuscripts every day. Qin Shi Huangdi probably became somewhat paranoid as the end of his life approached. As is often the case with overly powerful leaders, their desire for power often transforms into a powerful paranoia. For instance, Qin Shi Huangdi had numerous palaces near the capital to which he could move whenever he decided to do so. It is said that not even his closest companions knew about his whereabouts, which were kept secret; needless to say, some people knew about the emperor's location, and if they had let their tongues loose, they would have been executed.

China." p. 174

The most important markers of the Qin rule are also the most important causes of its downfall. The cruelty of the Qin regime caused the aristocracy of various states and the rural population to rebel. Moreover, instead of focusing on coming up with a cultural style that would unify all the different states, the empire focused more on the suppression of cultures perceived to be a threat to the regime. Both the first and second emperors were too cruel, too much within their own "bubble," and unable to hear the wise voices of the aristocracy and the populace. A regime's inability to juggle the power of the monarch, the power of the few, and the power of the many, as Polybius put it many years ago, destroyed many regimes. This inability was certainly behind the fall of the Qin.

SECTION FIVE:
THE HAN DYNASTY
(206 BCE–220 CE)

Chapter 16: Rise of the Han Dynasty

After the Qin dynasty fell, someone had to step in and stop another Warring States Period from wrapping China in centuries of war. China actually witnessed another, albeit much shorter, period of civil war. The war was fought primarily between two important leaders of the rebellion against the Qin: Liu Bang and Xiang Yu.[348]

Xiang Yu emerged as the supreme leader of the rebellion against the Qin and was seemingly the one to make decisions about how the Chinese states would coexist after the first empire was dismantled. He was subsequently remembered as a great leader and entered Chinese culture through numerous stories, legends, and operas.[349] He was a very powerful leader and came from the state of Chu.

After the Qin fell in 206 BCE, Xiang Yu started materializing his plan to divide what had been the Qin dynasty into a number of smaller states in a similar way to how China looked before the Qin prevailed. This plan, which did not stay in effect for long, is sometimes referred to as Eighteen Kingdoms. However, contentions broke out again, with war once again setting its foot firmly in China.

---

[348] Zhou, Minhwa, and Meihwa Zhou. "Wisdom and Strategy— An Example for Zhang Liang and Liu Bang." In 7th International Conference on Humanities and Social Science Research (ICHSSR 2021), pp. 941-943. Atlantis Press, 2021.

[349] Chen, Pauline. "History Lessons." *New York Times,* 1993.

One of the most important leaders of this new rebellion was Liu Bang. This man must have been a fearless and incredibly authoritative war leader in a similar way to Xiang Yu. But unlike Xiang Yu, Liu Bang had fairly humble beginnings. He was born far from the aristocratic homes, although when he eventually became the emperor, numerous stories about his divine origins were made up. Liu Bang initially worked for the Qin regime in his native Chu state as a sort of pavilion chief; in other words, he was a minor official. As the Qin regime weakened, Liu Bang understood what was happening and started organizing forces against the Qin in his jurisdiction. Slowly but steadily, his influence and war prowess grew, and stories about the incredible Liu Bang started to circle. Finally, he became the king of one of the eighteen states that were formed after the fall of the Qin, specifically the state of Han. In this state, Liu Bang would muster his forces and deal one final blow to Xiang Yu.

The Feast That Almost Killed Liu Bang

But prior to open animosities between Xiang Yu and Liu Bang, there was a curious event that almost saw Liu Bang dead—the so-called "Feast at Swan Goose Gate." After the Qin were defeated in their own capital, Xianyang, a large body of forces assembled outside the capital to celebrate the victory. By this time, there was already a certain degree of tension between Liu Bang and Xiang Yu. Namely, Liu Bang was the first to arrive in Guanzhong (a region in modern-day Shaanxi province) and the first to besiege Xianyang, which is found in this region. This was taken as a sign of Liu Bang's supremacy; in fact, there seems to have been a kind of "race to Guanzhong," and the winner would become the king of Guanzhong and, thus, the king of China.

In reality, Liu Bang was the first to arrive. When other forces, including those of Xiang Yu, arrived, a great feast started. But Xiang Yu had already made his decision about Liu Bang, whom he regarded as someone who ruined his chance of being the first to take Xianyang. Through a chain of informants, Liu Bang learned about Xiang Yu's wrath. However, when he received an invitation to Xiang Yu's banquet, he couldn't refuse. Prior to going to the banquet, Liu Bang sent messages to Xiang Yu, trying to tell the latter that he wasn't trying to declare himself the ruler of China.

Liu Bang, probably against the advice of his close associates, went to pay his respects to Xiang Yu. The seating arrangement and the whole tone of the banquet were carefully constructed to put Liu Bang in a subordinate role to Xiang Yu. Moreover, it's possible that Xiang Yu and his associates planned to kill Liu Bang right there and then since he was virtually unprotected and far from his army.

According to a legend, when one of Xiang Yu's subordinates started performing a sword dance but was actually getting ready to kill Liu Bang, another Xiang Yu's associate, who did not know of the plot to kill Liu Bang, got in the way by trying to participate in the dance. Liu Bang's closest advisor, Zhang Liang, stormed out and found Liu Bang's general, Fan Kuai. Zhang Liang instructed Fan Kuai to burst into the banquet, which he did, much to the surprise of Xiang Yu, who admired Fan Kuai's military demeanor and his armor.

This must have changed the tone of the banquet, and Liu Bang succeeded in getting out under the pretext of having to use the bathroom. However, he still wanted to get back and at least say goodbye to Xiang Yu before going to sleep, but Zhang Liang and Fan Kuai vehemently objected to this.[350] It was agreed that Zhang Liang would stay and wait for a while before returning to the banquet to give Fan Kuai and Liu Bang time to return to their camp. In the end, Zhang Liang brought jade presents to Xiang Yu, apologizing for Liu Bang's absence, who, as Zhang Liang assured, was already rather drunk and had to get some sleep. Xiang Yu accepted the presents, but Xiang Yu's advisor, understanding that the opportunity to assassinate Liu Bang was now lost, shattered the jade presents to pieces, predicting the fall of Xiang Yu and the rise of Liu Bang.

A mural depicting the famous feast at the Swan Goose Gate. The picture dates from the Eastern Han dynasty and is more of a typical representation of Chinese feasts than an exact account of how the Swan Goose Gate feast looked like. Daunting Tomb.

https://commons.wikimedia.org/wiki/File:Mural_Painting_of_a_Banquet_Scene_from_the_Han_Dynasty_Tomb_of_Ta-hu-t%27ing.jpg

---

[350] Sima, Qian. Records of the grand historian: Han dynasty. Columbia University Press, 1993.

Open Conflict between Xiang Yu and Liu Bang

Immediately after this event, Xiang Yu, perhaps trying to affirm himself as the leader of China, sacked and burned the Qin capital, Xianyang. Interestingly, Liu Bang, who, as mentioned, arrived first at Xianyang, refrained from burning and looting. Both leaders of the rebellion had similar aspirations (to become the supreme ruler of China) but had different *modi operandi.*

After amassing a vast fortune, Xiang Yu decided to return home to the state of Chu. There, he proclaimed himself king of Chu and "promoted" the previous king of Chu (Huai) to the rank of "righteous emperor." Of course, this title was merely symbolic, and in any case, the "righteous emperor" was soon assassinated on the orders of Xiang Yu.

Roughly in the same period (206 BCE), Liu Bang started preparing for an all-out rebellion against the forces of Xiang Yu. He started slowly taking newly formed kingdoms one by one. By 205 BCE, Liu Bang had amassed a force of around 560,000 men (according to ancient historian Sima Qian) and marched eastward toward the Chu capital of Pengcheng. Since Xiang Yu was busy fighting other rebellious groups, namely the Chi in the north, Liu Bang was able to take Pengcheng with little to no resistance.[351] The soldiers were enjoying the spoils of war, namely the fortunes of Pengcheng and its beautiful women, when Xiang Yu struck back and inflicted a catastrophic defeat on Liu Bang's Han army. The Han army started a disorderly retreat, which resulted in even more casualties. During this retreat, hundreds of thousands of soldiers perished in rivers, mountains, and ambushes, as they lacked even basic necessities. Sima Qian reports that when Liu Bang's soldiers were forced into a river called the Sui, the subsequent carnage left so many corpses that they dammed up the river.

Liu Bang found himself surrounded over the course of his retreat, and the circle was getting tighter and tighter. All of a sudden, a great storm overtook the battlefield. It was so powerful that it was able to make trees fall. Dust and debris filled the air, and the day turned into night. The subsequent chaos allowed Liu Bang to break through and save his life with as little as thirty cavalrymen.

But this wasn't the only close call. You may remember that Liu Bang was actually born in the state of Chu and had family there; in fact, his

---

[351] Ibid.

children, wife, mother, and father were all living in the state of Chu when Liu Bang came to defeat Xiang Yu. So, Liu Bang wanted to save his family as he was fleeing. His children, his wife, and his parents were already fleeing, and it was by pure chance that Liu Bang came across his son (future Emperor Hui) and daughter (future Princess Yuan) on the road. However, Liu Bang's caravan was spotted by Chu cavalrymen, and the two groups engaged in what must have been an incredibly tense chase. To make the scene even more dramatic, as Sima Qian reports, Liu Bang grew extremely worried about his children making the carriage heavier, which would make it easier for the Chu horsemen to catch up with them. So, he tried to push his children out of the carriage, but fortunately, Lord Teng, one of Liu Bang's closest associates, saved his son and daughter.

Liu Bang's wife, mother, and father weren't so lucky, as they were captured by the Chu forces.

The year 204 BCE saw Liu Bang regaining control over his forces, mustering new ones, and retreating to more friendly areas. He also ensured he had a road, which was important for moving provisions. The road meandered together with the Yellow River and connected less-well-supplied areas with the grain-rich Yellow River Basin.

Xiang Yu, who was advised by Fan Tseng, did everything he could to cut off this road and make life harder for the Han. It is at this moment and under the threat of having his main cities besieged by the Chu that Liu Bang decided to start negotiating with the Chu, aiming to buy himself some time before being able to recover his forces and deal a counterblow. An envoy arrived in the Han state, and Liu Bang started to unravel his plan to sow dissent in the heart of the Chu leadership. He first bestowed the Chu negotiators a grand feast. But then, he "learned" they had been sent by Xiang Yu. (Liu Band pretended that he thought these negotiators were sent by Fan Tseng independently of Xiang Yu to sow discord between the two.) Liu Bang ordered servants to carry away the lavish meals and drinks and instead bring in a much more modest dinner.

Needless to say, the Chu negotiators were astonished at this mistreatment and were suspicious as to why Liu Bang changed his demeanor once he "learned" that the negotiators were sent by Xiang Yu. They reported this to Xiang Yu, raising his suspicions about Fan Tseng. The latter was angered by these probably unjustified suspicions. He handed in his resignation but soon died of health complications related to an ulcerous sore.

Back in Han, the situation was going from bad to worse. Liu Bang was besieged in the city of Jung-yang, and it seemed that his final capture was imminent. But Liu Bang's general, Han Xin, stepped in. Han Xin decided to lead a decoy attack disguised as the king of the Han himself, making space for the real Liu Bang to escape. In order to make this decoy attack more believable, thousands of women from the city were dressed up in battle armor and led outside through the eastern gate. While Han Xin was handing in his "royal surrender" to Xiang Yu, Liu Bang fled through the western gate with a few dozen cavalrymen. Han Xin was burned alive.

This was a fairly smart move because Liu Bang managed to escape, and the city of Jung-yang was still in the hands of the Han. The defense of the city was now the duty of Chou Ko, Lord Tsung, and Wei Pao (who was a former enemy of the Han but now an ally). Chou Ko and Lord Tsung decided to kill Wei Pao since they didn't want an ex-enemy with them. The Chu army finally prevailed and took Jung-yang; when Chou Ko was offered the place of a Chu general, he decided to choose a more glorious yet more tragic fate. Chou Ko retorted, "If you do not hurry and surrender to the king of Han, you will be taken prisoner! You are no match for him!"[352] It is not surprising that Chou Ko was then boiled alive at the orders of Xiang Yu. Lord Tsung was executed as well, although not in such a dramatic fashion.

Liu Bang's Final Victory

The year 203 BCE saw Liu Bang take part in more military campaigns. Once again, he was besieged in a city, this time Cheng-kao. However, this time, he was forced to flee alone. After this, he was able to organize his forces and, most importantly, further cooperate with his allies, who were attacking the Chu and making it harder for the Chu to focus on destroying the Han. The forces of Peng Yueh were especially a nuisance to the Chu supply lines; they were also able to foment rebellion in Chu-controlled regions, such as the Liang region. Enraged by years of what seemed to be unsuccessful warfare against Liu Bang, Xiang Yu decided to boil Bang's father alive if Liu Bang didn't surrender immediately. Liu Bang's response, to say the least, was incredible:

"When you and I bowed together before King Huai and acknowledged our allegiance to him, we took a vow to be brothers.

---

[352] Ibid.

Therefore my father is your father, too. If you insist now upon boiling your own father, I hope you will be good enough to send me a cup of the soup!"[353]

Hsiang Po, Xiang Yu's new advisor, was against this drastic move, and Hsiang argued that boiling the old man alive would be futile since Liu Bang obviously didn't care about it, claiming the only thing he wanted was to rule the world. What then ensued was a fairly stable stalemate, with both sides making no notable moves. Xiang Yu, who was known for his valor and physical prowess, decided to challenge Liu Bang to a personal duel, just the two of them. Liu Bang was possibly aware that the odds were in Xiang Yu's favor, so he didn't agree to a duel.

Xiang Yu started sending his strongest and bravest men to challenge the bravest Han men to battle. There was a highly skilled horseback archer within the Han ranks who came from a barbarian tribe (Loufan) that lived close to the "civilized" Chinese world. This horse archer killed three of Yu's challengers. Xiang Yu was once again enraged and approached Cheng Kao, the city where Liu Bang and his forces were stationed, and challenged the Loufan horseback archer. It is said that the spectacle and incredible scream of Xiang Yu distressed the Loufan archer so much that he fled back to the city.

Liu Bang, having learned about this strange occasion, decided to leave the city and talk to Xiang Yu at a safe distance. Once again expressing his desire not to fight the much stronger Xiang Yu, the leader of Chu grew extremely frustrated and drew out a concealed crossbow, wounding Liu Bang, who fled back into the city.

More hostilities continued. The Han allies continued harassing the Chu, and Xiang Yu was forced to leave his generals to besiege Cheng Kao and Liu Bang, marching eastward to help fight the Han allies. One of the most important instructions to his generals was something along the lines of "Stay put, don't pitch battles, and don't fight battles when Liu Bang challenges you." After a few days of taunting and mocking, the Chu forces were led into battle by General Tsao Chiu. In order to meet Liu Bang's forces, the Chu forces had to cross the river Ssu. Liu Bang attacked them just as they were crossing the river, massacring the Chu men.

This was one of the turning points of the war. Xiang Yu was forced to march back and face Liu Bang's army, even though his own men were

---

[353] Ibid.

exhausted. Another round of negotiations was held. Xiang Yu offered the lives of Liu Bang's wife, father, and mother and a partition of Chinese lands. Liu Bang acquiesced. But Zhang Liang, Bang's closest advisor, saw an opportunity for a complete victory over the Chu. Zhang Liang argued that the Chu were exhausted and had almost no allies. The Han, on the other hand, had plenty of supplies and a lot of allies on their side. Now was the time to attack!

Liu Bang listened to this wise counsel and attacked the Chu in 202 BCE. However, he once again suffered a crushing defeat since his closest allies, Peng Yueh and Han Hsin, did not show up at the agreed time. Once again, the good counsel of Zhang Liang came to Liu's rescue. As Zhang Liang argued, both Peng Yueh and Han Hsin were unhappy since they had already done a lot for Liu Bang without receiving any territorial gains. If they received land, they would be more motivated to help Bang end this long war.

After receiving territorial grants, the allies continued their operation, and the circle around Xiang Yu grew smaller and smaller. His camp was encircled by the enemy, his provisions were thin, and morale was low. After hearing the sounds of Chu songs coming from the enemy camp, Xiang Yu understood that many of his men had joined the enemy's ranks. Saying his last farewell to his concubine, the beautiful Lady Yu, Xiang Yu drove out of the camp and broke the encirclement, along with a few hundred horsemen. But the group lost the way and was pursued by the Han horsemen. Realizing that everything had been lost and that the worthiest thing would be to make one last stand, Xiang Yu divided his men into several groups and ordered them to inflict as much damage as possible on the enemy. Xiang Yu is said to have slain up to one hundred men on his own.

He managed to break out and reach the Yangtze River with a few fellow soldiers. A village head offered to take them to the other side. Xiang Yu firmly believed that the heavens themselves wanted to take him down and bring Liu Bang to power and had already decided on how he would end his life. He wasn't going to try to flee as far as he could. Instead, he gave his beloved horse to the kind village head and returned to face the Han soldiers one last time. Once again, Sima Qian tells us that Xiang Yu killed hundreds of Han soldiers, suffering bitter wounds himself. Then, he spotted Liu Bang's cavalry commander, Lu Matung, and his entourage. Even in his last moments, Xiang Yu kept his honor and pride, saying, "I have heard that Han has offered a reward of a thousand catties of gold and a fief of ten thousand households for my head. I will do you the favor!"[354]

The Han soldiers then literally battled for Xiang Yu's body and head. The victors of this unworthy scuffle divided the rewards quite literally as they dismembered Xiang Yu's body. His death marked the end of a period of calamity, which had lasted ever since the Qin were overthrown some five years before. In 202 BCE, the Han, heralded by Liu Bang, finally gained supremacy over the whole of the Chinese civilized world. Liu Bang wasn't overly cruel when it came to finalizing his ascent to power. Namely, he spared the state of Lu, Xiang Yu's native state, and Xiang Yu's family.

The Han Emperor

Liu Bang, later known as Emperor Gaozu, is an incredibly interesting personality, so this short excerpt on him won't do him justice. Still, we'll try to sketch him as a person and lay out his most important achievements as emperor.

There are many poetic stories about Liu Bang's early life, and quite a lot of them firmly step into the mythical, legendary, or purely superstitious realms. For instance, Liu Bang's mother, Dame Liu, is said to have met a god prior to giving birth to her prodigal son. His father, who was looking for Dame Liu, eventually found her but saw a large dragon hovering over his wife. Dame Liu conceived Liu Bang after this event. Liu Bang is said to have had seventy-two moles on his left leg, and this number might have been a magical number since it's the product of two equally magical numbers in Chinese culture: eight and nine.

When the time came, Liu Bang passed an official exam and became the village head of the Ssu River region. Sometime around this period, Liu Bang showed his love of women and wine, often visiting brothels in his town. Sima Qian even mentions the poetic names of these places, such as Dame Wang's or old lady Wu's place. Liu Bang wasn't exactly a good customer, as he often drank and enjoyed the services of the ladies on credit. However, Liu Bang's prodigality once again stepped in. Even though he rarely paid, he had a sort of lucky allure with him; every time he came, the brothel's profits increased! What's more, when Liu Bang was exhausted from pleasure and fell asleep, people could notice a sort of

---

[354] Ibid.

dragon hovering over him.[355]

Then, there are stories about people "reading" great future deeds from the faces of Liu Bang and his family. In fact, this was how Liu Bang was married to his first wife, Lady Lu, who became Empress Lu. Her father, Master Lu, noticed that there was something great about Liu Bang, even though the latter was a simple village head. He decided to marry his daughter to Liu Bang. Later, when an elderly man was passing through Liu Bang's village, he saw Liu Bang's wife, son, and daughter, and he predicted a glorious future for all of them just by reading their faces.

It's certain that Liu Bang was an extraordinary man. Curiously, however, he wasn't an exceptional statesman or a worthy general. His talent lay elsewhere—he knew how to recognize talented and able individuals who could do the job and remain loyal to him. In fact, Liu Bang himself emphasized that he could not compare with Zhang Liang's strategic mind, nor could he measure up to Xiao He's ability as a statesman. However, Liu Bang knew how to control powerful individuals, and it's due to this ability that he ultimately conceived a powerful Chinese empire.[356]

But let's leave these stories now and rejoin our emperor where we left him, at the very start of his reign. In the year 202 BCE and after the death of Xiang Yu, Emperor Gaozu still had a lot of work to do to affirm himself as the great emperor of China. There were some revolts that needed to be quenched, and Gaozu also had to appoint the proper men as (nominal) heads of state. In 201 BCE, Liu Fei, the emperor's son, became the governor of the state of Qi. In 200 BCE, more revolts needed to be pacified, but the capital of the new empire was completed. It was called Chang-an (modern-day Xian, Shaanxi province) and was home to the "Palace of Lasting Joy" and infrastructure for the bureaucracy and public officials.

---

[355] Ibid.

[356] Hardy, Grant, and Anne Behnke Kinney. *The establishment of the Han empire and imperial China.* Greenwood Publishing Group, 2005.

Chapter 17: Western and Eastern Han Dynasties

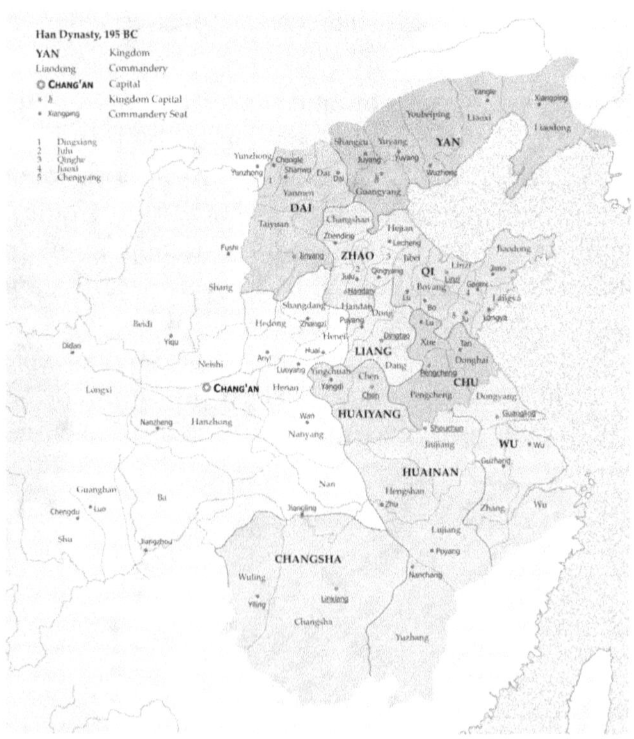

Early Western Han state.

Esiymbro, CC BY-SA 4.0 <https://creativecommons.org/licenses/by-sa/4.0>, via Wikimedia Commons; https://commons.wikimedia.org/wiki/File:Han_dynasty_Kingdoms_195_BC.png

Emperor Gaozu established a stable dynasty that ruled China for centuries to come (albeit with some breaks). Emperor Gaozu died in 195 BCE, leaving the throne to his young son, Lui Fei (Emperor Hui), who was only fifteen years old when his father died. So Gaozu's wife, Empress Lu, stepped in and served as regent. Empress Lu furthered the interests of her own clan, giving numerous members of her family important posts. Emperor Hui died of an illness in 188 BCE, which allowed Empress Lu to increase her influence even further. Two alleged sons of Emperor Hui, Liu Gong and Liu Hong, then became emperors. Both were very young and easily manipulated.

It's clear that Empress Lu tried to establish herself as the supreme ruler, but owing to the rules of the time, she could only be the regent of "real" emperors.

Empress Lu wasn't a bad ruler, but she did try to increase the influence of her own clan at the expense of Emperor Gaozu's clan. It is for this reason that after her death in 180 BCE, influential members of the Lu clan were massacred, and the supremacy of Liu Bang's clan was assured once again, this time thanks to Emperor Wen, who was one of the numerous sons Liu Bang had with his consorts.

The following forty years, during which time Emperor Wen (180–157 BCE) and his son Emperor Jing (157–141 BCE) ruled, were remembered as relatively peaceful and prosperous. During this period, the reach and power of the central government were further increased, and the power and influence of provincial kings were curbed. The influence of nobles also decreased, as the state would take over their possessions if they died without an heir or if they broke the law.

Next came Emperor Wu, who reigned between 141 and 87 BCE. His reign was also known for being peaceful, stable, and prosperous. The empire was expanded and protected by building the Great Wall, which helped stop the invasions of the northern barbarians. Emperor Wu is also presented in literature as the emperor who finally allowed an all-encompassing adoption of Confucianism in the court and government, although he did not outright reject the Legalist tradition.

During the long reign of Emperor Wu, Chinese astronomy became very important. First of all, one has to keep in mind the close relationship between philosophy, science, and myth in the ancient age. Specialization is a relatively modern thing, and erudition was much more common in ancient times (both in Europe and China, as well as elsewhere). So, intellectuals close to the court were well versed in practically all fields of knowledge, and astronomy/astrology was an important part of what Emperor Wu expected from his intellectuals. Back then, the observation of stars wasn't simply a scientific act. In the case of Emperor Wu, astronomy/astrology provided a way to inquire about the future and establish contact between people and higher entities. There was another, very specific goal as well: ensuring the emperor's immortality.[357]

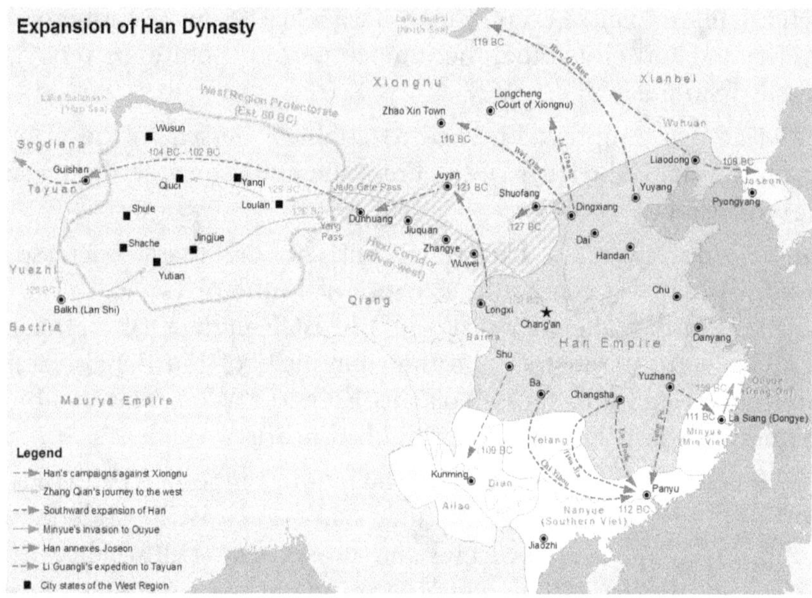

Expansion of the Han toward the north, south, and west during the reign of Emperor Wu. This would be the basis for subsequent contact between Chinese and faraway Asian and European civilizations.

SY, CC BY-SA 4.0 <https://creativecommons.org/licenses/by-sa/4.0>, via Wikimedia Commons; https://commons.wikimedia.org/wiki/File:Han_Expansion.png

It is somewhat ironic that a crucial incentive for the development of Chinese astronomy came as a result of the emperor's superstition. For instance, it's said that Emperor Wu once encountered a man who claimed to be hundreds of years old and who allegedly held the secret to eternal youth. This man was able to strike at the emperor's vanity and vivid imagination. He succeeded, like many who came after him, to profit by telling fantastic stories to Emperor Wu. Unfortunately, the emperor

---

[357] Cullen, Christopher. "Motivations for Scientific Change in Ancient China: Emperor Wu and the Grand Inception Astronomical Reforms of 104 BC." *Journal for the History of Astronomy* 24, no. 3 (1993): 185-203.

wasn't really that gullible, and he would see through these people's attempts to fool him by planting fake evidence and things like that. Everyone who was caught doing so or anyone with fake prophecies risked execution.

Emperor Wu was also obsessed with the mythical Yellow Emperor and started believing in stories of people who drew parallels between his reign and that of the Yellow Emperor.[358] In myth, the Yellow Emperor is a being that existed (or continued to exist spiritually during the times of Emperor Wu) in the intersection between the earthly and the divine. It's possible that the Yellow Emperor originated from Shang deities and has been translated into a real historical person over the course of time. Then, during the Qin dynasty, and especially thanks to Qin Shi Huangdi's megalomania, the myth of a Yellow Emperor who was also a god was once again revived. In fact, the "di" from Huangdi was commonly used to denote the qualities of a god.

One of these parallels between the Yellow Emperor and Emperor Wu was closely tied to astronomy and the Chinese calendar. Namely, some people claimed that such an ancient "holiday" during the reign of Emperor Wu fell on the same day as during the reign of the Yellow Emperor. In other words, the emperor's "need" to have good astronomers in the court came from his desire to relive the example of the Yellow Emperor.

Emperor Wu's ambitions, capabilities, and long reign resulted in the significant territorial expansion of China, especially westward. The vast, unexplored, and sparsely populated steppe highlands must have seemed alluring to Emperor Wu, who wanted to project his power as far as possible. Beginning in the times of Emperor Wu, the Chinese had considered the modern-day Xinjiang region (a very large central Asian region in the far west of China, bordering countries like Kazakhstan, Kyrgyzstan, and Tajikistan) as their sphere of influence. This was more of an exploratory expedition, and the primary goal was to establish diplomatic relations with whomever the Chinese explorers came across. And they came across the likes of the Dayuan and Kangju people, who inhabited the modern-day regions of Uzbekistan and Tajikistan.

The steppes might have been a simpler feat compared to Wu's southern conquests. During Emperor Wu's reign, Xinjiang and modern-

---

[358] Ibid.

day southern China came under the influence of the Han Empire. Provinces like Fujian, Guangdong, or Guanxi wouldn't have been within modern-day China if it hadn't been for Emperor Wu's southern excursions. To do this, Wu's army first had to defeat the states of Minyue and Nanyue.

Finally, Emperor Wu sorted out the problem of northern invaders by becoming the invading force. The Xiongnu group of nomadic tribes was the primary target. The Chinese civilization was threatened for centuries before and after by these tribes since they were drawn southward by the rich cities of China.

It is not an uncommon occurrence in history that after a particularly strong and authoritative leader comes a period of calamity and chaos. It didn't take long for China to enter such a period after Emperor Wu died in 87 BCE, although this time, things didn't end in centuries of civil wars. Emperor Wu's youngest son, Zhao, came to the throne, and during his reign, which ended in 74 BCE with his untimely death (he was only twenty years old), the power was essentially in the hands of Huo Gang, an important official under Emperor Wu.[359] Emperor Zhao didn't have a son who would inherit the throne, so Huo Gang first chose Liu He, Emperor Wu's grandson, as the heir. Liu He must have done something wrong since he was deposed after just about twenty days, and Wu's great-grandson, Emperor Xuan, came to the throne.[360] He was also chosen by Huo Gang. Huo Gang's final choice turned out to be for the better since Emperor Xuan's reign was known for its stability and prosperity. For some time, Huo Gang continued to be a close advisor to the emperor in spite of his intention to step down. Some good things happened during the reign of Emperor Xuan; for instance, he issued important reforms to the judicial system, which moderated the harshness of judges and made appeals easier. Meritocracy was at its height, with able people finding their way to the top offices. The emperor was also a friend of the arts, with numerous poets and literary workers being supported directly by the court. Emperor Xuan died in 48 BCE, and his son, Emperor Yuan, took over.

---

[359] Dreyer, Edward L. "Zhao Chongguo: A Professional Soldier of China's Former Han Dynasty." *The Journal of Military History* 72, no. 3 (2008): 665-725.

[360] Gao, Jiyi. "Emperor Xuan, Emperor Zhang and the Rise and Decline of Zhangju in the Han Dynasty." Hanxue Yanjiu (Chinese Studies) 25, no. 1 (2007).

Up until then, the Chinese empire remained fairly prosperous. Even during the times of Emperor Yuan and the subsequent domination of his wife, Empress Wang, China was fairly stable. Her influence increased after Emperor Yuan died in 33 BCE. A number of emperors sat on the throne, but Empress Wang, who became dowager empress, remained very influential and increased the influence of her own Wang clan.[361] This was possibly the main thing that pushed China back into chaos. Relatives of Empress Wang grew stronger and stronger, and it's entirely unsurprising that Wang Mang decided to depose the young and insignificant Emperor Ping and replace him with the even younger Ruzi Ying, who was formally in power from 6 to 9 CE. Eventually, Wang Mang decided to stop pretending and declared himself the first emperor of a new dynasty, the Xin.[362]

It is not possible here to dissect all the events that led to the short-lived Xin dynasty and the short-lived chaos that came soon after Wang Mang rose to the throne. Suffice it to say that this was a natural consequence of the Chinese political dynamics at the time, with ruthlessness, mischievousness, and insidiousness being equally important as political wisdom and real merit. Wang Mang wasn't necessarily going to be a bad emperor, and there are some indications that he had grand plans for China. But ultimately, his usurpation of the Han dynasty led to a civil war and the formation of a very peculiar group called the Red Eyebrows.

Wang Mang was also unlucky. Right when he was working hard to implement his grandiose reforms, there was a great flood in China that left a lot of farmers without much food. A revolt was unavoidable, and the Red Eyebrows and other groups finally sacked the capital of the Western Han, Chang'an, in 23 CE. Together with other groups of rebels, the Red Eyebrows chose a new emperor who was related to the Han named Gengshi. He didn't rule for long, as the Red Eyebrows overthrew him and placed a child whom they could more easily control. Finally, they were defeated by the founder of the Eastern Han, Emperor Guangwu, who chose a new capital city, Luoyang. Since Emperor Guangwu was related to the Western Han, he had the leverage needed to help him crush the

---

[361] Xiong, Victor Cunrui, and Kenneth James Hammond, eds. Routledge Handbook of Imperial Chinese History. Routledge, 2019. p. 25-38.

[362] L'Haridon, Béatrice. "WANG MANG 王莽 (c. 45 BCE–23 CE) AND CLASSICAL LEARNING AS PATH TO SUPREME POWER." *Early China* 45 (2022): 51-72.

rebels who were increasingly seeking to satisfy their own needs as opposed to the needs of the Chinese civilization.

Chapter 18: Cultural and Military Developments

Administrative Reforms

The foundations for the empire were partially inherited from older empires and partially laid by Liu Bang and his important officials. We already mentioned Zhang Liang, whose advice was crucial in the period of the establishment of the Han dynasty. Zhang Liang was more of a Sun Tzu type of advisor, aiding Liu Bang in politico-strategic decision-making. But there were other important advisors, such as Xiao He (or Ho), who focused more on law and administration. Xiao He became Emperor Gaozu's chancellor and was instrumental in the legal, cultural, and administrative improvements related to the early Han period. Even before 202 BCE and the final victory of the Han, Xiao He was very active, governing vast areas while Liu Bang was waging war. During this challenging period, Xiao He was tasked with simplifying laws, setting up district offices, and spreading Han propaganda and dynastic temples.

In 202 BCE, Xiao He was bestowed with the highest possible merits by Emperor Gaozu. Xiao He had so many privileges that other officials became envious, and the emperor had to remind everyone that it was Xiao He who had practically governed the whole empire for years. Under the guidance of Xiao He and other important officials, the Legalist tradition, which was characteristic of the Qin empire, was slowly augmented with the suppressed Confucian tradition.[363] Xiao He is also credited with the establishment of the Han code. Apart from being a great organizer and administrator, Xiao He was also a great connoisseur of the law. He took the existing Qin code, revised it, and quite possibly made it more humane.[364] His code consisted of nine chapters, with statutes on robbery and theft, arrest, dereliction, stables, and much else. It was a fairly complex code that was more attuned to the contemporary situation and most certainly more conducive to peace and stability in comparison to the old Qin code.

The early Han dynasty had an elaborate taxation system, which included both grain and labor. Provincial chiefs—so-called "kings" who were appointed directly by Emperor Gaozu—were instrumental in tax collection, defense from external enemies, and execution of laws. The empire itself was initially divided into thirds, with the eastern kingdoms (ten of them) constituting two-thirds of the empire. The western third of the country was divided into provinces or commanderies that were under the direct control of the central government. Initially, the "kingdoms" in the east were granted to numerous allies of Liu Bang. But many of these chiefs soon revolted against Emperor Gaozu, and fairly quickly, the emperor was forced to appoint people closer to him, usually his family members, as provincial chiefs.

The emperor also brought order to the nobility. Namely, Gaozu divided the elite into twenty distinct "levels" of nobility. Purportedly, the basic assumption of the new nobility was a meritocracy, and it's probable that this rule was enforced to a certain extent. Furthermore, the emperor appointed 150 marquises, the only hereditary noble title (excluding the imperial family) that could be passed directly to children. It goes without saying that noble children were given a chance to deserve higher positions, and many of them took that chance.

As far as the central government is concerned, it was separated into three government sectors: the civil service, military, and internal investigation service (usually tasked with monitoring the elites and spying on officials). On the local level, this division was more or less preserved,

---

[363] Dubs, Homer H. "The victory of Han Confucianism." *Journal of the American Oriental Society* 58, no. 3 (1938): 435-449.

[364] Xueqin, Li, and Xing Wen. "New light on the Early-Han code: a reappraisal of the Zhangjiashan bamboo-slip legal texts." *Asia Major* (2001): 125-146.

so there were county military and civil authorities as separate branches. A very important office was the county magistrate, who was, in essence, the civil representative of the central government. County magistrates had a very important mixture of powers. First of all, they were responsible for the collection of taxes, even though they didn't collect them personally. Next, they had both executive and judicial powers, meaning they were in charge of arrests but also judging and sentencing criminals. They were also in charge of infrastructure maintenance, specifically the maintenance of waterways.

County magistrates were supreme judges in their respective counties, so they also resolved civil disputes between individuals and were in charge of applying the central government's agenda when it came to, for instance, agricultural planning. To top it all off, they were in charge of the census, which means they assessed the size of the population in their county, the people's total possessions, etc.

County magistrates couldn't serve in their native counties, which must have been a way for the central government to reduce corruption and nepotism. Moreover, their salary was paid by the central government, and the pay was based on their job performance. County magistrates were closely monitored and had to send periodic reports on the state of things in their county to the central government.

Confucianism Came Back!

Besides this careful planning of state administration, there's another reason the Han dynasty functioned effectively and efficiently: Confucianism. You may remember that Confucianism was considered the most bitter enemy of the Qin. We may argue that their failure to understand the importance of Confucianism is one of the reasons for the Qin dynasty's downfall. The Han didn't repeat this mistake. However, if it was only up to Liu Bang, Confucianism might have remained underground. Initially, Liu Bang had a particular disdain for Confucian scholars. It is said that Liu Bang, who was a fairly simple and robust man, once encountered a Confucian scholar. He took off the man's cap and urinated in it![365]

Fortunately for his successors and the whole of China, Emperor Gaozu learned to appreciate Confucians, albeit not without nudges from

---

[365] Hardy, Grant, and Anne Behnke Kinney. *The establishment of the Han empire and imperial China.* Greenwood Publishing Group, 2005.

officials who were aware that years of warfare must have molded Liu Bang into a strict, no-nonsense, in-your-face type of person. The following nudge from an official pointed out in a very visual way why Liu Bang's old style of administration had to be adapted to suit the needs of the empire: "You may have won the world on horseback, but can you rule it on horseback?"[366]

However, Confucianism didn't become the official "religion" until sometime later. It wasn't the only creed or philosophical outlook. As we've seen, the Han took a lot from the Qin, such as their legal code and the essence of the Legalist tradition. But unlike the Qin, the Han knew how to combine Legalism and Confucianism (and other viewpoints), building a firm, authoritative government that wasn't too severe.

Confucian ethics and focus on ancient ceremonies provided an important cultural boost to Chinese elites and officials. The ancient ceremonies and rituals brought order to relationships between the imperial family and the elites, affirming the emperor's place within his own empire.

All these and other cultural developments had very palpable results. For instance, Xu Shen, an important Chinese scholar who lived in the 1st and 2nd centuries CE, composed the first Chinese dictionary around 100 CE.[367] This dictionary focuses on the graphic etymology of Chinese characters. The dictionary (often referred to as *Shuowen Jiezi*) shows the development of Chinese culture; reflecting on the language people use every day is no small intellectual feat.

Sima Qian has already been mentioned; this intellectual was instrumental in the development of Chinese historiography. His objective treatment of incredibly complex historical events spanning centuries still stands as a shining example of how historiographers should think about past times. Sima Qian was regarded by subsequent annalists as a "true" historian and the father of Chinese historiography. It is true that Sima Qian's father was also a revered annalist and that Sima Qian's writings bear marks of his own day and age. Sima Qian, much in accordance with the revivified Confucian values, considered furthering the cause his father had dedicated his life to as his ultimate goal. Intellectual rigorousness and

---

[366] Ibid.

[367] Bottéro, Françoise, and Christoph Harbsmeier. "The" Shuowen Jiezi" Dictionary and the Human Sciences in China." *Asia Major* (2008): 249-271.

objectivity, on the one hand, and filial piety and the sense of duty, on the other, are the two main dimensions of Sima Qian's work.

Sima Qian followed the true methods of historiography. He gathered evidence when he could, and when he was in doubt, he wasn't shy about indicating it. For his passage on Confucius, he relied heavily on his personal visits to Confucius's birthplace. He also sought people who had knowledge of past events, compiling different stories and trying to come up with the most logical descriptions of events. But there's also the emotional background: Sima Tan's (Sima Qian's father) unusual position as an intellectual/astronomer/astrologist in the court of Emperor Wu. Sima Tan wasn't treated that well by Emperor Wu, who seemed to have thrown Sima Tan in the same basket as musicians and jesters. Sima Qian must have been deeply shaken by this lack of respect for his father and sought to obtain the respect he believed his family deserved.

Here, we have to remind ourselves of the importance of filial piety in Han China. A very important Confucian dictum was that "a son does not consider that he has his own self."[368] This dictum is important in explaining Sima Qian's motivation to write his books. And on a much wider scale, it shows us the Confucian version of order and peace, where everyone and everything has its own place and purpose. In a way, this trait of Chinese culture remained and has served as a major point for the creation of our modern distinction between collectivistic and individualistic cultures.

The cultural developments of Han China served as a basis for important technological and scientific breakthroughs. Paper was invented in China in the early 2nd century CE.[369] The invention is often ascribed to Cai Lun, who was the head of the government's workshops in the eastern capital of Han, Luoyang. This invention was a big breakthrough because Chinese people mainly used bamboo slips or silk instead of paper, the former being cumbersome and the latter exceedingly costly. Beginning in the 2nd century CE, the Chinese started using hemp to produce relatively cheap paper. Hemp was readily available, cheap, and relatively easy to craft into pieces of paper ready for writing. Needless to say, the Chinese people continued experimenting with paper, and many different plants were used in the process.

---

[368] Nylan, Michael. "Sima Qian: A True Historian?." p. 206

[369] Cartwright, Mark. Paper in Ancient China. *World History Encyclopedia*, 2017.

Together with educational developments, owed primarily to the ascent of Confucianism and the opening of official schools, most importantly, the Imperial University (Taixue), the invention of paper propelled Chinese culture into a new era. It was now easier than ever before to obtain a good education (needless to say, a vast majority of people remained illiterate and uneducated). It was also easier than ever to obtain books and to actually practice writing, which, up until the invention of paper, had been very costly and thus only available to a few individuals. The education of women also progressed during the Han dynasty, although, of course, the most important lessons taught to women at this time were their manners and their role in the family.[370] The following excerpt from a correspondence between a Confucian scholar and a government official named Gongsun Hong and Emperor Wu shows the value of education and plans to further expand education early on in the Han period:

"In order to fill the offices of erudites we suggest that fifty additional students be selected and declared exempt from the usual labor services. The master of ritual shall be charged with the selection of students from among men of the people who are eighteen years of age or older and who are of good character and upright behavior in order to supply candidates for the quota of students of the erudites."[371]

The Han Army

Periods of relative peace and stability allowed for the development of vast public projects and initiatives. Conscription during the Han dynasty was fairly efficient and served three main purposes: men serving in the capital, men defending the borders of the empire, and men serving in their places of birth. Conscription was universal, and all males were supposed to serve in the capital, defend the borders, and retain law and order in their own regions. Military service started sometime around when males turned twenty.[372] It was taken seriously, and it was universal in

---

[370] Zhijie, Huo. "The significance of female education during the Han Dynasty." *Вестник Бурятского государственного университета. Гуманитарные исследования Внутренней Азии* 4 (2016): 54-59.

[371] Van Ess, Hans. "Emperor Wu of the Han and the First August Emperor of Qin in Sima Qian's Shiji." *Birth of an Empire* 5 (2013): 239.

[372] Ch'ien, Mu. *Merits and Demerits of Political Systems in Dynastic China.* Springer Berlin Heidelberg, 2019.

the real meaning of the word—some very high officials didn't hesitate to send their sons to serve in the military!

At any given moment, there were two large armies, with seventy thousand soldiers combined, stationed in the capital. One army, usually referred to as the South Army, was tasked with defending the imperial palace; the North Army was tasked with defending the capital itself. Serving in the capital wasn't such a bad thing, as the government covered all expenses, such as traveling to and back from the capital and food and drink, during the length of a man's service in the capital, which was around one year.

The frontier service was somewhat different. The Qin dynasty inherited a three-day frontier service from the smaller feudal states that it (forcibly) united. Before unification, a three-day frontier service functioned well since states were fairly small, and it didn't take too much time to arrive at the frontier from any place in the state. The Qin simply adopted this system, disregarding the fact that they led a much larger state. The Qin government still demanded the three-day frontier service in spite of sending men from one end of the empire to the other. It's possible that frustration concerning this particular service was one of the reasons for the fairly quick downfall of the Qin.

The Han were smarter and had a large enough administration to deal with the matter of frontier service. The service formally still lasted for only three days, but there was a possibility of paying not to serve at the frontier. So, the government amassed enough money to finance longer stays at the frontier for soldiers who were willing to do so.

Trade and Contact with Faraway Peoples

Increased security made it possible for trade to flourish further. And it wasn't only internal trade that flourished; the Chinese started establishing stable contact with Eurasian cultures. Zhang Qian, who served as a diplomat and an explorer under Emperor Wu (r. 141–87 BCE), was one of the first Chinese to explore central Asia and find new opportunities for trade and diplomatic relations. His travels to central Asia also brought modern-day Xinjiang province under China's sphere of influence. The Silk Road started to function thanks to Zhang Qian's explorations, and the concept of the bridge between China and the rest of the world continues to live today under the form of the modern Belt and Road initiative.

Because of the Parthian Empire, Chinese silk started reaching European states, and silk soon became a status symbol among Greeks and Romans. Note that there was still very little direct contact between Europeans and Chinese. Goods moved very, very slowly via the Silk Road, and the prospect of goods reaching their destination was precarious at best. But for all intents and purposes, China started opening up to the world. In the example of Zhang Qian, we can see that this was a calculated move coming from the very top, not something haphazard or transitory.

Chapter 19: The Fall of the Han Dynasty

As is the case with any dynasty, the Han dynasty had to finally cease existing at some point. This happened around 220 CE, but the reasons for the downfall of the Han go far back. We find stern criticism of the lack of meritocracy, a crucial prerequisite of the earlier success of the Han, in the works of Xu Gan, an important Confucian who lived in the final years of the Eastern Han dynasty.[373] While praising virtue, Xu Gan noted that times differ and, in certain periods, even the most virtuous men didn't get the praise they deserve. Xu Gan likely felt this way, as he lived during a time when court insidiousness, corruption, and constant strife for influence all reached their peak.

Aware of the roots of the Yellow Turbans and other rebels, Xu Gan saw the good things that came out of the Legalist movement, which was able to bring at least a transitory stability to the Chinese states that had been ravaged by centuries of war during the Warring States Period.

As is so often the case when there are numerous clandestine strivings for power and influence, the emperors turned to people who seemingly didn't belong to any party or clan, such as servants, eunuchs, slaves, etc. One of the last Han Chinese emperors, Ling-ti, relied heavily on his eunuchs when it came to governing his empire. This led to dissatisfaction

---

[373] McLeod, Alexus. "Philosophy in Eastern Han Dynasty China (25–220 CE)." *Philosophy Compass* 10, no. 6 (2015): 355-368.

from the elites, and as was so often the case in ancient (and not so ancient) China, a revolt heated up in the provinces as powerful individuals emerged, wanting to take advantage of the weak central administration.

A very logical conclusion of all this was the so-called Yellow Turban Rebellion, which was motivated by the weak government, natural agrarian disasters, and epidemics. The movement had a strong religious Taoist background and was led by three brothers. Yellow had a special meaning in Taoism, as it signified a new beginning. The movement preached the end of the Han and the coming of a new age, the age of "yellow heaven." The soldiers led by the Chang brothers wore yellow "turbans" or handkerchiefs wrapped around their heads as a way of distinguishing themselves from other groups, hence the name of the whole rebellion.

The Yellow Turbans soon took over a large chunk of the empire, up to two-thirds. The brothers weren't simply involved in religion. They also dabbled in medicine. In the countryside, which had been ravaged by famine, floods, and epidemics, their skills came in handy, allowing them to establish a good relationship with the peasants. To demonstrate how bad it was during this period, let's look at one popular ballad that must have been on every peasant's lips at the time:

"Great chaos in the empire,

The markets were desolate.

Mothers could not protect children,

Wives lost their husbands."[374]

On the other side, in the imperial palace, the emperor wasn't concerned with the growing influence of the Chang brothers, who quickly amassed a following of some 360,000 people by the 180s CE. It is also true that the influence of the Chang brothers reached the imperial palace, and some corrupt eunuchs started, in a way, lobbying in favor of the Yellow Turbans.

The unrest was eventually quenched by the central government around the year 185 CE. But China was already in a very precarious position, with the emergence of powerful warlords who were increasingly thirsty for power. The last Han emperor, Xian, relied heavily on one such warlord, Cao Cao, who was also the chancellor of the empire. Initially, Cao Cao

---

[374] Levy, Howard S. "Yellow Turban religion and rebellion at the end of Han." *Journal of the American Oriental Society* 76, no. 4 (1956): 214-227.

helped the Han dynasty to remain in power, fighting against the Yellow Turbans and other contenders. However, the status of the emperor was by now merely symbolic, and the real power lay in the hands of warlords like Cao Cao or others who managed to get a piece of the Chinese empire.

Cao Cao, like so many before him, possibly tried to unify China once again, but the decisive defeat at the Battle of Red Cliffs restricted his sphere of influence.[375] The Three Kingdoms Period started to emerge after the fall of the Eastern Han, Cao Cao's Wei, as well as Shu-Han and Wu, all led by powerful warlords. It didn't matter that Cao Pi, Cao Cao's son, was declared emperor in 220 CE, the same year when Cao Cao died. The great Han dynasty ceased to exist, as did the unified Chinese state.

There are many reasons for the ascension and downfall of the Eastern Han. It seems the early Eastern Han were able to keep a firm grip over the country, allowing the Chinese people to develop. But as the years passed and the memory of the Western Han's downfall became dimmer, the Eastern Han grew increasingly divorced from what was happening in their empire, caring more about carnal pleasures and their own vanity. By forgetting the big lesson of the Western Han, they were doomed to become another lesson for the next dynasty.

For the next sixty years, up until 280 CE, China would be divided into three spheres of influence until it was once again unified, this time under the Jin dynasty. This marked the end of ancient China and brings us to the end of our journey. However, this is the start of another story, the story of medieval China.

The period of the Three Kingdoms and the period that directly preceded it is remembered by the Chinese people as being fairly tumultuous. Old power hierarchies were abolished, and a window was opened for those who had the wits and courage to take their once-in-a-lifetime opportunity. Cao Cao was one such gentleman, even though he didn't live to see the fully fledged Three Kingdoms period. Cao Cao himself expressed the joys of this unpredictable but exciting period and lifestyle in the following passage:

---

[375] De Crespigny, Rafe. "Man from the Margin: Cao Cao and the Three Kingdoms." (1990).

"The swift steed in old age may rest in his stable,
But he still thinks of a thousand li journey;
When a hero comes to the end of his days,
Strong heart remains the same.
The time of our life and death
Is more than the whim of Heaven;
If a man is in harmony with himself
He may live for long years."[376]

---

[376] Ibid.

Conclusion

Cao Cao once wrote, "The time of our life and death is more than the whim of Heaven." This is true not only for human life but also for the life of nations, empires, and states. The history (and prehistory) of China is more than a set of haphazard circumstances. It's actually a highly intricate weaving of the fabric of time. Numerous threads make the canvas of Chinese history, and they sometimes intertwine and intermingle in unpredictable and almost incoherent ways.

Sometimes, the threads take their own paths, and what emerges isn't a unified picture but a set of smaller pictures whose complexity we sometimes lose due to the sheer distance of events and their microscopic size. But there's a trend in Chinese history, a trend of reunification (or, inversely, reseparation), where separate threads join and once again intertwine to form a much bigger and often more glorious picture.

From the earliest evidence of Chinese cultures, we can see the conflict between these two trends of unification and separation. They are still at work today, and no one involved, probably not even the main actors, knows where the weight of history will shift next.

However, one thing is certain: China will remain a very important global power, something this country most certainly owes to thousands upon thousands of years of continuous development. Ever since the early days of agriculture, which was where we began this book, the Chinese have heralded technological improvements that very early on made it one of the most populous "countries" in the world (we put "countries" in quotes because the concept of a country as we know it today is a fairly recent development and most certainly didn't exist in the early days of agriculture). The Chinese people quickly optimized the production of grain (not only rice), which made food more available to the people. Having learned the basics of effective agriculture, the Chinese people, in a very similar way to the Egyptians and Mesopotamians, mastered landscape planning, shifting the beds of whole rivers, draining areas important for agricultural production, and controlling the immense power of rivers.

The early days of Chinese culture are wrapped in this vaporous mist of constant battles against the power of water and inevitable floods. The Hebrews are not the only ones with a story of a great flood that came and swept the earth. The Chinese have their own version, and people living at the turning point between prehistory and history had to battle their environment much more than we have to today. No one knows how many Chinese cultures were swept away by torrential floods, but according to something that's still closer to legend than historical fact, Yu the Great, the founder of the legendary Xia dynasty, stopped the floods and provided a basis for the development of all subsequent dynasties.

Unfortunately, we're still in the realm of prehistory with the Xia, as the Chinese writing system took a little bit more time to develop. The Shang are still the earliest proven Chinese dynasty. Thanks to their mastery of writing and the ample evidence they left in the form of oracle bones and bronze vessel inscriptions, we learned quite a lot about the Shang and their way of life in the 2nd millennium BCE.

There is one deep truth linked to the Shang and their writing system, which was refined and further propagated in the millennia to come, resulting in the modern-day Chinese characters. The early writing in China was inextricably tied to the ritual world. There was certainly a practical incentive for developing the writing system. As agriculture, trade, and crafts developed, people started amassing goods. Contracts were established to exchange goods, which was made easier with the help of writing. But equally important, if not more so, was the ritual incentive, the implementation of writing in a carefully constructed system of rituals and beliefs. This is important evidence of the interconnection between the rational and the irrational. Much like thoughts wouldn't exist without emotions, rational, logical writing systems wouldn't exist without the world of mystical rituals. Thanks to discoveries related to the Shang, this deep truth shines even brighter.

The Chinese characters soon crossed the borders of China, whether one turned toward the east (Japan, Korea), south (Indochina), north (Mongolia), or west (Xinjiang, Tibet), helping with the transmission of ideas and data and heralding the cultural developments of whole societies. But the Shang didn't simply bequeath a writing system to their successors. They also left beautifully crafted bronze objects, and their craft of metal production and processing was adopted by surrounding cultures, including the Zhou, who took it to another level.

Learning how to produce and process various metals (especially during the Zhou dynasty when the production of iron was mastered), the Chinese launched themselves into the advanced Age of Metal, which was edified by the invention of their own writing system during the Shang dynasty. The Zhou were strong warriors with effective weapons, and they established a sort of feudal system with their subjugated neighbors, granting relative autonomy to regions that were fairly distant from their centers of power but still exerting strong cultural influence. This interplay between the center and the periphery continues to exist in China to this day. The size of China and its population (which was large even during the Zhou dynasty) made direct administration impossible. The Zhou established a system that worked for centuries, but the precarious balance was ultimately lost since their neighbors grew stronger and demanded more autonomy. Eventually, they demanded to be the next leaders.

One of the first known large-scale conflicts in China, the Warring States Period, ensued. The battles were fierce, long, and exhausting, and China plunged into centuries of conflicts over supremacy. Finally, a new dynasty emerged victorious: the Qin. This dynasty is credited with building the first Chinese empire. As we've seen, there were other Chinese dynasties that came before, but most historians don't dub them "empires." This is because the Qin were the first to systematically address the question of directly administering vast Chinese sub-states/provinces. Their solution, autocracy, was often unjust and ruthless, so the Qin didn't last long.

However, in a similar way to what the Romans were (roughly speaking) contemporaneously doing in Europe, the Qin quickly laid foundations— legal, administrative, and ideological—for an efficient empire.[377] The

---

[377] It has to be said the Romans really started building their empire, in the constitutional sense, by the end of the 1ˢᵗ century BCE, while the Qin came significantly earlier.

historical pendulum was now at the other extreme of its predictable trajectory. The Qin were determined to crush all rebellion and to once and for all unify China under one strong ruler. But when this strong ruler, the first Chinese emperor (Qin Shi Huangdi), died, a new conflict started, as the historical pendulum shifted back to a period of fragmentation. The people simply didn't want to tolerate a tyrannical government, and it seemed as if China was going to enter another Warring States Period.

Fortunately for the Chinese people, this time, the final victor and the new emperor, Liu Bang, knew how to lay the foundations for an empire that would last. He founded the famous Han dynasty, the first to build a strong, stable, and prosperous Chinese empire.

The Han dynasty inherited the foundations of the Qin and added a special ingredient, Confucianism, one of the most important "philosophical products" of China, the influence of which is still felt today in modern Chinese politics. Confucianism is a philosophy of societal order, harmony, and virtue. Confucius was also fond of ancient customs, traditions, and rituals, which were carefully preserved by later Confucians. Another important thought was altruism, the supreme love of fellow human beings.

Confucianism came into existence much earlier, during the Spring and Autumn Period, which preceded the Warring States Period. By the time of the Qin dynasty, Confucianism had spread throughout the Chinese states, but the Qin decided that this new philosophy was too dangerous for the new precarious Chinese empire. Much like Mao Zedong's regime persecuted intellectuals and was wary of free-thinking, the Qin decided to crush the Confucian school of thought, accepting the much more narrow-minded, stern, and unempathetic Legalist philosophy. It is actually the Legalist thought that laid the foundations for the first Chinese empire, asserting the emperor as an absolute, supreme ruler, almost a deity, and carefully defining one of the earliest Chinese codes of law. Legalism is not a historical coincidence; after years and years of brutal conflicts, someone had to bring an end to the carnage, but to do this, the first emperor had to be the most brutal of all.

The wisdom of Liu Bang and his successors lies not in their total rejection of Legalism and total acceptance of Confucianism but in their careful balance between the two.

The long period of relative stability allowed for exponential cultural developments. The Han dynasty gave us a fairly cheap way to make lots of paper, which would, combined with the later European printing press, help spread education to millions of people. And this was just a single contribution of the Chinese.

The level of organization in the Han empire was unmatched by anything that came before, even on a global scale. The sheer size of the Chinese population and the vast lands put an almost insurmountable challenge in front of Han statesmen. Practically every village had a chief who was appointed by the central government. He was responsible for applying the government's plan on the micro level. Conscription was universal, with a complex system of different sorts of service types. Trade also started to flourish.

During the Han dynasty, a stable connection, known as the Silk Road, was established between China and Europe. In light of the sheer size, cost, and influence of the modern Belt and Road initiative, this first contact between China and Europe and the establishment of initial trade routes gains even more importance. And the exchange between two large cultural spheres, Chinese and European, resulted in mutual benefits back in the day. Today the Western world, Asian, African, and Latin American countries all benefit from their relationship with China.

For thousands and thousands of years, China was one of the strongest countries in the world. Then, faced with the inevitable atavism of the imperial system, the whole country almost crumbled to pieces during the so-called "century of humiliation," which relates to the Opium Wars and the subsequent subjugation of China by European powers. It is at this point that the historical pendulum reached its extreme, as China dissolved into numerous smaller countries led by power-thirsty warlords. This wasn't a singular occurrence. We've seen in this book that the pendular oscillation between two extremes—fragmentation and unification—is more of a pattern than an exception in thousands and thousands of years of Chinese history (and perhaps even prehistory). And much like the Warring States Period was followed by the Qin dynasty and its incredibly stern tendencies, the chaos of the Warlord Era that took place during the last period of the empire early in the 20th century was followed by the authoritarian regime of Mao Zedong.

And history will continue to repeat itself, surely. The question is only when and how.

Part 3: Ancient Japan

An Enthralling Overview of Ancient Japanese History, Starting from the Jomon Period to the Heian Period

Introduction

What is not to like about the wonderful land of the rising sun? Ask a person who has just returned from visiting Japan about the things they like most, and their answers might be the unique Japanese culture, the wondrous buildings that were built many centuries ago, the pleasant weather (especially during spring when the Sakura start to bloom), or even the unbelievable cleanliness of the Japanese cities. To put it simply, words are not enough to describe Japan.

Today, Japan is home to over 125 million people. Many people claim that their advanced technologies are astounding and that their culture is definitely one of a kind. The world's first bullet train, Tōkaidō Shinkansen, for instance, is one of the most impressive inventions that originated in Japan; believe it or not, it takes slightly over three hours to travel from the capital city of Tokyo to Osaka, which is located more than 500 kilometers (310 miles) away. This 20th-century invention alone proved the nation's excellence in the world of technology. Meanwhile, sumo matches, calming traditional tea ceremonies, Shinto rituals, geisha, and kabuki theaters are some of the things that easily distinguish Japanese culture from the rest of the world. But has Japan always been this way? When did the archipelago first witness the birth of the Japanese civilization?

To the surprise of many, back in ancient times, Japan actually developed pretty late compared to its neighboring countries on the Asian mainland. Although the first groups of humans to ever inhabit the Japanese archipelago could be traced back to prehistoric times, it was not until the 4th century BCE that Japan was first introduced to iron technology and agricultural civilization. By this time, China was in the midst of warfare and military reforms, Alexander the Great had already conquered most of the Achaemenid Empire, and the ancient Greek philosopher, Plato, had already founded his academy, which became a place of study for Aristotle. However, Japan's late start did not stop the Japanese from growing. Although the nation was initially dependent on the influences brought by the immigrants who made their way from the Asian mainland and diplomatic envoys, the people gradually thrived, reaching a turning point by the 8th century CE.

The Japanese went from living as hunter-gatherers and rice farmers who could neither write nor read into a more civilized society, especially when they transitioned into the Heian period, which began in 794 CE. The two written records of ancient Japan, *Kojiki* and *Nihon Shoki*, clearly describe the flourishing cultures of the nation. Plenty of temples were constructed, each with a touch of the unique Japanese architecture that could not be seen anywhere else.

Of course, behind all of those great developments lay a great number of conflicts. Like many other nations in the world, ancient Japan had its fair share of vicious wars, battles, and assassinations. There were cases where imperial princes planned a coup to exterminate a ruling clan leader, a surprise siege laid upon the imperial castle late at night, and, not to forget, the birth of the samurai clans and their bloody skirmishes with each other.

With that said, this book wishes not only to provide readers with a captivating insight into the colorful culture of Japan and its origin but also the important incidents and conflicts that occurred throughout the centuries that shaped the nation into what it is today. Starting from the prehistoric period where the archipelago first welcomed its first inhabitants, readers will then journey through the ancient Jomon and Yayoi period before moving on to take a glimpse at the elaborate lives of the Japanese nobles in the Nara period and the early samurai warriors who made their first appearances in the 10th century CE.

Chapter 1 – Life in the Jomon Period

Certain people believed that the entire world was shaped by the hands of either mythical or celestial beings. The ancient Greeks suggested that the universe started off in the form of nothingness that they called Chaos, while the Norse people had almost the same belief except that they referred to the void as Ginnungagap. From these empty voids came primordial beings and, later on, the universe, skies, stars, the sun, the moon, clouds, mountains, islands, and so much else. But the Greeks and Norse people are not the only ones with myths about the beginnings of their worlds; the ancient Japanese people also believed that their lands were created by powerful mythical beings.

The Creation of the Japanese Islands

Izanami and Izanagi are a pair of gods often associated by the Japanese as the creators of their archipelago. It was said that it all started when the two celestial beings were walking along a bridge floating high up in the sky that connected heaven and earth. Staring down at the great ocean, where only nothingness could be seen, the two gods began to ponder on how to transform Chaos into a world of their own. Still focusing on the nothingness below them, the gods decided to make use of their jeweled spear known as Amenonuhoko, which was gifted to them by the elder gods. With the spear, the gods stirred the deep sea, and when they lifted it up, a small droplet at the end of the spear fell into the great ocean, thus creating the very first island of Japan. This mythical island is known as

Onogoroshima.

Izanagi and Izanami creating the islands of Japan.
https://commons.wikimedia.org/wiki/File:Kobayashi_Izanami_and_Izanagi.jpg

With the creation of Onogoroshima, the celestial pair finally had a land they could call home. Here, they built a legendary pillar, also known as the Heavenly August Pillar, which they later used in their rituals to start producing offspring. However, the gods started off on the wrong foot during the first ritual, which resulted in their first two children being born in the most twisted way possible. One of them was born without a single bone, almost resembling a leech. Disappointed, Izanami and Izanagi journeyed back to heaven, where they sought solutions for their misfortune from the elder gods.

Once the celestial pair had gotten the answers they needed, they traveled back to the island and performed the ritual again, correctly this time around. With the ritual a success, the two gods soon gave birth to many divine children, including the eight principal islands of Japan: Awaji, Shikoku, Oki, Tsukushi (later known as Kyushu), Iki, Tsu, Sado, and Oyamato.

How Japan Was Shaped

In contrast to the mythical legend of how the Japanese islands were shaped, science has suggested that Japan was initially attached to the eastern coast of the Eurasian continent. This was, however, over twenty million years ago. So, how did Japan get separated from the continent and transformed into a chain of islands?

Imagine our earth's continents as pieces of a jigsaw puzzle that could be attached and separated from each other at any time. Over two hundred million years ago, all the continents were attached together perfectly, just like a completed jigsaw puzzle, forming a supercontinent called Pangea. Fast forward to about fifty million years later, these continents began to drift apart, resulting in the positions we know today.

Thanks to the theory of plate tectonics, we now know that the continents are constantly on the move, drifting apart from each other. The same thing happened to Japan, which was initially a part of the Eurasian continent. About twenty thousand years ago, volcanic activity caused Japan to move eastward, taking its new position on the Pacific Ring of Fire, which explains the earthquakes and tsunamis that continue to terrorize the lands today. But if Japan was detached from the Eurasian plate many years ago, when did humans first set foot on the island chain? And how did they even travel to the archipelago?

The Discovery of the Japanese Paleolithic Age

While the ancient Japanese had Izanami and Izanagi to thank for the creation of their beautiful lands, archaeologists and historians are grateful for their discoveries of the various artifacts and fossils that reveal some stories of the past. However, many years ago, none of the Japanese believed that their lands went through the Stone Age due to the lack of evidence. Archaeologists spent their days and nights digging deep in their sites, hoping to find at least one artifact that could prove Japan did have a Paleolithic period. Their effort, however, was not very fruitful, leading to them believing that the Jomon people were the first group of humans to ever live on the islands.

But things would change right after the end of World War II. Tadahiro Aizawa was the first person to ever discover Japanese Paleolithic artifacts. Much to everyone's surprise, Tadahiro was only an amateur archaeologist, and he also happened to be a natto (fermented soybean) merchant. In 1946, while he was walking along the road on his way to conduct his daily business errands in Iwajuku, the amateur archaeologist came across a small flaked stone tool made out of obsidian, half-buried in a layer of red soil. He continued searching the area and found even more fragments of stone tools, which left him puzzled. The Japanese, at that time, believed that the Jomon were the earliest group of humans to arrive on the islands.

Three years after his discovery, Tadahiro once again found a fragment of a stone artifact; this time around, it was a stone arrowhead. He finally came to the conclusion that the islands of Japan had, in fact, been inhabited by humans way earlier than what was believed. The amateur archaeologist decided to meet a professor at one of the universities in Tokyo, hoping he could enlist more help from professionals to excavate the site. His first attempt, however, was unsuccessful, as the professor was not convinced by his findings. Many were unconvinced by Tadahiro's sudden discoveries except for one archaeologist from Meiji University who decided to assist his research. From there, full-fledged excavations were conducted, and just as the amateur archaeologist expected, more artifacts surfaced, and more sites were discovered, proving that the early inhabitants of Japan had lived through the Paleolithic period.

Tadahiro was not the only archaeologist known for the discovery of the Japanese Paleolithic period. In the 1970s, another amateur archaeologist was said to have found a number of artifacts, most of them originating from the Paleolithic period. His name was Fujimura Shinichi, and due to his remarkable discoveries at various sites, he was nicknamed the "Divine Hand." Although many other professional archaeologists were skeptical of his many findings, Fujimura's career flourished to the point where he held a position as a deputy director of the Tohoku Paleolithic Institute.

However, his success began to plummet when it was discovered that most of his findings were fraudulent. The archaeologist was caught red-handed when journalists from a newspaper managed to record footage of Fujimura planting fake artifacts at excavation sites. When the footage came to light, the archaeologist was forced to confess.

Nevertheless, through the artifacts discovered by other archaeologists—from those found by Tadahiro back in the 1940s to more recent ones—professionals have concluded that the Japanese archipelago first received inhabitants approximately forty thousand years ago. During this time, the world was at the peak of the Ice Age. Due to the sea level being 150 meters lower than what we see today, the Japanese archipelago was not

100 percent detached from the Asian continent; land bridges would have connected the islands with the continent. Since there were land bridges, humans could migrate to Japan without having to cross the sea.

It is plausible that the first humans to travel to the archipelago were following the migrations of animal herds, such as the Naumann's elephant and the giant elk. (Some claimed the first humans came from Southeast Asia based on skeletal analyses, while others suggest Northeast Asia.) Wild animals played a big role in the early humans' lives. Most of the time, their food depended on hunting. The Naumann's elephant (an extinct species of ancient elephant), for instance, weighed between four to five tons, and its meat could feed an entire settlement for a very long time. Because of that, these elephants became an attractive hunting target, which could be the reason humans decided to follow their migration over the land bridges. The discovery of the extinct elephant's fossils in Lake Nojiri further supports this theory.

The Lifestyle of the Paleolithic Japanese

Handless stone axes.

https://commons.wikimedia.org/wiki/File:JapanesePolishedStoneAxes.JPG

The Japanese Paleolithic period, also referred to as the Pre-ceramic era, was said to have taken place nearly forty thousand years ago and lasted until the end of the Ice Age. Not much is known about the lives of these ancient people except that they were big-game hunters and gatherers. When they were not out in the wilds hunting for animals or fishing, they spent their days foraging forests, collecting nuts and berries to add to their food supplies. Various tools were found by archaeologists.

One of them was the handless ax, which was possibly used to chop wood. They found a spearhead that was attached to driftwood, which would have been used for hunting, and a stone knife used to skin animals.

Since hunting was their main source of food, it is unsurprising to discover that these people moved from one place to another. They only occupied a specific location for a few weeks or months before they moved to another area, possibly following herds of animals. While some suggested that they took shelter in simple tents made out of animal skins, there are others who claimed that these people dwelled in caves, possibly in groups of ten or so. This is due to the discovery of Yamashita-Dojin, a limestone cave where the fossils of an eight-year-old prehistoric human were found. The remains were estimated to be approximately thirty-two thousand years old. Archaeologists also managed to excavate impressive fossils in a stone quarry located in Okinawa. This discovery of complete skeletons with skulls, feet, and hands received worldwide recognition. They are named Minatogawa people, and they are estimated to be seventeen thousand years old.

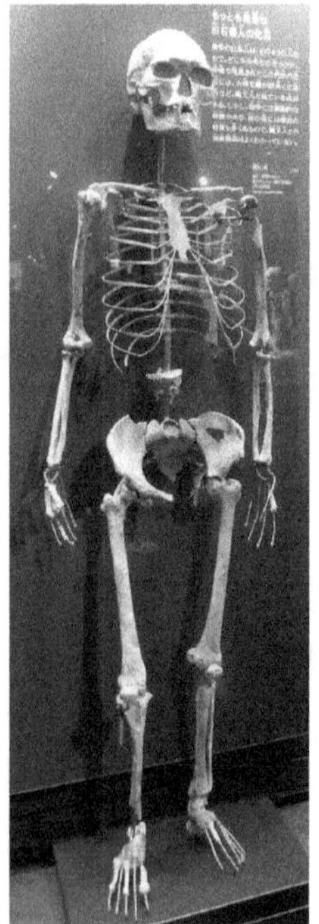

Fossil of the Minatogawa Man.
Photaro, CC BY-SA 3.0 https://creativecommons.org/licenses/by-sa/3.0 via Wikimedia Commons:
https://commons.wikimedia.org/wiki/File:Fossil_of_Minatogawa_Man.jpg

The Paleolithic age soon became a thing of the past, as the people in the Japanese archipelago experienced a gradual change in both their surroundings and lifestyle. Approximately twenty thousand years ago, warmth began to replace the earth's cold climate. Later on, the glaciers began to melt, and the sea level rose, marking the end of the Ice Age. This was also when Japan was completely separated from the Asian mainland. The gradual change in the climate affected a few beings. The number of large animals, especially the Naumann's elephant and the giant elk, began to drop. Without these massive animals to hunt, the people in Japan began to modify their tools and hunting weapons. Although the tools were smaller, they remained useful.

The era following the Japanese Paleolithic age is known as the Jomon period. When these people transitioned into this new period remains debatable. Some historians believe that the Jomon period began at least twelve thousand years ago, while there are others who claim that it started as early as sixteen thousand years ago when the land bridges still existed. The word Jomon is simply translated as "cord-markings" and is named after the unique characteristics of the pottery found during this period. The Jomon period lasted for nearly ten thousand years, and it is divided into six different phases: the Incipient phase (10,500–8000 BCE), the Initial Jomon (8000–5000 BCE), Early Jomon (5000–2500 BCE), Middle Jomon (2500–1500 BCE), Late Jomon (1500–1000 BCE), and Final Jomon (1000 BCE–300 BCE).

The Incipient Phase and Initial Jomon

The Incipient phase, which took place as early as 10,500 BCE, is often categorized as the transitional phase where the Jomon people were starting to change their way of life to better suit the climate change and their surroundings. Aside from living in simple surface dwellings, the early Jomon people were believed to be hunter-gatherers.

With the end of the Ice Age, the archipelago's vegetation faced some great transformations. The southwestern region of Honshu, Shikoku, and Kyushu saw the growth of broadleaf evergreen trees filling up every corner of the lush forests. Several different tree species, such as buckeyes, chestnuts, oaks, and beeches, began to prosper, making nut-gathering activities possible. Those who took shelter in the northeastern part of these regions focused on fishing activities to sustain their families. Salmon and various shellfish were their main sources of food, while sika deer and wild boars were also hunted for their meat.

Incipient Jomon pottery.
https://commons.wikimedia.org/wiki/File:JomonPottery.JPG

Pottery first emerged during these two phases of the Jomon period. They were mostly used as cooking containers, and pottery with pointed bottoms was a common sight. Each of these containers featured unique cord markings, which were normally carved using sticks and sometimes shells. Flat-bottomed pots also existed, which were typically used to boil food.

Early Jomon

The Early Jomon period was when the population of the Japanese archipelago began to flourish, growing from 20,000 to approximately 100,000 people. With the growth of the population, bigger villages started to emerge across the lands. Their shelters developed from simple surface dwellings into much sturdier structures. They lived in pit houses that could fit up to five people at once. Supported by wooden pillars, the pit houses were usually built surrounding a fireplace. Villages established by the sea depended mostly on fishing, while those who lived farther inland resorted to hunting and gathering activities.

A Japanese pit house at Dōnosora site, Gifu prefecture, Japan.
Alpsdake, CC BY-SA 4.0 https://creativecommons.org/licenses/by-sa/4.0 via Wikimedia Commons: https://commons.wikimedia.org/wiki/File:Pit-house_of_D%C5%8Dnosora_site.JPG

Cord-marked cooking containers continued to be used by the Jomon people, except the pottery had more intricate patterns and shapes. Narrow-necked jars, shallow bowls, and deep storage vessels were common, while bone needles and woven baskets were created for daily use. Pottery in the shape of animals and human figurines also emerged during this phase.

Middle Jomon

As the years passed, the Japanese archipelago welcomed yet another phase of the Jomon period. During the Middle Jomon, the population of the Japanese lands continued to increase greatly, leading to the establishment of bigger villages. Pit houses were widely used; some even featured paved stone floors. The rise in the temperature, however, caused many of the communities to move to mountainous regions. Hunting, fishing, and foraging were still their main activities for food. Rabbits, ducks, deer, and bears were common targets for hunters, while gatherers would often spend their time collecting different types of berries, mushrooms, and nuts. Some historians even claimed that the earliest plant cultivation might have happened during this phase, although it was most likely uncommon.

The Jomon people also began to bury their deceased in shell mounds, with various ritualistic practices slowly emerging within their communities. While their pottery continued to evolve into more sophisticated designs, human figurines became even more common. Archaeologists suggest that they were probably used in ritualistic ceremonies.

Late Jomon

The Jomon people once again moved their villages to another location due to climate change. With the temperature drop, these people chose to settle in an area closer to the sea; most of them would often live somewhere along Honshu's eastern shores. Because of this, the Late Jomon period witnessed an explosion of fishing activities, which resulted in new fishing tools and technology. Deep-sea fishing techniques were introduced, and the creation of a toggle harpoon, an ancient fishing tool, made it possible for the Jomon people to fish larger marine animals. By this time, whales and seals had become a part of their diet.

The discovery of circular ritualistic sites filled with a number of intricate figurines and assembled stones also suggests that the Jomon people held strong beliefs. It could be plausible that they had begun believing in a number of spirits and magic. Their ceremonial sites would often feature a sophisticated female figurine, which could have been used to symbolize the goddess of earth or fertility. Their beliefs, however, varied, depending on the many tribes and communities scattered throughout the archipelago.

Final Jomon

While the population of the Jomon thrived, especially by 5000 BCE, a climate change that occurred by 1000 BCE caused their population to decline drastically. The shortage of food supplies and other environmental issues might also have played a role in this sudden decline.

However, during this period, the Japanese archipelago began to receive contacts from the Asian mainland, particularly the Korean Peninsula. By 900 BCE, settlements influenced by the Koreans started to emerge around the western region of Kyushu. Pottery styles similar to those from the peninsula were also introduced. Not only did these settlers from the Asian mainland establish new settlements across the archipelago, but they also brought precious knowledge in rice cultivation and metalworking. Later on, hunting and foraging activities slowed down as rice cultivation became more widespread. This marked the end of the Jomon period.

Chapter 2 – Art, Culture, and Transition

The earth is indeed full of mysteries. Life sprung up at least tens of thousands of years ago, but it is hard for us to imagine how the world was back then. However, thanks to the many artifacts that have survived through the years, archaeologists and scholars have managed to put the pieces together and provide us with an insight into the lives of many ancient beings. The Jomon pottery, for instance, could tell us about the daily lives of the Jomon people in great detail.

When exactly the Japanese archipelago transitioned from the Paleolithic Age to the Neolithic Jomon period is disputed, but it is safe to say that the usage of pottery is what distinguishes the two periods. The first person to ever discover the unique and ancient Japanese pottery was a 19th-century American zoologist and archaeologist named Edward S. Morse. He was also the same person responsible for naming their pottery "Jomon," which simply means cord pattern in Japanese. The origins of the pottery, however, remain debatable. Since the title of the earliest type of ceramic vessels in East Asia is given to China, it is plausible that Jomon pottery was somehow influenced by Chinese techniques and traditions.

Since the Jomon period lasted for tens of thousands of years, scholars divided the period into different phases. Each of these phases featured different kinds of pottery, beliefs, and cultures. Some of the oldest Jomon pottery were the ones excavated from Shinonouchi, Nagano, as well as another site in Amouri called Odai-Yamamoto. These ancient artifacts can be traced back to 13,000 BCE, making them some of the oldest pottery in the world. During the early Jomon period, pottery was created in a rather simple design; they typically featured pointed bottoms, hollow bodies, and, of course, a distinctive rope pattern imprinted on the exterior surface. They were normally used as storage vessels and cooking containers.

Since a potter's wheel did not yet exist during the ancient period, the Jomon created these clay vessels using only their hands. Using the coil method, these people would shape their pottery layer by layer. Once the process of shaping the pottery was done, twines, ropes, grasses, and sometimes even seashells were imprinted on the wet clay to produce designs on the exterior surface. To finish them, the pottery had to go through a firing process, but due to the lack of a kiln, the Jomon would expose the pottery under the scorching sun before firing it in a bonfire that had a temperature no higher than 900°C (1652°F). To ensure they were waterproof, these vessels were usually covered with a lacquer made out of sap from the tree *Rhus verniciflua*.

By the Middle Jomon period, the pottery had evolved, featuring more intricate designs and shapes. Scholars divided the pottery into six different categories: *fukabachi* (deep bowls), *asabachi* (shallow bowls), *hachi* (medium-depth bowls), *sara* (plates), *tsubo* (narrow vessels with long necks), and *chuko* (spouted vessels). The pottery in the Middle Jomon evolved from pointed ends into flat bottoms, allowing them to be placed on flat surfaces easily.

An intricate Jomon flame vessel.
Cleveland Museum of Art, CC0, via Wikimedia Commons:
https://commons.wikimedia.org/wiki/File:Clevelandart_1984.68.jpg

The most famous type of Jomon pottery, called flame ware, was first introduced during this phase. Mostly found in central Honshu, these flame wares typically sport an opening wider than their base. Since they were most likely used in cooking activities, especially in boiling food, the reason behind the structure was to avoid having the contents boil over. These elaborately decorated pottery pieces were still made using the coil method and were also covered with thin rolls of clay, which were shaped into swirls, crests, and even holes. Although widely used as cooking pots, archaeologists suggest that they were also used in ritualistic ceremonies from time to time, especially in burial rites.

In the Late Jomon period, however, these highly decorated pottery pieces became less common. The Jomon people began to prioritize a vessel's functionality instead of intricate designs. Spouted pottery, round-bottomed vessels, short ceramic containers, and even incense burners began to emerge widely across the archipelago. While the finer pottery still existed, they were only used in ritualistic practices.

Round-bottomed pottery from the Final Jomon.

The Final Jomon saw the birth of yet another piece of pottery that was unique to the archipelago. Dogū, which literally translates as "earthen figure," was first discovered in the 17th century. It has a rather peculiar appearance. While Dogū could be in any sort of form—be it an animal or a human—the most popular Dogū ever discovered was the one from

Kamegaoka, Aomori Prefecture. Its prominent features include its coffee bean-shaped eyes, tiny nose and mouth, and an elaborate crown placed on its oval head. The size of these figurines varies; some measure at least forty centimeters (about sixteen inches) tall, while others stand at one meter (about three feet). The Dogū was often painted in red pigments and featured a complex detail on its body that perhaps indicated tattoos, scarring, body paint, or jewelry.

Dogū excavated from Ebisuda Site in Tajiri, Miyagi Prefecture, Japan.
World Imaging, CC BY-SA 3.0 https://creativecommons.org/licenses/by-sa/3.0 via Wikimedia Commons: https://commons.wikimedia.org/wiki/File:Dogu_Miyagi_1000_BCE_400_BCE.jpg

The purpose of this clay figurine, however, is not clear. Some claim that it was once used as a talisman for good health and safe childbirth, while others suggest that it was an item of worship the Jomon people prayed to in order to be blessed with an abundance of food. It might have also been used as an offering for a specific goddess and spirit. It is even possible that it was not to religious practice at all and was merely used as a children's toy. Nevertheless, the discovery of the Dogū is indeed valuable since it tells us of how expressive and creative the Jomon people were, despite the lack of advanced tools and technology.

The Beliefs of the Jomon People

The increasing number of figurines, stone circles, rods, and other ritualistic objects created during the Late and Final Jomon suggest that these ancient people had already established their own beliefs and religious practices. Although we cannot be sure what kind of ritualistic ceremonies the Jomon people participated in, it is likely that most of them were performed to commemorate or celebrate bountiful hunting catches and harvests. Archaeologists also managed to excavate pit houses that were filled with an array of clay figurines, ritual masks, highly decorated vessels, and even phallic stones, which might indicate that they belonged to shamans who were responsible for leading religious ceremonies.

Late Jomon clay head, possibly used in ritualistic ceremonies.

Animism beliefs and animal worship might have also been practiced by the Jomon people. Pottery featuring animal motifs, especially snakes, were found around the Yatsugatake Mountains in Nagano Prefecture. Due to the discovery of this pottery, experts arrived at the conclusion that certain tribes of the Jomon people—mostly those who lived within the mountains and coastal areas—were part of snake cults. They might have practiced certain rituals presided over by female shamans. It is possible that the snake motifs carved onto the clay pottery were depictions of the mamushi or Japanese pit viper, the most venomous snake in Japan. However, snakes were not the only animals to be depicted on their pottery, as archaeologists have also discovered clay figurines that resembled rodents.

Some of the clay figurines even came with highly complex details on their body, face, and arms, which led scholars to believe that the Jomon people were familiar with tattoos. Some suggest that they actually tattooed themselves on both their bodies and faces. In fact, the Ainu people, who are believed to share the same DNA as the Jomon people, were known for their tattoos, although the tradition of tattooing body parts and faces was mainly for women.

An Ainu woman with a facial tattoo.

The discovery of Jomon skulls with missing teeth also indicates that they might have practiced tooth ablation, a ritualistic practice that involves the removal of a person's healthy teeth. This ritual first took place during the Late Jomon period, and it was even practiced by some of the Yayoi people. To the Jomon people, tooth ablation was considered crucial since their altered look signified their status and age; the sets of teeth extracted from a person who had just reached puberty differed from those who had just been married. There were also cases where tooth ablation was done after the death of a loved one, either one's parents or spouse.

Burial Rites of the Jomon People

Of course, there are no intricate details about what happened when death occurred within a tribe or village. But with the discovery of the many stone circles, along with other ritualistic tools that indicate the strong beliefs of these ancient people in spirits and magic, it is safe to assume that a particular ritual or ceremony must have taken place to honor the dead. It is possible that they also buried animals, especially dogs, which were sometimes kept as pets.

Early on, the dead would be buried in shell mounds with their legs folded close to their chest, but as the years passed, the Jomon began using burial pits and jars. The latter were commonly used to bury children, infants, and unborn fetuses. Burial sites were normally placed at the center of a village, with most of them featuring grave markers. Archaeologists suggest that these ancient people had a particular way of marking the graves of their loved ones; they would place stones in a circular arrangement known as *kanjo-haiseki-bo*. Cremations also existed during this era, but they were rarely practiced. In some cases, the body of the deceased would be buried underneath the floor of their pit dwelling. Some also suggest that the body was placed directly on the floor before being covered with shell layers. Since death was considered unlucky and impure, the family members of the deceased would move out of the dwelling, abandoning it entirely.

Children might have had a special place in the hearts of the Jomon people since they took great care when it came to burying their lifeless bodies. Instead of being buried the same way as the adults, deceased children, infants, and unborn fetuses had their own burial tradition. They were buried in a curled-up position in burial jars made out of clay. Although some adults were buried in burial jars, by the starting of the Final Jomon period, this method was commonly used for infants, especially those who had died at the age of thirty-eight weeks or so. The Sanai Maruyama site alone had nearly eight hundred burial jars that contained the remains of children and infants.

At the start of this ancient period, the Jomon people would often bury their dead along with common items typically used in their daily lives. This included things like stone tools, arrowheads, and simple clay vessels. However, by the beginning of the Middle Jomon, their burial customs began to evolve, with the people burying their dead with an abundance of more elaborate items, such as ornaments and jewelry like shell bracelets, stone and shark tooth pendants, earrings, and jade beads. Ritualistic items, such as complex pottery vessels, figurines, clay tablets, and stone rods, were also included in graves, suggesting that these people probably believed in life after death.

Chapter 3 – The Yayoi Period

It is plausible that the Jomon period ended by the 3rd century BCE when its population plummeted and food sources were scarce due to their diet being fully dependent on hunting and foraging. Soon, another group of people arrived in the land of the rising sun, and they brought useful knowledge of rice cultivation and metalworking with them. We could say that Japan developed pretty late compared to other parts of the world. In the 3rd century BCE, China was constructing the Great Wall. Ancient Egypt had just finished building the Lighthouse of Alexandria. Nevertheless, on the islands of Japan, the 3rd century BCE marks the start of the Yayoi period, which lasted for at least five to six centuries. Unlike the word Jomon, which was named after the period's pottery style, Yayoi was named after a district in Tokyo. Here, the first artifacts originating from this period were discovered back in the 19th century.

The Origins of the Yayoi People

Many studies have been conducted to determine whether or not the Yayoi people were related to those from the Jomon period. The skull shapes of these two people groups were analyzed and compared, and their DNA was extracted for research. It was then revealed that there were, indeed, distinct differences between the two groups of people. While the Jomon people shared a little in common with the modern Japanese—although they did have some small similarities with the indigenous Ainu—the Yayoi people were the ones believed to be directly linked to the modern Japanese. But unearthing the roots of the Japanese is far more complicated than one might expect since there are many conflicting theories. In fact, no one is even sure what happened to the Jomon people after the Yayois' arrival. Were they violently replaced, or was there any intermarriage between the two groups?

Although where the Yayoi people came from remains a topic of debate today, scholars, historians, and archaeologists alike suggested that it involved migrations of people from either the Korean Peninsula via the Tsushima Strait or northern China across the Yellow Sea. Since the land bridges that connected Japan to the Asian continent had already been submerged due to the rising sea, it is safe to assume that sea-faring migrations were involved. The Yayoi culture was also said to first emerge in Kyushu, and in just a blink of an eye, it spread to the other part of the archipelago, first to the east and then up north.

Since the origin of wet rice farming can be traced back to China's Yangtze River, it could also be possible that the Yayoi people were initially farmers from this area who decided to migrate to the archipelago. To test this theory, research was carried out by Satoshi Yamaguchi, a researcher from Japan's National Museum of Nature and Science. The remains of the Yayoi people discovered in two Japanese prefectures, Yamaguchi and Fukuoka, were thoroughly examined and compared with the remains from Jiangsu, a Chinese province. At the end of the three-year research, they found that the remains bore many similarities, especially in their skulls and limbs.

The Legend of Xu Fu

Other than migrations of rice farmers from the Asian continent, some of the Japanese also believed that the advanced techniques of farming were actually brought into their lands by Xu Fu, who also introduced the knowledge of traditional medicines to the native on the islands.

Xu Fu, also called Jofuku by the Japanese, was an alchemist who called the ancient Chinese state of Qi his homeland. The alchemist served Qin Shi Huang, the founder and first emperor of the Qin dynasty, as a court sorcerer. Since Xu Fu was an alchemist and an explorer, it is not surprising to learn that Xu Fu held much knowledge. He somehow learned that there were three celestial islands in the world where their inhabitants were all immortals. These lands were named Penglai, Fangzhang, and Yingzhou. The immortals were said to be thousands of years old, and they lived in a gold palace nestled within the mountains. On the island of Penglai, one could feast night and day without having to worry about their bowls getting empty. The enchanted fruits growing in the area could also grant eternal youth.

And so, when the emperor—who was famously known to have an obsession with immortality— learned about the existence of these magical lands, he ordered the alchemist to set sail and search for the key to immortality: the elixir of life. Some say the emperor's obsession with immortality had to do with his extreme fear of death, especially since so many people wanted to spill his blood. In fact, he was believed to have survived two murder attempts. Another reason could also be the ominous message Qin Shi Huang saw on a meteor that hit Dongjun back in 211 BCE. The message stated that he would soon die and that all of his lands would be divided, which somehow came true since the emperor died in 210 BCE after possibly consuming an elixir containing mercury prepared by his own court alchemists and physicians. To make matters worse, the Qin dynasty collapsed about five years after his death, and his lands were, indeed, divided.

Xu Fu set sail under the order of his emperor and began his expedition across the East Sea in search of the celestial island. The alchemist brought along a few thousand men, women, and children. The expedition, however, was nothing but a waste of time, as Xu Fu never found any islands or mountains of the immortals. And so, he set sail back to his homeland. When questioned by the emperor about his adventure and whether he had gotten the elixir of life, Xu Fu answered that he was forced to retreat, as there was a massive sea creature underneath the deep sea patiently waiting to attack his ship. Upon hearing the alchemist's explanation, the emperor sent highly skilled archers to the sea, where they killed the creature believed to be blocking Xu Fu's way.

Xu Fu's expedition for the elixir of immortality.
https://commons.wikimedia.org/wiki/File:Xu_Fu_expedition%27s_for_the_elixir_of_life.jpg

With the creature gone, the emperor again sent Xu Fu across the ocean to retrieve the magical elixir. This time around, Xu Fu had a total of three thousand men, women, and children on board, along with many provisions, seeds, and silks. However, just as last time, Xu Fu never found Penglai. He was well aware that he could never return home since the emperor would want to have his head on a plate for failing his task. So, Xu Fu never returned, and that was the last time anyone ever heard of him or his crew.

Legend has it that Xu Fu and his crew actually landed in Japan, thinking Mount Fuji to be the celestial Mount Penglai. Some believed that upon landing on the archipelago, the alchemist shared much of his knowledge with the people there. This includes the techniques of rice cultivation. The Japanese people eventually worshiped the alchemist as their god of farming; statues honoring him can be found in Japan today. Some even believe that he was the same person as Emperor Jimmu, Japan's first emperor, as recorded in the *Nihon Shoki* and *Kojiki*.

The Daily Lives of the Yayoi People

With the precious knowledge of wet rice cultivation, the Japanese archipelago became extremely valuable to the Yayoi people. Agriculture was considered their main source of food, and choosing the right land to set up a settlement was, of course, one of their highest priorities. During the early times of the Yayoi period, the people would often choose healthy lands that featured either high terraces or valleys surrounded by rolling hills and mountains. The Itatsuke site in Fukuoka Prefecture is one of the examples that had all of the above features. However, as more and more settlements were built and rice farming began to spread throughout the islands, land became more limited, and the people had no other choice but to settle on the alluvial plains.

Although the art of agriculture and metalworking were still new to these ancient Japanese, the Yayoi people had no problem with developing technologies to improve their fields. Once they had gathered enough wood, the farmers would carve and create wooden stakes, which they used to outline their rice fields. To provide a continuous water supply and irrigate the rice fields, the farmers built canals and waterways. Some settlements even went the extra mile by constructing canals right under their rice fields, thus making water recycling possible. Wells were also built in close proximity to the farming fields to ease the process of obtaining water.

Stone tools such as hoes and knives were widely used at first, probably due to the minimal supplies of iron and metal, but it did not take long for them to develop proper and sturdier tools to aid in their farming activities. Later on, the blades of their stone knives were replaced with iron, and they would use them to harvest rice. Other tools that the Yayoi people used in their daily farming activities include *geta*, a pair of wooden clogs often used to walk through marshy grounds; *eburi*, which was used to smoothen the paddy fields; and *ooashi*, a paddy field tramper. These wooden tools were first discovered by archaeologists at the Toro site in Shizuoka. Believe it or not, these useful wooden tools are still used today. The harvested rice was then gathered and stored in storage jars before being kept in underground pits or elevated wooden storehouses.

Rice was not the only thing found on the farms of the Yayoi people, although it was their main source of food. Archaeologists found a total of thirty-seven other plants cultivated on their lands, including adzuki beans, barley, foxtail millet, and gourds. Hunting activities and foraging were not completely replaced, as some of them hunted for wild animals and journeyed into the wilds every now and then. They also weaved textiles on a daily basis and tended to the wild boars that they kept in their villages.

With the introduction of agricultural activities, the population of the Japanese archipelago skyrocketed, reaching almost two million people at its peak. The Yayoi people began settling permanently and lived in bigger communities. Early on, their houses were pretty much identical to those originating from the Jomon period. Pit houses featuring thatched roofs and earthen floors were a common sight during this time. As time passed and their technology advanced, these groups of dwellings were surrounded by moats to prevent attacks. Other structures were built, such as granaries and wooden storehouses, which were typically used to store rice and other crops.

Reconstruction of a Yayoi village with an elevated granary.
Pekachu, CC BY-SA 4.0 https://creativecommons.org/licenses/by-sa/4.0 , via Wikimedia Commons:
https://commons.wikimedia.org/wiki/File:Habu_Ancient_Ruin_restored_houses_and_a_warehouse.jpg

Many pottery pieces were also found at various sites. While pottery in the Jomon period was known for its intricate shapes and designs, those originating from the Yayoi period are simpler; it seems the Yayoi prioritized usefulness. Long-necked storage vessels, round-mouthed cooking pots, pedestalled dishes, and serving bowls were common pottery during this period. While scholars believed that the shapes of pottery and jars might have come from Korea since they bore similarities with Mumun pottery, others suggest that Jomon influences played a role.

Religion, Beliefs, and Burial Ceremonies of the Yayoi Period

By the 1st century BCE, bronze started to be widely used by the Yayoi people. While iron and metal were commonly used to create farming tools, weapons, and armor, bronze was often smelted to make ritual items. Dōtaku, for instance, were huge bells made out of bronze. According to Japanese folklore, dōtaku were actually emergency bells that were used by the sentinels whenever they spotted a threat coming their way. Once a dōtaku was rung by the sentinels, warriors would prepare themselves to defend their settlements. However, certain scholars and historians have suggested that these bronze bells were not used to sound emergencies. Dōtaku have rather thin walls, and because of that, it would not resonate like a fully functioning bell. So, they came to the conclusion that dōtaku were, in fact, ritual items.

A bronze dōtaku.
https://commons.wikimedia.org/wiki/File:Dotaku_LACMA_M.58.9.3_(2_of_2).jpg

Most of these bronze bells were found with images of various animals, such as wild boars, dogs, birds, praying mantises, and even dragonflies, carved on the surface. But the most prominent animals featured on these bells were deer and cranes; carvings of deer were also featured on some of the Yayoi pottery. This reason alone led archaeologists to believe that the Yayoi people already had their own beliefs.

We have learned that the origins of Shintoism can be traced back to the Yayoi period. By this time, they already had shamans and priests. This fact is not at all surprising, especially since experts discovered that certain animals were considered sacred to the Yayoi people and played an important role when it came to agriculture. Farmers performed a ritual where they would sow seeds in deer blood, as they believed that deer could help improve the growth of rice. A deer's antlers are known for their rapid growth; they shed and grow new antlers every year. In spring, their antlers begin to grow and continue to develop all throughout the year until winter, when antlers are supposed to shed, repeating the entire cycle again. This cycle was believed to be connected to the growth of rice and other plants.

Apart from using blood to enhance the growth of their plants, these people would also transport the dōtaku to an isolated location away from their settlements and bury the bronze bells deep underground to receive the earth's life force. This holy rite was to ensure that their lands remained fertile.

Indeed, the Yayoi people valued their agricultural growth more than anything, but they performed rituals for other things too. It is believed that when a person died in a settlement, the entire village would enter a mourning phase that lasted for ten days. During that time, the villagers were said to dress in hemp clothes and restrict themselves from eating any sort of meat. The leader of the settlement would then wail as others participated in a ritual where they sang, danced, and drank. Once the mourning period was over, the family members of the dead would head into the waters and perform a type of purification to cleanse themselves from all the impurities of the dead.

As for the dead, their last stop would be at the burial mounds. They would be buried in wooden coffins, although some sources suggest that this method was only used during the early years of the period. Some were also buried in burial jars along with various kinds of items, such as weapons, pottery, jewelry, and ritualistic items like bronze mirrors and swords. These items were often only in the graves of those who held higher positions in a settlement.

Social Classes, Wars, and Relationship with China

Since Japan had no writing system during this period, the earliest written documents that describe the ancient Japanese are from China. These old documents are known as *Wei Shu* (*Book of Wei*) and *Han Shu* (*Book of Han*). Referring to Japan as Wa, historians from ancient China tell us that by the late Yayoi period, Japan had over one hundred different communities or states, with each one of them ruled by wealthy landowners or chieftains.

Those who possessed more metal, bronze, glass, and even silk were considered elite members of a settlement. Men with higher status were said to have many wives compared to the commoners, and those from lower classes were required to show their respect. Whenever someone with an elite status walked by, commoners had to step to the side of the road and make way for them. This was practiced by the Japanese until the 19th century CE.

As the Yayoi people strived toward civilization, they became more accustomed to war and conquest. Iron and bronze were melted, and wood was gathered to create more weapons, shields, and armor. More settlements emerged, and the land became even more limited, so these people were left with no choice but to fight each other in order to conquer fertile lands to house and support their growing population. With the increasing number of wars, the people began to fortify their settlements by digging dry moats and installing *sakamogi* or sharp wooden stakes to keep their enemies at bay. Watchtowers were built, and sentinels were stationed to keep an eye on invaders from afar.

The ancient Chinese records also mentioned that certain communities from the lands of Wa would send tribute to the Chinese emperors from time to time. In 57 CE, the state of Nu (now located on Hakata Bay, Kyushu) once sent emissaries to the emperor of the Han dynasty. In return, the emperor granted them a golden seal as a sign of a diplomatic relationship. The golden seal was lost for thousands of years, but it was later rediscovered by a farmer in 1784.

The golden seal sent by Emperor Guangwu of Han in 57 CE.
https://commons.wikimedia.org/wiki/File:King_of_Na_gold_seal.jpg

The Kingdom of Yamatai

Another decade replaced the other, and the Japanese archipelago was plagued by numerous wars and violence. Kingdoms waged wars with each other, and swords clashed no matter the time of day. However, according to the Chinese records, there was one kingdom that stood out; it was known as Yamatai. The kingdom rose to power when it successfully conquered a total of thirty states of the Japanese islands and ruled over them peacefully.

The kingdom of Yamatai was led by a shaman queen who went by the name Himiko. She was first put on the throne by her own people and was believed to possess religious powers. Some even claimed that the queen was, in fact, a direct descendant of the Shinto sun goddess, Amaterasu, while others also suggested that Himiko was the same figure as the legendary Empress Jingū.

However, only a few ever got a chance to see Himiko in person, as she resided in her palace, which was well-guarded by dozens of guards and watchmen. She was tended by a thousand female servants, and her younger brother was often the only one to meet her face to face.

Himiko never married, and she never left her palace. Since she preferred to devote herself entirely to shamanism, the queen conveyed her orders through her younger brother, who would pass them to the people of her kingdom. Under Himiko's reign, peace was possible, and more states acknowledged her as a ruler. To solidify her power, Himiko sent envoys to China with slaves and fine pieces of cloth as tributes. Noticing her influence over the lands of Wa, the Chinese Wei dynasty honored her with the title "Queen of Wa, Friendly to Wei." Along with the title and in return for her generous tributes, Himiko was gifted with a golden seal, a hundred bronze mirrors, and swords. And so, Queen Himiko became the first ruler of Japan.

Queen Himiko managed to restore peace and rule the lands of Japan for over fifty years. According to the Chinese records, Japan transformed into an organized kingdom with political stability. Law was established, and punishments were invented. The queen, however, finally passed away in 248 CE, and her remains were interred in a massive tomb, which archaeologists believed to be located in Nara Prefecture. The death of Queen Himiko also marked the end of the Yayoi period.

Chapter 4 – Shintoism

Upon looking at their first child, both Izanagi and Izanami were horrified. The child who they called Hiruko— soon known as Ebisu—was the very first kami to be born in Japan, but his appearance at birth was rather twisted. He was born without a single bone in his body, which explains why his name also meant the "Leech Child." Hiruko was later placed in a boat of reeds by his parents, who then set it adrift into the open sea. Although the kami had been born with deformities, it was said he grew a pair of legs and other limbs at the age of three. When he first washed ashore after his parents abandoned him, Hiruko was found and taken in by a group of Ainu people. He learned how to walk, talk, and smile. Soon, Hiruko went by the name Ebisu and became the patron god of fishermen as well as one of the Seven Lucky Gods or Shichifukujin.

It turns out that Ebisu's deformities were caused by none other than Izanagi and Izanami themselves. To produce offspring, the two deities participated in a ritual where they had to circle around the Heavenly August Pillar in the opposite direction. When they neared each other, Izanagi was supposed to greet his partner first; however, during their first ritual, Izanami was the one who spoke before her husband. This mistake resulted in the unfortunate birth of Hiruko.

However, the two deities managed to perform the sacred ritual correctly after consulting the elder gods in heaven, who explained what had gone wrong. With the ritual performed perfectly the second time around, Izanami gave birth to many other kami, including the eight principal islands of Japan, Watatsumi (kami of the sea), Kukunochi (kami of the trees), Oyamatsumi (kami of the mountains), and Kagutsuchi (kami of fire). Although the ritual was fruitful, resulting in the birth of many kami, Izanami had to pay a heavy price—death.

Izanami faced her fate when she gave birth to Kagutsuchi. Being the kami of fire, Kagutsuchi burned his mother to death as soon as he was delivered. Enraged, Izanagi unsheathed his legendary sword, Ameno Ohabari, and killed his son. He chopped Kagutsuchi's remains into eight pieces and scattered them throughout the islands, resulting in the eight major active volcanoes of Japan. From Kagutsuchi's blood dripping from the great sword came several more kami. The most prominent one is Takemikazuchi, the kami of thunder often associated with martial arts and believed to be the creator of sumo.

Izanagi's journey and the birth of many new kami did not stop there. Driven by extreme sadness and sorrow, Izanagi decided to venture into the underworld or Yomi, hoping to bring his wife back to the world of the living. After urging Izanami to leave the underworld and return home, Izanagi was informed that his wife had already eaten the food of the underworld, thus making her one with the land of the dead. Izanami, however, tried pleading with the gods and asked for their permission to return home with Izanagi. In the meantime, she made Izanagi promise that he would never try to look at her. Missing his beloved wife, Izanagi eventually became impatient and broke his promise by looking at her. But instead of feeling joy at seeing his long-lost wife, he was terrified, as Izanami's entire body was already decomposing and covered with wriggling maggots.

Shocked by the horrifying state of his wife, Izanagi ran away and decided to return to the world of the living without Izanami. Learning of her husband's intentions to abandon her, Izanami, along with the demons of thunder (Yakusanoikazuchi) and the ugly hags of the underworld (Yomotsu-shikome), chased after the terrified man. Luckily for Izanagi, he successfully escaped the underworld and quickly blocked the entrance to Yomi with a massive boulder, thus separating the two lands.

To cleanse himself of the underworld, Izanagi performed a ritual in the River Woto. This cleansing ritual is called *harae*, and it is one of the most important rituals in Shintoism. As Izanagi performed the purification ritual in the river, he gave birth to more kami: Amaterasu, the goddess of the sun and the mythical ancestor to Japan's emperors; Tsukuyomi, the god of the moon; and Susanoo, god of storms. These kami, along with the purification ritual, are some of the most important aspects of Shintoism.

But what exactly is Shintoism, and where did it come from? Before the arrival of Buddhism in Japan in the 6th century, its people believed in Shintoism. Shintoism was even acknowledged as the state religion back in the Meiji period. During this time, priests were appointed as state officials, and the building of shrines was put first. People would also worship their emperor since they believed that the imperial line descended from the most important kami in Shinto, Amaterasu. This, however, only lasted until the end of World War II. Today, both Shintoism and Buddhism coexist peacefully.

Although known around the globe as another type of indigenous religion, the Japanese tend not to classify Shintoism as one. Unlike other major world religions, Shintoism has neither a founder nor sacred texts like the Bible or the Quran. There is neither right nor wrong in Shintoism. Humans are believed to be born good and pure, and evil is caused by malevolent spirits.

To put it in simple words, no one knows when Shintoism exactly surfaced. But with archaeological evidence, scholars and historians believe that many of its practices began during the Yayoi period, although the earliest writing about Shintoism dates back to 712 CE. It is called *Kojiki (Record of Ancient Matters)*. The prehistoric people, including the earliest inhabitants of Japan, were familiar with animism; they believed that everything in this world—from mountains to grasses, rocks, wild animals, places, and even the weather—possessed a spiritual essence. In Shintoism, it is believed that a spirit dwells in every single thing surrounding us.

Torii gates, a traditional Japanese gate placed at the entrance of a Shinto shrine to mark the transition from our world to a sacred site.

Balon Greyjoy, CC0, via Wikimedia Commons: Balon Greyjoy, CC0, via Wikimedia Commons: https://commons.wikimedia.org/wiki/File:20181110_Fushimi_Inari_Torii_10.jpg

Shinto simply means the way of the kami. As the translation suggests, those who practice this two-thousand-year-old religion worship kami. But what exactly is a kami? Some might translate the word as either deities or gods, but a kami is not restricted only to godlike figures. In Shinto beliefs, kami can be anything, such as the forces of nature or the spirits of dead ancestors. The river has a kami, and so do the towering volcanoes, waterfalls, and trees growing in the middle of a lush forest. Shintoism teaches that the physical world itself is sacred and needs to be respected at all times.

Amaterasu, the Most Important Kami in Shinto

Amaterasu, whose name means the "Shining in Heaven," was born from Izanagi's left eye as he performed the purification ritual after his return from the underworld. Appointed as the ruler of the High Celestial Plain (Takamagahara) by her father, Amaterasu is also the elder sister to the mischievous yet impetuous god of storms, Susanoo. Besides being widely known as the ancestor of the imperial line of Japan, Amaterasu was also said to have taught humans how to weave cloth and plant rice. But those were not the biggest blessings that the kami bestowed upon the universe. Amaterasu was the goddess of the sun, and without the magnificent light shining out of her, both the world of humans and the heavens would plunge into total darkness, which had already happened once.

It all began when Susanoo was expelled by Izanagi when he was said to have caused nothing but nuisance upon the world. Before leaving Takamagahara, the mischievous storm god decided to meet Amaterasu at her palace just so he could bid her farewell. This event, however, turned into chaos, as the two siblings ended up in an argument. Susanoo, who was known for his temper tantrums, wreaked havoc across the celestial plain; he burned Amaterasu's rice fields, destroyed parts of her palace, and defecated on her high seat. Seeing that his sister's reaction was not what he had hoped for, Susanoo came up with more mischief. The god first flayed a beautiful spotted horse alive. Then, standing on top of the roof, Susanoo threw the flayed horse into Amaterasu's weaving hall. The poor horse fell helplessly on the floor and terrified a few of Amaterasu's sacred weaving maidens, who had peacefully been weaving clothes for the gods. More chaos ensued when one of them accidentally struck herself against a weaving shuttle and died.

Learning about the death of one of her beloved weavers, Amaterasu was overwhelmed with anger and sadness. And so, the goddess of the sun decided to leave her palace and lock herself in a cave called Ama-no-Iwato. Since she had blocked the entrance of the cave with a massive boulder, none could enter, and her shimmering light soon disappeared from the universe. With the sun gone, Takamagahara and the earth fell into darkness. Crops began to wither, food supplies deteriorated, and evil spirits started to roam the world, causing all kinds of trouble.

Realizing that the catastrophe was happening due to the absence of Amaterasu's radiant light, the kami of Takamagahara began plotting ways to persuade the goddess to leave her hiding. Omoikane, the Shinto god of wisdom, first suggested they place roosters in front of the cave, hoping that their crows would trick Amaterasu into thinking that it was finally dawn. Then, they planted a sakaki tree—a sacred evergreen in Shintoism—right in front of the cave entrance and placed a huge mirror on its trunk.

Amaterasu was puzzled when she heard the roosters crow since it was impossible for dawn to emerge without her light. Moments later, the goddess heard loud laughter coming from the many kami who had gathered in front of the cave. The laughter got louder as Amenouzume, the patron goddess of dancers, performed a wild dance on an upturned tub. One of the deities also announced that another shining goddess had arrived who was just as magnificent as the goddess of the sun herself. Finally curious, Amaterasu slowly moved the boulder blocking the cave entrance and peeked through the gap. The first thing she saw was her own radiant reflection in the sacred mirror.

Amaterasu was in complete awe, thinking the reflection was the newly arrived deity. Without delaying a single moment more, Ame-no-tajikarao, the kami known for his strong hands, yanked the sun goddess out of her hideout. The cave entrance was then sealed with Shimenawa, a straw rope, which later became an item used in Shinto purification rituals. As Amaterasu got closer to the mirror, she finally realized that she was looking at her own beautiful reflection. The goddess now knew of her important role in the universe and how wrong it was to deprive the world of her glorious light.

Amaterasu emerging out of her cave, shining the entire world with her radiant light.
https://commons.wikimedia.org/wiki/File:Amaterasu_cave.JPG

And so, with Amaterasu out of hiding, the world was blessed with her light. Crops began to prosper, the evil spirits went back to where they came from, and joy filled the air yet again.

The Story of Hōsōgami, the Kami of Smallpox

Although most of the kami worshiped by Shinto practitioners are generally good spirits who wish to see humans flourish and prosper, there are also kami associated with evil and sickness, such as Hōsōgami, the kami of smallpox. This particular kami is often depicted as an old man carrying a torn Japanese traditional fan (*uchiwa*) or small demons. This kami traveled from one village to another, spreading smallpox to the unfortunate villagers. Despite being pictured as temperamental spirits or demons, Hōsōgami were said to have some weaknesses; they are terrified of dogs and the color red. The latter was due to the color red being a symbol of good health. Because of that, villagers back then would often be seen hanging *aka-e*, a red woodblock print, in their houses. Some of these prints even feature a picture of Shōki, a mythical god said to have the ability to vanquish evil spirits and ghosts. Aside from the prints, other protective talismans include toys in the shape of dogs and red clothing.

Even though Hōsōgami brought nothing but sickness to the villagers, some also believed they could stop smallpox from terrorizing their family by performing rituals and providing offerings to the evil kami. Rather than putting up red prints of protective deities, some villagers would erect a shrine specifically for Hōsōgami. In these shrines, they prayed and begged for the kami to spare them from his terrible infection.

Some even believed that the kami was not at all the cause of the infection; instead, he was their savior. Those who survived the disease would sometimes give offerings to the kami as a sign of gratitude. Those who did not build a shrine for Hōsōgami would erect one for either Sukunabikona, the Shinto god of healing, or the legendary samurai named Minamoto no Tametomo, who was believed to have once driven a sickness out of the land.

If offerings and prayers did not manage to fend off the evil spirit, the villagers would turn to another ritual called hōsōgami okuri. They would gather around and parade through the streets, beating on drums and bells and creating tunes from their flutes in the hopes they could entertain Hōsōgami and prevent the kami from infecting them.

There are so many stories that revolve around the Shinto gods and spirits, but, of course, some have already been lost in history. While there is said to be a total of twelve Olympians in Greek mythology and about sixty-six gods in the Old Norse belief, Shinto has eight million kami—which is a Japanese phrase describing infinity—and each one of them is to be respected. If one treats a kami with full respect, one will gain many benefits, be it in terms of health, success, wealth, and even examination results. Failure to do so might result in shinbatsu, retribution, which often came in the form of sickness and sometimes even death. When developers decided to cut down a seven-hundred-year-old tree growing in the middle of Kayashima Station back in 1972, many Japanese who strongly believed in Shintoism held a protest. The old tree was said to house a kami, and to let it get cut down by the developers would only bring them terrible misfortune.

Some said that the tree itself began to portray its protest against those who wished it harm. A man was believed to contract hay fever when he tried cutting one of the tree's branches, while some reported seeing a white snake—a type of snake associated with Shinto gods—slithering through the tree branches. Some even spotted smoke coming out of the tree. In the end, none dared to cut down the sacred tree, and it is still standing in the middle of Kayashima Station today.

Purification Rituals

Purification rituals are the central aspect of Shintoism. Indeed, there is no heaven or hell in Shinto, but it is believed that one can never gain blessings from the kami if they remain impure. These impurities can come in many forms. They are called *kegare* and *tsumi*. While *kegare* includes impurities that occur naturally, such as death, disease, menstruation, and filth, *tsumi* focuses more on the violation of legal or religious laws, such as murder, theft, disrespecting a place of worship, and even talking back to your parents. All of these impurities can be cleansed by performing *harae*, a ritual that was first performed by the creator kami, Izanagi.

Purification rituals are also done before taking a step into a Shinto shrine and performing any kind of religious ceremony. The simplest form of purification that can be done before interacting with a kami is called *temizu*. If you ever find yourself in Japan, you should approach the purification fountain called *temizuya* placed at the entrance of a shrine. Use the wooden ladle to draw water from the fountain and then rinse your left hand, followed by your right hand. Pour some water into your hand, and use it to rinse your mouth. Once the purification is done, one is free to enter the shrine and interact with the kami.

Purification can also be done in the form of misogi, which requires a person to cleanse themselves in the ocean or by standing under a cascading waterfall. Shubatsu, on the other hand, is a form of *harae* that uses salt as a purification agent. Shubatsu is often seen at the start of a sumo wrestling match, as the sumo fighters purify the wrestling ring by sprinkling salt around it. Other than water and salt, a ritual wand could also be used to purify not only a person but also objects and land.

Ise Grand Shrine

There are many Shinto shrines scattered throughout the Japanese archipelago. One could find a shrine dedicated to all different kinds of kami, from the kami of rice to money, poetry, and even hair. However, the most sacred Shinto shrine is the one and only Ise Grand Shrine, which is dedicated to none other than the supreme kami of the sun, Amaterasu.

Also known as Ise Jingu, the origins of the shrine go back two thousand years, when Japan was under the reign of Emperor Suinin. According to the *Nihon Shoki*, the emperor requested his daughter, Yamatohime-no-mikoto, set out on a mission in search of a location where they could permanently build a place of worship for the sun goddess. And so, without delaying a single moment, the princess left her dwelling and wandered through the regions of Omi and Mino for over twenty years. She could not find the perfect place for the shrine, so she continued her journey until she suddenly heard the voice of the goddess herself. It was believed that Amaterasu had whispered to the princess of a location where she wished to dwell. This pleasant land chosen by the supreme goddess is known as Ise, and it is located in modern-day Mie Prefecture. Honoring the sun goddess's wish, Yamatohime-no-mikoto placed fifty bells surrounding the area, marking the place for Amaterasu. The princess herself became the first high priestess of the shrine, kicking off the tradition of appointing the emperor's daughter as a high priestess of the Ise Grand Shrine.

Ise Grand Shrine (Naikū).

With the discovery of the land, the inner shrine or Naikū was first built to properly enshrine the sun goddess and house the sacred mirror. This was the same mirror used by the ancient gods to lure Amaterasu out of her cave after the terrible incident with Susanoo. Later on, the same mirror was gifted to the first legendary emperor of Japan, and it remains the imperial regalia of Japan today. About five hundred years after the construction of Naikū, the outer shrine, known as Gekū, was added. It was built six kilometers (about four miles) away from Naikū and is dedicated to Toyouke-Ōmikami, the kami of agriculture and industry who was also said to hold the responsibility of offering sacred food to the sun goddess. While there are over 125 shrines found around Ise, both Naikū and Gekū are what make up the Grand Ise Shrine. However, today, visitors are restricted from entering these two main shrines and are only allowed to roam around the forests and their surrounding areas.

Since the outer and inner shrines are the most sacred sites in Shintoism, they both go through reconstruction once every twenty years. This reconstruction ceremony is known as Shikinen Sengu. It first took place in 690 CE, and the process of rebuilding both shrines takes at least eight years. The entire ceremony also consists of thirty-two rituals, the first one being a ritual that involves cutting the first few trees for the reconstruction of the structures. The last ritual involves the transfer of Amaterasu's sacred mirror into the newly built shrine.

Chapter 5 – The Kofun Period and Early Tomb Building

Queen Himiko was believed to have restored order across the lands of Japan back in the Yayoi period. Before she was chosen by her people to rule, Japan was divided into over a hundred states or tribes, each ruled by a different leader. War was nearly everywhere, as the people were beginning to crave more power and lands for their growing agricultural activities and population. Peace was, no doubt, established when the shaman queen rose to power, as most of the tribes across the islands acknowledged her as a ruler—all except for the Kingdom of Kuna (Kuna-koku)

Little is known about Kuna-koku. The only record that tells its story is about its dispute with the Kingdom of Yamatai. Archaeologists and historians believe that at some point, Himiko sought help from the Chinese to settle the issues going on between the two kingdoms. However, the queen died shortly after. No one has been able to find the reason behind Himiko's death, but we do know that with Himiko gone, peace across the archipelago died as well.

When the queen passed away, another figure rose to power—a king, this time around. But few were fond of the new king, resulting in more bloodshed across Japan. Violent wars erupted yet again, and murder and assassination became the norm. It is believed over a thousand people perished. It seems like with just a snap of a finger, peace was reversed, and the archipelago was in a state of chaos. This continued until people agreed that another woman should be put on the throne. This woman is known in ancient Chinese records as Iyo. She happened to be Himiko's relative; historians believe she was Himiko's niece. At the age of thirteen, Iyo reigned over Japan. She restored order just as Himiko did and maintained a close relationship with China.

In 266 CE, Japan is no longer mentioned in the Chinese records. It was not until the 5th century that Japan would be mentioned again, but by this time, Japan already had its own emperor. No one knows what happened to the Kingdom of Yamatai after Iyo's reign. In fact, even its exact location remains disputed today. If one was to faithfully follow the directions that lead to Yamatai as recorded by the ancient Chinese historians, you would end up south of Japan, right in the middle of the vast Pacific Ocean. Ever since the Edo period, scholars have been trying to trace the location of Yamatai. There are two possible theories today. Himiko's mysterious kingdom could have been located on the west coast of Kyushu or within the central area of Japan, once known as the Yamato region (now known as Nara Prefecture, Honshu).

If the latter theory is taken into account, then it could be possible for researchers to conclude that the Hashihaka Tomb found in the prefecture belonged to none other than the legendary Queen Himiko. And if the massive tomb was, indeed, where the queen was interred, then we could say that Yamatai had some sort of ties with the Yamato, a powerful clan during the Kofun period that gave birth to the imperial house of Japan.

Kofun Tombs and the Birth of a New Period

The Kofun period, which marks its beginning around 250 and lasted until 538 CE, derived its name from the unique burial mounds (also known as kofun) scattered throughout the archipelago. As of today, there are nearly thirty thousand kofun tombs in Japan that have been discovered by archaeologists and scholars. Unlike normal graves and burial mounds, a kofun was initially built only to bury the remains of those who held power and status, such as emperors and powerful clan leaders. Early in this period, the tombs were simpler; they were built on natural mounds and did not have specific designs. However, as time passed, people began building tombs on flat grounds, and more complex designs were introduced, with the most popular one being the keyhole pattern.

These exceptional tombs varied in size, with the smallest measuring about 15 meters (49 miles) in diameter and the biggest measuring at least 821 meters (2,693 miles) long while being encircled by three moats. The latter was also considered the largest kofun with a keyhole design, and it belonged to Japan's sixteenth emperor, Nintoku. Given its massive size, it is not a surprise that the construction took nearly twenty years to complete. Inside of a kofun is normally a stone-lined chamber that often houses a coffin containing the remains of the deceased. Since the ancient Japanese believed in life after death, they would fill the tombs with various precious items, ranging from swords, armors, and shields to bronze mirrors, bracelets, and beads. Haniwa, a type of terracotta clay figure, were also placed around a kofun since they were believed to have the ability to protect the deceased from any kind of danger in the afterlife.

The kofun of Emperor Nintoku.

Copyright © National Land Image Information (Color Aerial Photographs), Ministry of Land, Infrastructure, Transport and Tourism, Attribution, via Wikimedia Commons: https://commons.wikimedia.org/wiki/File:NintokuTomb.jpg

Although Emperor Nintoku's kofun is believed to be the biggest of all, it was not the oldest one ever found. The Hashihaka kofun located in Nara Prefecture is the oldest keyhole kofun ever discovered, but whose remains were interred there remains a mystery. While some believed that the ancient tomb belonged to the first king of the Yamato Kingdom, the records in the *Nihon Shoki* claim that the tomb belonged to a princess named Yamato-totohi-momoso-hime-no-mikoto.

An aerial view of the Hashihaka kofun.

The princess, who was the daughter of Emperor Kōrei, the seventh legendary emperor of Japan, was also believed to be the wife of Ōmononushi, a Shinto kami of Mount Miwa. The pair, however, never met each other during the day, as the kami refused to appear before his wife in his true form. And so, every night, Ōmononushi would travel to meet with the princess until one day, she demanded him to reveal his true form. Agreeing to the request, Ōmononushi hid in a box—some sources suggest he made his way into the princess's comb case—but the princess was terrified to discover that her husband's true form was a snake. Embarrassed that his wife's reaction upon seeing him was to scream aloud, Ōmononushi slithered his way back into the mountains. The princess was no doubt saddened by the incident. As she took a seat, she accidentally sat on a pair of chopsticks, which stabbed her in her private parts, leading to her death. Her remains were buried in the tomb called Hashihaka, which directly translates to "Chopstick Grave."

There is another theory involving the mystery of this tomb. Some archaeologists claimed that the Hashihaka tomb was actually built for Queen Himiko, who could be the very same person as Princess Yamato-totohi-momoso-hime-no-mikoto. According to Chinese records, a massive tomb was built by the people of Yamatai. It measured at least a hundred paces in diameter, which is almost the same size as the Hashihaka kofun. However, this is but a theory; as of now, no one can conclude whose remains were interred in the tomb. But we can safely say that whoever was buried in the kofun definitely played a role in the rise of the Yamato Kingdom.

The Rise of the Yamato Kingdom

Like the legendary Kingdom of Yamatai, almost every single clan across the Japanese archipelago was led by a religious figure. This includes the Yamato clan. Around the 4th century CE, the Yamato clan rose to power and successfully spread its wings to many other regions in Japan. Legend has it that their success had something to do with a folk hero that went by the name of Yamato Takeru. His entire story was told in the Japanese chronicles of *Kojiki* and *Nihon Shoki*. Yamato Takeru, who was born Prince Ōsu, was one of the sons of the twelfth emperor of Japan, Emperor Keiko.

His story began when he brutally killed his older brother named Ōsu with only his bare hands. Upon discovering the murder, Emperor Keiko decided to punish his son but not with his own hands. Fearing his temper, the emperor sent Yamato Takeru on a mission to conquer the other regions of Japan while secretly hoping that his own son would die while doing so. The prince was sent to the region of Kumaso, where he easily defeated its leaders while they were at a drinking party. With his mission a success, he returned to the emperor, who soon sent him out again on another quest in the eastern region, where he was to eliminate those who opposed the imperial court.

An illustration of Yamato Takeru and the legendary Kusanagi sword.
https://commons.wikimedia.org/wiki/File:Yamato-Takeru-with-Sword-Kusanagi-no-Tsurugi-by-Ogata-Gekko.png

Finally learning that his father had wished nothing but death upon him, Yamato Takeru journeyed to Ise Province and met with the high priestess of Amaterasu, Yamatohime-no-mikoto, who was also his aunt. There, he lamented his father's ill intentions. Feeling sorry for the prince, the high priestess granted him the Kusanagi sword, a sacred weapon obtained by Susanoo, the kami of storms. And so, he continued his quest to the eastern region, where he was suddenly caught in the middle of an ambush. Thanks to the sacred sword, Yamato Takeru successfully countered the attacks, and he managed to conquer many regions in the east. Despite his success, the hero was said to have done atrocious things to the kami of Mount Ibuki, which led him to be cursed with a mysterious illness that soon led to his death.

While the story of how Yamato Takeru conquered the regions is mostly considered a legend, history tells us that the Yamato clan possibly rose to power due to their blossoming agricultural activities. Intermarriage happened between the Yamato people and powerful figures from other clans throughout the Japanese archipelago. Later on, more and more kofun tombs emerged across the islands. These tombs were considered a symbol of the Yamato; at the time, only those from this clan would be buried in this method. This signifies the growing power of the Yamato clan. The Yamato eventually conquered almost all of Japan, from Kyushu to Tohoku.

During this period, Japan welcomed many immigrants from the Korean Peninsula, who brought new tools and precious knowledge of farming. The Yamato employed these immigrants in their lands and made use of the new farming knowledge they brought with them. With the help of the immigrants, the Yamato Kingdom managed to boost its agricultural economy and wealth. The Yamato rulers realized that they were a step closer to unifying Japan since they had most of the regions under their grasp. However, during this time, Japan was more of a confederation of many other clans. The Yamato ruler was placed on top of this hierarchy, but other clans had their own power and could control their lands how they preferred. Some clans even owned more lands than the imperial family. And so, the Yamato rulers introduced a new bureaucratic ranking system.

In the Yamato court, the head of the Yamato clan took the mantle as an emperor, and only those descended from the clan were able to sit on the Chrysanthemum Throne. As for the other powerful clans or uji, they were granted a kabane, a nobility title. The old clans, such as the Soga and the Katsuragi, were given the kabane title of Omi, which was also a title given to those who had blood relations with the imperial family. Another kabane title, Muraji, was given to the clans of Otomo, Nakatomi, and Mononobe, which claimed to be descendants of the gods. Then, a single influential figure or leader of these two kabane, Omi and Muraji, would be chosen to carry the title of Ōomi and Ōmuraji, respectively. These two figures acted as direct advisors or ministers to the Yamato court and held a very high position in the government. Aside from these top-tier clans, the mid-level clans were also granted their own kabane, such as Kimi or Atae.

Life in the Kofun Period

While kabane titles were bestowed upon those who held power in a certain clan, the lives of the commoners were not much different compared to the previous period. Most of them still lived in simple dwellings with thatched roofs, except this time around, they replaced their fire pits with a proper earthen stove called a kamado. This kind of oven lasted throughout the centuries and is still used today. The people supported themselves by farming, fishing, and sometimes hunting. Iron became even more common in this period, and it was often used to create farming tools, such as spades, hoes, and sickles.

The people also devoted themselves to nature, a belief they carried over from the Yayoi period. Purification was turned into one of the most important aspects of their beliefs to the point where, every now and then, the Yamato court would send out religious officials to different regions to recite prayers to the communities and rid them of impurities. Other than purification, religious practices during this period included exorcisms and divination rituals, as well as fortune-telling by using burned animal bones.

Punishment systems were further developed, with flogging and banishment being the most common punishments. There were, however, more harsh punishments that existed in this period. When someone committed serious crimes, such as adultery, arson, or murder, the person was almost always sentenced to death. The perpetrator would either be half-buried in the ground before being stoned to death or had their heads sawed off by a piece of bowstring. But how did the community decide who was guilty and who was innocent?

Whenever a dispute between two people could not be resolved privately, they had no other choice but to go through the trial of ordeal or kugatachi. In this trial, the two people accused of being involved in a certain crime were to stand in front of a pot of boiling water and swear their innocence to the gods. Once that was done, they had to put their hands into the boiling water. The one whose hand was wounded the most was considered guilty, as the people believed the gods would protect only the innocent one. The legendary Japanese statesman, Takenouchi no Sukune, was said to have cleared his name from an accusation using this method. The boiling water could also be replaced with a pot containing a poisonous snake. The person who got bitten by the snake would be the one guilty of the crime and must accept their punishment.

Contact with China and Korea

The Kofun period was when Japan started to move toward a more cohesive state. The influences and new knowledge brought by those from the Asian mainland had no doubt helped the people realize their goal, which was to become a more recognized state. By the end of the 4th century, the Yamato state was entangled in a rivalry between three kingdoms in the Korean Peninsula.

The map of the ancient kingdoms of Korea.

Myself, CC BY-SA 3.0 https://creativecommons.org/licenses/by-sa/3.0 via Wikimedia Commons: https://commons.wikimedia.org/wiki/File:History_of_Korea-476.PNG

These kingdoms were known as Goguryeo (Koguryo), which was the largest among the three; Silla, which dominated the southeastern part of the peninsula; and Baekje in the southwest. On the southern tip of the peninsula was a loose confederation of smaller states known as the Kaya region, which also acted as a doorway for the Yamato to the Korean Peninsula.

The main reason behind the Yamato government's involvement in the war was so they could secure the many sources of iron found in the Korean Peninsula. The Yamato state formed an alliance with the

Kingdom of Baekje and went against both Silla and Goguryeo. The Yamato managed to expand their power in some regions in the Korean Peninsula, but they were forced to withdraw by the 6th century CE due to the increasing power of Silla's military forces, which were aided by the Tang dynasty of China.

As for Yamato's contacts with China, the *Book of Song*, a collection of historical records in the Liu Song dynasty, mentioned that five Yamato kings had actively sent them tribute in order to gain recognition and solidify their status as kings or emperors. According to scholars, some of the five Yamato kings could have been the same legendary emperors of Japan named in the *Nihon Shoki*.

By the 5th century CE, the Yamato state once again welcomed another set of migrants from the Asian mainland. These people, also referred to as Toraijin, decided to migrate to the archipelago to escape the raging wars and famine plaguing their homeland. With this migration, the lands of Japan were introduced to new technologies and knowledge, such as irrigation and reservoir construction techniques, shipbuilding, and blacksmithing. Most of the Toraijin were employed by the Yamato court and earned their own kabane titles.

The Kingdom of Baekje also shared a wide variety of knowledge with the Yamato state. Horses were introduced to the archipelago during this period. Through a messenger, the king of Baekje sent a few gifts to the Yamato court. These gifts were literary works called the *Analects of Confucius* and the *Thousand Character Classic*, which is a poem written in Chinese characters. With these two literary works, the Japanese kanji system was born. Japan was finally able to send written diplomatic documents and engraved items to friendly states.

However, the writing system was not the only thing that was introduced by the king of Baekje. A statue of Buddha and Buddhist scriptures were also sent to the court of Yamato, which kickstarted the spread of Buddhism across Japan. This caused a serious quarrel between the state's two main clans.

Chapter 6 – Haniwa and Its Importance

Funeral customs and burial rites have come a long way. Even in this modern world of ours, we can find more than a dozen different ceremonies taking place after the death of a person. If we travel back to ancient times, however, we can discover many funerary practices that might appear normal to those ancient civilizations but perhaps seem strange to our modern minds.

The ancient Egyptians, for instance, had a rather lavish approach to death; they believed that death was not the end and that they would resume their life in the Field of Reeds. Thus, they would often bury the deceased in a tomb filled with goods, ranging from glimmering jewelry to food and weapons. The goods left in these graves acted as supplies for the dead, allowing them to move on to their next life in the celestial field. The ancient Greeks, on the other hand, believed in the underworld or the Land of the Dead. According to legends, the dead must pay a fee to the ferryman named Charon so that they can be transported across the River Styx and reach the underworld. So, when a person died, they would often be buried with an obol, a type of ancient coin that was put inside of the deceased's mouth or over their eyes.

The ancient Japanese also had their own funeral customs. Pit and jar burials were common during the Jomon period, and historians even claim that there were cases where the dead would be buried under a pit house, although the house would then be abandoned. Over time, the ancient

Japanese changed the way they honored the dead, especially those who had high status and power. Soon, burial mounds and more complex tombs could be seen scattered throughout the archipelago, especially near the end of the Yayoi period and throughout the Kofun period.

As explained in the previous chapter, the Kofun period earned its name from the distinctive tombs and burial mounds discovered in Japan. While most of these tombs were significantly massive and could span hundreds of meters, another unique feature that made them even more interesting was the terracotta clay figures surrounding the upper section of these tombs. They are known today as Haniwa.

Although archaeologists have discovered many of these clay figures around the tombs, no one is entirely certain of the origins of Haniwa. A writing system did not yet exist during this period, so there was no written record that could tell us the purpose of these clay figures. Some suggest that its origins could be traced back to the Jomon period when the Japanese people created the Dogū, a type of humanoid figure also made out of clay. However, the production of Dogū stopped as soon as the period ended, as archaeologists have not yet found one that dates back to the Yayoi period. The only story that tells us the origin of Haniwa can be seen in the *Nihon Shoki.* The record, however, was written centuries after Haniwa was first introduced, so whether or not the story bears the truth remains unknown.

The Man Possibly Responsible for the Creation of Haniwa

Emperor Suinin, the eleventh legendary emperor of Japan, was said to have contributed several things to Japan. He was the one who instructed his daughter, Yamatohime-no-mikoto, to create a shrine for Amaterasu, leading to the construction of the Ise Grand Shrine. He is also regarded as the one who created sumo wrestling, as the first-ever sumo match was held during his reign.

The story of the first creation of Haniwa began when Emperor Suinin received the news of his half-brother's death. During his reign, it was completely normal for a great number of attendants or servants to follow their lords to the grave. Some suggest that these people were buried alive in the burial mounds, while others claim that they were buried only up to their necks so that they could mourn and wail for the death of their lord. This tradition could even be seen when Queen Himiko died; at least a hundred of her servants were sacrificed for her burial. As for Emperor Suinin, this tradition was carried out when his brother died. Witnessing the many sacrifices, he began to wonder if there was a way to replace the old tradition.

Emperor Suinin was later devastated due to yet another death of a loved one. This time around, it was his wife, Empress Hibasuhime. Once again, the thought of replacing the sacrificial tradition came to mind. The emperor then consulted his ministers and asked for advice regarding the tradition. They suggested sticking with the old ways. Shortly after, the emperor heard another idea from Nomi no Sukune, the legendary sumo wrestler. He suggested that they leave the tradition behind, especially since they were aiming to create a more humane government. He then went on to gather three hundred potters and instructed them to create clay figures.

After being presented with the clay figures, Emperor Suinin agreed to replace the old sacrificial tradition. Instead of sacrificing servants and loyal attendants, the clay figures were used to accompany the dead. To thank Nomi no Sukune for his brilliant idea, the emperor granted him the kabane title of Haji. He would be responsible for overseeing the pottery workers and funeral customs.

How Haniwa Were Made and the Theories of What They Were Used For

Somewhat similar to the previous pottery items found in the Jomon period, the process of making a Haniwa started with a lump of water-based clay. The Japanese used a specific technique called wazumi, which required them to create the image of the Haniwa one layer at a time. The basic shape of the Haniwa, which was normally under a meter tall, was created first. Once it was done, the potters would move on to shape the protruding parts of the figure before they were attached to the main body of the Haniwa created earlier. Other carvings were then added to create more details, and any rough surfaces were smoothed out with a wooden paddle. When they were done with the design, the Haniwa would then be fired at a low temperature.

Since the clay figures had to be fired at a relatively low temperature, it would have taken a long time until you could finally see the end result. So, most emperors and elite members of the ruling family would often plan ahead for their tombs. Haniwa would be prepared way before their deaths so that everything would be ready when death finally came to take these people away from the land of the living.

While the *Nihon Shoki* briefly explained that Haniwa were used to replace an old tradition where slaves were sacrificed and buried with their masters, another theory suggests that these clay figures were actually used to protect the deceased. There is also another theory that claims the opposite; instead of defending the remains of the dead and ensuring the tomb was never disturbed, the Haniwa were actually arranged surrounding a kofun tomb so that they could protect the living from the spirits of the dead. Science, however, suggests that Haniwa were used to avoid corrosion, but which one of these theories is the most accurate remains unknown.

The Evolution of the Haniwa

Aside from providing us with an insight into the evolving art and culture of the Kofun period, the shapes and images of these clay figures also give us a chance to take a glimpse into the early lives of the Japanese people: how they were dressed, what their houses looked like, what their beliefs were. In the early years after the introduction of Haniwa (250–450 CE), they were only made in simple shapes. Many cylindrical Haniwa were discovered by archaeologists, and these are considered to be the earliest forms. As the years passed and bigger kofun tombs started to emerge throughout the archipelago, the Haniwa evolved into more elaborate structures—some even measured more than 1.5 meters (nearly 5 feet) tall.

The Haniwa began to appear in the forms of animals, humans, and even buildings. Clay figures in the shape of a horse were discovered by archaeologists. The horse's tack, collar, saddle, and what seems to be bells resembled those of the Korean Peninsula. Birds, monkeys, wild boars, rabbits, and ships were also common shapes of a Haniwa. Although the outer perimeter of the kofun tombs was often surrounded by cylindrical Haniwa, certain mounds feature house-shaped Haniwa at the center, which could be purposely arranged to resemble a small village or settlement once overseen by the owner of the kofun. These house-shaped Haniwa normally had a thatched roof, a square base complete with simple walls, an entrance, and a couple of rectangular holes as windows.

A Haniwa in the form of a horse.
Gary Todd from Xinzheng, China, CC0, via Wikimedia Commons:
https://commons.wikimedia.org/wiki/File:Haniwa_Terracotta_Figurine_(29768242740).jpg

A house Haniwa.
Gary Todd from Xinzheng, China, CC0, via Wikimedia Commons:
https://commons.wikimedia.org/wiki/File:Haniwa_Terracotta_Figurine_(30028141366).jpg

Perhaps the most famous Haniwa figure is the warrior dressed in early Japanese-style armor called *kikkō*. Excavated from a site in Gunma Prefecture, this Haniwa warrior stands on an elevated cylindrical base and has a height of over 130 centimeters (53 inches) in total. In one of his hands is a sword, while the other could be holding a broken piece of a bow. The wrist guard on his left arm was probably worn to protect himself from the bowstring once he shot an arrow. At the back of the Haniwa was a bow quiver, which further suggests that he was an archer.

Due to this, it is thought that fully armored soldiers had already existed during this period. It could also be a depiction of a soldier from the Mononobe clan, who was entrusted by the emperor to oversee the Yamato Kingdom's military affairs. Some also suggest influence from the Asian mainland; its hip-length armor, gauntlets, and riveted helmet resembled the soldiers of the Chinese horsemen of the Six Dynasties period.

Of course, the designs of Haniwa were not only limited to warriors and soldiers. There were also figures that resembled working farmers, musicians, dancers, and mothers carrying her child in her arms. A female shaman was one of the most intricate forms of Haniwa ever discovered by archaeologists. They would often be seen with a flat headdress and a colored tattoo on their faces. The protruding pendants could symbolize either stone or glass beads, and the flat, circular discs hanging from the Haniwa's belt could represent mirrors, especially since they were considered sacred in Shinto beliefs.

Haniwa of a female shaman.

Haniwa in the Modern World

The number of kofun tombs might have declined as the years passed, and so did the existence of Haniwa. Indeed, it took many years for Haniwa to be rediscovered by modern archaeologists, but its unique design and mysteries did not only invite us to take a look at the early lives of the ancient Japanese but also opened the door for modern artists to appreciate the arts of the ancient Japanese people. Many began to show interest and saw the aesthetic significance in Haniwa. Isamu Noguchi, a renowned American artist in the mid-20th century, fell in love with the beauty of Haniwa when he first saw one during his visit to Kyoto Museum in 1931. From then onward, the American artist began to study more about the clay figure to the point where he had created several masterpieces heavily inspired by Haniwa. *Time* even named Haniwa a form of "pure art."

By the end of the 20th century, Haniwa began to receive even more attention from the world. It is safe to say that Haniwa are now forever immortalized, as they have been featured in an array of entertainment mediums, ranging from films, tv shows, video games, and even trading cards, though they are often depicted in a less complex form compared to the ones discovered from excavation sites and displayed behind glass in a museum.

Chapter 7 – Life in the Asuka Period

Assassinations, murders, conflicts, great changes, and the spread of Buddhism—these are the words that might come to mind whenever the Asuka period is mentioned. The Asuka period only lasted nearly two centuries (538-710 CE), but one cannot deny that it brought many changes to Japan, allowing it to become the flourishing country that we know today. Although the period started off rough, with clans constantly at each other's throats, spilling blood for the sake of power, the Japanese archipelago soon witnessed a gradual improvement in both political and social organizations as time passed. Buddhism was introduced to the Japanese people, greater ties were made with China, new ruling systems were established to minimize corruption in the Yamato government, and new art, architecture, and other facets of culture surfaced.

The Conflict between the Soga and Mononobe Clans

The origins of the Soga remain uncertain. They claimed to be descendants from a powerful clan named Katsuragi, while some scholars believe they were initially a family from the Korean Peninsula that eventually made the Asuka region their base. They then went on to form alliances with the Toraijin clans and made use of their knowledge to establish themselves as one of the greatest clans in the Yamato state. The Soga clan rose to greater heights of power during the reign of Emperor Kinmei. Soga no Iname, the clan's leader, who also held the title of Ōomi, was said to have strengthened his clan's power and ties to the imperial family by marrying his two daughters to Emperor Kinmei. To Soga no Iname's delight, his two daughters eventually bore children with the emperor; three of them sat on the Chrysanthemum Throne. Through marital relationships, Soga no Iname successfully increased the Soga clan's status and influence throughout Japan.

The Mononobe clan, on the other hand, claimed to be descendants of the gods, and like the Nakatomi, they held strong Shinto beliefs. Since this was another influential clan in the Yamato state, the position of Ōmuraji was often filled by the leaders of the Mononobe clan, which means they were put in charge of military matters.

When a statue of Buddha arrived in the archipelago in 538 CE, the ruling emperor at that time, Emperor Kinmei, was torn between spreading the new religion to his people or rejecting it completely and sticking to Shintoism. So, he consulted his two high ministers, the Ōomi, Soga no Iname, and the Ōmuraji, Mononobe no Okoshi. Soga no Iname had close contact with people from the Asian mainland, and he right away agreed to accept the new religion. Mononobe no Okoshi strongly disagreed, as he claimed that adopting Buddhism would anger the Shinto gods. After listening to both of his ministers' explanations, the emperor decided to entrust the Buddha statue to Soga no Iname for the time being. Soga no Iname soon built a brand-new Buddhist temple. The Ōomi kept the Buddha statue in the temple and began to adopt the new religion. At the same time, a terrible plague took over the lands, killing many of the inhabitants.

Mononobe no Okoshi saw the plague as a misfortune brought by the Shinto gods as a result of blindly accepting the new religion. He voiced this belief to Emperor Kinmei, who later gave him permission to resolve the matter. Without delay, Mononobe no Okoshi burned down the Buddhist temple built by his rival and cast the Buddha statue into the river, thus starting a war between the Soga and Mononobe clans.

Many years passed by, and the conflict between the two clans had only gotten worse. After the death of Soga no Iname, his son, who went by the name Soga no Umako, continued his legacy. Meanwhile, the title of Ōmuraji passed to Mononobe no Moriya. When Emperor Yōmei (the son of Emperor Kinmei and the thirty-first emperor of Japan) died, another dispute erupted between the two powerful clans. Soga no Umako was planning to place his nephew on the throne, while Mononobe no Moriya decided to enthrone another candidate, Prince Anahobe.

However, the dispute came to an end when Soga no Umako assassinated Prince Anahobe, which allowed his nephew, Sushun, to ascend to the Chrysanthemum Throne.

The feud between the two clans did not stop there. Soga no Umako decided to end the conflict once and for all, and he rallied his allies in the imperial court and attacked the Mononobe residence. War was waged with Mononobe no Moriya, who led his troops while firing arrows from on top of a tree. The Soga were forced to retreat more than once; the Mononobe clan was quite powerful when it came to their military. However, legend has it that the tides were about to turn when the fourteen-year-old Prince Shōtoku, a devout Buddhist, began to pray for Soga's victory. Perhaps Prince Shōtoku's prayer was heard, as shortly after, an arrow struck Mononobe no Moriya, which led to his death. With their leader gone, the Soga clan managed to destroy the entire Mononobe family. The victory of the Soga marked the beginning of the spread of Buddhism across Japan.

The fall of the Mononobe clan also meant the abolishment of the Ōmuraji title. Soga no Umako no doubt held the highest power in the imperial court, and his growing influence somehow worried Emperor Sushun. One day, a wild boar was presented before the emperor, and as he held a *kōgai* (a type of Japanese hairdressing tool) to stab the boar's eye, he muttered something that drew Soga no Umako's attention. The emperor said that one day, he would kill a man that he hated just as he killed the poor boar. Soga no Umako quickly came to the conclusion that he was the person the emperor was speaking of and that, sooner or later, he would be deposed and replaced by someone else. So, the Ōomi planned another assassination. The emperor was killed by a man named Yamato no Aya no Koma. With a vacancy on the throne, Soga no Umako put his niece, who was also the younger sister of Emperor Yōmei, on the throne. The empress was known by the name Suiko.

Empress Suiko

Toyomike Kashikiya hime no Mikoto, more famously known as Empress Suiko, was the thirty-third ruler of Japan and the first woman to ascend to the Chrysanthemum Throne. The empress ruled after the murder of her half-brother, Emperor Sushun, in 592 until she passed away in 628. Like those from the Soga clan, Empress Suiko was also pro-Buddhist. Some even claimed she had taken the vows of a Buddhist nun before accepting the throne. She highly encouraged the influence of

Chinese culture across the archipelago.

The following year after her ascension to the throne, a regent was appointed to assist her; this position was given to none other than Prince Shōtoku. Empress Suiko and her regent are often credited with the spread of Buddhism in Japan. In just the span of two years, the empress issued the Flourishing Three Treasures Edict, which established Buddhism as Japan's national religion. From there, the religion thrived throughout every part of the archipelago, and new temples were constructed. More Buddhist monks and scholars were employed by the government, with most of them carrying influences from China. These foreign cultures then blended with the Japanese traditional cultures, resulting in the Asuka culture.

The empress, however, did not shun those who still held strong beliefs in Shintoism. In fact, Buddhism and Shintoism coexisted peacefully during her reign. It was said that when a devastating earthquake struck Yamato Province back in 599, the empress ordered several constructions of Shinto shrines in honor of the earthquake kami.

Although many viewed her as merely a puppet under the influence of Soga no Umako, the empress was actually a strong political leader. Soga no Umako once requested Kazuraki no Agata, an imperial territory, to be granted to him, but the empress had no issues rejecting the Ōomi's request. This shows that the empress was not entirely powerless.

Asuka Culture, Art, and Architecture

Foreign influences, especially those from China and Korea, played a prominent role in developing the unique Asuka culture. At that time, Japan employed many Korean architects to construct new structures and even gardens. Empress Suiko once commissioned a Korean craftsman to build the very first palace garden in Japan. Heavily influenced by China, the garden featured a pond and an artificial mountain that represented Mount Mera, a sacred five-peaked mountain in Buddhist cosmology. Buddhist structures and statues were also common in Japan by this period, with most of them being created out of wood and gilded bronze.

Japan absorbed influences from other parts of the globe, such as ancient Greece and India. This can be seen in Hōryū-ji Temple, which was built by Prince Shōtoku in 607. It featured pillars similar to those found in ancient Greece's Parthenon. The Tori style, named after Japan's first and greatest sculptor, Kuratsukuri Tori, also emerged during the Asuka period. Influenced by sculptures from the Northern Wei, Tori's best masterpiece was the Shaka Triad, which was built in 623 and served as a memorial for Prince Shōtoku.

Hōryū-ji in Nara Prefecture, Japan.

The Asuka period also introduced many unique paintings that were influenced by Buddhism. One example was Tamamushi-no Zushi, also known as the Jewel-Beetle Shrine. Resembling a miniature shrine, Tamamushi-no-Zushi housed a Buddha sculpture, where people often placed a range of offerings in front of it, such as rice, vegetables, tea, and flowers. Unfortunately, we can no longer take a glimpse of the old Buddha statue since it has been lost; some said that it was stolen in the 10th century.

However, the most prominent feature of the shrine can still be found today. On the lower part of the shrine were several panels containing paintings that depicted scenes from the previous lives of Buddha. One of the most popular ones is a painting of Prince Mahasattva jumping off a cliff to save a tigress and her cubs from starvation.

A panel on the lower left of Tamamushi-no Zushi depicting Prince Mahasattva sacrificing himself to save a starving tigress.

https://commons.wikimedia.org/wiki/File:Tamamushi_Shrine_(lower_left).jpg

With the existence of a writing system, which was introduced during the late Kofun period, the Japanese, especially the nobles and elites, were now able to read, write, and keep written records of history and literature. This no doubt led to a more developed nation. The art of poems also began to see its beginnings during this period, which was later compiled in the *Manyoshu* circa 760.

The Twelve Cap Ranks

Before the establishment of the Twelve Cap Ranks in the imperial court, the title of kabane was mostly hereditary. If one was born into a mid-level clan, it was nearly impossible to obtain a higher rank, no matter one's achievements and success. The Twelve Cap Ranks system was created to rectify this. Instead of earning titles based on family lines, this system allowed a person to be promoted based on their merit and individual achievements.

The written Japanese records did not exactly mention who established the system, but many historians believe that, under the blessings of the empress, Prince Shōtoku and Soga no Umako were the ones who reinforced this new system after witnessing it being used by the Sui dynasty of China and the kingdoms of Korea, Baekje and Goguryeo.

Under this system, officials were required to wear silk caps of different colors that signified their ranks. Some say that it was the color of the feather on their caps that differentiated them, not the cap itself. Nevertheless, each of the ranks was named after six Confucian virtues, and each of them was divided into two lower ranks.

The Seventeen Article Constitution

In 604, a year after the introduction of the Twelve Cap Ranks, came the Seventeen Article Constitution. Drafted by Prince Shōtoku, who infused the influences of Confucian principles and the understandings of Buddhism, the constitution's sole purpose was to ensure a smoothly running government. Japan was moving toward a unified state, one that was ruled by a single sovereign. Through this constitution, the emperor's position was strengthened, as they were regarded as the highest authority in the hierarchy.

Since the emperor or empress was placed on top, their subjects were to respect and obey their decisions and actions at all times. The imperial court's officials were to be employed based on their merits instead of heredity. The constitution also highlighted the responsibilities of the ruler and their officials.

Envoys to the Sui Dynasty

A century after Japan's last envoy to China, which had been deployed by the five kings of Wa, Prince Shōtoku (during the reign of Empress Suiko) was believed to have sent the first embassy to the Sui dynasty in 600. This event, however, was not recorded in the *Nihon Shoki*, but it was mentioned in the Chinese record called the *Book of Sui.*

During the embassy's visit, Emperor Wen asked the Japanese messenger about the nation's customs and government. After receiving an answer, the emperor was said to have had a different opinion of the way Japan was governed at that time. He thought the ruling system lacked justice and was completely irrational. Emperor Wen then urged the messenger to return to his land and have his king rectify his customs. This unfortunate embassy was probably the reason the visit was not included in the Japanese records. It could also be plausible that Prince Shōtoku decided to devise his two main reforms—the Twelve Cap Ranks and the Seventeen Article Constitution—in response to Emperor Wen's comments.

Another envoy was again sent to the Sui dynasty seven years later, and it was led by Ono no Imoko. When Ono no Imoko arrived in China, he presented a letter to Emperor Yang, the ruling emperor of the Sui dynasty at that time. The said letter began with the sentence: "The emperor of the land of the rising sun sends this letter to the emperor of the land where the sun sets."

This particular sentence irritated Emperor Yang due to the Japanese ruler using the word "emperor," which somehow indicated that they were on the same level. So, the Chinese emperor told his ministers of his wish to never set eyes on such a horrible letter ever again. But despite the emperor's response, the diplomatic relationship between China and Japan did not end there, as the Sui dynasty sent an embassy in return to Japan. This embassy was led by Hai Seisei. Although Emperor Yang did not give any direct response, the embassy sent to Japan showed that the Sui dynasty somehow recognized the ruler of Japan as an independent sovereign.

It is also believed that Emperor Yang sent a letter to the Japanese ruler through Ono no Imoko, but the diplomat claimed that the letter was lost at sea. Scholars suggest that he intentionally destroyed the letter, knowing that the unpleasant contents would enrage the empress. His action resulted in exile. However, Ono no Imoko was given amnesty soon after, and he had the honor of being promoted to the first grade of the Twelve Cap Ranks for his excellent service.

The following year, another embassy led by Ono no Imoko was sent to the Sui dynasty to accompany Hai Seisei back to his homeland. This time around, Ono no Imoko brought along several scholars and monks who extended their stay in China to gather new knowledge and skills. All of the knowledge obtained by the scholars were used to benefit Japan and kickstarted the many unique customs in Japan that we see today.

The Overbearing Power of the Soga Clan That Led to Their Destruction

After accomplishing many achievements in his life as a regent, Prince Shōtoku was finally laid to rest in 622. With the legendary prince gone, the power in the imperial court was almost entirely monopolized by the Soga clan. The clan was now led by Soga no Emishi, the son of Soga no Umako.

Soga no Emishi first displayed his disobedience and craving for power when he appointed his own son, Soga no Iruka, into the imperial court without consulting the empress and other high officials. The father and son then proceeded to construct residences high up on a hill, overlooking the imperial palace. This irritated many since it signified that they were above the imperial family. Soga no Iruka even went to the extent of referring to his sons as princes.

To make matters worse, Soga no Iruka laid an attack on the residence of Prince Shōtoku's son, Prince Yamashiro. The incident went horribly. Prince Yamashiro and his family were forced to commit suicide, thus ending the great Prince Shōtoku's direct bloodline.

These changes in the state were eyed by Nakatomi no Kamatari, an important statesman and aristocrat. After witnessing the growing power of the Soga clan and knowing that it could possibly lead Japan to its doom, Nakatomi decided to put an end to the clan's greedy monopoly once and for all. And so, he began plotting a strategy to overthrow the Soga clan by conspiring with the imperial prince, Naka no Ōe.

On July 10th, 645, Soga no Iruka attended a court ceremony in Daigokuden (the Great Hall of State), where he welcomed the diplomats arriving from the Korean kingdoms. Prince Naka no Ōe had hidden a spear in the hall. He bribed several palace guards and was waiting for an opportunity to get rid of Soga no Iruka. He had initially ordered four men to ambush Iruka, but it became clear that they had cold feet. The prince did not want to waste the opportunity, so he grabbed the hidden spear and severely wounded Iruka. The latter, however, did not die on the spot. He claimed to be innocent and begged Empress Kōgyoku (the ruling empress at this time) to hold an investigation. The empress agreed, and as she left the hall, the four armed men suddenly emerged and immediately killed Soga no Iruka.

The news of his son's death reached Soga no Emishi shortly after. He could not contain his despair, so he burned his entire residence and committed suicide. With that, the Soga clan was permanently erased, and the Japanese government was finally free of its power. However, this bloody incident (known in history as the Isshi Incident) was not the only thing planned by Prince Naka no Ōe and Nakatomi no Kamatari. Having successfully removed the Soga clan, the two men then moved on to the next step: reconstructing the Yamato government and transitioning into a new era.

Chapter 8 – The Spread of Buddhism

When speaking of Buddhism and its religious practices, many would immediately think of meditation, karma, reincarnation, and perhaps massive Buddha statues, which were built for Buddhism's many temples around the world. But truth be told, Buddhism is way more than just that. In fact, this two-and-a-half millennia religion consists of many complex yet amazing religious practices, beliefs, and principles that changed the course of many nations, including Japan. The origins of Buddhism can be traced back to the 5th century BCE, which makes it one of the oldest religions in the world. Today, Buddhism is practiced by over five hundred million people around the globe, with its influence most prominent in both East and Southeast Asia.

The Origin of Buddhism and How It Was Spread to the World

Buddhism began with a man who went by the name Siddhartha Gautama. He was initially a son of King Suddhodana and Queen Maya, the rulers of the ancient city named Kapilavastu. After his birth (circa 563 BCE), the king and queen were said to have been approached by an old hermit named Asita, who also served the king as his advisor. The hermit informed the royal pair of a prophecy, saying that their son bore a magnificent destiny. He would grow up to either become a powerful king or a spiritual leader if he ever saw the lives of those outside the palace compound.

As soon as King Suddhodana heard the prophecy, he decided to protect his son from seeing the sufferings of the world to prevent the prophecy from coming true. So, the prince remained within the palace for twenty-nine years of his life without having a single glimpse of life outside the palace gates. Not once did he ever witness suffering or any unpleasant experience. Some say that the king even went to the extent of sweeping away the fallen petals of a wilting flower and sending his sick and old servants away. Because of this, the prince was completely unaware of the process of aging, death, and even sickness.

However, it all changed one day when the prince listened to a musician sing about the wonders of the world. Enthralled by what could be on the other side of the palace walls, Siddhartha Gautama went to see the king and informed him of his wish to travel and see the world. Although the king was hesitant at first, he finally granted his son's wish. King Suddhodana told his son that in order to prepare himself to be the future king, he must see the world that he would soon be ruling.

During his travels, Siddhartha Gautama encountered the first of the Four Signs—a man who was coughing continuously. Since the prince had never witnessed any type of sickness before, he asked his royal charioteer about the man's condition. He was told that the man was battling a sickness and that it was completely normal since everyone would get sick at some point in their lives. The prince was, of course, surprised by this revelation, but he continued his journey across the kingdom.

Shortly after, he encountered the second and third of the Four Signs: an old man and a person who had just died. Again, the prince turned to his charioteer, who explained that these events were inevitable. Again, this revelation saddened Siddhartha Gautama, and he finally came to the realization that he, too, would experience the events he had just witnessed, as would the ones he loved most. Continuing on his adventure, Siddhartha Gautama encountered the fourth and last of the Four Signs: a wanderer who was sitting still. The wanderer had explained to the prince that he was meditating and that he had left all his material things behind to embark on a spiritual journey to discover an escape from life's suffering.

Inspired by the wanderer, Siddhartha Gautama began his own quest to search for ways to end suffering. After renouncing his wealth and nobility, he traveled far from his kingdom, trying to gain more and more knowledge until he finally decided to join five ascetics who were meditating deep in the woods. There, Siddhartha Gautama devoted himself to extreme deprivation, believing that he could finally achieve enlightenment this way. He fasted for six years and only survived by consuming a few grains of rice each day. However, Gautama soon realized that this deprivation was making his state worse than before. His ribs were visible due to long-term starvation, and his mind had slowed down. So, he left the ascetics and encountered a woman who offered him rice and milk. After restoring his energy, Siddhartha Gautama came to the conclusion that neither indulgence nor extreme deprivation could provide a path to enlightenment. It had to lay between those two extremes. This idea was later developed into the Middle Path.

Continuing his journey, Siddhartha Gautama came across a fig tree (now known as the Bodhi Tree), and he sat underneath it. After meditating for forty-nine consecutive days under the tree, Siddhartha Gautama finally attained enlightenment. At the age of thirty-five, Gautama became the "Awakened One," although he is more famously known as the Buddha.

The Buddha then returned to the five ascetics in the woods and shared his knowledge. This was when he delivered the first dharma and shared the Four Noble Truths. With his teachings, the ascetics soon became the first members of the Sangha (the Buddhist community), and Buddha went on to spread his teachings across the Gangetic Plain, doing so until he passed away at the age of eighty. Despite his death, Buddhism still spread throughout the world. Buddha's teachings were recorded in texts known as the sutras, which were later spread around the globe. They traveled from the Ganges region to Sri Lanka and other regions in Southeast Asia before moving on to both Central and East Asia. From there, Buddhism made its way to Mongolia, Russia, and finally to the countries in the west.

Buddhism in Japan

Japan saw the arrival of Buddhism through a diplomatic relationship with the Korean Peninsula. Ironically, when Buddhism, a religion often associated with peace and enlightenment, first emerged in the Japanese archipelago, it somehow caused a feud between two of the most important clans of the Yamato Kingdom. This was because Buddhism was not only used as a religion but also in political matters. Soga no Umako, for example, wished to spread the religion not only because of its teachings but also because he saw it as an opportunity to bolster his authority. Wars were waged, and blood was spilled. After the issue was resolved, the religion was spread to every corner of the islands, allowing Japan to embrace a more civilized and organized way of life.

Japan already had its own governing system before the arrival of Buddhism. The Yamato clan was the first to rise to power and claim the throne of Japan. They called themselves kings and queens—the term emperor was not officially used until the reign of Emperor Tenmu—but their power was often overshadowed by the powerful clan chieftains. However, with the arrival of Buddhism, the nation started to make some great changes, focusing more on solidifying the emperor's power and moving toward a centralized government.

Buddhism was then made the nation's official religion almost immediately after Empress Suiko first sat on the Chrysanthemum Throne. A proper constitution was compiled by Prince Shōtoku; it heavily relied on the combination of Buddhist beliefs and Confucian principles. Emperors and empresses were put at the top of the hierarchy, and they were to be obeyed and respected at all times. New ranking systems were introduced to appoint and promote officials. Moral codes were emphasized, and due to a more organized and stable political system, contacts were made with China. Monks were often sent there to learn and bring back knowledge in various fields.

Aside from the nation's governing system, Buddhism also greatly affected culture, art, and architecture. The level of literacy skyrocketed with the arrival of Buddhism, which had been introduced by Baekje. Japan finally had a writing system, and historical records could be compiled. The Japanese people, especially the elites and nobles, could now read and write. Paintings and sculptures became more intricate and complex, and they were heavily influenced by the new religion. Bronze statues of Buddha became a normal sight, along with paintings that depicted the previous lives of bodhisattvas (beings who delay their enlightenment to assist others). However, the most obvious change after the arrival of Buddhism could be seen in the construction of many temples across the Japanese islands.

After scoring a victory against the Mononobe clan and contributing to the establishment of Buddhism in Japan, Soga no Umako built Hōkō-ji (now known as Asuka-dera), one of the first and oldest fully-fledged Buddhist temples in Japan. Prince Shōtoku also honored his promise and erected a temple named Shitennō-ji in modern-day Osaka. By the 6th century CE, the archipelago housed a huge number of Buddhist temples and monasteries. The number continued to grow after the end of the Asuka period. Emperor Shōmu, who ruled during the Nara period, for instance, suggested the construction of provincial temples across the Japanese archipelago. He believed that Buddhism could put a stop to the political turmoil that was happening during his reign.

These temples were a sign of power. Before the arrival of Buddhism, kofun tombs were built for powerful chieftains, emperors, empresses, and the royal family. The size of these tombs signified their power and status, but as Buddhism spread, the construction of these massive tombs greatly decreased. Instead, temples were built, and they soon replaced the tombs. Bigger and greater temples meant powerful and influential emperors.

Buddhism vs. Shintoism

Although both Buddhism and Shintoism are closely knit together, there are still several differences that remind us that they are, indeed, two separate religions. True, Shintoism originated from Japan itself while Buddhism originated in India, but the biggest difference that completely distinguishes the two religions is their purpose.

Shintoism is the way of life. Its devotees hold their beliefs in the kami. They believe that by respecting the kami, their lives will be blessed. People are believed to be born as pure as the driven snow. The only thing that could stop them from receiving blessings is impurities. To put this in simple words, the purpose of Shintoism is for its devotees to lead an honest life and respect the kami. In return, their lives are blessed.

However, in Buddhism, the purpose is to reach enlightenment. Buddhists believe that life itself is a cycle of suffering. So, those who practice Buddhism strive to achieve a state of enlightenment so that they do not have to experience another cycle of suffering.

Other differences can be seen in the deities that are worshiped. Buddhism does not have any deities, although there are supernatural beings that can help guide someone to enlightenment. On the other hand, Shintoism has an unlimited number of kami since they believe that a spirit dwells in all of our surroundings. Buddhism also has clear doctrines and rules, while Shintoism has neither specific texts nor teachings and doctrines.

The two religions have interesting differences in the description of their lands of the dead or the underworld. Shinto's underworld is called Yomi, but unlike hell, it is not a place where the deceased face their mistakes and get punished. It is also not heaven; rather, it is merely a place where the dead carry on.

Buddhism has its own version of the underworld, and it is known as Jigoku. Buddhists believe in reincarnation, and they also believe that the state of their rebirth is intertwined with karma. If a person lived a life filled with good actions and deeds, they would be reborn in one of the heavenly realms. Bad karma, however, can lead a person to be reborn in Jigoku, although they won't remain there permanently. According to the scrolls made in the Heian period, Jigoku consisted of several different hells, each reserved for different types of crimes and wrongdoings. Murdering another human being or even an animal will cause the person to end up in Toukatsu Jigoku or the Reviving Hell, where they would be beaten to death repeatedly by an oni (a demon-like figure). The punishment will only stop when the karma of the misdeeds is all used up. Only then would the person be reborn into a better realm.

How Buddhism and Shinto Coexist

Shintoism was never erased from the lands of Japan with the arrival of Buddhism. In modern Japan, one can easily see a Shinto shrine placed side by side with Buddhist temples. Some Japanese people might identify themselves as Buddhist while still practicing Shinto rituals and attending Shinto-related ceremonies. Many even have Shinto shelves and Buddhist altars in their home. Wedding ceremonies often include Shinto rituals, while funeral rites tend to be entrusted to Buddhism. This proves that Buddhism and Shinto coexist peacefully.

But when exactly did the lines between these two religions blur? The amalgamation of these two religions is called Shinbutsu-shūgō, and it began during the Nara period when a *jingū-ji* or a shrine temple was first built. Before the people erected Daibutsu (Giant Buddha) in Tōdai-ji Temple, a Buddhist priest was said to have visited the Ise Grand Shrine to inform the kami Amaterasu of the construction. To help protect the temple, the priest installed a shrine of Hachiman, the Shinto kami of war and culture, in the compound of Tōdai-ji. Ever since this event, Shinto shrines have been constructed near Buddhist temples.

A depiction of Hachiman in Buddhist monk attire.
https://commons.wikimedia.org/wiki/File:S%C5%8Dgy%C5%8D_Hachiman.jpg

Later on, priests and monks began to link Shinto kami to Buddhas, as they believed that kami were actually reincarnations of the Buddha. They even suggested that the kami were suffering from the cycle of birth and that they needed to achieve enlightenment. From then on, monks would often read sutras to the kami to assist them in attaining enlightenment. The Shinto god Hachiman was absorbed into Buddhism, where he was also known as Hachiman Daibosatsu. In Buddhism, Hachiman was described as a kami who had become a bodhisattva, a being who had already attained enlightenment but delayed it so they could assist others. While he is often pictured wearing the official garments of an emperor or in full samurai armor while riding a horse, a depiction of Hachiman in Buddhist monk attire also exists.

Buddhism and Shintoism were separated again by order of the government during the Meiji period, as these rulers sought to minimize the spread of Buddhism. Many of the *jingū-ji* were destroyed during this time. However, many years later, the two religions began to coexist again, and it remains this way today.

Chapter 9 – Prince Shōtoku (574– 622)

Japan is renowned for its many legendary figures, both historical and mythical. Emperor Jimmu, for instance, is known as the first emperor of Japan mentioned in the *Nihon Shoki* and *Kojiki*. He was said to be a descendant of Amaterasu through her grandson Ninigi and had ascended to the throne as early as 660 BCE. However, due to the lack of archaeological evidence, historians and scholars alike agree that Jimmu and the eight other emperors who reigned after him did not exist and were merely myths. The same, however, cannot be said about Prince Shōtoku, another famous figure in Japanese history, although there are a few who question whether or not he was a real person.

Sometimes referred to as the founder of the Japanese nation and known as the father of Japanese Buddhism, Prince Shōtoku was, no doubt, the most well-known figure in Japan. Due to his efforts, Buddhism flourished throughout the Japanese archipelago, and his drive to establish a harmonious nation led to the introduction of the Twelve Cap Ranks and the Seventeen Article Constitution. These two political reforms set the foundation for Japan to move into a much more developed and organized nation. Prince Shōtoku's continuous efforts also led to Japan strengthening its relationship with China.

The Early Life of Prince Shōtoku

Prince Shōtoku was the son of Japan's thirty-first emperor, Emperor Yōmei, and his consort, who also happened to be his younger half-sister,

Princess Anahobe no Hashihito. Born in the year 574, the prince, according to the *Nihon Shoki,* was said to possess a variety of wonders. The prince was originally named Umayado no ōji; the name means the prince of the stable door (the prince was born in front of a stable). Legend has it that the prince had the ability to speak the moment he entered the world. It was also said that he performed a Buddhist prayer as soon as he turned two years old. The miracles did not stop there, as the ancient semi-mythical record even claims that Prince Shōtoku could listen to ten men speaking simultaneously. Not only was he able to comprehend each of the men's speeches, but he could also easily provide solutions that were rarely wrong.

But, of course, historians agree that these are but myths written to exaggerate the prince's early life. Rather than being born with exceptional gifts—some even claimed he was the reincarnation of Buddha—Prince Shōtoku was said to have been raised within the palace, spending most of his days gaining knowledge from a Korean monk. As he grew up, Prince Shōtoku became well-versed in Buddhist doctrine. Like the elites and nobles, the prince could read and write.

By the age of fourteen, Prince Shōtoku was already involved in the chaotic struggle between the two powerful Soga and Mononobe clans. The Soga clan, which was pro-Buddhist, was adamant about spreading Buddhism across Japan, while the Mononobe wished to remain true to Shinto beliefs. This disagreement resulted in terrible bloodshed, in which the Mononobe had the upper hand due to their experiences in military affairs. Upon witnessing the Soga clan retreat from the war multiple times, Prince Shōtoku, who was already a devout Buddhist at the time, decided to turn to the Shitenno (Four Heavenly Guardians of Buddhism) for help.

The young prince was said to have sat on the ground and spent hours carving statues of the Buddhist deities. Once Prince Shōtoku was done, he prayed to them for the Soga clan's victory. In exchange for their help, he promised to build a temple dedicated to the Four Heavenly Guardians as soon as the war was over. Miraculously, shortly after the prayer, a warrior from the Soga clan shot an arrow that hit the clan leader of the Mononobe right in the chest, which immediately marked the fall of the entire Mononobe clan. With this victory, Japan saw the birth of Buddhism, with Prince Shōtoku soon at the helm.

After the assassination of Emperor Sushun, Soga no Umako's own nephew, the throne was passed to Empress Suiko. She was said to have reigned over Japan for thirty-five years and oversaw great developments. But some believed that the empress could not have achieved her success without the help of Prince Shōtoku. A year after she was chosen as the empress, Prince Shōtoku was appointed as a regent, thus beginning the story of his many accomplishments that made him a famous historical figure.

Prince Shōtoku's Accomplishments and Contributions

When Prince Shōtoku rose to power, he was often pictured wearing Chinese-style court clothes, complete with official headgear and a pair of aristocratic shoes. It was also said that he carried a jeweled sword, which was an imperial symbol of power and authority. At times, the prince would be depicted in ceremonial attire, especially when he was lecturing on the Buddhist sacred texts.

As a regent, the prince went to extra lengths to ensure that his wish to turn Japan into a harmonious state came true. In 600, the ancient Chinese records state that Prince Shōtoku sent an envoy to China, where one of his messengers was asked by the Chinese emperor about Japan's customs. Upon discovering how the Japanese government ruled their lands at that time, the emperor immediately expressed his negative opinion. Some believed that Prince Shōtoku began to work on two of his biggest political reforms in response to the Chinese emperor's critics. And so, three years after the diplomatic envoy returned to the land of the rising sun, Prince Shōtoku introduced Japan to the Twelve Cap Ranks, as well as the first-ever Japanese constitution, the Seventeen Article Constitution, the following year.

Through the Twelve Cap Ranks, Prince Shōtoku made it possible for anyone to get promoted into higher positions in the imperial court, no matter their family lineage. By drafting the Seventeen Article Constitution, the prince managed to solidify the status of the emperor or empress and promote Buddhism as the state's official religion. Ever since he was young, Prince Shōtoku had been heavily influenced by both Buddhist teachings and Confucian principles. He put a lot of emphasis on the importance of harmony, so it is not a surprise that the constitution highlighted moral codes and social behavior. During his lifetime, the corruption rate was said to have decreased compared to the previous periods. No one was allowed to impose taxes on the people unless it was the emperor or empress. Indeed, not every single point in the constitution was practiced during the Asuka period, but it surely played a role in shaping the government in the later periods.

Prince Shōtoku also sent many monks and scholars abroad to gather useful knowledge and skills. He introduced the Chinese-style calendar to Japan and encouraged ties with China. Throughout his time as a regent, Prince Shōtoku sent at least five diplomatic missions to China. He invited scholars from the Asian mainland to Japan so that they could spread knowledge in astronomy, medicine, and geography. The prince himself turned into a scholar, as he has been credited with authoring the commentaries on the three Mahayana Buddhist scriptures: the Lotus Sutra, the Vimalakirti Nirdesa, and Queen Srimala Sutra.

As you might expect, Prince Shōtoku was a busy man. Staying true to his promise when he first carved the wooden statues of the Shitenno, Prince Shōtoku immediately started the construction of the Shitennō-ji Temple with the help of a few skilled carpenters from the Kingdom of Baekje. The temple, now named one of the oldest temples in Japan, still stands today, although it has gone through multiple restoration projects. With the completion of the Shitennō-ji Temple in 593, the prince then moved on to yet another project. He commissioned another Buddhist temple in Nara Prefecture, which we know as Hōryū-ji Temple. However, an account in the *Nihon Shoki* suggests that lightning once struck the temple, destroying it. But thanks to a reconstruction project done over a thousand years ago, we can still see it today.

The main hall and pagoda of Shitennō-ji.

Another important temple built by the regent prince was the Daruma-ji Temple in Kitakatsuragi. Founded in 613, this particular temple was believed to have been linked to a legend of a prince and a beggar. Before the existence of Daruma-ji, Prince Shōtoku was said to have met a beggar who was lying helplessly on the side of a road. Looking at the beggar, the prince decided to ask for his name, but the only response he received was complete silence. The beggar then claimed that he was dealing with extreme starvation. The prince, who was known for his compassion and selflessness, offered the starving beggar some food, drink, and a piece of his own clothing. The beggar, however, died shortly after, and Prince Shōtoku decided to give him a proper burial. A few days later, Prince Shōtoku returned to the very same spot where the beggar had been buried, but to the prince's surprise, his tomb was empty. He then noticed a piece of clothing that he had lent to the beggar earlier. It was perfectly folded and lying on the empty coffin. This mysterious event led many to believe that the beggar was, in fact, a reincarnation of Daruma Daishi, an important monk in Japanese Buddhism. After this incident, Prince Shōtoku built the Daruma-ji Temple at the same location as the tomb to honor the Buddhist figure.

Throughout his life, Prince Shōtoku was believed to have built a total of forty-six Buddhist temples and monasteries in Japan. Most of them not only served as places of worship but also as hospitals and places of lectures.

The Last Years of Prince Shōtoku's Life

In 620, Prince Shōtoku was believed to have worked with Soga no Umako to compile a collection of Japanese history. These compilations were known as *Kokki* (the "Record of the Nation") and *Tennōki* (the "Record of the Emperors"). Not much is known about these two records, except that they were later entrusted to the Soga clan. The *Tennōki* was completely destroyed years after it was compiled; this happened when Soga no Emishi committed suicide by burning his entire residence after hearing the news of his son's assassination. Although archaeologists reportedly found the remains of Soga no Emishi's burnt residence back in 2005, there was no sign of the ancient record. The *Kokki*, on the other hand, was saved from the fire by a person named Fune no Fubitoesaka, and it was later given to Prince Naka no Ōe.

Two years after the compilation of Japanese history, Prince Shōtoku fell ill. He passed away peacefully in his residence. He was only forty-eight years old. His family and the entire population of Japan grieved his death. An account in the *Nihon Shoki* says that everyone lamented the prince's death until their weeping echoed throughout the streets. No one was able to eat, as their appetite was replaced with ultimate sadness. The old cried as if they had lost their dearest child, while the young wept as if they had just witnessed their parents' passing. Even farmers let go of their hoes, spades, and sickles to wipe the tears from their gloomy faces. Everyone knew they had lost a great soul, but although Prince Shōtoku could no longer be seen walking the earth, his legacy lives on. His name is forever immortalized.

The Fate of Prince Shōtoku's Family

Since polygamy was the norm back in ancient Japan, especially among the elites and nobles, Prince Shōtoku was believed to have married more than one woman. Some sources suggested that he had at least four wives, with some of them being descendants of Empress Suiko and Soga no Umako's daughter. Prince Shōtoku's most well-known wife was named Kashiwade no Hokikimi no Iratsume, and she died a day before the prince. She was buried in the same mausoleum as her beloved husband.

It is uncertain how many children the prince had, but the most prominent one was his eldest, Prince Yamashiro. When Empress Suiko finally passed away, the Chrysanthemum Throne was yet again in dire need of a new ruler since she did not name a successor, although she did call upon Prince Yamashiro and Prince Tamura (the grandson of Emperor Bidatsu) to give them some advice. So, again, another dispute arose within the imperial court; Prince Yamashiro had all the rights to claim the throne, but so did Prince Tamura. The latter, however, gained the support of Soga no Emishi. To solve the dispute, an attack led by Soga no Iruka was carried out on Prince Yamashiro's residence, which resulted in the prince and his family committing suicide. This marked the end of Prince Shōtoku's bloodline, at least as far as we know.

Prince Shōtoku in the Modern World

Prince Shōtoku's tomb can be found in Taishi, a small town in Osaka, which is also where the remains of several emperors and their families were buried, such as Emperor Bidatsu, Kōtoku, and Yōmei. Once the news of Prince Shōtoku's death spread throughout the Japanese archipelago, Empress Suiko immediately instructed her subjects to build Eifuku-ji, a temple that could protect the prince's tomb. The temple, however, was burned down in the late 16th century, but most of the buildings were reconstructed afterward. Enshrined statues of the prince can be found in many of the temple's halls.

Prince Shōtoku's tomb is located at the end of the temple complex, and it has been visited by many important Buddhist monks over the years. Of course, like many other mausoleums of powerful figures in Japan, visitors are not allowed to enter the tomb and can only view it from a distance.

We can also find a great number of institutions named after the prince, such as the Shōtoku Gakuen University, Seitoku Junior College of Nutrition, and Seitoku University in Matsudo. His portraits were featured on Japanese yen, and many of his sculptures and paintings have survived. One of the most famous ones is a 13th-century sculpture of the prince when he was two years old. This sculpture was discovered in 1936 and is now safely housed in the Harvard Arts Museum (Cambridge, Massachusetts, USA). Interestingly, a number of sacred items were found stashed within the sculpture's body. Some of them were writings of prayers and poems and smaller sculptures.

An old sculpture of Prince Shōtoku at the age of two.
Daderot, Public domain, via Wikimedia Commons:
https://commons.wikimedia.org/wiki/File:Prince_Shotoku_(574-
622 AD) at Age Two, Japan, Kamakura period, c. 1292 AD, cypress, polychromy, rock-
crystal inlaid eyes - Arthur M. Sackler Museum, Harvard University - DSC01169.jpg

A special ceremony is held once a century to honor the prince. The ceremony is normally held at Hōryū-ji, the same temple founded by Prince Shōtoku himself, and it is often filled with many monks, musicians, and visitors. Ancient music is played throughout the ceremony, with various traditional dances accompanying the tunes.

It is safe to say that Prince Shōtoku's name will continue to echo throughout every corner of Japan. Some might say that certain parts of his life were only a myth, while others believe that he was extraordinarily gifted. But most would agree that Prince Shōtoku was a prominent figure in ancient Japan and that his contributions played a great role in shaping the nation.

Chapter 10 – The Taika Reforms of 645 CE

With the assassination of Soga no Iruka and the death of Soga no Emishi, the Yamato Kingdom could finally break free from their monopolistic power. Prince Naka no Ōe and his conspirator, Nakatomi no Kamatari, might have been able to let out a huge sigh of relief due to their success in overthrowing the Soga clan, but Empress Kōgyoku could not relax. The empress, who was also the mother of Prince Naka no Ōe, was shocked when the news about the two Soga leaders' deaths reached her, especially since one of them was murdered right in front of her throne. So, the empress decided to renounce her position as sovereign and urged her son, Prince Naka no Ōe, to replace her. Although it was an honor to be offered such a high position, the prince refused to take the position of emperor since he knew that after the Isshi Incident, all eyes were on him. He did not want the people to think that he slew Soga no Iruka because of his desire for the Chrysanthemum Throne. Thus, he passed the offer to his uncle, who soon became Emperor Kōtoku.

With Emperor Kōtoku installed on the throne in 645, a new era in Japan was born. The Taika era (also known as the era of great change) was proclaimed by the emperor himself, along with Prince Naka no Ōe and Nakatomi no Kamatari. It was Japan's first named era in history. While Naka no Ōe's uncle wore the crown, the prince stepped in as the nation's crown prince. Nakatomi no Kamatari, on the other hand, was appointed as Naidaijin, or the Interior Minister. With this new system, both the titles of Ōmuraji and Ōomi were abolished. They were replaced with the positions of Udaijin (Minister of the Right) and Sadaijin (Minister of the Left). The emperor also appointed two monks in the imperial court to serve as state scholars. These titles were given to Takamuko no Kuromaro and Minabuchi no Shōan, both of whom had traveled to China for a diplomatic mission in 608. The two stayed in China for over three decades and brought back valuable knowledge of political law and culture from the Asian mainland.

Taika Reforms

Modeled after Tang China, the Taika reforms were a set of doctrines established by Prince Naka no Ōe and Nakatomi no Kamatari. While they wished to unite Japan, extinguish corruption, and maintain an orderly and fair government system, the Taika reforms' main purpose was to exert the emperor's dominion throughout Japan and minimize the clan leaders' excessive power. In addition to the two state scholars, four articles were developed as part of the reforms:

I. The Abolishment of Private Land Ownership and the Kabane System

The central government introduced a new system called Kochi Komin sei, which directly translates to the public land system. Through this newly introduced system, clan leaders and members of the imperial family were no longer able to possess their own lands and subjects—they belonged to the state. Prince Naka no Ōe volunteered and surrendered his lands and estates to the government. The others followed in his footsteps and did the same thing.

The hereditary kabane titles, such as Ōmuraji and Ōomi, were no longer in use. Instead, the emperor was the only person who could grant titles and lands to someone. Those who served in the court as bureaucrats were also given a type of salary called Jikifu by the central government.

II. The Establishment of Provincial Governing Offices

The Japanese archipelago was divided into 66 imperial provinces and 592 counties. Instead of a single clan member, each province was overseen by a governor. Guardsmen called the sakimori were placed in the outer provinces, and post stations complete with stables and horses were constructed. These horses would be used by the guards across the country, especially if there was an urgent need to deliver messages and information.

III. Census Records

Under this article, the government was to conduct a census and keep records of not only the population but also information and data about land use. Rice cultivating lands known as kubunden were redistributed to every person across the country. They had to farm these lands and pay taxes to the government.

IV. Introduction to the New Tax System

The previous tax systems imposed by the local clan leaders in their respective territories were completely abolished and replaced with a uniform tax system called soyocho. This new system required all subjects to pay taxes in the form of rice and local specialty products. Later on, another tax system was introduced known as zoyo, which was paid in the form of conscripted labor. The number of days for mandatory labor differed according to the person's age. It was fifteen days for males aged between seventeen and twenty, thirty days for males older than sixty years old, and sixty days for those aged between twenty-one and sixty.

The reforms, of course, were not implemented as soon as it was established, but Prince Naka no Ōe's true aim was crystal clear; he wanted to unite the nation under a centralized government, allowing the emperor to hold absolute power over the nation.

Emperor Kōtoku's Death

When the emperor first rose to power, which was only two days after the Isshi Incident, he commissioned the construction of a new city in Naniwa (now known as Osaka). The capital was then moved to the new city under the order of Emperor Kōtoku. The emperor even sent diplomatic envoys to Tang China eight years after he ascended the throne, but most of the ships were said to have been lost at sea.

In the same year, however, the relationship between the emperor and the crown prince began to deteriorate. Prince Naka no Ōe had requested the emperor to move the capital back to the Yamato Province, but the emperor disagreed. Not taking no for an answer, the prince decided to move out of the current capital with many of his supporters and court courtiers. Emperor Kōtoku's wife, Empress Hashihito, was also said to have moved out of Naniwa. The emperor, who was now living in an almost empty palace, finally succumbed to illness in 654. The reactions of his subjects were unknown, although the *Nihon Shoki* describes the emperor as a gentle king, so it is likely some tears were shed. There was another vacancy on the throne. Many expected the crown prince would ascend next, but it was actually his mother who took the mantle, this time around under the name Empress Saimei.

The Battle of Baekgang

The three kingdoms of Korea had been engaged in wars with each other for over six centuries. Goguryeo owned a lot of territories in the north of the Korean Peninsula, and its people were known for their military prowess. Baekje, on the other hand, was well known for its wealth since it controlled the trade route between Korea, China, and Japan. The last kingdom of the three, Silla, was said to be the weakest among them. However, it finally formed an alliance with a powerful force in 650 and unexpectedly turned the tide of the centuries-long war.

The Kingdom of Silla first saw an opportunity to take control of the peninsula with the news of a newly formed dynasty in China. Silla formed an alliance with the Tang dynasty, which was already in a vicious rivalry with the Kingdom of Goguryeo. The joint forces raised their troops and successfully invaded Baekje in 660. The king was captured in the aftermath of the invasion. Baekje attempted to resist, but it failed terribly. However, another resistance movement was created, and this time around, the rebels sent messages to Japan, requesting military assistance to drive the united forces of Tang and Silla back to where they had started.

The call for help reached Empress Saimei, and she hastily gave orders to her subjects to prepare for a massive war. She even left the capital to oversee the preparation herself. Along with Prince Naka no Ōe, the mother and son duo began raising many troops and oversaw the construction of many warships. Japan had a close tie with Baekje—the kingdom played a great role in Japan's development—so the Japanese were not planning on laying low while the Korean kingdom was facing destruction.

The empress wished to lead the military expedition, but it never came true, as she passed away the following year. Nevertheless, in October 663, a total of 800 warships and 42,000 troops were sent by the Yamato Kingdom to face the forces of the Tang dynasty, which consisted of only 170 ships and 13,000 army troops. The Japanese troops, which most likely already imagined their victory due to their bigger numbers, launched an attack on the Tang forces at least three times in a day. The Tang army, which was led by extremely disciplined generals, managed to hold their position every single time despite being outnumbered.

The attack went on for so long that it finally exhausted the Yamato troops, opening an opportunity for the Tang forces to launch their counterattack. In just a snap of a finger, many of the Japanese ships sank into the deep water while the rest burned in bright flames. While many had fallen off their ships and drowned, a great Yamato general named Echi no Takutsu fought valiantly. He was believed to have cut down dozens of his enemies in close combat before death came knocking at his door. Near the end of the war, at least four hundred Japanese ships had reached the bottom of the sea, and ten thousand Japanese soldiers had perished. The war was, no doubt, one of the most devastating events that the Yamato Kingdom had ever been involved in.

The Kingdom of Baekje completely fell apart, and Goguryeo soon surrendered to the joint forces of Silla and Tang China. The Baekje nobles who escaped to Japan were absorbed into the Yamato court, while the commoners who made it to the archipelago served as professional artisans. As for the Japanese themselves, they began to work day and night under the order of their emperor to fortify their lands in case Silla or Tang ever shifted their focus to Japan. However, some historians claim that these fortification projects were completed mostly by Baekje refugees. The fortification projects went on for years and only stopped in 701 when the people finally realized that Silla and Tang had broken their alliance and turned on each other.

The Jinshin War

After Empress Saimei's death in August 661, Prince Naka no Ōe finally sat on the throne, going by the name of Emperor Tenji. He reigned over Japan for eleven years, but he did manage to implement some parts of the Taika reforms that he had developed. The emperor successfully conducted Japan's first national census and compiled a collection of law codes named Omi-Ryo. Consisting of a total of twenty-two volumes of administrative codes, the Omi-Ryo was considered by historians to be the first-ever Japanese legal code. However, many historians doubt its existence. Aside from the fact that archaeologists have been unable to find physical evidence of its existence, the collection of laws was not described in the *Nihon Shoki* and was mentioned only briefly in *Tōshi Kaden,* a historical record of the Fujiwara clan written between the 8ᵗʰ and 9ᵗʰ centuries.

One of the few people that the emperor never forgot was, of course, Nakatomi no Kamatari, his most loyal friend and ally. Nakatomi no Kamatari continued to support his friend until he drew his last breath. To honor his service and loyalty, Emperor Tenji granted him the rank of Taishōkan and a new family name, Fujiwara. Nakatomi passed away on November 14ᵗʰ, 669. The emperor drew his last breath three years later.

However, to avoid more political turmoil from appearing in the imperial court, Emperor Tenji had named his successor before his death. During his early years as emperor, he was said to have written his brother's name, Prince Ōama, as his successor; he was even appointed as crown prince. The emperor lacked a suitable son who could take his place, and most of his children were born to mothers who came from lower-ranking families. So, the only possible candidate for the throne was Prince Ōama. But eventually, Emperor Tenji happened to welcome another son named Prince Ōtomo into his family. As his favorite son grew older, the emperor soon began to change his mind about his successor. By 671, Emperor Tenji had bestowed upon his son the rank of Daijō-daijin and soon showed signs of an obsession to put Prince Ōtomo on the throne and continue his legacy. This sudden change most likely worried Prince Ōama and affected his relationship with the emperor.

Word had been going around saying that Prince Ōama could be in danger. When this rumor reached the prince's ears, he immediately resigned from the imperial court and informed the emperor of his wish to become a monk and leave the political world behind. Prince Ōama began his journey and traveled to the secluded parts of the mountains in Yoshino. The prince brought along his sons and one of his many wives, Princess Unonosarara, with him.

The months passed, and Emperor Tenji finally died of illness in January 672. With that, his twenty-four-year-old son ascended to the throne and changed his name to Emperor Kōbun.

Although Prince Ōama and his family adjusted to living in the mountains as best they could, another rumor kept the prince awake at night. The rumor said that the current emperor refused to sit still as long as he knew that Prince Ōama was alive and well. Suspecting that Emperor Kōbun might have already cooked up a plot to end his life, Prince Ōama gathered his allies and made preparations for war. This war is known as the Jinshin War, and it was the biggest one to explode in pre-modern Japan.

After sending messengers to both Ise and Iga Provinces in the east to rally the clan leaders to his side, Prince Ōama then instructed a portion of his army to march to the north and block a major route. This was done to make sure that Emperor Kōbun could never gather allies from the northern provinces. While Prince Ōama had already gained the support of the provinces in the north and the east, Emperor Kōbun sent word to the clan leaders in Kibi and Tsukushi. His hope, however, was immediately crushed, as the governor of Tsukushi refused to aid him, claiming that they could not leave their posts in case of any threats arriving from the Asian mainland.

The war took place in various locations in central Japan, with Prince Ōama emerging victorious each time. The last battle was fought on the Seta-no-Karahashi Bridge, and it was won yet again by Prince Ōama. The young emperor saw his soldiers lying lifeless on the ground, and he immediately lost hope. Emperor Kōbun had only ruled Japan for eight months, but he soon committed suicide, leaving the door open for his uncle to step in and finally take the throne.

Emperor Tenmu

After defeating his nephew, Prince Ōama ascended to the throne in 673 and gained the name Emperor Tenmu. The first thing he did as a sovereign was pretty much the same as the other emperors: he moved the capital. Since the Japanese believed in the concept of purification, it became a priority for a newly ascended emperor to move his capital to another region since the previous capital was considered impure. And so, the capital was moved back to Asuka.

New governing systems were established during Tenmu's reign, although most of them did not stray far from the Taika reforms. Instead of appointing new officials to serve as his ministers, Emperor Tenmu employed his own sons in the imperial court, while his wife carried the title of empress. A new kabane system called Yakusa no Kabane was established, and it consisted of a total of eight new kabane titles, with some of them being even higher than the previous titles of Ōmuraji and Ōomi. These titles are Mahito, Asomi, Sukune, and Imiki, and they were bestowed only upon those in the top tier. With the change in the governing structure completed, the emperor then shifted his focus to constructing another capital, which was located to the north of Asuka. Influenced by the organized arrangement of the capital in China, Emperor Tenmu's new capital, Fujiwara-kyō, was built according to the Chinese-style grid plan.

Unfortunately, despite the emperor's ambitious plans, he never got to see his new capital, as he passed away on October 1st, 686. The throne passed to his wife, Empress Jito, who proceeded to oversee the completion of Fujiwara-kyō before finally moving the capital there.

Art and Culture

The culture during this time was referred to as the Hakuho culture, and many of its architectural designs and the arts were heavily influenced by Tang China. A small portion was indirectly influenced by Gupta art in India; the latter can be seen in the exquisite wall paintings found in the kondo (Golden Hall) of the Hōryū-ji Temple. They bear a striking resemblance to the old murals found in the Ajanta Caves, Buddhist rock-cut cave monuments in India.

Painting on the ceiling of the Ajanta Caves, India.
Piyal chatterjee, CC BY-SA 4.0 https://creativecommons.org/licenses/by-sa/4.0 via Wikimedia Commons: https://commons.wikimedia.org/wiki/File:Life_circle_of_Lord_Buddha_-_A_marvel_of_painting_inside_Ajanta_Cave.jpg

A mural in the Golden Hall of Hōryū-ji.
https://commons.wikimedia.org/wiki/File:Amidhaba_paradise_Horyuji_Mural.JPG

More and more temples emerged as the years went by; historians claim that over a hundred temples and monasteries were built in this period alone, especially when Buddhism began experiencing rapid growth throughout the archipelago. The Hōryū-ji Temple, which had first been commissioned by Prince Shōtoku, was reconstructed around this time due to a lightning incident that affected almost every part of the temple complex. The Kawara-dera and Daikandai-ji were some of the new Buddhist temples constructed during this period, and they all featured some magnificent touches influenced by the architectural designs of Tang China.

Before his death, Emperor Tenmu commissioned a beautiful temple called Yakushiji to be constructed in Fujiwara-kyō, though it was later relocated to Nara. It was said that the emperor was devastated upon learning that his wife had fallen terribly ill. He began to pray to the Buddha of healing, Yakushi Nyorai, and decided to establish a temple in the deity's honor. Emperor Tenmu never got to see the finished temple, but his wife continued the project and oversaw its completion.

Yakushiji Temple in Nara.
https://commons.wikimedia.org/wiki/File:Yakushiji_panomara.jpg

Considered to be one of the most beautiful temples to ever exist in Japan, the Yakushiji's famous features were the symmetrical layout and the two finely constructed pagodas accompanying each side of the main hall. Unfortunately, in 973, a fire engulfed most of the temple's structure, which was followed by another fire in 1528 that destroyed the main hall. However, massive reconstruction projects were arranged in the 20th century. The only original structure of the temple that still stands today is the three-story East Pagoda.

Aside from the fine architectural designs seen in temples and the flourishing poetry brought by the Baekje aristocrats who came to Japan after the fall of their kingdom, funerals during this period also began to see some changes. Buddhist-style cremation funerals became more popular, especially when the government restricted the construction of massive burial mounds. Thus, the number of new kofun tombs began to drop drastically until they completely disappeared.

Chapter 11 – Tōdai-ji and the Bronze Buddha

Tōdai-ji (the "Eastern Great Temple") is one of the Buddhist temples constructed during the ancient Nara period that still stands today. Initially commissioned by Emperor Shōmu in 728, the great temple was actually built as an appeasement for the troubled spirit of Prince Motoi, the emperor's late son.

Prince Motoi was born to Emperor Shōmu and Empress Kōmyō in November 727. He was the emperor's first son, and he was appointed as the nation's crown prince at the age of thirty-two days, which was a rare occurrence, although there was not yet a minimum age in place for an appointment in the imperial court. Unfortunately, despite his parents' joy and tender care, the infant crown prince fell terribly sick and passed away shortly after. He was less than a year old when his remains were buried on Mount Naho.

With the crown prince's death, the imperial court had lost their next heir to the throne. To make matters worse, a rumor spread, suggesting that the late crown prince's mysterious sickness and death were actually caused by some kind of magic by Prince Nagaya, who served the court as Sadaijin at the time. He was the next possible successor to the Chrysanthemum Throne. So, the emperor, who was still in mourning over his only son, began to distrust Nagaya. Without strong evidence, the Fujiwara Four (the sons of Fujiwara no Fuhito) took matters into their own hands; they pressed charges against Prince Nagaya and forced him to commit suicide. His wife and children were killed at the same time. Prince Nagaya's death was believed to have started a curse, as the Japanese archipelago was then overwhelmed by several terrible incidents in the next following years.

Six years after the slander and death of Prince Nagaya, the Japanese archipelago was struck with a smallpox epidemic. Beginning in a city in Northern Kyushu, the illness was said to have plagued a Japanese fisherman who had returned to the archipelago after being stranded in the Korean Peninsula. From there, the plague spread throughout Northern Kyushu, leading to many deaths. Crops failed to grow, and agricultural activities drastically decreased. Famine greatly affected the people, and the economy declined.

By 736, several officials from the imperial court had passed through the infected area in Northern Kyushu. As a result, the party was immediately infected. While some of them perished, the remaining officials returned to the capital, thus spreading the disease to Nara. By 737, the plague had slowed down. It was reported that nearly 35 percent of Japan's population had died of smallpox, including the Fujiwara Four, who had driven Prince Nagaya and his family to their deaths.

The disaster, however, did not stop after the terrible plague. Emperor Shōmu's kingdom was yet again in chaos when Fujiwara no Hirotsugu started a rebellion against the government. However, Fujiwara no Hirotsugu claimed that his war was only with Kibi no Makibi and Genbo, who, according to Hirotsugu himself, was the reason the Fujiwara clan's influence in the court had been suppressed. The rebellion was successfully handled by the government's forces. Hirotsugu was captured and killed, and his supporters were imprisoned, flogged, and exiled.

Emperor Shōmu somehow believed that he was the one responsible for all the terrors happening in his kingdom. And so, he began to show signs of becoming a devout Buddhist; he believed that the nation could be cleansed, saved, and protected by Buddhism. In 741, he issued an edict that required the construction of a temple in all sixty-six provinces of Japan, as well as the construction of Tōdai-ji's Great Buddha Hall. This would come to house the colossal bronze Buddha known as Daibutsu. To make sure the project went well, a Buddhist priest named Gyoku traveled throughout the entire archipelago seeking donations. Over two million people provided wood, metal, cloth, and rice. The priest also returned with at least three hundred thousand laborers who would later work on the bronze Buddha and its great hall. Although the emperor himself had provided financial support for the construction from his royal coffers, the construction of these temples, especially the Tōdai-ji, nearly led the Japanese state into bankruptcy. Special taxes were imposed on everyone to ensure the completion of Tōdai-ji, which caused many to suffer, including those in the higher social classes.

Although the Tōdai-ji Temple was commissioned as early as 728, it was not actually opened until about twenty-four years later. Standing at the east of the palace, the Tōdai-ji was made the provincial temple of Yamato Province after the issuing of an edict (*kokubunji*) by Emperor Shōmu. It also served as the headquarters for the other provincial temples in the archipelago. It housed offices for all six Buddhist schools in Japan: Hosso, Kegon, Jōjitsu, Sanron, Ritsu, and Kusha. Other than being a place of worship, the temple was used as a learning center; it featured both a college and a library, which were often used by monks and priests to translate Buddhist sutras. The Tōdai-ji was also the very first Buddhist temple to install an image of the Shinto kami of war and culture, Hachiman, as it was believed that the kami had the ultimate ability to protect the sacred temple.

Daibutsu, the Largest Bronze Buddha in the World

Daibutsuden, the Great Buddha Hall of Tōdai-ji.
Wiiii, CC BY-SA 3.0 https://creativecommons.org/licenses/by-sa/3.0 *via Wikimedia Commons:*
https://commons.wikimedia.org/wiki/File:T%C5%8Ddai-ji_Kon-d%C5%8D.jpg

The Tōdai-ji Temple was indeed built to impress, despite the project first being commissioned by the emperor as a means to protect the kingdom against chaos. At the center of the temple complex, one could find the grand hondō or the main hall named Daibutsuden (the Great Buddha Hall). In this very hall, the largest bronze Buddha statue in the whole wide world stood. Measuring almost fifteen meters (forty-nine feet) tall and weighing at least five hundred tons, this sitting Buddha statue was a representation of Dainichi Nyorai (also known as Vairocana), one of the most important Buddhas in the Kegon sect. The Buddha statue sits on top of a bronze lotus pedestal with his right hand raised, which symbolizes a gesture of teaching. The Buddha's snail-curled hair is said to have been made out of 966 bronze spheres, while the base of the lotus pedestal features the unique engravings of *Rengezō sekai*, also known as the Lotus Treasury World. By the Buddha's sides are two of his bodhisattvas; on his left is the bodhisattva, Kokuzo Bosatsu, which was built in the early 18th century.

The bronze Buddha of Tōdai-ji (Nara Daibutsu).

The construction of the Buddha statue took a few years to complete. The first construction site was in Shigaraki, and it was later moved to Nara after the emperor relocated the capital back to Heijō-kyō. After the completion of the years-long construction, an "Eye-Opening Ceremony" was held in 752 to consecrate the image of the Vairocana Buddha. Overseen by Empress Kōken, the ceremony was attended by nearly ten thousand monks and four thousand dancers from the Asian mainland. At that time, it was considered the largest international event ever held in East Asia. The retired Emperor Shōmu and his consort, Kōmyō, were also among the respected guests of the ceremony.

Music filled the air, which was followed by several dance performances by dancers from Korea and China. When it was finally time to enshrine the newly constructed Buddha statue, the officiating monk, who was a respected Indian priest named Bodhisena, painted the pupils of the Buddha by using a special brush named *kaigan kuyo-e*, thus imbuing the Buddha with life. Then, former Emperor Shōmu was believed to have sat in front of the Buddha and made a vow to completely devote himself to the Three Treasures of Buddhism: the Buddha, the Dharma (Buddhist law), and the Sangha (the Buddhist monastic community).

In 855, slightly over a century after the completion of the statue's construction, an earthquake struck the Japanese archipelago, destroying a part of the bronze Daibutsu. Its massive head fell to the ground. The statue, however, was restored under the order of the central government soon afterward. When one of Japan's biggest conflicts, the Genpei War, exploded in 1180, the statue was once again destroyed. The leader of the Taira clan instructed his men to torch the complex since the Buddhist monks showed their support to the clan's worst rival, the Minamoto. Unlike the damage done by the earthquake centuries before, the Genpei War seriously damaged the Tōdai-ji complex. Not only did it severely destroy the massive Buddha image, but it also caused heavy casualties.

The Taira clan destroyed another temple during this time, but the imperial government could focus on restoring one temple at a time since it was drowning in financial problems. And so, the constructions of the Tōdai-ji and the Daibutsu were prioritized. Under the supervision of former Emperor Go-Shirakawa, a restoration project was launched. The former emperor appointed an obscure monk named Chōgen to travel across the Japanese lands and collect funds to ensure the restoration project ran smoothly. The monk was believed to have devoted over twenty years of his life working on the restoration of the Daibutsu and other important structures of the Tōdai-ji.

The project continued even after the end of the Genpei War. Under the supervision of the victorious Minamoto, Tōdai-ji was finally restored in 1195. However, due to some financial difficulties, the temple was built on a smaller scale compared to the original.

Since Japan is situated on the Pacific Ring of Fire, it is not surprising that Japan was hit by yet another terrible earthquake in 1709, resulting in the destruction of the Great Buddha Hall. It was rebuilt soon after, and it still stands in Nara Prefecture today. Just as before, the reconstruction of the hall was costly. Because of that, the hall was reconstructed on a smaller scale; it measured about 57 meters (187 feet) long and 48 meters (157 feet) tall. Nevertheless, the hall is still named the largest wooden building in the world today.

Other Structures at Tōdai-ji

As one of the largest temple complexes in Japan, the Tōdai-ji comprises several other magnificent structures. The main gate of the temple, known as Nandaimon ("The Great South Gate"), measured at least twenty-one meters (sixty-nine feet) long and features an impressive double hip-and-gable roof—an architectural design popular during the Kamakura period. Although the gate was first constructed in the Nara period, it was, unfortunately, destroyed by a typhoon several years later. However, thanks to the reconstruction project launched in the early 12th century, the gate still exists today.

A wooden sculpture of one of the Niō guardians that protect the temple complex from evil spirits.
Lisa Beké, CC BY 3.0 https://creativecommons.org/licenses/by/3.0 via Wikimedia Commons:
https://commons.wikimedia.org/wiki/File:20100716_Nara_Todaiji_Nandaimon_2252.jpg

To protect the temple from being infested with evil spirits and demons, two wooden sculptures of Niō guardians measuring eight meters (twenty-six feet) tall were added in 1203 CE. About four years after the construction of the Niō guardians, a 12th-century Zen priest named Yōsai added an exquisite bell tower called Shoro to the temple complex. The structure houses the second largest bell in Japan, and it weighs over twenty-six tons.

Shoro, which houses the second largest bell in Japan.

To the west of the Great Buddha Hall stands the Nigatsu-dō (the "Hall of the Second Month"). First erected in the 8th century, the hall is where the Omizutori, the sacred water-drawing festival, takes place every second month of the lunar calendar (around March 1st until March 14th). Since the hall is located on top of a hill, one can feast their eyes on breathtaking views from there.

To the south of Nigatsu-dō is another grand hall known as the Hokke-dō (the "Lotus Hall"). Just like the Nigatsu-dō, Hokke-dō was founded in the 8th century. The structure features two separate halls: the worship hall and the image hall. The latter, which houses an impressive collection of Buddhist statues, appears to be darker than the other since minimal light is allowed to shine through. This is to ensure all of the 8th-century statues remain well preserved. While the 3.6-meter (12-foot) statue of Fukukenjaku Kannon is the highlight of Hokke-dō's image hall, there is another unique clay sculpture hidden away from visitors. The statue of Shūkongōjin is only made available for viewing once a year (every December 16th), and because of this extreme preservation measure, the sculpture is said to have maintained its original state. The shape is as exquisite as ever, and not a single color has faded.

Statue of Fukukenjaku Kannon inside the Hokke-dō.
Ismoon (talk) 15:49, 10 February 2019 (UTC), CC BY-SA 4.0
https://creativecommons.org/licenses/by-sa/4.0 , via Wikimedia Commons: I, KENPEI, CC BY-SA 3.0 https://commons.wikimedia.org/wiki/File:Todaiji_Monaster_Fukuken-saku_Kannon_of_Hokke-do._Todai-ji.jpg

Chapter 12 – The Nara Period Explained

The Nara period took place in 710 when the capital was moved to Heijō-kyō, Nara. The Nara period lasted for slightly over eighty years, and writing exploded during this time. The *Kojiki* and *Nihon Shoki*, two of the most important written records of Japanese history, were finally compiled. The *Kojiki*, which was commissioned by Empress Genmei in 712, features the story of the imperial court during its early days up until the reign of Empress Suiko, as well as various religious practices and ceremonies held during ancient times. The record, however, is considered semi-historical since most accounts are fused with legends and myths. The same could also be said about the *Nihon Shoki*, although it contains a more detailed account of ancient Japanese history. Initially commissioned by Emperor Tenmu during his reign, the *Nihon Shoki* was written in classical Chinese and tells the story of how the world was shaped, followed by accounts of dozens of emperors—both legendary and historical—and various events that took place until the 8th century.

Beautiful works of poetry also began to appear during the Nara period. Ōtomo no Yakamochi, a government official and poet, was believed to have compiled 4,516 different poems into a collection called Man'yōshū. While his own works were also included in the collection, some of the poems were written by emperors, nobles, and even court ladies.

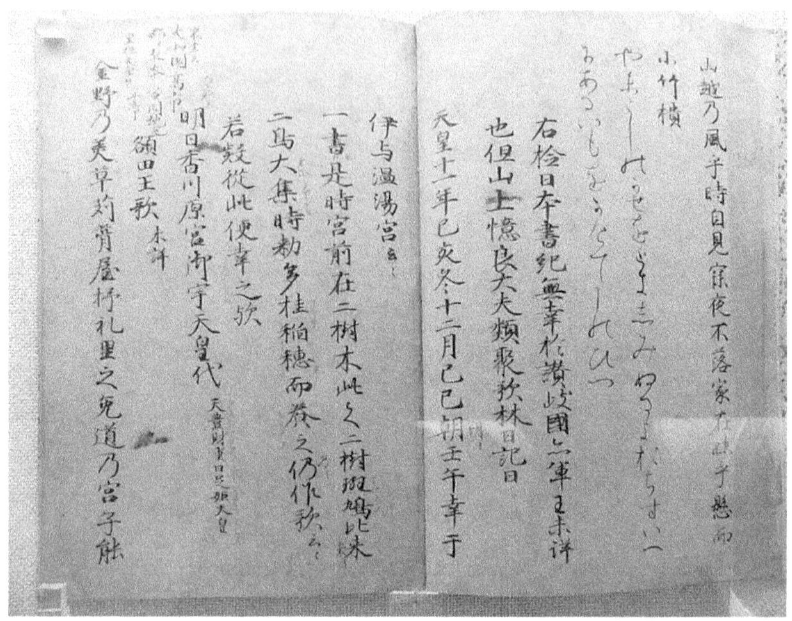

A page of the Man'yōshū, which is kept in the Tokyo National Museum.

Reiji Yamashina, CC BY-SA 3.0 https://creativecommons.org/licenses/by-sa/3.0 , via Wikimedia Commons: https://commons.wikimedia.org/wiki/File:Genryaku_Manyosyu.JPG

Japan also maintained its international relations. Diplomatic envoys or *kentōshi* were sent to Tang China every twenty years. More knowledge and cultural influences were brought back, and several of the students who returned from the Asian mainland were promoted to high ranks in the Yamato court. The Japanese archipelago also accepted many visitors from other parts of the world, ranging from India to Vietnam, Indonesia, and Malaysia. When foreign visitors arrived at the main gates of the kingdom, they were often welcomed with grand ceremonies filled with music and dance performances.

Although great art and literature were some of the prominent features of the Nara period, the life of the commoners only slightly improved. While the elites lived lavishly in their estates, the lower classes were still plagued by poverty, and most of them still lived in rural villages. They supported themselves with agricultural activities, though their technology remained the same as in previous periods. Shintoism was widely practiced by the commoners, while the nobles held strong beliefs in Buddhism, especially Emperor Shōmu, who was known for issuing the massive construction of the bronze Buddha, which almost dried out the nation's wealth.

The Aftermath of Emperor Tenmu's Death

Right after Emperor Tenmu's death, the Japanese archipelago was ruled by his wife, Empress Jito, although she did not rise to the throne officially at this time. The empress was said to have been a great ruler, something she had already demonstrated before her husband's death. But Empress Jito did not plan to rule for too long, which could be the reason she did not officially take the throne. The empress was actually planning to install her own son, Prince Kusakabe, on the Chrysanthemum Throne.

Ever since he was young, the prince was groomed by his royal parents to become an emperor. He was absorbed into the imperial court at a young age and was taught how to handle administrative work. He was also appointed as crown prince during his father's reign. Empress Jito was, no doubt, confident that her son would be a great fit for the throne. However, one problem kept her awake at night; Prince Kusakabe had some health issues.

Later, another contender surfaced and began to quickly gain support from the other officials in the Yamato court. His name was Prince Ōtsu, and he was also the son of Emperor Tenmu. Described as a modest man who had a good physique and was very skillful in sword fights and martial arts, Prince Ōtsu gained favor from many, from those working in the ministry office to the peasants working the lands. We could say that everyone liked him—everyone except for Empress Jito.

While everyone was enthralled by Prince Ōtsu's polite manners, Empress Jito saw him as an obstacle. Word soon reached the empress, informing her that Prince Ōtsu was quietly planning a rebellion. Not wanting to miss this golden opportunity to get rid of him, the empress charged Prince Ōtsu with treason. He was immediately captured and killed at his residence; some claimed he was forced to commit suicide. But was Prince Ōtsu really planning a rebellion? Or was it actually a plan devised by the empress? We may never know for sure.

Nevertheless, the empress had successfully removed the obstacle, leaving a clear way for her beloved son to step up as emperor. Unfortunately, her effort was for nothing, as Prince Kusakabe soon died of his illness. With her son gone, Empress Jito had no other choice but to take the mantle and rule the kingdom officially.

Continuing her late husband's work, Empress Jito moved the capital to Fujiwara-kyō after the city's completion. The new capital was the first one to be used by three consecutive rulers, breaking the old tradition of capitals being moved every time a new emperor took the throne. The empress oversaw the completion of many temples, especially the Yakushi-ji. A new law code was enacted under her reign, and another census was conducted. Since social classes became even more important during this era, the records obtained from the census were considered valuable; the government could now keep track of everyone's lineage and bloodline. From this point on, a census had to be conducted once every six years.

Later on, Empress Jito would abdicate her throne in favor of her grandson, who was the son of Prince Kusakabe. He rose to the throne as Emperor Monmu in 697. Influenced by Tang China and realizing the idea of the Taika reforms, the new emperor established the Taihō-ritsuryō (Code of Taihō) in 701. It included both punishment and administrative laws. The government was also improved and transformed into a much more organized structure, with two offices placed right under the emperor himself, followed by eight different ministries. Each of these positions was filled by reliable chieftains and members of the imperial line.

Life under Emperor Monmu's reign

During this time, commoners still lived in villages. Most of the time, they engaged in agricultural activities to survive. Taxes were collected from them no matter their living situation. Women and slaves only had to pay a certain amount of rice, but men had to pay with rice, cloth, specialty products, and manual labor for sixty days. To make it harder on them, the villagers had to deliver their payment to the capital themselves. This could have been a long journey depending on where one lived.

Adult males were drafted for three-year periods of guard duty, where they would be sent to specific regions across the archipelago to keep an eye out for possible invasions from the Asian mainland. Although they were exempted from taxes during this time, these people still had to finance their own equipment, travel, and supplies. Due to high taxes and military drafts, there were cases of census fraud. Men would lie and register themselves as women so they could avoid the burdens placed upon them by the government.

The Rise of the Fujiwara Clan

The Fujiwara clan was founded by none other than Nakatomi no Kamatari after he gained a new surname from Emperor Tenji a couple of years before his death. Although the Fujiwara clan had long been established in the Yamato court, it rose to even greater heights when

Fujiwara no Fuhito (the son of Kamatari) gained favor from Empress Jito. To further strengthen their ties with the imperial line, Fuhito married his daughter to Emperor Monmu, and they soon bore a son named Obito.

Emperor Monmu, however, only lived until the age of twenty-five. He died in 707, leaving the throne empty and ready to welcome another ruler. Of course, Fuhito was obsessed with putting his grandchild, Prince Obito, on the throne, but it was not that easy. Since his mother was not the late emperor's main consort, Obito could not claim the throne since it was prioritized to the emperor and his main consort's sons. But this did not stop Fuhito; he eventually came up with a plan that made it possible for Prince Obito to step up as the next emperor, although he did not live long enough to witness his grandson sit on the throne. The other officials in the court were no doubt unhappy with this turnaround, especially the Sadaijin, Prince Nagaya.

However, since Obito was merely a child, he was unable to rule. So, his grandmother ascended the throne as Empress Genmei and ruled until her grandson reached an age fit to govern. Under the empress's rule, the capital was moved from Fujiwara-kyō to Nara, marking the start of the Nara period. The first Japanese coins were introduced during this era. Archaeologists have found the remnants of coins older than the ones from the Nara period; however, they were probably used only in rituals and not as currency.

Rice and cloth were used as currency before coins came along. In 708, two years after the enthronement of Empress Genmei, silver and bronze coins were introduced to the public, although few agreed with the change. The nation only had a limited supply of silver, which made the production of silver coins pretty rare. Counterfeits were common, as people would often mix cheaper metals to create silver coins. Thus, the production of silver coins ended, and the government started to use bronze coins for nearly everything. Construction workers who had spent day and night building temples and shrines were paid with a certain number of bronze coins, as were the government officials. Soon, coins could even be used to exchange for a rank in the court.

The oldest Japanese bronze coin, *Wadōkaichin*.
PHGCOM, CC BY-SA 3.0 https://creativecommons.org/licenses/by-sa/3.0 , via Wikimedia Commons: https://commons.wikimedia.org/wiki/File:Wadokaichin_copper_coin.jpg

By 707, Prince Obito had reached the age of fourteen, but Empress Genmei thought it was not the time for him to take the throne since he was still too young to handle the pressures of being an emperor. Obito was instead appointed as crown prince, and the empress herself abdicated in the following year in favor of her daughter, who became Empress Genshō. Empress Genshō ruled for nine years before she finally passed the throne to the twenty-three-year-old Prince Obito, who became Emperor Shōmu.

Fujiwara no Fuhito, on the other hand, was appointed as Udaijin, but he later died in 720. He did leave behind a legacy: his four sons, who later founded the four houses of the Fujiwara clan. With Fuhito's death, power in the court was seized by none other than Prince Nagaya. He had spent years trying to erase the Fujiwara clan's influence in the court, but he was forced to stop when Fuhito's four sons stepped in to end the rivalry once and for all. He was falsely charged with treason in 729 and forced to commit suicide. His family was also killed, and his loyal supporters were exiled. Legend has it that before committing suicide, Prince Nagaya cursed the living with misfortunes and death.

Now that Prince Nagaya was gone, the power in the court shifted yet again. It was completely dominated by Fuhito's four sons. Their methods of removing obstacles in their way were no doubt ruthless, but they did gain the public's favor. Thanks to the brothers, taxes were greatly reduced, military drafts were abolished, and more hospitals and charitable institutions were built. But, of course, the public's perception of the Fujiwaras was not the only thing that mattered. To further solidify their influence in the imperial court, their younger sister, Kōmyō, was married to Emperor Shōmu. Although Kōmyō did not have royal blood in her veins, she was later promoted to empress consort, which made it possible for her son with the emperor to take the throne in the future. With this, the Fujiwara clan had scored a huge win in the imperial court. But perhaps Fuhito's four sons really could not escape from the curse of Prince Nagaya, as they all perished when the smallpox epidemic hit Japan in 737. However, their deaths did not mean the end of the Fujiwara clan.

Conflicts, Power Struggles, and More Murders

Schemes, plague, and continuous struggles continued during the reign of Emperor Shōmu. In fact, a terrible plague had turned him into a devout Buddhist, resulting in the emperor issuing many constructions of Buddhist temples across the archipelago. Soon, the ongoing disasters and political feuds led the emperor to move the capital several times until his subjects' rejections could be heard loud enough that he returned the capital back to Nara. Emperor Shōmu finally had enough of the pressures of the political world, and he abdicated the throne in favor of his daughter, who reigned as Empress Kōken. As for Shōmu, he decided to enter the priesthood and devote his life to Buddhism.

In the imperial court, another clan rose to power after the death of Fuhito's four sons. This clan was called Tachibana, and it was led by an influential figure named Tachibana no Moroe. On the other side of the court was Fujiwara no Nakamaro, who had risen through the ranks with the help of Empress Kōken's mother, Empress Kōmyō. Unable to sit still while Moroe gained more power each day, Nakamaro dreamed of getting rid of him. One day, the officials attended a party, where Moroe accidentally expressed his comments about the current ruling empress. Seeing this incident as an opportunity, Nakamaro spread the word about Moroe starting a revolt. He then forced Moroe to resign. Moroe soon complied, as he feared his life was on the line.

The event angered Moroe's son, Tachibana no Naramaro, who planned revenge in response to his father's forced resignation. And so, he devised an ambitious strategy to take down Nakamaro and replace Empress Kōken. However, his plans turned out to be a failure before they could even begin. When Naramaro gathered allies to participate in his scheme, one of them decided to turn on him and informed high officials of his plans. Word spread faster than lightning, and he was soon questioned by the empress herself. Holding his ground, Naramaro admitted to having forged the plan and continued to criticize the government's failure as a means to justify his actions. In response, Empress Kōken exiled him, but that was not enough for Fujiwara no Nakamaro. He ordered his men to murder Naramaro, even though he had already been sentenced to exile. Some claimed that Naramaro died slowly and painfully, as Nakamaro's men had beaten him to death with wooden canes.

With Naramaro's death, Nakamaro could easily control the court. Later on, Empress Kōken stepped down. Some suggest that Nakamaro, with the help of Kōmyō, persuaded her, while others claim that the empress was ill. Nevertheless, with Empress Kōken out of the picture, Emperor Junnin was installed on the throne. The new emperor was nothing more than a puppet, as the real power was in the hands of Nakamaro and Kōmyō.

Things were going well for Nakamaro until Kōmyō suddenly passed away in 760. This opened the door for Kōken to gain the throne again. With the strong influences she had gained during her time as empress, she proclaimed that she would be the one to oversee state matters. This, of course, shocked Nakamaro, who had already begun to lose support from many of his followers. To put an end to Kōken, he started a rebellion. He gathered his own military forces and met with a fortune teller to help him decide a date for the rebellion to take place. The fortune teller, however, turned on him and informed Kōken of his plans. After rewarding the fortune teller for this information, Kōken stripped Nakamaro of all his power and positions, including his surname: Fujiwara. Nakamaro attempted an escape while trying to gather more allies, but he was soon cornered by Kōken. He was killed along with his entire family, and his remaining allies were exiled.

Emperor Junnin, on the other hand, was banished to Awaji Island, as he was charged with conspiring with Nakamaro. Some suggest that the former emperor attempted an escape but failed miserably and was assassinated. With zero obstacles lying ahead, Kōken rose to the Chrysanthemum Throne for the second time. She reigned as Empress Shōtoku with the help of a mysterious man named Dōkyō.

How Dōkyō Almost Turned Japan into a Theocracy

Who exactly was Dōkyō, and how did he manage to get on the empress's good side? Dōkyō was actually a Buddhist priest who had crossed paths with the empress when she was seriously ill. The priest was said to have saved her life; it was believed that he cured her using magical Buddhist powers. Ever since then, they became extremely close to the point that many claimed they became lovers.

Due to his close relationship with the empress, Dōkyō was able to rise through the ranks with ease. Historians believe that Dōkyō wished to change the Japanese government and convert it into a theocracy, with Buddhist priests placed on top of the pyramid instead of a single emperor. He even went to the extent of persuading the empress to make changes in the current government system so that it was more in line with Buddhist beliefs. Monks and priests started to get employed more in the imperial court. A number of lands were restricted, so the nobles could not own land without the court's permission. Instead, more land was provided to construct temples.

As the days went by, people began to worry that the empress might abdicate the throne in favor of the Buddhist priest who had no blood ties to the imperial family. To make matters worse, Dōkyō himself had started to act like a ruler of the nation; he wore clothes with the same standard as the imperial family and ate the same things they did. He even had his own special palanquin, which was only used for those with royal blood.

Later, the nation was shocked by a prediction made by an oracle from Usa Hachimangu Shrine. It was said that the kingdom would only achieve peace if Dōkyō was put on top. This sudden prediction quickly enraged many, especially since Dōkyō was not related to the imperial family. To quench the noise of her subjects, the empress sent an official to the shrine so that they could confirm the prediction. This time around, however, the oracle stated that none should ever rise to the Chrysanthemum Throne except for those who belonged to the imperial family.

So, when Empress Shōtoku died in 770, the Fujiwara clan members took matters into their own hands and immediately exiled the ambitious priest, thus saving both the imperial line and the kingdom from being transformed into a theocracy. Female royals were also prohibited from sitting on the throne—at least for eight hundred years—after this incident. As for the Fujiwara clan, this meant that their power continued to grow in the imperial court, and they would soon prosper even more during the Heian period.

Chapter 13 – The Shosoin Repository and Its Many Treasures

Ever since Buddhism arrived in the Japanese lands, temples began to adorn every corner of the archipelago. Following the completion of Asuka-dera (formerly known as Hōkō-ji), which was built as early as the late 6th century, many more temples were constructed throughout the years, each with its own uniqueness that distinguishes it from the others. Today, Japan houses over eighty thousand Buddhist temples, with the world-famous Tōdai-ji being the largest of them all.

While the Tōdai-ji was best known for its impressive grand hondō and the colossal bronze Buddha that sits inside it, the temple complex also features an 8th-century storehouse that protected many artifacts, trinkets, and documents from Japan's ancient past. The storehouse, often referred to as the Shosoin Repository, stands at the northwestern corner of the Grand Buddha Hall and has been there ever since the Nara period (710–784 CE). Although the exact date of its construction remains unknown, the Shosoin Repository's initial purpose was to store treasures belonging to the imperial family, particularly those of Emperor Shōmu and his empress consort, Kōmyō.

Front view of the Shosoin Repository.

Empress Kōmyō was first married to Shōmu in 716 when he held the title of crown prince. Kōmyō was the mother of both Empress Kōken and Prince Motoi, who died a year after his birth. The empress was believed to have embraced the Buddhist faith. It is thought that she was the one who advised the emperor to construct the Tōdai-ji following the many disasters that had terrorized the archipelago. She was also highly skilled in calligraphy; she was responsible for producing the *Gakki-ron,* one of the oldest copies of a text by Wang Xizhi, a famous Chinese calligrapher from the 4th century CE. The empress consort was also an influential political figure, as she played a prominent role alongside her husband. It is safe to assume that the imperial pair had a close relationship.

So, when Emperor Shōmu died in 755, the mourning empress consort decided to dedicate over six hundred treasures to the bronze Buddha of Tōdai-ji as an offering to ensure the spirit of her deceased husband was at peace. The offerings were done in the span of several years. To preserve the state of the treasures, they were kept within a room in the Shosoin Repository.

The storehouse itself was built using a unique Japanese architectural style called Azekura-zukuri. Resembling a sturdy log cabin, this particular style has actually been around ever since the ancient Yayoi and Kofun periods, although, back then, this kind of simple yet durable wooden cabin was typically used to store rice and other agricultural harvests. The Shosoin was made out of age-darkened cypress, which is a type of timber known for its high durability. The entire structure did not feature a single nail or bolt. The triangular wooden beams that came together in each corner of this rectangular building are what make the Shosoin so special.

In fact, this construction method without nails saved the structure from being destroyed by earthquakes. While the Shosoin has gone through minor restoration processes and repairs, most of its structures remain unaltered. It witnessed a number of destructions during ancient times, including the torching of the Tōdai-ji by the Minamoto clan and the siege of Nara in the Heian period, but thanks to its durability, the storehouse is still intact and has managed to preserve almost all of its treasures.

The triangular wooden beams that come together at the corner of the structure.
ignis, CC BY-SA 3.0 http://creativecommons.org/licenses/by-sa/3.0/ , via Wikimedia Commons: https://commons.wikimedia.org/wiki/File:Azekura-dukuri_JPN.JPG

Since its main purpose was to preserve centuries-old artifacts, a lot of effort was put into its construction. Only the highest quality of timber could be used to build the repository, as this would allow it to expand and contract according to the weather conditions. The storehouse measures about fourteen meters (forty-six feet) tall, and it is poised on top of forty sturdy columns so that it is raised over two meters (six feet) above the ground. The elevation was done to avoid dampness and protect the entire structure from being infested with vermin and destructive pests. The repository also features a hip-and-gable roof covered in traditional ceramic tiles; the roof has the ability to shed water and repel fire. The Shosoin also lacks stairs to prevent thieves from easily entering the storehouse. The treasures, on the other hand, were kept in elevated wooden chests made out of cedarwood. This protected the artifacts from being exposed to unnecessary light, which explains their marvelous state. Most of the precious artifacts still remain in their original states; the ancient paintings are as vibrant as ever, the exquisite fabrics are still in perfect condition, and the inks on the old manuscripts are still clearly visible.

The Treasures of the Shosoin Repository

The interior of the Shosoin Repository was separated into three parts. The Northern Room was historically reserved for all of the gifts and offerings made by Empress Kōmyō to the bronze Daibutsu. Both the middle and southern rooms were used by high-ranking Buddhist monks to store various ceremonial objects and important articles and documents belonging to the central government. This included tax records, censuses, and poetry books, with most of them originating from the 8th century.

Over the years, the repository housed over nine thousand treasures of the past, with some of them originating from different countries all over the world, such as China, kingdoms in Southeast Asia, and the Middle East. These items are divided into different categories: *Butsugu* (Buddhist objects), *Fukushoku* (clothing pieces and accessories), *Chōdo Hin* (furniture), *Yūgi Gu* (games), *Gakki* (musical instruments), and *Buji* (weaponry). Each of these items preserved in the storehouse reveals a lot about the economy of ancient Japan, as well as the social and cultural lives of the Japanese people, especially during the Nara period.

Torige ritsujyo no byōbu, an old painting preserved in the Shosoin Repository.
https://commons.wikimedia.org/wiki/File:%E9%B3%A5%E6%AF%9B%E7%AB%8B%E5%A5%B3%E5%B1%8F%E9%A2%A81.jpg

The Torige ritsujyo no byōbu, for example, is a well-preserved folding screen that features a painting of a young lady, possibly a depiction of someone from Tang China, under a tree with her flowy garments beautifully decorated with colorful bird feathers. Through this rare painting alone, we can get an insight into the feminine beauty standard of a noblewoman during the Nara period. Cut glass bowls (Hakururi no wan) possibly originated from the Middle East, and there were pitchers and cups from Persia, highly intricate musical instruments from Tang China, a silver incense burner (Odo no Gosu), ceramic drum body, lacquered ewer, and a golden Buddhist scepter (Saikaku no nyoi) made out of the horn of a rhinoceros. These items prove that ancient Japan had connections with the Silk Road.

An 8ᵗʰ-century incense burner.
https://commons.wikimedia.org/wiki/File:Silver_Incense_Burner_Shosoin.JPG

A lacquered ewer measuring over forty-one centimeters (sixteen inches) tall.
https://commons.wikimedia.org/wiki/File:LACQUERED_EWER_Shosoin.JPG

The most popular treasure stored in Shosoin, however, is a musical instrument called Kuwanoki no genkan. This rare lute is believed to have originated from China and is made out of mulberry wood with an inscription of the word "Todaiji" on the back of its round body. This four-string lute also features a detailed motif of three Chinese men playing Go, a traditional board game that was first made famous in China about 2,500 years ago.

Another musical instrument that survived the many centuries is the Raden Shitan no Gogen Biwa, a five-stringed biwa lute of Indian origin; the one stored in the repository is, in fact, the only one left of its kind. Almost like the Kuwanoki no genkan, this ancient biwa is adorned with a motif that depicts a man riding a camel. Made out of red sandalwood, this musical instrument is exquisitely decorated with nacre or mother-of-pearl, as well as golden and silver motifs in the shapes of birds, flowers, and trees.

Through the donations made by Empress Kōmyō as a dedication to her late husband, many of Emperor Shōmu's personal belongings survived through the years. A Buddhist robe, a fine embroidered armrest, a bronze mirror inlaid with mother-of-pearl, silk fabrics, and intricate swords are among the six hundred treasures donated by the empress consort. A sword named Kingin Denso no Karatachi was one of the emperor's most prized possessions. The hilt of the sword is made out of white sharkskin and is adorned with crystals, glass, and golden lacquer. However, its complex sheath is what makes the sword unique. It was created using a technique known as *makkinru*, and it features fine depictions of animals, along with two hanging ornaments known as *ashikanamono*.

A lacquered bronze mirror with mother-of-pearl inlays.
https://commons.wikimedia.org/wiki/File:8Lobed_Mirror_Inlay_Shosoin.jpg

Believed to have arrived in Japan from Tang China, there were initially a hundred swords made in the *makkinru* method. Most of them, however, have not been found, most likely because they were used as weapons by Fujiwara no Nakamaro in his rebellion. In 2010, two of these long-lost ancient swords were found buried underneath the pedestal of the bronze Buddha of Tōdai-ji. Out of a hundred, only three—including Kingin Denso no Karatachi—were ever discovered and safely stored in the Shosoin.

Although the Shosoin was designated as a national treasure of Japan in 1997 and was registered as a UNESCO World Heritage Site, the ancient treasures were no longer kept there by the 20th century. In 1953 and 1962, two modern repositories were built in close proximity to the Shosoin Repository; they are known today as the East Repository and West Repository. Instead of timber, these two modern structures were constructed using reinforced concrete and structural steel. To further preserve the conditions of the rare treasures, the interior of the repositories is equipped with HVAC systems. Textiles are stored in the East Repository, while most of the other treasures are kept safely in the West Repository.

The public is, of course, not allowed to enter these repositories; it is strictly sealed under the order of the imperial family. However, every autumn, the Nara National Museum holds an exhibition for the public that lasts for two weeks. It contains approximately sixty ancient treasures from the Shosoin.

Chapter 14 – The Heian Period (794–1185)

The Heian period marked its beginning when the official capital of Japan was relocated from Nara to Heian-kyō (modern-day Kyoto). Emperor Kanmu (Japan's fiftieth emperor) was the one responsible for the relocation. By the end of the Nara period, Buddhism had strongly spread its influence across the archipelago, with more and more temples filling up the central region of the capital. Noticing that their influence was spreading too fast, the emperor began to express his concern about the state of the government. He did not wish to see history repeat itself; remember, the imperial court had almost been taken over by the Buddhist priest Dōkyō many years prior. It was possible it could happen all over again. And so, in 784, Emperor Kanmu relocated the capital to Nagaokakyō.

The construction of the new capital was overseen by Fujiwara no Tanetsugu, the emperor's advisor. However, a year after the relocation, Tanetsugu was found dead, murdered by an unknown assassin. Questions were asked, and investigations were carried out, but no one had witnessed the incident. Not a single soul knew who the culprit was until shocking news reached the imperial court. Someone stepped up and claimed that the murderer was none other than Crown Prince Sawara, the emperor's younger brother. He was soon arrested, although he was adamant about his innocence. As a protest, Prince Sawara starved himself during his imprisonment until he was somehow proven guilty and sent to exile on

Awaji Island. However, he never set foot on the island, as he died due to starvation on the way. After this incident, more misfortunes fell upon the state. For instance, there were deaths of the imperial family, and a terrible flood occurred. Seeing the chaotic events as a curse by his late younger brother, Emperor Kanmu decided to relocate once more. And so, in 794, the capital was moved to Heian-kyō, kicking off a new era in Japan.

Art, Culture, and Literature during the Heian Period

The Heian period lasted for nearly four hundred years, and it was known as the last classical period in Japanese history while also being considered the turning point for the nation. Fine arts, culture, and literature were at their peak during this period. Most of the culture imported from the Asian mainland was, no doubt, vigorously infused to shape the Japanese culture, but when diplomatic missions to Tang China were forced to a halt in 894, Japan witnessed the birth of a new culture that contained little to zero influence from foreign lands.

Writing systems in Japan had been heavily influenced by the Chinese ever since the nation had started making contact with the Asian continent. Most documents were written in Chinese ideograms (kanji), but during the Heian period, the Japanese finally developed their very own script. Most of the Chinese characters were different from Japanese sounds. Although it was still based on Chinese characters, writers and priests worked together to create two Japanese writing systems. Consisting of approximately fifty characters, the two Japanese forms of writing or kana are known as katakana and hiragana; the latter is written in a cursive style.

Men preferred to use Chinese characters to create poems and various documents, although some of them did switch to using kana since it was simpler than kanji. Women would often produce their literature masterpieces using kana since few were familiar with kanji. This was due to a tradition where women would often be excluded from learning to write since they were not allowed to gain positions in the government. Nevertheless, the development of these two writing styles led to an increased number of literary works. Perhaps the most well-known piece of literature created in this period is the one by Murasaki Shikibu, a lady-in-waiting in the imperial court who had exceptional writing gifts. She was the author of *Genji Monogatari* or *The Tale of Genji*, the world's first novel. Consisting of fifty-four chapters, the novel tells the story of Genji, the son of an emperor. It includes the story of his love life as well as a great description of the lavish lifestyle of the aristocrats during the Heian period.

Yamato-e, a form of painting, originated during the Heian period. Simply translated as "Japanese painting," Yamato-e was often painted on scrolls, folding screens, and panels. This painting style involves vivid color schemes and depictions of the lives of nobles. The human figures in a Yamato-e painting appear small while its surrounding scenes are painted in great detail, combined with large bands of "floating clouds" covering the empty spaces or separating a scene. To depict multiple scenes in different spaces indoors, a technique called *fukinuki yatai* was used. Directly translated as "blown off roof," the technique involves painting a certain building or structure without its roof or using partitions to expose its interior and provide the viewer with an artistic perspective of a bird's eye view.

A Yamato-e painting on folding screens.
https://commons.wikimedia.org/wiki/File:Soutatsu_Matsushima.jpg

A Yamato-e painting featuring the *fukinuki yatai* technique.
Metropolitan Museum of Art, CC0, via Wikimedia Commons:
https://commons.wikimedia.org/wiki/File:MET_2015_300_27ai_Burke_website.jpg

Architectural designs also blossomed during this period, especially when it came to palaces, estates, and mansions belonging to those of the elite class. Most of these structures were built based on a Japanese design called shinden-zukuri. The main features of this design include traditional Japanese blinds called sudare. It serves as a cover for an opening of a building from sunlight and rain. While it is typically made out of wood, palaces often use sudare made out of high-quality bamboo complete with silk and gold embroidery for decorative purposes. Some even feature a Yamato-e painting.

Shitomi, timber lattice shutters, were also common in the *shinden-zukuri* style, along with *tatami*, a type of flooring only found in mansions. The Heian Palace (modern-day Kyoto Imperial Palace) as well as the two Buddhist temples called Byōdō-in and Hōjō-ji, were some of the buildings that featured the *shinden-zukuri* design; the latter, however, was destroyed in a fire in 1053.

Traditional Japanese blinds, *sudare*, installed at the Kyoto Imperial Palace.

Shitomi, traditional Japanese shutters.

The Life of the Common People in the Heian Period

By the middle of the Heian period, Japan's population had skyrocketed, reaching approximately six to seven million people. The capital alone was home to about a hundred thousand people, of which only a thousand or two belonged to the elite social class. While the aristocrats called the capital their home, the commoners still lived outside of the capital, where they mostly engaged in agricultural activities, especially rice farming. They lived in loose settlements instead of a crowded village, with houses placed at least a hundred meters away from each other. A house typically had around eight to ten people living in it at the same time.

Centuries after rice cultivation arrived in the Japanese archipelago, the farmers finally decided to change their rice farming methods. Instead of direct seeding, they started to become familiar with the transplanting method. Although the method had already been introduced to Japan way before the beginning of the Heian period, it was not entirely implemented since it seemed to be more complicated and time-consuming than direct seeding.

Farmers would start planting the seeds into a dry seedbed and wait for them to grow. Once the seeds turned into seedlings, the farmers had to take them out and transfer each one of them into a flooded field. Indeed, transferring one seedling at a time and making sure they were planted in neat and organized rows would take a lot of time and energy. However, this method guaranteed higher harvests since no weeds would disturb the growth of the rice. It also required more people, which explains why they lived in big groups.

This time-consuming rice farming process could also be the reason why newlyweds did not move into a new home and live together right away. Instead, they would continue living in their parents' house, and husbands would only visit their wives every once in a while at night. Children were also raised in the wife's household. For some couples, this situation would last their entire lifetime, although there most people would eventually leave their parents' house—typically after five or six years of marriage—and move in together.

Fashions of the Nobles and Elites

Clothing played an important part in identifying the nobles' rank in the imperial court. They dressed pretty much the same as those from the Nara period, but changes began to happen during the second half of the Heian period. *Jūnihitoe*, or the twelve-layered robe, was one of the garments popular during the era. It was worn only by the highest-ranking women in the `imperial court. Despite its name, the wearer was not obliged to don exactly twelve layers of robes. In fact, the number of layers varied according to seasons, occasions, and ceremonies.

Jūnihitoe, the twelve-layered formal robe worn by high-ranking women during the Heian period.
https://commons.wikimedia.org/wiki/File;Junihitoe.jpg

The counterpart to the *jūnihitoe* was the *sokutai*. It was worn by elite men during formal events such as weddings and enthronement ceremonies. A *sokutai* has an outer robe (*ho*) and a black silk hat that was sometimes decorated with a chrysanthemum crest. The men would hold a flat ritual scepter called a *shaku*. Other garments worn by noblemen include *noshi* (everyday wear) and *kariginu* (hunting dress). The latter was also worn at Shinto and Buddhist rituals.

Sokutai, formalwear worn by high-ranking men during the Heian period.
https://commons.wikimedia.org/wiki/File:Tsukuba_Fujimaro.jpg

Dyeing techniques were also improved during this period, leading to an explosion of colors in fashion. While there were many color schemes, a specific dye named *kurenai* or scarlet was reserved only for women in the imperial line, while another dye called *aka* or red was restricted for men holding a certain rank in the court. The different colors in their clothing were aimed not only to portray their ranks but also their age, marital status, and reputation.

White skin was considered attractive for a woman in ancient Japan, so she would apply rice powder on both her face and neck. To ease the process of applying the rice powder to their face, the nobles, especially women, would pluck or shave their natural eyebrows before drawing them slightly higher on the forehead using a type of powdered ink named *haizumi*. This practice of removing eyebrows is known as *hikimayu*.

White teeth, however, were not a popular look back then. The Heian aristocrats were known for their pitch-black teeth. *Ohaguro* is an ancient Japanese custom that involves dyeing teeth black. This tradition was believed to have emerged during the Kofun period, but it was common among the Heian elites.

But despite the vibrant fashions and cosmetic looks, it was considered rude for men to look directly at a woman's face. Because of that, bamboo curtains hung from the ceiling, and painted fans were used to cover women from their sight. The only thing they could see was the edges of the women's sleeves.

Yamato State vs. the Emishi People

The Yamato court had long spread its power all over Japan except for the northeastern Honshu region, which was the home of the Emishi people. While the origins of the Emishi remain debatable, some suggest that they were descendants of the Jomon people, while others claim that they were related to the Ainu people. Nevertheless, these people strongly resisted the expansion of the Yamato state.

The Yamato often thought of the Emishi as barbarians and uncivilized people. It wished to expand its power and move toward an even more centralized state, which resulted in a conquest mission. Back in the Nara period, the central government had proclaimed its power over the region of northeastern Honshu by installing two provinces called Dewa and Mutsu in these lands. Later on, outposts were established in these regions in an attempt to assert their influence over the Emishi. Settlements were also built farther in the regions, and stockades defended by the government military began to appear. The Yamato state even went to the length of inviting the chiefs of the Emishi to the capital, where they absorbed them into the imperial court and gave them bureaucrat ranks. Some of them decided to migrate and join the state; those who were not convinced stayed behind.

However, as more settlements were built in the northeastern Honshu region, the Emishi people began to become irritated as the Yamato's attempt to invade their territories became clearer. And so, they began to sharpen their spears and arrows to get ready for a possible war. The Emishi people were divided into several tribes, and some of them even waged war against each other once in a while. But to push the Yamato forces back to their capital, these tribes were left with no choice but to unite. They began raiding the Yamato settlements scattered throughout their territories and killed the provincial government officials, leading to several small-scale wars with the Yamato court in the early 8th century CE.

The conflict between the imperial court and the Emishi tribes only became worse as time passed. Eventually, war was officially declared by the Yamato court in 774. The long, terrible conflict is known as the Thirty-Eight Years' War, and it undoubtedly caused heavy casualties on both sides. Victory, however, looked like it was siding with the Emishi people. They managed to burn down not only the villages of the Japanese but also Taga Castle, which was the imperial court's main base of operation in the north. In response, the imperial court recruited at least twenty thousand military forces to fend off the Emishi tribes, which only had three thousand warriors. An attack was launched against the Emishi in 776, but it ended terribly for the Japanese. Again, in 789, another battle ensued between the two factions; this one is known as the Battle of Koromo River. The Japanese forces were once again defeated by the Emishi tribe, which was led by a powerful general named Aterui.

However, a ray of light finally shone upon the imperial court when the Japanese forces welcomed a new skilled shogun general named Sakanoue no Tamuramaro into their long battle. The general launched another attack against the Emishi using well-trained horse archers. The relentless war eventually came to an end when Aterui was forced to surrender in 802, thus ending the long war between the imperial court and the Emishi people. After the victory, Sakanoue no Tamuramaro brought Aterui and his lieutenant back to the imperial capital as prisoners, where he suggested the emperor spare their lives. The shogun general claimed that their skills in war could be put to good use and benefit the government. The emperor was not pleased with the suggestion since the state had faced much destruction from the terrible war. So, instead of a royal pardon, Aterui and his loyal companion were executed. Although there was still slight resistance by the Emishi after the defeat of Aterui and his forces, the Yamato state successfully pushed its border farther to the north.

The Dominance of the Fujiwara Clan and the Establishment of a Cloistered Government

The Fujiwara clan was divided into four different houses; each one of them had been founded by the four sons of Fujiwara no Fuhito. These main houses were known as Nanke (Southern), Hokke (Northern), Shikike (Ceremonial), and Kyoke (Capital). But when Japan transitioned into the Heian period, the Hokke rose to power and eventually dominated the entire imperial court. They asserted their power by marrying Fujiwara women to the emperors. Fujiwara no Yoshifusa, for instance, married his daughter to Emperor Montoku (the fifty-fifth emperor of Japan). The two bore a son, who later became the emperor's crown prince.

When Emperor Montoku died in 858, his crown prince, who was only nine years old at the time, was enthroned as the new emperor. Since he was merely a child, Fujiwara no Yoshifusa grabbed the opportunity and made himself a regent or *sesshō*. He would govern the state on behalf of the young Emperor Seiwa. This was also the first time the position of regent was given to a person outside of the imperial line. Since a *sesshō* was only appointed to rule on behalf of a child emperor, they had to step down once the emperor came of age. The Fujiwara, however, was not planning to give their power away so easily. They established another title called *kampaku*, which is essentially a regent for adult emperors. Many in the court opposed the idea since it would mean that the emperor was no longer placed on top of the pyramid and only acted as a figurehead. But these oppositions were a waste of time. Both titles of *sesshō* and *kampaku* eventually became permanent and were only reserved for those belonging to the Hokke Fujiwara clan. This marked the dominance of the Fujiwara, and it lasted for the next two hundred years.

The clan's power soon began to wane when Emperor Go-Sanjō rose to the throne in 1068. Being the first emperor since the 9th century who was not born from a Fujiwara mother, he was indeed against the Fujiwara's dominance in the imperial court. He began to establish a couple of reforms and offices in hopes of curbing the clan's power. Four years later, the emperor abdicated the throne in favor of his son, Shirakawa, and went on to establish the office of the retired emperor (*In no chō*). The retired emperor planned to continue his efforts of erasing Fujiwara power by starting a cloistered rule—a form of government where retired emperors held the true power. But unfortunately, he passed away a few years later. His plan was then resumed by his own son, Emperor Shirakawa, who successfully set the cloistered rule system into motion, thus greatly weakening the dominance of the Fujiwara clan.

Minamoto and Taira Clans: The Origin of the Samurai

Although the Heian period was when the unique Japanese culture began to flourish, the government was surprisingly in the midst of financial difficulties. One of the reasons for these financial problems was the never-ending imperial line. The ancient emperors of Japan were well known for having a long list of children. Emperor Kanmu, for instance, had thirty-six children in total, while Emperor Saga had forty-nine. Each of the members of the royal family was given an allowance, which had seriously drained the royal coffers.

So, to solve the problem and save government funds, Emperor Kanmu began to demote many of his descendants; this method was also practiced by his successors. He removed at least a hundred of his descendants from the imperial house, gave them the title of nobles, and sent them to live in different provinces across the Japanese archipelago. These demoted imperial members were, of course, no longer in line for the throne, and they were also given new surnames: Minamoto and Taira. The latter was given to the grandchildren of Emperor Kanmu, while Taira was bestowed upon the descendants of Emperor Saga. Although these two clans started off as demoted members of the imperial family, they soon evolved into warriors. Today, we know them as samurai.

While the Taira clan remained in the shadows, the Minamoto clan first gained fame in the archipelago when the central government was in need of military forces on the field against the Abe clan in Mutsu Province. The Abe clan was initially tasked by the government to oversee the Emishi people and collect taxes from them. However, things got worse when the Abe started to take matters into their own hands. They stopped sending tax money to the central government and began causing trouble with the governor of Mutsu, which eventually led to violence in 1051.

The government appointed two powerful figures from the Minamoto clan to lead their troops against the rebellious Abe. Without delaying more time, Minamoto no Yoriyoshi and his son, Minamoto no Yoshiie, mounted their horses with bows and arrows at the ready and easily demolished the Abe clan. Minamoto no Yoshiie was known for his exceptional skills in archery and horseback riding. He had emerged victorious in dozens of battles to the point that he became the kami of the Minamoto clan. The Minamoto forged an alliance with the Fujiwara clan to remove anti-government rebels. Men from the Minamoto clan were regarded as being the greatest warriors in the Heian period.

The Minamoto clan's power, however, began to spiral out of control after the death of Yoshiie. Troubles arose when one of Yoshiie's sons,

Minamoto no Yoshichika, started a rebellion against the government and violently murdered several government officials. Hoping to put the issue to rest, the imperial court hired the leader of the Taira clan named Taira no Masamori, who managed to execute Yoshichika and the other Minamoto rebels. From this point onward, the Taira clan began to gain more power, thus starting a long rivalry with the Minamoto clan.

Chapter 15 – Fudō Myō-ō and Amida

Esoteric Buddhism, also known as Tantric Buddhism, can be traced back to ancient India. In the 8th century CE, the teachings were spread to other parts of the world. It was brought to Tibet by the guru Padmasambhava, while China welcomed a few Tantric masters from India, which led to the establishment of Mi-tsung or the School of Secrets. Later on, in 804, the Japanese monk named Kukai set sail to Tang China, where he became a student of Hui Guo, a Chinese Mi-tsung teacher. After a couple of years in Tang China, where Kukai obtained knowledge and teachings passed down by Hui Guo, he finally returned to the Japanese archipelago. He greatly wished to spread the knowledge that he had just mastered. Although his lessons did not get much attention at first, it was believed that through his exquisite calligraphy skills, those in the imperial court and the emperor himself began to notice his teachings. Eventually, the emperor became his patron, and Japan saw the birth of Shingon, one of the major schools of Japanese Buddhism.

With the birth of a new school of Japanese Buddhism in the 9th century came a group of Buddhist deities known as the Myō-ō. Corresponding to the Vidyaraja in Sanskrit, the Myō-ō were initially Hindu deities who were then absorbed into the pantheon of Esoteric Buddhism. Despite being considered protective Buddhist deities and messengers of Dainichi Nyorai, the supreme Buddha of Shingon Buddhism, the Myō-ō are often depicted with menacing appearances.

They are believed to have the ability to fend off and frighten evil spirits and vanquish blind cravings. There are a total of five deities of the Myō-ō: Go Sansei, Dai Itoku, Gundari-yasha, Kongō-yasha, and the most prominent one, Fudō Myō-ō.

A seated statue of Fudō Myō-ō.
https://commons.wikimedia.org/wiki/File:Fudo_Myoo_Museum_Rietberg_RJP_21.jpg

Featuring ferocious and wrathful facial expressions complete with a piercing stare, Fudō Myō-ō, also known as the Immovable One, is a form of the Buddha Vairocana and is regarded as the central deity of the Myō-ō. Aside from his intimidating facial expression, Fudō Myō-ō is often pictured in various threatening postures while being accompanied by a burst of bright orange flames behind him. The flames signify a process of purification of the mind from material desires, and his fierce face not only scares off evil spirits but also frightens nonbelievers and leads them toward the teachings of the Buddha Vairocana. Fudō Myō-ō also carries a sword called a *hōken* in one of his hands, which he uses to cut through both ignorance and ugly delusions. In his left hand is a *kensaku*, a lasso that is used to capture and bind the evil spirits. The deity is also sometimes depicted with a pair of fangs; one fang faces upward while the other faces downward.

Statues of Fudō Myō-ō are often placed deep in the mountains, caves, or near cascading waterfalls. The temple in Kyoto, Kiyomizu-dera, is one of the many temples that houses a statue of Fudō Myō-ō. It is placed near

Otowa-no-taki, a waterfall with three separate streams associated with love, success, and longevity. Visitors and believers are allowed to drink from the streams should they wish to be blessed with either of the attributes associated with each of the streams. However, it is important to choose only one stream, as drinking water from each of them at the same time is considered greedy—a behavior that a Buddhist must avoid at all times should they wish to obtain enlightenment.

To purge evil desires and bad karma and purify negative thoughts, a traditional ritual involving fire is often performed. Known as Goma Taki, this specific ritual is only practiced in the Shingon sect. Taking place in Gomado, the hall where a sculpture of Fudō Myō-ō is housed, the ritual is often performed by priests every morning or afternoon. The traditional ritual involves the burning of wooden plates containing various wishes and prayers inscribed on them. The flame signifies the Buddha's wisdom, while the burning itself symbolizes the destruction of both evil desires and bad karma.

As a protector of Buddhism, it is not a surprise that Fudō Myō-ō became an important deity for warriors, especially for the samurai. The samurai were said to have carried images of Fudō Myō-ō on the battlefield. Images of the fierce deity were placed on either their breastplates or helmets, as it could act as a protection for the vital organs in those areas.

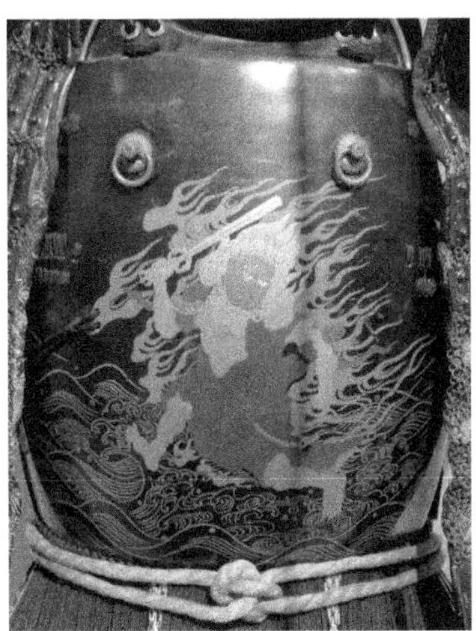

A samurai armor plate featuring a depiction of Fudō Myō-ō.
Marshall Astor, CC BY-SA 2.0 https://creativecommons.org/licenses/by-sa/2.0 via Wikimedia Commons: https://commons.wikimedia.org/wiki/File:Hotoke_dou.jpg

Legend has it that the Japanese monk Kukai was once saved by Fudō Myō-ō. After mastering the teachings of Esoteric Buddhism in Tang China, the monk was preparing to embark on the long journey back to the Japanese archipelago. Sailing through an open sea is still not an easy task, as one must go through various weather systems. And a disastrous storm was in store for Kukai back in the 9th century. A heavy storm was believed to have caused a lot of trouble for the monk and the entire crew on board. An hour passed, then another, yet there was no sign of the storm subsiding any time soon. Instead, the wind was only getting stronger, and the ship continued to fight against the massive rolling waves.

Seeing that the weather was only getting worse by the minute, Kukai decided to turn to Fudō Myō-ō and began to pray. He prayed to the deity for protection; he wished for nothing but a safe return home so he could soon spread his teachings across the archipelago. Later on, the devout monk was said to have been bestowed with a vision. He saw the fierce deity ferociously cutting through the rolling waves that stood in the way, thus ending the storm completely. Perhaps Fudō Myō-ō did hear the monk's prayer after all, and thanks to him, Kukai and the rest of the crew on the ship could return to the land of the rising sun safe and sound.

Amida and Pure Land Buddhism

Amida Nyorai (referred to in Sanskrit as Amitabha Tathagata) is one of the most prominent Buddhist deities, especially in East Asia. Also known as the Buddha of Immeasurable Light, Amida, like Gautama Buddha, had also gone through a long journey before finally reaching enlightenment and entering the state of Buddhahood. The Infinite Life Sutra stated that Amida was once a king who went by the name of Dharmakara. He was believed to have renounced his throne and lifestyle when he came across the Buddhist teachings by Lokesvararaj, the fifty-fourth Buddha in history; he came long before Gautama Buddha. Impressed by his teachings, Dharmakara chose to live his life as a monk and focused on obtaining enlightenment.

After countless lives and reincarnations, Dharmakara finally accumulated enough merit to achieve enlightenment. Upon attaining Buddhahood, Dharmakara went on to create *Buddhasetra* ("Buddha Land"), a celestial land or paradise positioned in the west, beyond the boundaries of our world. He also took a total of forty-eight vows; for instance, the Buddha promised that he would grant anyone passage to his blissful land should they call upon his name. The Buddha even vowed that he and his two bodhisattvas would appear before those who had died while faithfully calling upon his name. The Buddha was also described as being gentle and accepting, which made him one of the most well-known Buddhist deities, especially in Japan when Pure Land Buddhism was established.

Buddhism was first introduced to the Japanese archipelago by the Kingdom of Baekje back in the 6th century CE. With Prince Shōtoku at the helm, the religion quickly flourished and was accepted by many, except, of course, for the Mononobe clan, which was strongly against it. However, the early forms of the religion that arrived in Japan at that time were mainly practices from Mahayana and Esoteric Buddhism, which mainly focused on the concept of universal salvation through an array of specific rituals. It was only by the mid-Heian period that the Japanese were more familiar with the practice of Pure Land Buddhism, which is notable for the spiritual field associated with the Buddha of Eternal Life, Amida.

The history of Pure Land Buddhism can be traced back to the 2nd century CE, when it was first developed in India. The teachings then continued to gain many new followers, especially in Kashmir and several other regions in Central Asia. By 147, Pure Land Buddhism made its way to China, where a Kushan Buddhist monk, Lokakṣema, translated the sutras into Chinese. In Japan, Pure Land Buddhism was introduced by a Tendai monk named Honen Shonin, who founded the Japanese Buddhist school called Jodo Shu (School of the Pure Land).

Buddhists sought only two things: to put an end to suffering and attain enlightenment. The journey to reach enlightenment is not an easy task, though. However, in Pure Land Buddhism, it is believed that one can effortlessly attain enlightenment by gaining entrance to Sukhavati ("Blissful Land"). But what exactly is Sukhavati, and how does one enter it?

According to the Pure Land sutras, Sukhavati, also known as the Pure Land of Amida Buddha, is a world that is filled with nothing but joy and pleasantness. The world was said to have trees growing with precious jewelry and golden bells hanging from them, while the surroundings are continuously accompanied by the soft tunes of birds chirping and whistling. At the center of the world, one could lay their eyes on Amida Buddha, who would probably be sitting calmly on a lotus floating in the middle of a terrace pond while being attended by two bodhisattvas:

Avalokiteshvara and Mahasthamaprapta. Sukhavati is also where all wishes are made true. It is a place those who put their faith in Amida Buddha would enjoy before attaining enlightenment with ease.

To be reborn in the joyous world of Sukhavati, Honen taught his followers that they must practice *nembutsu*, a practice that involves chanting the name of Amida Buddha while putting absolute faith and trust in the deity. However, there is no specific way of chanting the name of the deity; it can be done alone or in groups, silently or aloud, and with or without prayer beads. Honen himself was said to have chanted Amida's name at least sixty thousand times a day. Through his teachings, the monk claimed that everyone could achieve salvation. The simplicity of *nembutsu* allowed aristocrats, devout monks, and those living in rural villages to take a step closer to enlightenment. Chanting the name of Amida Buddha did not require ultimate intelligence or proficiency; all that was needed was for a person to repeatedly chant "Namu Amida Buddha" ("Save me, O Amida Buddha").

While Honen received many new followers from various levels of Japan's social classes, his teachings also invited a few negative critics, especially from other Buddhist schools that had long been established on the archipelago. To add salt to the wound, two imperial ladies-in-waiting decided to convert to Honen's teachings. Elites were worried that Honen's teachings of Pure Land Buddhism might grow too influential and eventually surpass the influence of the other Buddhist schools, so Honen and his loyal followers were exiled in 1207. The monk, however, continued to spread his lessons to every single person he met—be they farmers, fishermen, peasants, or even prostitutes. He was eventually pardoned four years after his exile and allowed to return to the capital. A year after his return, Honen passed away. Some claimed that he passed away peacefully while chanting the name of Amida Buddha, thus allowing him to be reborn in the joyous world of Sukhavati. Despite the monk's death, Pure Land Buddhism continued to prosper and has become one of the most well-known Buddhist schools in Japan.

Chapter 16 – Preparing for the Age of the Samurai

The Heian period lasted for nearly four hundred years, and it saw the birth of many things. The Japanese writing systems were created in this era, leading to an explosion of literature masterpieces and arts. New architectural styles emerged that featured only a little influence from the Asian continent, and new Buddhist schools were established by monks who had returned from China, which resulted in the construction of many temples. The central government had faced several major changes as well. After engaging in wars with the Emishi people, the Yamato government succeeded in expanding its power to the north. Later on, the Fujiwara clan rose to even more power, which allowed them to hold the imperial court firmly in their hands. Two centuries later, though, the power in the court shifted again with the establishment of cloistered rule. The conflicts did not stop there, as the Heian period was also when the samurai began to emerge from the shadows and take their first steps to transform the state into a shogunate (a military dictatorship).

Hōgen Disturbance

Emperor Toba, the seventy-fourth emperor of Japan, was only four years old when he first rose to the Chrysanthemum Throne. Under a cloistered government, the emperor was merely a figurehead; the real power was held by his grandfather, the retired Emperor Shirakawa. Soon, the retired emperor married Emperor Toba off to Fujiwara no Tamako, who later bore a child named Sutoku. Continuing the tradition of enthroning a young emperor in the court, Shirakawa forced his grandson, who had just turned twenty years old, into abdicating the throne in favor of his infant son Sutoku.

However, there are sources that claim Emperor Toba was not fond of his eldest son, the young Emperor Sutoku. This was due to a rumor saying that Sutoku's real father was, in fact, Emperor Shirakawa. Although it remains unsure whether or not the rumor is true, the retired Emperor Toba surely seemed to have bought it since he began to treat Sutoku coldly.

When Emperor Shirakawa passed away in 1129, six years after Sutoku's ascension to the throne, the retired Emperor Toba was finally able to step out of his grandfather's shadow and assert his political power. He forced Emperor Sutoku to step down. The young emperor complied, although he was unsatisfied with the decision. Toba placed Emperor Konoe, another one of his sons, on the throne. Unfortunately, Konoe was a sickly man, and he died of a disease thirteen years after his succession. There was another vacancy on the throne, and Sutoku hoped his son would rise as an emperor. However, much to his disappointment, the retired Emperor Toba enthroned Emperor Go-Shirakawa, another one of his sons with Fujiwara no Tamako. Realizing that it was becoming impossible for his heir to sit on the Chrysanthemum Throne, Sutoku decided to take action, which resulted in a serious dispute with the current emperor, Go-Shirakawa.

Upon noticing the heightened dispute between the retired Emperor Sutoku and the current Emperor Go-Shirakawa, the Fujiwara clan decided to become involved in the issue, hoping it could be a stepping stone for them to reinsert their power into the imperial court. However, two of the most powerful members of the Fujiwara clan, Fujiwara no Tadamichi and Fujiwara no Yorinaga, were not on good terms. The latter supported Sutoku, while his brother, Tadamichi, sided with Emperor Go-Shirakawa. To prepare for battle, the two factions (Sutoku and Go-Shirakawa) turned to the two most powerful samurai clans: Minamoto and Taira. Minamoto no Tameyoshi, the leader of the Minamoto clan, was quick to announce his support for the retired emperor and Fujiwara no Yorinaga. To raise enough troops for the upcoming battle, Tameyoshi tasked his own son, Minamoto no Yoshitomo, with traveling across the archipelago and enlisting as many warriors as possible. Yoshitomo succeeded in building a massive army, but he did not present them to his father. Yoshitomo instead abandoned his father and swore his bow to

Emperor Go-Shirakawa and Fujiwara no Tadamichi.

Something similar happened to the Taira clan. The leader, Taira no Kiyomori, chose to support Go-Shirakawa, while his uncle, Taira no Tadamasa, sided with Sutoku. The dispute over the imperial throne reached its peak when Emperor Toba died in 1156 due to an unknown sickness. Legend has it that the retired emperor met his fate after he was cursed by his favorite courtesan, Tamamo-no-Mae, who was later revealed to be none other than the famous yōkai, the nine-tailed fox.

Those who had allied with Sutoku gathered at his palace, while Go-Shirakawa's loyal supporters and his massive samurai troop raised a defense within another palace nearby. When it was time to discuss a strategy for the battle, Minamoto no Tameyoshi suggested that they lay a surprise attack on Go-Shirakawa's palace at night. Although their forces were smaller than Go-Shirakawa's, Tameyoshi was confident with the plan since he had his other son, Minamoto no Tametomo, by his side. Tametomo was described as a legendary archer. Some claimed that he was able to sink a whole ship with only a single arrow and that his left arm was slightly longer than his right, allowing him to draw his bow better than any average archer.

However, Fujiwara no Yorinaga was against Tameyoshi's war strategy. He claimed that the only honorable way to defeat their enemies was to attack head-on instead of deploying a surprise attack when the skies were dark. Many agreed with Yorinaga's plan to hold their positions and wait for their enemies to arrive so that they could fight each other in a fair battle. Unfortunately, his plans were immediately foiled. Go-Shirakawa's forces laid a surprise attack at night. They charged toward Sutoku's palace gates, and a chaotic battle ensued.

The legendary archer, Minamoto no Tametomo, led his troops to defend the palace. On horseback, he began firing arrows at his opponents. The victory looked as if it belonged to Sutoku's forces at the beginning of the battle; however, everything spiraled out of control when an arrow lethally struck Fujiwara no Yorinaga, which soon resulted in his death. This was followed by the torching of Sutoku's palace. After witnessing the huge flames rapidly devouring every inch of the palace gates, Tametomo, Sutoku, and his remaining allies were forced to flee.

Emperor Go-Shirakawa emerged victorious, and it was not long until his rivals faced their fates. The ambitious retired emperor, Sutoku, was exiled; he died soon after. Some believed that he died unpleasantly, turning into an evil spirit that wished nothing but only misfortune upon those who wronged him. Minamoto no Tametomo, on the other hand, had the tendons in his left arm severed so that he could no longer fire an arrow precisely. He was then banished to an isolated location. His honor was severely tarnished, and he had lost his skills. The legendary archer slashed his own abdomen, committing the first seppuku (ritual suicide) in history.

The remaining allies of Sutoku were sentenced to death; however, Minamoto no Yoshitomo pleaded to the emperor to spare his father, Minamoto no Tameyoshi. Seeing all the destruction caused by the short civil war and not wanting to risk a situation where his enemy could regain his power, Emperor Go-Shirakawa showed no mercy. Yoshitomo had no other choice but to execute his father. The same thing happened to Taira no Kiyomori, who was forced to end his uncle's life.

With the rebellion a failure, the Japanese government remained under the rule of the retired emperor. Go-Shirakawa stepped down from the throne three years after his reign, but he remained in power behind the scene while his eldest son, Emperor Nijō, sat on the Chrysanthemum Throne. As a reward for their service and loyalty, Minamoto no Yoshitomo and Taira no Kiyomori were given promotions. However, their new ranks within the imperial court were not equal. The imperial house seemed to have favored the Taira over the Minamoto. And so, a bitter rivalry between the two samurai clans continued for years to come.

Four years after the Hōgen Disturbance came another bloody rebellion spearheaded by Minamoto no Yoshitomo, who had sealed an alliance with Fujiwara no Nobuyori. Upon receiving news that the head of the Taira clan, Taira no Kiyomori, and some other supporters of the imperial family were about to depart from Heian-kyō (Kyoto) for a religious pilgrimage, Yoshitomo began plotting. Yoshitomo and Nobuyori raised an army—approximately five hundred men strong—and marched toward the Sanjō Palace. There, the samurai kidnapped the retired Emperor Go-Shirakawa and his son, Emperor Nijō, before setting the palace on fire. Their next target was Go-Shirakawa's loyal supporter Fujiwara no Michinori, who had already made his escape earlier to the mountains near the capital. Unfortunately, it did not take long for the rebels to trace him. He was decapitated shortly after.

A painting of the night attack on Sanjō Palace.

https://commons.wikimedia.org/wiki/File:Heiji_Monogatari_Emaki_-_Sanjo_scroll_part_5_-_v2.jpg

Manors and estates were set aflame. The screams could be heard from far away, and much blood was spilled. No one saw any semblance of peace for at least two weeks. Soon, Taira no Kiyomori returned to the chaotic capital. He and his son, Taira no Shigemori, managed to rescue Go-Shirakawa and his son, Emperor Nijō, from the Minamotos' grasp. A battle ensued between the two samurai clans later on, and the Minamoto clan was again defeated. Yoshitomo managed to escape to Owari Province, where he found refuge in the residence of Tadamune Osada, his retainer. But Yoshitomo's journey ended there, as he was eventually betrayed by his own retainer and murdered while he was bathing. Three of Yoshitomo's sons, Yoritomo, Noriyori, and Yoshitsune, were spared and banished.

Taira no Kiyomori had not only successfully strengthened his clan's position as the strongest and most powerful warrior clan in the entire Japanese archipelago, but he had also proved to be a master politician. Through the former emperor, Go-Shirakawa, Kiyomori managed to rise through the ranks and hold the title of chancellor (Daijō-daijin). He married his daughter into the imperial family, appointed those from the Taira clan as provincial governors, and gathered many Japanese to serve under his rule. Taira no Kiyomori's power soon began to overshadow the retired Emperor Go-Shirakawa.

By 1180, Kiyomori installed his two-year-old grandson, Antoku, on the Chrysanthemum Throne. Prince Mochihito, the son of the former

Emperor Go-Shirakawa, was enraged by this decision, especially since his opportunity to step up as emperor had been snatched away by an infant. The prince soon discovered that Taira's sudden domination over the central government had irritated many Japanese throughout the archipelago, especially those from the Minamoto clan and some other Buddhist warrior monks who had been wronged by Kiyomori the past few years. And so, Prince Mochihito put up a call to arms for anyone who was against the Taira. This marked the very beginning of the famous Genpei War, which lasted for five years.

The Genpei War

The first figure to answer Prince Mochihito's call to arms was none other than Minamoto no Yorimasa. The first battle of the Genpei War took place in Uji. When word about Prince Mochihito's plot to overthrow the Taira reached Kiyomori, he sent his troops to demolish the rebels. The prince, Yorimasa, and his few troops were left with no choice but to retreat to Mii-dera, a Buddhist temple located at the foot of Mount Hiei. Realizing that they arrived too late to defend the temple, the Minamoto troops, Prince Mochihito, and several remaining Buddhist warrior monks fought their way to Byōdō-in, another Buddhist temple in Uji.

An illustration of the Battle of Uji.
https://commons.wikimedia.org/wiki/File:Ukiyo-e_War.jpg

Right after crossing the Uji River, the Minamoto clan immediately destroyed the bridge behind them, hoping that the pursuing Taira clan would not be able to reach them. The Taira troops remained insistent on their goal of defeating the Minamoto, and they were said to have crossed the river on their horses. Accepting that defeat was around the corner,

Prince Mochihito attempted an escape, but it was not to be; he was captured and executed. Minamoto no Yorimasa, on the other hand, retreated behind the walls of Byōdō-in and committed seppuku. It is believed that after Yorimasa let out his last breath, one of his loyal followers unsheathed his blade and cut off Yorimasa's head. He tied his lord's severed head to a stone and threw it into the river. This was done to ensure that his lord's head would never become a trophy for the Taira.

The Taira emerged victorious yet again after defeating Yorimasa and his samurai troops. But this incident was only the beginning of the terrible war. The Taira victory eventually drew the attention of Minamoto no Yoritomo and his brothers, Noriyori and Yoshitsune—these were the banished sons of Minamoto no Yoshitomo who had grown up over the years and were ready to cleanse their tarnished clan's name. Not long after the Battle of Uji, Kiyomori witnessed the rise of many rebels throughout the Japanese provinces. It turns out that the Taira clan, despite its growing power, had made a lot of enemies.

Minamoto no Yoritomo had witnessed his father's murder and was expecting to be executed by the Taira clan. But somehow, Kiyomori decided to show mercy and spared the thirteen-year-old boy and his two brothers; some claimed that he only spared them due to his stepmother's request. And so, Yoritomo was exiled and sent to Izu Province, where he was raised and cared for by the Hōjō clan, another branch of the Taira clan. Yoritomo stayed in the shadows for nearly twenty years, and he even married the daughter of the Hōjō clan's leader. Thinking that the boy was no longer a threat, Kiyomori let out a sigh of relief since he did not have to keep his eyes on him anymore. This was a mistake that he would soon regret.

The terrible aftermath of the Battle of Uji fed Yoritomo's anger, and he sought to overthrow the Taira once and for all. Supported by the Hōjō clan, Yoritomo gathered allies from the warriors of Izu Province and raised his own samurai army. Noriyori and Yoshitsune, who had been exiled to different parts of Japan, joined forces and supported their brother's mission. Soon after, Yoritomo bravely declared war against the ruling Taira.

The first small-scale battle ensued; however, Yoritomo's forces faced their first defeat. After Yoritomo was forced to retreat, he came up with another plan; he would establish an independent warrior state in the Kanto region. Back then, the Kanto region was full of skilled warriors who harbored deep hatred toward the unfair central government. Even the first known samurai, Taira no Masakado, once attempted to remove the central government from the region. Promising the warriors of the Kanto region land and freedom under his rule, Yoritomo gradually earned enough support to the point where he managed to establish a base in Kamakura. His next move was to remove the government headquarters scattered throughout the region. Those who had supported the Taira clan began to see his potential, and many of them switched sides and became loyal followers of the rising leader of the Minamoto clan. In just a short span of time, Yoritomo had successfully conquered the region. He welcomed those who chose to support him and annihilated those who strongly opposed him.

The Taira was well aware of Yoritomo's growing power, but due to an unfortunate famine taking over the lands of Japan, they were forced to delay their attack. When the time finally came, the Taira troops marched toward Fujikawa to face Yoritomo's forces. The Taira samurai soon realized they were heavily outnumbered, and they immediately retreated. Legend has it that the Taira began to doubt their victory once they noticed dozens of fires emerging from the darkness. They assumed that the fires were from the Minamoto camps when it was, in fact, cooking fires lit by peasants who were taking shelter from the upcoming war. The Tairas' fear grew even stronger when they were startled by the thunderous sound of a flock of birds suddenly flying in the skies. The Taira thought it was the Minamoto galloping on their horses to lay a surprise attack on them. And so, many of them left their campsites and retreated back to the capital.

With the retreat of the Taira army, Yoritomo shifted his focus back to his base in the Kanto region. While he worked on solidifying his position, conquest missions and battles were left to Kiso Yoshinaka, who is also known as Lord Kiso. According to *Heike Monogatari* (*The Tale of the Heike*), a compilation of events during the clash of the two samurai clans, Lord Kiso had a powerful supporter by his side. She was known by the name Tomoe Gozen, and she served under Lord Kiso as an onna-musha or a female warrior specially trained in martial arts and combat. Aside from her extreme beauty, Tomoe was said to possess exceptional skills in archery, sword fighting, and horseback riding. She was often appointed as the lord's first captain or commander. Tomoe would often ride to war wearing full armor and was equipped with a bow and an oversized sword that she would use to decapitate her enemies.

With Tomoe by his side, Lord Kiso launched several attacks against the samurai troops from the Taira clan and expanded his influence across much of the archipelago. His name soon echoed throughout the capital, and the Taira began to take notice.

An illustration of Tomoe Gozen in battle.
https://commons.wikimedia.org/wiki/File:Battle_of_Awazugahara.jpg

The Taira, on the other hand, had lost their leader, Taira no Kiyomori, to a serious fever in 1181. Honoring his father's wish, Taira no Munemori became the clan's leader, while his brother, Taira no Tomomori, served as the chief commander for the war. Under this new leadership, the Taira enjoyed victory after victory against the Minamoto in a couple of battles. Buddhist temples, such as Tōdai-ji, Mii-dera, and Kōfuku-ji, were burned since the monks supported the Minamoto clan. Their victory, however, did not last long, especially once the retired emperor, Go-Shirakawa, defected to the Minamotos. There was also an invasion of the capital led by Lord Kiso.

The ongoing war between the two warrior clans was paused when the archipelago was plagued by horrible disasters. First, there was a typhoon, and then came extreme famine. The people were desperate, and it wasn't just the peasants who were suffering. Death was nearly everywhere, and bodies lined the streets. Those who were still breathing decided to move to the mountains in hopes of saving their lives. There, they could live off of fishing and hunting. The elites began trading their valuables for food supplies, although few would give up their food in exchange for shiny jewelry during this unfortunate time.

The war eventually resumed in 1183 when the famine finally subsided. The Taira launched an attack on Lord Kiso, who eventually lured them into a narrow valley called Jigokudani. Lord Kiso's troops managed to surround the Taira, and they clashed swords and fired arrows at one another. Legends even claim that Lord Kiso annihilated the Taira by using oxen. The lord was said to have gathered a herd of oxen nearby and tied burning torches on their heads before causing a stampede into the Taira army. How true this story is remains unsure, but we do know that Lord Kiso successfully defeated the Taira army, thus opening an opportunity for him to march toward the capital.

After the Taira received the news that Lord Kiso and his samurai army were en route to the capital, they donned their armor and began searching for more allies to support them. They even turned to the Buddhist monks for support, but they all refused to support them due to the burning and destruction of their temples. The Taira, knowing that they were outnumbered, decided to flee from the capital. They brought the young emperor, Antoku, and three of the imperial regalia—the Kusanagi sword, the jewel named Yasakani no Magatama, and the sacred mirror called Yata no Kagami—with them.

In the absence of the Taira and the young emperor, Lord Kiso could freely wander around the capital without having to worry about getting attacked. However, there was only room for one leader in the Minamoto clan. Lord Kiso's growing power worried Minamoto no Yoritomo. So, Yoritomo forged an alliance with the former emperor, Go-Shirakawa, who was not at all fond of Lord Kiso and the terror that he had brought to the capital. To suppress Lord Kiso's power entirely, Yoritomo sent his two brothers, Yoshitsune and Noriyori, to the capital. This resulted in the Battle of Awazu. Lord Kiso and his most loyal followers perished.

Through Go-Shirakawa, Kamakura was recognized as a military state. The court then issued an order to demolish the entire Taira clan, most of whom had fled the capital, along with the young emperor. Without sparing a moment, Yoritomo sent his brothers to destroy the Tairas' remaining posts and attack their base. The long rivalry between the two clans reached its peak during the naval Battle of Dan-no-ura, which took place in the Strait of Shimonoseki.

An illustration of the naval Battle of Dan-no-ura.

https://commons.wikimedia.org/wiki/File:AntokuTennou_Engi.7%268_Dannoura_Kassen.jpg

The Taira was well known for their exceptional seafaring skills. However, they were far outnumbered by the Minamoto—the Taira only had about 500 ships, while the Minamoto, under the command of Yoshitsune, had nearly 840 ships. Realizing that the Minamoto clan was quickly gaining the upper hand in the battle, one of the Taira generals named Taguchi Shigeyoshi decided to betray his own clan. He managed to turn his men against the Taira lords and swear their bows to the Minamoto instead. The Taira faced a terrible defeat at Dan-no0ura. The clan's leader, Taira no Munemori, was executed. The chief commander Tomomori committed suicide by tying an anchor to his feet and leaping into the deep sea. The grandmother of the young Emperor Antoku took him in her arms and leaped into the sea as well, where they drowned.

The ruling Taira clan was no more, and the Minamoto finally emerged victorious. This ended the Heian period and kicked off a whole new era: the Kamakura period. Following the war, Yoritomo established the very first shogunate, a military government that dominated the Japanese archipelago for centuries.

Conclusion

Japan has come a long way. Ten thousand years ago, the nation was only a chain of islands filled with rich nature and hunter-gatherers who lived in simple tents made entirely out of animal skins. As the centuries went by, these prehistoric inhabitants of Japan began to evolve as new technologies were introduced. From foraging forests and hunting boars, they focused on plant cultivation, especially rice. More ritualistic ceremonies took place, and later on, Shinto beliefs were established. Dozens of clans and tribes emerged, with each of them showcasing their power over the many regions of Japan. Wars exploded, and bloodshed became the norm. Then, the first line of the imperial family was born. They strived to unite the entire archipelago under a centralized government, an effort that took many centuries to come to fruition.

Many might agree that China and Korea played an important role in Japan's development. The art, culture, and even religious beliefs were heavily influenced by the Asian mainland. For instance, Buddhism came to Japan via one of the three ancient Korean kingdoms, the imperial capitals were constructed mainly using the Chinese grid system, constitutions and laws were created based on Buddhism doctrines combined with Confucian beliefs, and even *biwa,* a traditional Japanese lute, was influenced by the Chinese musical instrument called *pipa.* However, despite all of the influences that arrived on the archipelago, Japan was not subjected to foreign political control. The people were free to choose what foreign ideas they should adapt and infuse into their traditions and beliefs, thus creating cultures and customs unique to the country.

Today, Japan is considered to be one of the most advanced countries in the world. Despite all the complex new technologies and modern lifestyles, the Japanese are still deeply connected to their ancient roots. The busy metropolitan city of Tokyo might be packed with endless modern structures, skyscrapers, towers, and shopping complexes with neon lights lighting up during nighttime. But traditional houses with *tatami* floorings, *shoji* (the traditional Japanese sliding door), and *sudare* (traditional Japanese window coverings) are not an uncommon sight. Many Buddhist temples dated from the ancient periods are still intact today, and the existence of over 100,000 Shinto shrines across the archipelago tells us that the ancient religion has not been forgotten; in fact, Buddhism and Shintoism continue to peacefully coexist to the point that it is common for someone to practice both beliefs and ritualistic rituals. Kimonos, traditional Japanese clothing that originated from the Heian period, are still widely used by the Japanese, as are geta, a pair of wooden clogs typically worn with the traditional Japanese socks called tabi.

Important events that took place during ancient times are recalled in the forms of theatrical performances, traditional dances, and songs to ensure the efforts of their ancestors are never forgotten. All of those incidents, battles, and conflicts definitely paved the way for Japan to become what it is today. Starting off only as a small kingdom isolated from the Asian mainland, Japan is now known as one of the most influential countries in the whole world. Its colorful history, traditions, and culture are known by many. More movies, books, artwork, and even video games have adopted stories of Japan's ancient past. Because of this, Japan's ancient history has been kept alive within its people, and it has also been forever immortalized among those outside of the archipelago. To put it in simple words, the history of ancient Japan is unlikely to ever disappear.

Free limited time bonus

Stop for a moment. We have a free bonus set up for you. The problem is this: we forget 90% of everything that we read after 7 days. Crazy fact, right? Here's the solution: we've created a printable, 1-page pdf summary for this book that you're reading now. All you have to do to get your free pdf summary is to go to the following website:

https://livetolearn.lpages.co/enthrallinghistory/

Once you do, it will be intuitive. Enjoy, and thank you!

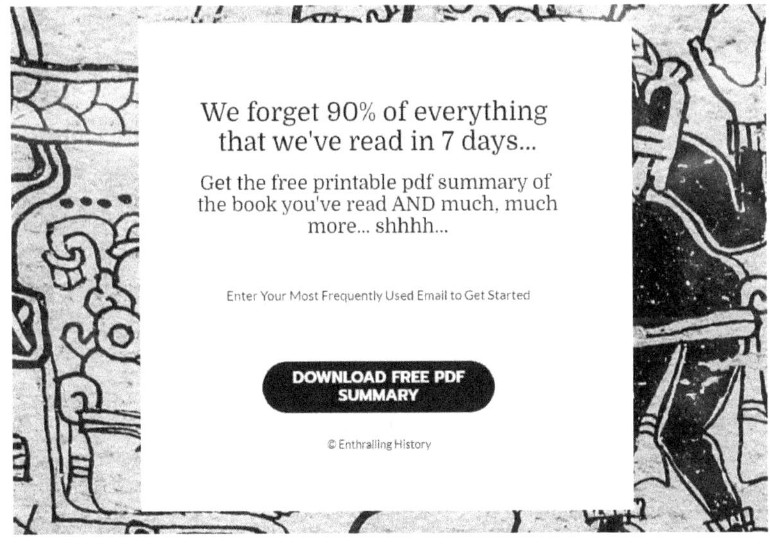

Bibliography

Allchin, F. Raymond, Srivastava, A.L., Alam, Muzaffa, Dikshit, K.R, Thapar, Romila, Spear, T.G. Percival, Champakalakshmi, R, Schwartzberg, Joseph E., Subrahmanyam, Sanjay, Wolpert, Stanley A. and Calkins, Philip B. "India." Encyclopedia Britannica, June 29, 2022. https://www.britannica.com/place/India.

Amruta, Patil. "Agriculture During Indus Valley Civilization - Ancient India History Notes." University of North Dakota. Prepp, July 6, 2022, https://prepp.in/news/e-492-agriculture-during-indus-valley-civilization-ancient-india-history-notes

Anand. "Socio-Religious Life of the Harappan People." Your Article Library, n.d., https://www.yourarticlelibrary.com/history/socio-religious-life-of-the-harappan-people/47142.

"Ancient Irrigation System." Indus River Valley Information, n.d., https://indusrivervalleyinformation.weebly.com/ancient-irrigation-system.html.

Atmaca, Dogukan. "Roman Baths as Social Congregation Places and Roman Bathing Culture." Mediterranean History & Culture by Dogukan Atmaca. July 3, 2019, https://www.doatmaca.com/post/roman-baths-as-social-congregation-places-and-roman-bathing-culture.

B., Kanika. "Early Indus Civilization and Its Trade Relations." HistoryDiscussion.net, n.d., https://www.historydiscussion.net/history-of-india/indus-valley-civilisation/early-indus-civilization-and-its-trade-relations-india-history/7058.

Basak, Saptarshi. "Deconstructing the 'Aryan Invasion' Debate Surrounding IIT Kharagpur's Calendar." The Quint, December 30, 2021, https://www.thequint.com/news/india/deconstructing-the-aryan-invasion-debate-surrounding-iit-kharagpurs-calendar

Bhagat, Sonya. "A Study of the Harappan Pottery Tradition in Saurashtra (With Special Reference to Padri and Tarasara, Shavnagdar District, Gujarat)." Bulletin of the Deccan College Research Institute 64/65 (2004): 359–64. https://www.jstor.org/stable/42930666

Biswas, Soutik. "Harappa Grave of Ancient Couple Reveals Secrets." BBC, January 9, 2019, https://www.bbc.com/news/world-asia-india-46806084.

Borland, William, Borz-Baba, Luca, and Farid, Sulmon. "Indus Valley Timeline." Sutori, 2017, https://www.sutori.com/en/story/indus-valley-timeline--wT3cJeHpx6TxYUQbC5ZTNXpD.

Brisch, Nicole. "Mother Goddess (Ninmag, Nintud/r, Belet-ili)." Ancient Mesopotamian Gods and Goddesses, Oracc and the UK Higher Education Academy, 2013, https://oracc.museum.upenn.edu/amgg/listofdeities/mothergoddess/.

Britannica, T. Editors of Encyclopedia. "Bronze Age." Encyclopedia Britannica, May 13, 2022. https://www.britannica.com/event/Bronze-Age.

Britannica, T. Editors of Encyclopedia. "Great Bath." Encyclopedia Britannica, January 26, 2018. https://www.britannica.com/place/Great-Bath-Mohenjo-daro.

Britannica, T. Editors of Encyclopedia. "Mohenjo-daro." Encyclopedia Britannica, May 16, 2021. https://www.britannica.com/place/Mohenjo-daro.

"Burial Methods of the Indus Valley Civilization." Unacademy. Sorting Hat Technologies Pvt Ltd, n.d., https://unacademy.com/content/bpsc/study-material/history/burial-methods-of-the-indus-valley-civilization/#:~:text=More%20than%20two%20hundred%20bodies,sites%20after%20all%20these%20years.

Burki, Shahid J. and Ziring, Lawrence. "Pakistan." Britannica, July 1, 202, https://www.britannica.com/place/Pakistan

Chase, Brad. "Family Matters in Harappan Gujarat." Academia, 2018, https://www.academia.edu/37391121

Chhatrapati Shivaji Maharaj Bastu Sangrahalaya. "Harappan Miniature Pottery." Indian Culture, n.d., https://indianculture.gov.in/artefacts-museums/harappan-miniature-pottery#:~:text=Harappan%20pottery%20was%20made%20of,basin%2C%20casket%20and%20so%20on.

Cracker, KAS. "Indus Valley Civilization - Town Planning." Midukkan Tony, March 28, 2021, https://www.midukkantony.com/post/indus-valley-civilization-town-planning.

Dales, George, F. "Civilization and Floods in the Indus Valley" Expedition Magazine 7.4 (1965): n. pag. Expedition Magazine. Penn Museum, 1965 Web. 23 Aug 2022 <https://www.penn.museum/sites/expedition/?p=1010>

Dalley, Stephanie M. "Sargon." Encyclopedia Britannica, January 5, 2021. https://www.britannica.com/biography/Sargon.

"Dancing Girl (Mohenjo-daro) from the Indus Valley Civilization." Joy of Museums Virtual Tours, 2022, https://joyofmuseums.com/museums/asia-museums/india-museums/national-museum-new-delhi/dancing-girl-Mohenjo-daro/.

Dangi, Vivek and Uesugi, Aninori. "A Study on Harappan Painted Pottery from the Ghaggar Plains." The Journal of the Indian Archaeological Society, No. 43, 2013, https://www.academia.edu/9718951/A_Study_on_the_Harappan_Painted_Pottery_from_the_Ghaggar_Plains

Deepak, Prabeer. "Agriculture and Economy of Indus Valley Civilization." Guru, 2020, https://www.ownguru.com/blog/indus-valley-civilization-agriculture/#:~:text=Agriculture%20in%20the%20Indus%20valley,rice%20were%20grown%20in%20summer.

"Disappearance of the Indus Valley Civilization." LumenCandela. Lumen Learning, n.d., https://courses.lumenlearning.com/suny-hccc-worldcivilization/chapter/disappearance-of-the-indus-valley-civilization/.

"Domestication Timeline." American Museum of Natural History, n.d., https://www.amnh.org/exhibitions/horse/domesticating-horses/domestication-timeline

"Do We Have Any Evidence of a Migration from the Indus to South India?" Harappa, n.d., https://www.harappa.com/answers/do-we-have-any-evidence-migration-indus-south-india

"Early Civilization in the Indus Valley." Ancient Civilizations Online Textbook. UsHistory.org, 2022, https://www.ushistory.org/civ/8a.asp.

EIA Editors. "Indus Valley Terracotta Animal Figurines." Map Academy, n.d., https://mapacademy.io/article/indus-valley-terracotta-animal-figurines/.

Elshaikh, Eman. "Indus River Valley Civilizations." Khan Academy, 2017, https://www.khanacademy.org/humanities/world-history/world-history-beginnings/ancient-india/a/the-indus-river-valley-civilizations

Garg, Divya. "Case Study - City Planning and Organization of Indus Valley Civilization." Ischools.org, 2015, https://ischools.org/resources/Documents/Discipline%20of%20organizing/Case%20Studies/IndusValley-Garg2015.pdf.

"Geography of the Ancient Indus River Valley." Students of History, 2022, https://www.studentsofhistory.com/the-geography-of-ancient-india#:~:text=The%20Indus%20River%20Valley%20is,steady%20supply%20of%20fresh%20water.

Glencairn Museum News. "Sacred Adornment: Jewelry as Belief in Ancient Egypt." Glencairn Museum, November 2, 2020, https://www.glencairnmuseum.org/newsletter/2020/3/6/sacred-adornment-jewelry-as-belief-in-ancient-egypt.

Halverston, Dean. "An Overview Definition of Animism." The Traveling Team. International Students, Inc, 2004, https://www.thetravelingteam.org/articles/animism-overview.

"Harappan Architecture." Fum. Wiki, n.d.,

"Harappan Burials." Worldhistory.biz, January 8, 2015, https://www.worldhistory.biz/ancient-history/67121-harappan-burials.html.

 "Harappan Culture." Students of History, n.d., https://www.studentsofhistory.com/harappan-planned-cities#:~:text=They%20used%20wheeled%20carts%2C%20boats,from%20the%20north%20in%20Afghanistan.

Hawkes, Jacquetta. The First Great Civilizations: Life in Mesopotamia, the Indus Valley, and Egypt. The History of Human Society. New York City, NY: Random House, Inc, 1980.

Hays, Jeff. "Great Cities of the Indus Valley Civilization." Facts and Details, September 2020, https://factsanddetails.com/india/History/sub7_1a/entry-7116.html

Hirst, K. Kris. "Harappa: Capital City of the Ancient Indus Civilization." ThoughtCo., September 20, 2019, https://www.thoughtco.com/harappa-pakistan-capital-city-171278

Hirst, K. Kris. "Mehrgarh, Pakistan and Life in the Indus Valley Before Harappa." ThoughtCo., May 30, 2019, https://www.thoughtco.com/mehrgarh-pakistan-life-indus-valley-171796.

History.com Editors. "Hinduism." History. A&E television Networks, May 19, 2022, https://www.history.com/topics/religion/hinduism

"Indus Valley Civilization." Cultural India, n.d., https://www.culturalindia.net/indian-history/ancient-india/indus-valley.html.

 "Indus Valley Wheeled Ram Toy," in World History Commons, n.d., https://worldhistorycommons.org/indus-valley-wheeled-ram-toy

IvyPanda. "The History of Indus and Chinese Civilizations Interaction." November 2, 2021. https://ivypanda.com/essays/the-history-of-indus-and-chinese-civilizations-interaction/.

"Jewellery." Sindhishaan, 2012, https://www.sindhishaan.com/gallery/jewellery.html.

Karuga, James. "What is a Furrow (In Agriculture)?" World Atlas, April 25, 2017, https://www.worldatlas.com/articles/what-is-a-furrow-agriculture.html.

Kenoyer, Jonathan M. "Uncovering the Keys to the Lost Indus Cities." Scientific American, January 1, 2005, https://www.scientificamerican.com/article/uncovering-the-keys-to-the-lost-ind/#:~:text=The%20earliest%20village%20settlement%20at,wealth%20in%20mud%2Dbrick%20tombs.

Kiprop, Joseph. "Interesting Facts about the Great Bath, the World's Oldest Public Pool." World Atlas, January 10, 2019, https://www.worldatlas.com/articles/interesting-facts-about-the-great-bath-Mohenjo-daro-the-world-s-oldest-public-pool.html.

Koch-Westenholz, Ulla. "Mesopotamian Astrology." CNI Publications. Museum Tusculanum Press, 1995.

Mani, B.R. "The 8th Millennium BC in the "Lost" River Valley. Friends of ASI, 2013, https://friendsofasi.wordpress.com/writings/the-8th-millennium-bc-in-the-lost-river-valley/

Marcus334. "Shiva Pashupati." World History Encyclopedia. World History Publishing, April 26, 2012, https://www.worldhistory.org/image/361/shiva-pashupati/.

Mark, Joshua J. "Indus Valley Civilization." World History Encyclopedia. World History Publishing, October 7, 2020, https://www.worldhistory.org/Indus_Valley_Civilization/

Mark, Joshua J. "Mesopotamian Religion." World History Encyclopedia. World History Publishing, February 22, 2011, https://www.worldhistory.org/Mesopotamian_Religion/.

Marsh, Matthew G. "Tools of Agriculture in the Indus Civilization." History of Applied Science & Technology, 2017, https://press.rebus.community/historyoftech/chapter/tools-of-agriculture-in-the-indus-civilization/

Meadow, Richard H. and Kenoyer, Jonathan, M. "Early Developments of Art and Symbol and Technology in the Indus Valley Tradition." Harappa, 2022, https://www.harappa.com/indus3/e2.html.

Menon, Arathi. "An Indus Seal." Smart History, April 22, 2020, https://smarthistory.org/indus-seal/.

"Mesopotamia Sumerian City-States." History's Histories, n.d., https://www.historyshistories.com/mesopotamia-sumerian-city-states.html

"Mesopotamia Trade: Merchants and Traders. History on the Next, Salem Media, 2022, https://www.historyonthenet.com/mesopotamian-merchants-and-traders.

Mhackworth. "No Interest in War: The Harappan Civilization." Real Archaeology. Vassar. September 22, 2017, https://pages.vassar.edu/realarchaeology/2017/09/22/no-interest-in-war-the-harappan-civilization/#:~:text=This%20is%20the%20Harappan%20civilization,ancient%20cities%20to%20do%20so.

Mishra, Sampadananda. "Pashupati is not the Lord of Animals." Bhagavadgita.org, March 27, 2018, https://bhagavadgita.org.in/Blogs/5ab5f10f5369ed0e343a7ca0

 Mukhopadhyay, Bahata A. "Ancient Tax Tokens, Trade Licenses and Metrological Records?: Making Sense of Indus Inscribed Objects Through Script-Internal, Contextual, Linguistic, and Ethnohistorial Lenses." Delivery PDF, n.d.,https://papers.ssrn.com/sol3/papers.cfm?abstract_id=3189473.

Nag, Oishimaya Sen. "Dholavira: Ancient Wonder of Gujarat." World Atlas, January 25, 2021, https://www.worldatlas.com/articles/dholavira-ancient-wonder-of-gujarat.html

Pandey, Jhimli M. "900 Year Drought Wiped Out Indus Civilization: IIT-Kharagpur." The Times of India, April 16, 2018, https://timesofindia.indiatimes.com/india/900-year-drought-wiped-out-indus-civilisation-iit-kharagpur/articleshow/63776710.cms

Pathania, Shivam. "Toys of Indus Valley Civilization." Amar Chitra Katha Media, June 25, 2021, https://www.amarchitrakatha.com/history_details/toys-of-indus-valley-civilization/#:~:text=Animal%20figurines%2C%20utensil%20sets%2C%20puzzle,other%20visuals%2C%20was%20the%20bull.

Pattanaik, Devdutt. "Was Harappan Civilization Vedic or Hindu?" Daily Beta. India Today Group, December 15, 2016, https://www.dailyo.in/variety/harappan-civilisation-hinduism-vedic-age-dharma-aryans-hindu-supremacists-marxists-14564

Perkins, McKenzie. "What Is Animism?" Learn Religions, April 5, 2019, https://www.learnreligions.com/what-is-animism-4588366

Possehl, G. L. "The Early Harappan Phase." Bulletin of the Deacon College Research Institute, 60/61, 2003.

Prabhakar, V. N. "A Survey of Burial Practices in the Late/Post-Urban Harappan Phase during the Second and First Millennium BCE." Journal of Multidisciplinary Studies in Archaeology 3 (2015): 54–83.

Rao, S.R. "Shipping and Maritime Trade of the Indus People." Expedition Magazine 7.3 (1965): n. pag. Expedition Magazine. Penn Museum, 1965 Web. 29 Jun 2022 <https://www.penn.museum/sites/expedition/?p=995>

"Sculpture in the Indus Valley." GK Today, December 17, 2013, https://www.gktoday.in/topic/sculpture-in-indus-valley-civilization/#:~:text=Terracotta%20Sculptures,-The%20terracotta%20figurines&text=The%20terracotta%20figurines%20of%20Indus,the%20female%20were%20more%20common.

"Seals of Harappan Civilization." Byju's Exam Prep, 2022, https://byjus.com/free-ias-prep/seals-harappan-civilization/#:~:text=Thousands%20of%20seals%20have%20been,shape%20with%20a%202X2%20dimension.

Siddiqui, Muhammah H. "Assignment on Sandstone Reservoir in Pakistan." Department of Earth and Environmental Sciences. Bahria University, Islamabad, Pakistan, November 5, 2015, https://www.academia.edu/18491035/Sandstone_Resorvior_in_Pakistan.

Sparavigna, Amelia. "Icons and Signs from the Ancient Harappa." Dipartimento di Fisica, Politechnico di Torino, n.d., https://web-archive.southampton.ac.uk/cogprints.org/6179/1/icons-and-signs-harappa.pdf

Subrahmanyam, S., Thapar, Romila, Spear, T.G., Percival, Calkins, Philip B., Wolpert, Stanley, A., Srivastava, A.L., Schwartzberg, Joseph E., Champakalashmi, R., Allicin, Frank Raymond, Dikshit, K.R., and Alam, Muzaffar. "India." Encyclopedia Britannica, July 13, 2022, https://www.britannica.com/place/India

Taub, Ben. "Was the Indus Valley Civilization Really a Non-Violent, Egalitarian Utopia?" IFL Science, September 19, 2016, https://www.iflscience.com/indus-valley-civilization-really-non-violent-egalitarian-utopia-37974.

"The Great Granary of Indus Valley Civilization Has Been Discovered by Which Site." Unacademy. Sorting Hat Technologies Pvt Ltd, 2022, https://unacademy.com/content/question-answer/gk/the-great-granary-of-indus-valley-civilization-has-been-discovered-by-which-site/#:~:text=Ans%3A%2D%20Granary%20is%20a,largest%20building%20discovered%20at%20Mohenjodaro.

Tiwari, Soymya V. "Music to the Years: Musical Instruments from the Indus Valley Civilization." Hindustan Times, August 16, 2016, https://www.hindustantimes.com/music/music-to-the-years-musical-instruments-from-the-indus-valley-civilisation/story-WuViIqOST8WMNCSkkayuuN.html

V., Jayaram. "Death and Afterlife in Hinduism." Hinduwebsite.com, n.d, https://www.hinduwebsite.com/hinduism/h_death.asp/

V., Jayaram. "The Religion of the Indus Valley Civilization." Hinduwebsite.com, 2019, https://www.hinduwebsite.com/history/indus.asp

Vahia, Mayank. "Is There Any Relation Between Vedic and Indus Civilization as many Indus and Saraswati Sites Have Been Found in the Region Which is Called Saptasindu in Vedas?" Harappa, n.d., https://www.harappa.com/answers/there-any-relation-between-vedic-and-indus-civilization-many-indus-and-saraswati-sites-have.

"Water Buffalo." Johne's Information Center. University of Wisconsin-Madison, 2022, https://johnes.org/other-animals/water-buffalo/

"What Did the Indus Valley People Trade?" Tutorials Point, July 30, 2019, https://www.tutorialspoint.com/what-did-the-indus-valley-people-trade#

Wood, Michael. *In Search of the First Civilization.* London: BBC Books, BBC Worldwide LLC 2005.

Chang, Kwang-Chih. "In Search of China's Beginnings: New Light on an Old Civilization: A Golden Age of Archaeology is piecing together a new Chinese prehistory and history that differ in fundamental ways from the traditional story." American Scientist 69, no. 2 (1981): 148-160.

Wang, Qian, and Li Sun. "Eightieth year of Peking Man: Current status of Peking Man and the Zhoukoudian site." Anthropological Review 63 (2000): 19-30.

Pu, Li, Chien Fang, Ma Hsing-Hua, Pu Ching-Yu, Hsing Li-Sheng, and Chu Shih-Chiang. "Preliminary study on the age of Yuanmou man by palaeomagnetic technique." Scientia Sinica 20, no. 5 (1977): 645-664.

Boaz, N., and R. Ciochon. "The scavenging of "Peking Man." Natural History 110, no. 2 (2001): 46-51.

Gao, Xing. "Paleolithic cultures in China: uniqueness and divergence." Current Anthropology 54, no. S8 (2013): S358-S370.

Freud, Sigmund. Moses and monotheism. Leonardo Paolo Lovari, 2016.

Yang, Xiaoyan, Zhikun Ma, Jun Li, Jincheng Yu, Chris Stevens, and Yijie Zhuang. "Comparing subsistence strategies in different landscapes of North China 10,000 years ago." The Holocene 25, no. 12 (2015): 1957-1964.

Jing, Yuan. "The origins and development of animal domestication in China." Chinese Archaeology 8, no. 1 (2008): 1-7.

Bestel, Sheahan, Yingjian Bao, Hua Zhong, Xingcan Chen, and Li Liu. "Wild plant use and multi-cropping at the early Neolithic Zhuzhai site in the middle Yellow River region, China." The Holocene 28, no. 2 (2018): 195-207.

Guoping, Sun. "Recent research on the Hemudu culture and the Tianluoshan site." A companion to Chinese archaeology (2013): 555-573.

Wang, Jiajing, Jiangping Zhu, Dongrong Lei, and Leping Jiang. "New evidence for rice harvesting in the early Neolithic Lower Yangtze River, China." Plos one 17, no. 12 (2022): e0278200.

Zhang, Haiwei, Hai Cheng, Ashish Sinha, Christoph Spötl, Yanjun Cai, Bin Liu, Gayatri Kathayat et al. "Collapse of the Liangzhu and other Neolithic cultures in the lower Yangtze region in response to climate change." Science Advances 7, no. 48 (2021): eabi9275.

Ling, Qin. "The Liangzhu culture." A companion to Chinese archaeology (2013): 574-596.

Runnels, Curtis N., Claire Payne, Noam V. Rifkind, Chantel White, Nicholas P. Wolff, and Steven A. LeBlanc. "Warfare in Neolithic Thessaly: A case study." Hesperia: The Journal of the American School of Classical Studies at Athens 78, no. 2 (2009): 165-194.

Liu, Li, Jiajing Wang, Maureece J. Levin, Nasa Sinnott-Armstrong, Hao Zhao, Yanan Zhao, Jing Shao, Nan Di, and Tian'en Zhang. "The origins of specialized pottery and diverse alcohol fermentation techniques in Early Neolithic China." Proceedings of the National Academy of Sciences 116, no. 26 (2019): 12767-12774.

Thorp, Robert L. "Erlitou and the search for the Xia." Early China 16 (1991): 1-38.

Bunker, Emma C. "The Beginning of Metallurgy in Ancient China" Web Archive. Available at: https://web.archive.org/web/20070206143502/http:/exhibits.denverartmuseum.org/asianart/articles/metalwork/art_li_mat.html

Dono, Tsurumatsu. "ON THE COPPER AGE IN ANCIENT CHINA." Bulletin of the Chemical Society of Japan 7, no. 11 (1932): 347-352.

Chen, Minzhen. "Faithful History or Unreliable History: Three Debates on the Historicity of the Xia Dynasty." Journal of Chinese Humanities 5, no. 1 (2019): 78-104.

Allan, Sarah. "The myth of the Xia Dynasty." Journal of the Royal Asiatic Society 116, no. 2 (1984): 242-256.

Mark, Joshua J. "Ancient China." Ancient History Encyclopedia (2012).

Allan, Sarah. ""When Red Pigeons Gathered on Tang's House": A Warring States Period Tale of Shamanic Possession and Building Construction set at the turn of the Xia and Shang Dynasties." Journal of the Royal Asiatic Society 25, no. 3 (2015): 419-438.

Hou, Liangliang, Yaowu Hu, Xinping Zhao, Suting Li, Dong Wei, Yanfeng Hou, Baohua Hu et al. "Human subsistence strategy at Liuzhuang site, Henan, China during the proto-Shang culture (~ 2000–1600 BC) by stable isotopic analysis." Journal of Archaeological Science 40, no. 5 (2013): 2344-2351.

Guangkuo, Yuan. "The discovery and study of the Early Shang culture." A companion to Chinese archaeology (2013): 323-342.

Shelach, Gideon. "The Qiang and the question of human sacrifice in the late Shang period." Asian Perspectives (1996): 1-26.

Keightley, David N. "Shang divination and metaphysics." Philosophy East and West 38, no. 4 (1988): 367-397.

Qian, Sima. "Records of the Grand Historian of China" Available at: https://archive.org/stream/in.ernet.dli.2015.532974/2015.532974.records-of_djvu.txt

LI, Xiaobing (ed.). "China at War: An Encyclopedia." ABC-CLIO, 2012.

Boltz, William G. "Early Chinese writing." World Archaeology 17, no. 3 (1986): 420-436.

Huang, Chun Chang, Shichao Zhao, Jiangli Pang, Qunying Zhou, Shue Chen, Pinghua Li, Longjiang Mao, and Min Ding. "Climatic aridity and the relocations of the Zhou culture in the southern Loess Plateau of China." Climatic Change 61 (2003): 361-378.

Rawson, Jessica. "Ordering the exotic: ritual practices in the late western and early eastern Zhou." Artibus Asiae 73, no. 1 (2013): 5-76.

Khayutina, Maria. "Western Zhou cultural and historic setting." The Oxford Handbook of Early China (2020): 365.

Childs-Johnson, Elizabeth, ed. The Oxford Handbook of Early China. Oxford University Press, USA, 2020.

Wagner, Donald B. "The earliest use of iron in China." BAR International Series 792 (1999): 1-9.

Cartwright, Mark. Crossbows in Ancient Chinese Warfare. World History Encyclopedia.

Shaughnessy, Edward L. Sources of Western Zhou history: inscribed bronze vessels. Univ of California Press, 1992.

Tu, Wei-Ming. "Confucius and Confucianism." Confucianism and the Family: A Study of Indo-Tibetan Scholasticism (1998): 3-36.

Strickmann, Michel. "History, anthropology, and Chinese religion." (1980): 201-248.

Hsiao, Kung-chuan. "Legalism and autocracy in traditional China." Chinese Studies in History 10, no. 1-2 (1976): 125-143.

Tzu, Sun. The Art of War. Available at: https://sites.ualberta.ca/~enoch/Readings/The_Art_Of_War.pdf

Cartwright, Mark. Warring States Period. World History. Available at: https://www.worldhistory.org/Warring_States_Period/

Fiskesjö, Magnus. "Terra-cotta conquest: The first emperor's clay army's blockbuster tour of the world." Verge: Studies in Global Asias 1, no. 1 (2015): 162-183.

Britannica. Meng Tian. Available at: https://www.britannica.com/biography/Meng-Tian

Kulmar, Tarmo. "On the nature of the governing system of the Qin Empire in ancient China." Folklore: Electronic Journal of Folklore 59 (2014): 165-178.

Guo, Yanzi. "Contingency and Historical Inevitability in the Development of the Qin Dynasty." Journal of Education, Humanities and Social Sciences 8 (2023): 1367-1372.

Zhou, Minhwa, and Meihwa Zhou. "Wisdom and Strategy— An Example for Zhang Liang and Liu Bang." In 7th International Conference on Humanities and Social Science Research (ICHSSR 2021), pp. 941-943. Atlantis Press, 2021.

Chen, Pauline. "History Lessons." New York Times, 1993.

Hardy, Grant, and Anne Behnke Kinney. The establishment of the Han empire and imperial China. Greenwood Publishing Group, 2005.

Cullen, Christopher. "Motivations for scientific change in ancient China: Emperor Wu and the Grand Inception astronomical reforms of 104 BC." Journal for the History of Astronomy 24, no. 3 (1993): 185-203.

Dreyer, Edward L. "Zhao Chongguo: A Professional Soldier of China's Former Han Dynasty." The Journal of Military History 72, no. 3 (2008): 665-725.

Gao, Jiyi. "Emperor Xuan, Emperor Zhang and the Rise and Decline of Zhangju in the Han Dynasty." Hanxue Yanjiu (Chinese Studies) 25, no. 1 (2007).

Xiong, Victor Cunrui, and Kenneth James Hammond, eds. Routledge Handbook of Imperial Chinese History. Routledge, 2019. p. 25-38.

L'Haridon, Béatrice. "WANG MANG 王莽 (c. 45 BCE–23 CE) AND CLASSICAL LEARNING AS PATH TO SUPREME POWER." Early China 45 (2022): 51-72.

Dubs, Homer H. "The victory of Han Confucianism." Journal of the American Oriental Society 58, no. 3 (1938): 435-449.

Xueqin, Li, and Xing Wen. "New light on the Early-Han code: a reappraisal of the Zhangjiashan bamboo-slip legal texts." Asia Major (2001): 125-146.

Hardy, Grant, and Anne Behnke Kinney. The establishment of the Han empire and imperial China. Greenwood Publishing Group, 2005.

Bottéro, Françoise, and Christoph Harbsmeier. "The Shuowen Jiezi Dictionary and the Human Sciences in China." Asia Major (2008): 249-271.

Nylan, Michael. "Sima Qian: A True Historian?" Early China 23 (1998): 203-246.

Cartwright, Mark. Paper in ancient China. World history encyclopedia, 2017.

Zhijie, Huo. "The significance of female education during the Han Dynasty." Вестник Бурятского государственного университета. Гуманитарные исследования Внутренней Азии 4 (2016): 54-59.

Van Ess, Hans. "Emperor Wu of the Han and the First August Emperor of Qin in Sima Qian's Shiji." Birth of an Empire 5 (2013): 239.

Ch'ien, Mu. Merits and Demerits of Political Systems in Dynastic China. Springer Berlin Heidelberg, 2019.

Juping, Yang. "The Relations between China and India and the Opening of the Southern Silk Road during the Han Dynasty." The Silk Road 11 (2013): 82-92.

McLeod, Alexus. "Philosophy in Eastern Han Dynasty China (25–220 CE)." Philosophy Compass 10, no. 6 (2015): 355-368.

Levy, Howard S. "Yellow Turban religion and rebellion at the end of Han." Journal of the American Oriental Society 76, no. 4 (1956): 214-227.

De Crespigny, Rafe. "Man from the Margin: Cao Cao and the Three Kingdoms." (1990).

An Overview of Shintoism and Buddhism in Japan – Differences and History. (2021, September 30). Japan Wonder Travel Blog. https://blog.japanwondertravel.com/an-overview-of-shintoism-and-buddhism-in-japan-differences-and-history-20672

Armstrong, K. (2022, January 5). *History of Kimono: Classical Japan (Nara and Heian Periods).* Owlcation. https://owlcation.com/humanities/History-of-Kimono-Part-2-Nara-and-Heian-Periods

Buddhism: Pure Land Buddhism. (n.d.). BBC. Retrieved October 2, 2002, from

https://www.bbc.co.uk/religion/religions/buddhism/subdivisions/pureland_1.shtml

Cartwright, M. (2022, April 8). *Amaterasu.* World History Encyclopedia.

https://www.worldhistory.org/Amaterasu

Cartwright, M. (2022, April 8). *Heian Period.* World History Encyclopedia.

https://www.worldhistory.org/Heian_Period

Cartwright, M. (2022, April 9). *Fujiwara Clan.* World History Encyclopedia.

https://www.worldhistory.org/Fujiwara_Clan

Cartwright, M. (2022, April 9). *Genpei War.* World History Encyclopedia.

https://www.worldhistory.org/Genpei_War

Cartwright, M. (2022, April 9). *Kofun.* World History Encyclopedia.

https://www.worldhistory.org/Kofun

Cartwright, M. (2022, April 10). *Minamoto Clan.* World History Encyclopedia.

https://www.worldhistory.org/Minamoto_Clan

Cartwright, M. (2022, April 11). *Asuka Period.* World History Encyclopedia.

https://www.worldhistory.org/Asuka_Period

Cartwright, M. (2022, April 11). *Buddhism in Ancient Japan*. World History Encyclopedia.

https://www.worldhistory.org/article/1080/buddhism-in-ancient-japan

Cartwright, M. (2022, April 11). *Haniwa*. World History Encyclopedia.

https://www.worldhistory.org/Haniwa

Cartwright, M. (2022, April 11). *Izanami and Izanagi*. World History Encyclopedia.

https://www.worldhistory.org/Izanami_and_Izanagi

Cartwright, M. (2022, April 11). *Queen Himiko*. World History Encyclopedia.

https://www.worldhistory.org/Queen_Himiko

Chakra, H. (2021, April 17). *Yamato Clan and State, The Birthplace of the Japanese Political State. About History.* https://about-history.com/yamato-clan-and-state-the-birthplace-of-the-japanese-political-state/?amp

D. (2016, January 1). *The Controversial Iwajuku Site and the Argument for the Japanese Paleolithic Period. Ancient Origins.* https://www.ancient-origins.net/ancient-places-asia/controversial-iwajuku-site-and-argument-japanese-paleolithic-period-005081

Fudo Myo-o (Fudou Myou-ou) - Wrathful Messenger Who Protects & Serves Dainichi Buddha, Japanese Buddhism Art History. (n.d.). Copyright 1995 Onmark Productions.Com. All Right Reserved.
https://www.onmarkproductions.com/html/fudo.html

Goma Fire Ritual. (n.d.). Seattle Koyasan.
https://seattlekoyasan.com/services/goma-fire-ritual

The Great Buddha Hall. (n.d.). The Tōdai-ji.
http://www.todaiji.or.jp/english/map02.html

Great South Gate (Nandai-mon). (n.d.). Tōdai-ji.
http://www.todaiji.or.jp/english/map01.html

H. (2013, March 5). *Shoso-in Exhibition Treasures*. Heritage of Japan.

https://heritageofjapan.wordpress.com/2011/09/22/shoso-in-exhibition-treasures/amp

Haniwa Tomb Figure of a Soldier. (n.d.). Wellesley College.

https://www.wellesley.edu/davismuseum/artwork/node/36990

Hays, J. (n.d.). *JOMON PEOPLE (10,500–300 B.C.): RELIGION AND BURIAL CUSTOMS.*

Facts and Details. https://factsanddetails.com/japan/cat16/sub105/entry-5607.html

Hays, J. (n.d.). *JOMON PERIOD (10,500–300 B.C.)*. Facts and Details.
https://factsanddetails.com/japan/cat16/sub105/item2764.html#chapter-3

Hays, J. (n.d.). *ORIGIN OF THE YAYOI PEOPLE (AND MODERN JAPANESE)*. Facts and Details. https://factsanddetails.com/japan/cat16/sub105/entry-5284.html

Hays, J. (n.d.). *WA AND EARLY CONTACTS BETWEEN CHINA AND JAPAN*. Facts and Details. https://factsanddetails.com/japan/cat16/sub105/entry-5289.html#chapter-6

Hays, J. (n.d.). *WRITING AND LITERATURE IN THE HEIAN PERIOD (794–1185)*. Facts and Details. https://factsanddetails.com/japan/cat16/sub106/entry-5313.html#chapter-5

History of Japan: Heian Period (794–1185). (2021, September 30). Japan Wonder Travel Blog. https://blog.japanwondertravel.com/history-of-japan-heian-period-24207#toc4

HimikoHistory.com Editors. (2021, September 15). *Buddhism*. HISTORY. https://www.history.com/.amp/topics/religion/buddhism

Hoang, T. (2022, April 11). *Jomon Period*. World History Encyclopedia. https://www.worldhistory.org/Jomon_Period/Japanese Amida Buddha

K. (2020, March 18). *Hashihaka Kofun and Japan's Beginnings*. Kansai Odyssey. http://kansai-odyssey.com/hashihaka-kofun-and-japans-beginnings

K., & K. (2018, May 13). *The Isshi Incident*. Samurai World. https://samurai-world.com/the-isshi-incident

Kayashima: The Japanese Train Station Built Around a 700-Year-Old Tree. (2018, January 17). Colossal. https://www.thisiscolossal.com/2017/01/kayashima-the-japanese-train-station-built-around-a-700-year-old-tree

Kessler, P. L. (n.d.). *Early Japanese Cultures*. The History Files. https://www.historyfiles.co.uk/KingListsFarEast/JapanCultures.htm

Lane, V. (2015, June 17). *Jigoku and Yomi No Kuni: Exploring Japanese Hell*. Tofugu. https://www.tofugu.com/japan/japanese-hells

Lisina, E. (2021, December 13). *Fudo Myo*. JapanTravel. https://en.japantravel.com/blog/fudo-myo/68296

M. (2020, May 21). *Hōsōgami*. Yokai.Com. https://yokai.com/housougami

Mason, R. H. P., & Caiger, J. G. (1997). *A History of Japan: Revised Edition* (Revised ed.). Tuttle Publishing.

National Geographic Society. (2012, October 9). *Continental Drift*. https://www.nationalgeographic.org/encyclopedia/continental-drift

National Geographic Society. (2020, July 7). *Buddhism* https://www.nationalgeographic.org/encyclopedia/buddhism

Power of Plate Tectonics: Pangaea. (n.d.). American Museum of Natural History. https://www.amnh.org/explore/ology/earth/power-of-plate-tectonics/pangaea

S. (2020, January 20). *Naumann Elephant and Lake Nojiri.* Official Travel Guide of Shinanomachi, Nagano. http://shinanomachi-nagano.jp/en/wp/?p=281

Shingon - Japanese Esoteric Buddhism. (2017, March 6). Learn Religions. https://www.learnreligions.com/shingon-449632

Shinto. (2022, March 22). Japan-Guide.Com. https://www.japan-guide.com/e/e2056.html

Thomson, D. J. (2020, December 29). *Ise Grand Shrine: Everything You Need to Know about Japan's Most Sacred Shinto Shrine.* JRPass.Com. https://www.jrpass.com/blog/ise-grand-shrine-everything-you-need-to-know-about-japans-most-sacred-shinto-shrine

Who is Amida Buddha? - Buddhism for Beginners. (2020, April 25). Buddhism for Beginners. https://tricycle.org/beginners/buddhism/who-is-amida-buddha

Wikipedia contributors. (2021, December 18). *Battle of Uji (1180).* Wikipedia https://en.wikipedia.org/wiki/Battle_of_Uji_(1180)

Wikipedia contributors. (2022, March 23). *Geology of Japan.* Wikipedia https://en.m.wikipedia.org/wiki/Geology_of_Japan

Wikipedia contributors. (2022, March 23). *Tomoe Gozen.* Wikipedia https://en.wikipedia.org/wiki/Tomoe_Gozen

Won, J. (2022, March 30). *An Ancient Battle Where Japan Fought for Korean Independence.* Medium. https://historyofyesterday.com/an-ancient-battle-where-japan-fought-for-korean-independence-436590117e19

Wright, G. (2021, November 19). *Ebisu.* Mythopedia. https://mythopedia.com/topics/ebisu

Yasuka, A. (2021, February 3). *Empress Suiko: The First Empress Regnant of Japan.* KCP International. https://www.kcpinternational.com/2015/12/empress-suiko-the-first-empress-regnant-of-japan

Yayoi linked to Yangtze area: DNA tests reveal similarities to early wet-rice farmers. (2008, July 2). Heritage of Japan. https://heritageofjapan.wordpress.com/yayoi-era-yields-up-rice/who-were-the-yayoi-people/yayoi-linked-to-yangtze-area-dna-tests-reveal-similarities-to-early-wet-rice-farmers